Approaches to Teaching Austen's *Mansfield Park*

Approaches to Teaching
World Literature

For a complete listing of titles,
see the last pages of this book.

Approaches to Teaching Austen's *Mansfield Park*

Edited by

Marcia McClintock Folsom

and

John Wiltshire

The Modern Language Association of America
New York   2014

© 2014 by The Modern Language Association of America
All rights reserved
Printed in the United States of America

MLA and the MODERN LANGUAGE ASSOCIATION are trademarks owned
by the Modern Language Association of America. For information about
obtaining permission to reprint material from MLA book publications, send your
request by mail (see address below) or e-mail (permissions@mla.org).

Library of Congress Cataloging-in-Publication Data

Approaches to Teaching Austen's Mansfield Park / edited by
Marcia McClintock Folsom and John Wiltshire.
    pages cm. — (Approaches to Teaching World Literature Series ; 135)
    Includes bibliographical references and index.
  ISBN 978-1-60329-197-2 (hardback) — ISBN 978-1-60329-198-9 (paper) —
    ISBN 978-1-60329-199-6 (EPUB) — ISBN 978-1-60329-200-9 (Kindle)
1. Austen, Jane, 1775–1817. Mansfield Park.   2. Austen, Jane, 1775–1817—Study
and teaching.   I. Folsom, Marcia McClintock, editor.   II. Wiltshire, John, editor.
                    PR4034.M33A67 2014
                 823'.7—dc23   2014028799

Approaches to Teaching World Literature 135
ISSN 1059-1133

Cover illustration for the paperback and electronic editions: *Fond Memories*,
by Charles Haigh-Wood (1856–1927). Oil on canvas.

Published by The Modern Language Association of America
26 Broadway, New York, NY 10004-1789
www.mla.org

CONTENTS

For our grandchildren
August and Lorenzo and Alejandro Folsom
Angus and Oscar Wiltshire

Part One

MATERIALS

Editions

The first edition of *Mansfield Park* was issued in 1814 by Thomas Egerton, a small publisher of military books, and was badly printed. The second, published by the prestigious house of John Murray and including corrections by the author, came out in 1816. Most editors of reprints since the mid–nineteenth century have used the second edition as the copy text.

For over eighty years, the Oxford edition, first published in 1923 and edited by R. W. Chapman, was the standard and is cited in many critical articles and chapters on *Mansfield Park*. This edition is "in the main a reprint" of the second edition (J. Austen, *Mansfield Park* [ed. Chapman] 541) but uses the first when the editor found printers' errors in the text of the second; the Oxford edition also emends when both first and second editions seem incorrect. With the exception of the Penguin edition, edited by Kathryn Sutherland and first published in 1996, all current paperback editions use the second edition as copy text. Sutherland's Penguin includes a note defending her choice of 1814: "There is a freshness and freedom about *MP* (1814) which is lost in the regulizations and 'corrections' begun in *MP* (1816) and continued by Chapman," she argues (J. Austen, *Mansfield Park* [ed. Sutherland] xliii).

Chapman's edition gathered additional notes when Mary Lascelles revised it for the 1965–66 impression of the third edition. It remained the basis for James Kinsley's Oxford University Press edition of 1970, which became the Oxford World's Classics edition of 1980, which in turn was reissued in 1990 (with an introduction by Marilyn Butler) and was the basis for Tony Tanner's Penguin edition of 1966.

There are many paperback and even cheap hardback editions of Austen's novel currently available, but students should be discouraged from using editions that don't preserve the original division into three volumes. One of the cheapest, the Wordsworth Classics edition (2000) lacks this division, though it contains a good introduction and notes. College teachers, and the contributors to this volume, usually use and choose to recommend one of four publications: the Oxford World's Classics, the Penguin, the Broadview, or the Norton.

The current Oxford World's Classics edition, first published in 2003, has an introduction and notes at the back of the volume by Jane Stabler, a bibliography and chronology as well as appendices on "*Lovers' Vows*" (though not the play text), "Rank and Social Status," "Dancing," and the navy. The Penguin edition has an excellent introduction and notes at the back of the volume and reprints Tanner's original Penguin introduction. The Broadview edition contains an excellent introduction and footnotes together with extracts from contemporary sources.

The Norton edition, edited by Claudia L. Johnson in 1998, is the most compendious. It contains a map of England in the nineteenth century, a brief introduction, a note on the value of money in Austen's lifetime, and "A Note on

Austen and the Text of *Mansfield Park*." The footnotes are sometimes too succinct to be helpful. This edition includes the full text of *Lovers' Vows* and, as Norton Critical editions do, a selection of context materials and edited extracts from nine critical articles, three of which are on the topic of slavery. Johnson's edition prefers the 1816 text in several instances where Chapman reverted to the 1814, but where other editors emend even when both agree, it tends to stay with the originals. For example, Johnson does not emend "usual" in the last sentence of volume 1, to "unusual," as all the other editors, including Sutherland, do. Editions like the Norton, which provide students with ready-made reading in secondary materials, may discourage them from doing their own research. Instructors must decide whether it is good teaching practice to use such editions.

Electronic reading devices, like the Kindle and Nook, are appearing in classrooms. The texts at present available on these are of dubious provenance, and students should probably be discouraged from using them, especially as some of the widely available paperback editions of *Mansfield Park* are quite cheap. Teachers should consult the illuminating essay by Laura Carroll in this volume about these e-books.

All citations of *Mansfield Park* in this volume, unless otherwise noted, are to the new standard edition from Cambridge University Press, edited by John Wiltshire (2005). This edition supersedes the Oxford edition edited by Chapman and Lascelles and all the recent paperback editions. Part of the nine-volume Cambridge edition of the *Works of Jane Austen*, it is a scholarly edition, which in footnotes shows variants between the 1814 and 1816 editions. It includes a long introduction and nearly a hundred pages of explanatory notes, many of them covering matters not dealt with elsewhere. It contains the full text of *Lovers' Vows* and has a useful introductory note to the play. Because of its extensive and reliable introduction, complete notes, a chronology contributed by Deirdre Le Faye, complete text of *Lovers' Vows*, and authoritative text, we encourage teachers to consult this edition, though it is too expensive to require for students. To facilitate teachers' use of citations from the novel in this volume, when we give page numbers for this Cambridge edition, they are followed by volume and chapter numbers (e.g., 450; vol. 3, ch. 8).

The introduction to the 2005 Cambridge edition begins with sections on the novel's composition and publication and on the 1814 and 1816 editions, arguing (with Le Faye) that the composition of *Mansfield Park* probably began in the spring of 1812. These sections review all Austen's references to the writing of the novel in her letters and consider the probable reasons for delays both in composition and publication. They also offer an analysis of differences between the first and second editions and a chronicle of Austen's own involvement in the publication of both. The essay in this volume by Laura Carroll further explores the significance of the differences between the two editions of the novel.

Another section of the introduction to the Cambridge edition examines issues in the dating of the action of the novel, explaining the reasons for controversy about whether Austen imagined the time when Fanny is eighteen to be 1808 and 1809, which was Chapman's conclusion ("Chronology"), or 1812–13, which was Brian Southam's ("Silence" [*Mansfield Park*] 494). Carefully reviewing the internal and external evidence, Wiltshire concludes that Chapman's is the correct dating but that Austen may not have intended the reader to conceive that the action took place in "a precise year or years" (Introduction xlv). A recent article by A. J. Downie provides compelling evidence that the period of the novel is 1808–09 ("Chronology").

A section on contextual and intertextual issues examines the possible sources and fascinating resonances of the names chosen for characters and places in *Mansfield Park*. It also considers the novel's use of real places and historical events; explains its reflection of a new seriousness in English culture during the time of the novel's composition; and traces the novel's allusions to, echoes of, and direct mentions of other literature—poetry, novels, plays, and the King James Version of the Bible.

The section on critical reception is a helpful review of the criticism of *Mansfield Park* from the comments of Austen's own family members and friends through the nineteenth- and twentieth-century debates about the novel. In our survey of the novel's critical reception, we offer a shorter version of this review but include works published since Wiltshire's edition. Teachers wanting to understand the history of critical commentary on the novel should consult the comprehensive and well-illustrated review in the introduction.

The last section of the introduction to the Cambridge edition offers an analysis of *Mansfield Park*'s literary significance that will help teachers and readers identify the range of concerns and innovative narrative techniques that distinguish the book. The provocative conclusions of this analysis, about the ways Fanny Price represents a completely new kind of character in fiction, about the novel's command of space and management of characters in both indoor and outdoor settings, about its ambitious reach into historical realities, and about its experiment in introducing tragedy into the romantic novel, can spark classroom discussion and student writing.

Critical Reception

There were no reviews of *Mansfield Park* when it first appeared in 1814, and when Walter Scott wrote the first appreciative account of Jane Austen's novels in the *Quarterly Review* in 1815, he did not even mention it (Rev. of *Emma*). (Perhaps to compensate for this neglect, she collected the opinions of the novel of her family and friends ["Opinions"].) The neglect was remedied in the same journal in 1821, through a review by Richard Whately that devoted most of his discussion of Jane Austen's art to *Mansfield Park*. He wrote perceptively of

Fanny's "passion," of "the slender hopes and enjoyments by which it is fed," and of the "restlessness and jealousy," which, for her, "tinges every event and every recollection" (329). And he pointed out how daring is Austen's risking the creation of a heroine like this. It was to be many years before this novel would find a critic as able to meet its challenges as Whately.

In the Victorian period, though Austen's reputation grew and though writers like George Eliot's partner, G. H. Lewes, praised her in the intellectual magazines (see his "Great Appraisal"), there is little sustained attention to *Mansfield Park*. In 1862, however, Julia Kavanagh, a popular novelist, surprisingly declared that *Mansfield Park* "in the opinion of many" was Austen's "most perfect novel." She noted Fanny's "silent grief, her struggles, her jealousy, in spite of all [Edmund's] kindness" and that "[s]elfishness and egotism prevail, in this tale, over the folly" that characterized figures in Austen's previous novels (366). It was only in the twentieth century that formal and sustained criticism of *Mansfield Park* started to appear.

This criticism began, to all intents and purposes, with a lecture the great Shakespearean critic A. C. Bradley gave in 1911. "Jane Austen," published in his *Miscellany* (1929), balances the strengths and weaknesses of *Mansfield Park*, such as the authorial "justice" that prevails despite the novel's moral program or the "exceptionally delicate and subtle development" of Fanny Price's character despite Bradley's uncomfortableness with the heroine (211, 212). But it was Reginald Farrer's influential but flashy centenary essay on Austen's work, published in the *Quarterly Review* in 1917, that set the tone for many twentieth-century treatments of the novel. "Fiction holds no heroine more repulsive" than Fanny Price "in her cast-iron self-righteousness and steely rigidity of purpose," Farrer wrote and followed this statement with a characterization of Mary Crawford as "by far the most persistently brilliant of Jane Austen's heroines" (192). His narrow, character-based assessment of the novel was essentially replicated by several later writers, most remarkably by D. W. Harding, whose essay "Regulated Hatred: An Aspect of the Work of Jane Austen" (1940) is rightly considered one of the key documents of Austen criticism.

The publication of Chapman's Oxford edition of Austen's novels in 1923 (*Novels*) was instrumental in her elevation to serious, classic status. Carefully edited, with appendices and illustrations "from contemporary sources," the volume of *Mansfield Park* featured a frontispiece view of Harleston Park, Northamptonshire (with the implication that Harleston Park represented the fictional Mansfield), the full text of *Lovers' Vows*, and appendices on the chronology of the novel, on "improvements," and on carriages and travel. Chapman's edition effectively set the stage for criticism in the next decades. Essays appeared exploring the relation between Mrs. Inchbald's play and the novel, and *improvement* in its many senses became a major concern of criticism, most notably in Alistair Duckworth's *The Improvement of the Estate* (1971).

The prestige of *Mansfield Park* increased further with Edmund Wilson's pages on the novel in "A Long Talk about Jane Austen," in his *Classics and Com-*

mercials (1950). Dismissing the "familiar" reaction of critics who dislike Fanny Price (199), Wilson concentrated instead on the novel's narrative techniques, and it was he who encouraged Vladimir Nabokov to give a lecture on *Mansfield Park*, which appeared in Nabokov's *Lectures on Literature* (1980). His notes, which have never been published in full, include a floor plan of the house at Mansfield and even a sketch of the precise type of geranium Fanny tends.

Lionel Trilling's important essay "Jane Austen and *Mansfield Park*," first published in 1954 and very widely reprinted, is cited by several contributors to this volume. Affecting at first to share most readers' dislike of the novel and its heroine, Trilling turns the tables on them with the striking remark, "Yet *Mansfield Park* is a great novel, its greatness being commensurate with its power to offend" ("In *Mansfield Park*" 44). The novel, he contends, is a searching expose of modern culture and its values and the first novel in English to explore the complex and difficult moral life of modernity. In the same year, but hardly noticed, appeared Q. D. Leavis's essay on *Mansfield Park*, as an introduction to an Illustrated Classics edition. This is a brief but striking presentation of the novel as a searching and tragic work, to be compared with Shakespeare. Like Trilling and implicitly Nabokov, Leavis argued that Austen was on a level with the masters of the nineteenth-century European novel.

Many serious essays were written about *Mansfield Park* in the next decades, most of them explicating the novel's treatment of character and morality. Thomas R. Edwards's "The Difficult Beauty of *Mansfield Park*" (1965) is probably the article that most retains its usefulness. Avrom Fleishman's *A Reading of Mansfield Park, An Essay in Critical Synthesis*, first published in 1967, is a short book-length study that looks at the novel from a variety of angles. Written in a clear and forthright style, it is worth consulting.

Another powerful and widely influential reading, by Tanner, was first published as an introduction to the Penguin text in 1966. As "The Quiet Thing: *Mansfield Park*" it became a chapter of Tanner's *Jane Austen* (1986), a book that in 2007 was reissued with a new preface and notes. Like Trilling's essay, Tanner's is a rehabilitation of the novel. "In the debilitated but undeviating figure of Fanny Price we should perceive the pain and labour involved in maintaining true values in a corrosive world of dangerous energies and selfish power-play," Tanner writes (171–72). He celebrates Fanny's "incredible moral strength" in a changing world that Austen renders as threatening to the inner life (175). Butler's reading of *Mansfield Park* in her *Jane Austen and the War of Ideas* (1975) sees the novel as a paramount conservative text in a revolutionary age, in which Fanny undergoes a series of tests of her moral values. Treating the novel as an almost didactic narrative, Butler ignores its representation of Fanny's inner struggles with inconvenient feelings, and the chapter (219–49) is possibly now of historical interest only. Both Tanner's and Butler's treatments of the novel's heroine are discussed in our section "Fanny Price" below.

Much of the criticism of *Mansfield Park* in the ensuing decades was feminist in spirit. Margaret Kirkham in *Jane Austen: Feminism and Fiction* (1983), aligning Austen with Mary Wollstonecraft, describes *Mansfield Park* as far from "the work of conservative quietism that much twentieth-century criticism has turned it into" and claims that it is in fact Austen's "most ambitious and radical criticism of contemporary prejudice in society and in literature" (119). Kirkham was the first writer to link the novel's title to the Mansfield decision against slavery in England, which became a key platform of postcolonial readings of the novel in the 1990s. Also notable was Mary Poovey's *The Proper Lady and the Woman Writer* (1984). Johnson's "*Mansfield Park*: Confusions of Guilt and Revolutions of Mind" appeared in her *Jane Austen: Women, Politics, and the Novel* (1988). Like Kirkham, Johnson contests the then prevailing view of the novel as a vindication of conservative values; she suggests that, in effect, Austen is sabotaging the Bertram family and their values through the persistent exposure of their capacity for self-deception.

"Jane Austen and Empire," Edward Said's chapter on *Mansfield Park* in his *Culture and Imperialism* (1993), is referred to by several writers in this volume and in effect inaugurated the postcolonial readings of the novel that have been widely published in the past twenty years. His complex, thoughtful, and even troubled argument rejects "the rhetoric of blame" that has powered some postcolonial accounts (96): his essay has fed into the feminist, postcolonial, and historicist synthesis that governs much published criticism of *Mansfield Park*. In this volume, three essays offer ways of incorporating a postcolonial reading of *Mansfield Park* into the classroom. They take as a starting point John Wiltshire's "Decolonising *Mansfield Park*" (2003), which reviews and appraises the influential postcolonial arguments of Said and of Southam.

Wiltshire's chapter on *Mansfield Park* in *Jane Austen and the Body* (1992), "'Eloquent Blood': The Coming Out of Fanny Price," analyzes the ways that Fanny's inadmissible feelings of envy, jealousy, even rage, may be discerned in Austen's prose, in her presentation of Fanny's body and her blushes. His close readings of specific passages—for examples, the scene when Edmund guides Mary on Fanny's horse, the scene in the drawing room when Fanny has retreated to a distant sofa, or the scene in the East Room when Fanny is confronted by Sir Thomas—are detailed and psychologically astute and can be directly translated into classroom reading aloud and analysis.

Roger Sales's *Jane Austen and Representations of Regency England* (1994) contains "*Mansfield Park*: The Regency Crisis and the Theatre," a long chapter that continues the effort to place Austen's novel in historical context; Sales in fact calls it a "Condition-of-England novel" (87). In particular, his analysis of the relatively unstudied character Tom Bertram as the regent of Mansfield Park suggests that Austen's hatred of the profligate prince regent of England is figured in Tom's gambling, interest in cross-dressing, and interest in theater. Sales contrasts Tom's apparent indifference to women with Henry Crawford's preoccupation with them, and he argues that in Henry, Austen figures the Regency dandy. Sales's analysis of *Mansfield Park* emphasizes the novel's complexity and resistance to interpretation. In *Imagining Characters: Six Conversations about*

Women Writers (1997), A. S. Byatt and Ignês Sodré open their book with a discussion of *Mansfield Park*. This informal "conversation" between a well-known novelist and a psychotherapist about the novel raises interesting issues and includes many unusual but perceptive comments. It is a good source for vividly expressed views that would provoke class discussion.

Several essays in this volume indicate the usefulness of Austen biographies for students and teachers. Claire Tomalin places *Mansfield Park* in historical context in her *Jane Austen: A Life* (1997), also arguing that it is "about the condition of England" during the Regency, when the princes were able to live "with a total disregard for justice, religious principles, or the sanctity of marriage" (224). Tomalin suggests that perhaps Austen's intentions changed as she wrote this novel, creating confusion for readers trying to figure out the Crawfords or to decide whether Fanny is priggish; for her, too, the strength of the novel is that it is "open to different and opposing interpretations" (228). The psychologically perceptive Tomalin biography presents the Austen family and its forebears; the worlds of Steventon, Bath, and Chawton; the relations among the family and its neighbors, friends, and extended kin; and connections among Austen's early and later works. Park Honan's *Jane Austen: Her Life* (1987), has also proved useful for teachers: in particular, his chapter 4 suggests a connection between Austen's cousin Eliza de Feuillide and Mary Crawford (and Henry Crawford, too) that could be the basis for a student presentation.

Another attempt to place *Mansfield Park* in historical context is Mary Waldron's *Jane Austen and the Fiction of Her Time* (1999), which considers this novel in relation to the novels of Hannah More (*Coelebs* and *Thoughts*), Fanny Burney, Sarah Burney, Maria Edgeworth, and Mary Brunton. Knowledgeably tracing Fanny's dilemmas alongside those of such virtuous heroines as Emmeline, Cecilia, Camilla, Clarentine, and Belinda, Waldron offers close readings of Fanny's inner turmoil in such scenes as the theatricals, in her talk with Mary in Mrs. Grant's shrubberies, and the dinner party at the Grants'. "In *Mansfield Park*," Waldron argues, "Austen transforms the late-eighteenth-century conduct novel, making a strong bid for the liberation of fiction from its obligations to provide single, unequivocal moral readings" (111).

In the first edition of Edward Copeland and Juliet McMaster's *The Cambridge Companion to Jane Austen* (1997), Wiltshire offers a three-part essay on the three novels composed at Chawton, capturing succinctly how psychological depth in exploration of many characters and narrative innovations make *Mansfield Park* a "milestone in the English novel" ("*Mansfield Park*" 65). In that collection, the essays by McMaster on class, Copeland on money, and John F. Burrows on style are excellent resources for teachers. In the second edition of *The Cambridge Companion* (2011), Jocelyn Harris compares *Pride and Prejudice* and *Mansfield Park* and considers the importance of the theatricals to the meaning of *Mansfield Park* ("*Pride and Prejudice* and *Mansfield Park*"). Paula Byrne's *Jane Austen and the Theatre* (2002) has a helpful analysis of all the plays that the Crawfords and Bertrams consider performing, indicating Austen's extensive knowledge of late-eighteenth-century drama and the implications of characters' preferences for various proposed choices. Penny Gay's *Jane Austen and the Theatre*, published in the same year, refutes the criticism (mainly of *Mansfield Park*) that Austen was antitheatrical. Instead, Gay demonstrates how Austen in her last three novels reveals her extensive knowledge of eighteenth-century drama, her enjoyment of dramatic dialogue and situation, and her ability to translate dramatic convention in her fiction.

Another thoughtful study of Austen's relation to contemporary literary culture is William Deresiewicz's *Jane Austen and the Romantic Poets* (2004). Attempting to account for the difference between Austen's first three novels and the last three, Deresiewicz argues that her "encounter with the Romantics deepened her art, darkened it, made it more intuitive, ambiguous, and unsettled, but also more bold and mature" (3). His chapter on *Mansfield Park* considers the ways that Wordsworthian concerns of memory, substitution, loss, and attachment underlie patterns of the novel, especially in Fanny's feelings. He argues that Fanny is "an extremely passionate young woman . . . the most passionate figure Austen ever created" (74)—a modern critic at last amplifying the insight of Austen's first perceptive critic, Whately.

Sarah Emsley's *Jane Austen's Philosophy of the Virtues* (2005) has a chapter entitled "Fanny Price and the Contemplative Life," and Emsley offers a clear argument why Fanny cannot be viewed as submissive. In her *Cambridge Introduction to Jane Austen* (2006), Janet Todd begins by admitting that *Mansfield Park* "is rarely anyone's favourite Austen work." Nevertheless, she argues that the novel is "Austen's most serious look at childhood as influence on personality" (89).

The 2006 annual general meeting of the Jane Austen Society of North America, held in Tucson, Arizona, was called "Fresh Perspectives on *Mansfield Park*," and an issue of the society's journal, *Persuasions* (28 [2006]), contains nineteen essays on the novel originally given at that conference. The online version of *Persuasions* (27.1 [2006]) contains six more essays on *Mansfield Park*. Of particular interest to teachers might be Miriam Rheingold Fuller's "Crawfords on the Couch: A Psychoanalytical Exploration of the Effects of the 'Bad School' on Henry and Mary Crawford"; paired essays, by Alison Shea and by David Monaghan, debating Patricia Rozema's *Mansfield Park* film; a close reading of chapter 11 in volume 1 of *Mansfield Park*, by Maggie Lane ("Star-gazing"); June Sturrock's essay on the significance of the West Indies connection; and Johnson's examination of Fanny in the East Room ("Jane Austen's Relics").

Julia Prewitt Brown's *The Bourgeois Interior: How the Middle Class Imagines Itself in Literature and Film* (2008) begins with a chapter on Austen called "Fanny's Room." In a telling contrast, Brown compares Austen's examination of Elizabeth Bennet's consciousness as Elizabeth reads Darcy's letter and the way that Austen reveals Fanny's consciousness through her connection to physical objects. Brown's essay in this volume suggests how this contrast might be developed in the classroom.

In a fascinating pairing, *Jane Austen and Charles Darwin: Naturalists and Novelists* (2008), Peter W. Graham works out numerous insights about the Austen and Darwin families and the influence of sibling development ("'Entangled Bank'"). In an argument similar to Kay Souter's essay in this volume, Graham sorts out the family dynamics of the Ward sisters in *Mansfield Park*, and the sibling relationships of the Bertram, Price, and Crawford children in the next generation, in the light of Frank Sulloway's theory of sibling differentiation. In *Two Guys Read Jane Austen*, an offbeat, short book by Steve Chandler and Terrence N. Hill (2008), the writers chat back and forth in e-mail messages as they read *Pride and Prejudice* and *Mansfield Park* together, commenting as they go on their own lives, prior prejudices, and new discoveries. To their credit, they find *Mansfield Park* the greater novel.

Mansfield Park Films

The three films made so far of *Mansfield Park* offer strikingly different solutions to the opportunities presented by using the novel as a starting point. These films provide fascinating evidence of filmmakers' and directors' decisions about how to conceive of Fanny Price as heroine and how to envision the Bertrams' lives and estate. All three are currently available on compact disc: the 1983 BBC television miniseries in six episodes (dir. Giles), the 1999 Miramax film written and directed by Patricia Rozema, and the 2007 ITV television movie (dir. MacDonald). Most students recognize that film is a quite different medium from a written text and that the challenges of making an adaptation of a novel are considerable. If time allows, a discussion of how different directors meet these challenges can raise interesting questions about both the films and the novel. It can also be helpful for students to know that the adaptation of classic texts like *Mansfield Park* has its own history.

The movie of *Pride and Prejudice* made in Hollywood in 1940 is a precedent for later Austen adaptations. This American production rewrites the novel, invents new scenes between Elizabeth and Darcy, dispenses with the Pemberley visit, and changes some of the characters. However, until the 1980s, British television adaptations of Austen's novels were made with an expectation of faithfulness to the original text. Minor changes were acceptable, but on the whole the adapter and producer sought to reproduce the novel as far as possible. Television was felt to be an intimate medium; watching a television dramatization was akin to the reading of the novel. This tradition of fidelity was broken by the BBC miniseries of *Northanger Abbey* made in 1986. Influenced by the cinema of Fellini, it introduced new characters and added mysterious gothic suggestions that altered the antiromantic emphasis of the novel. Adaptations of classics for both cinema and television began to be seen as an opportunity for the screenwriter and director to present original and contemporary readings of foundational works, transforming them for a modern audience.

The BBC miniseries of *Mansfield Park* of 1983 belongs to the earlier phase of adaptation. The dramatization keeps close to the novel's text, and its characterization of Fanny as a modest, gentle, but on occasion surprisingly firm figure is close to the novel's. Students used to the constantly moving camera of modern cinema may find this series slow-moving and often tedious. There are several stationary shots of carriages driving off along gravel driveways, which imply but do not show a world outside the confined scenes of this largely studio-bound production. Still, there is sometimes mobility to the camera work. When *Lovers' Vows* is being cast, the camera focuses on and follows Mary Crawford as she wanders about the room, balancing a teacup in her hand, and this action reveals her inward musing about the best tactic to persuade Edmund to act with her. The production here shows more of Mary's interiority than the novel does, perhaps in order to invite the audience into a greater intimacy with the figure.

This playacting sequence is fully presented in episode 3 (the DVD lists scenes: the title of the first of three dealing with the theatricals is "Theatrics of Poetry"). These can be drawn on by teachers, as Gay suggests in this volume. They dramatize extracts from *Lovers' Vows* that Jane Austen left to her readers' imagination: Tom as the rhyming Butler; the opening dialogue between Frederick and Agatha, which allows Henry and Maria to embrace; and Edmund and Mary rehearsing the dialogue that culminates in Amelia's "What is the subject?" and Anhalt's response, "Love," while Fanny, as prompter, looks on.

This miniseries was the only one of *Mansfield Park* that the British broadcaster ventured to make in a period that saw four television versions of *Pride and Prejudice* and three of *Emma*. The challenges of adapting this novel to the screen, evidently greater than the challenges posed by Austen's other books, center on the character of the heroine. The first and so far only movie version of the novel, written and directed by Rozema, was released by Miramax in 1999. It followed the films of *Sense and Sensibility* in 1995 and *Emma* in 1996, each of which, but especially *Sense and Sensibility*, was successful in both commercial and critical terms. Rozema decided to make a film that would create a new narrative out of several Austen sources. As the opening title sequence puts it, the film is "based on Jane Austen's *Mansfield Park*, her letters and early journals." It offers a clearly revisionist, modern interpretation of the text, altering some characters, drawing on sophisticated cinematic techniques, and addressing the interests of a contemporary audience.

Rozema's approach involved a radical revision of the character of Fanny Price, who was reinvented as a forthright, active young woman. Writing in her East Room to her sister Susan, this Fanny is satirical and highly critical of the Bertram family into which she has been adopted. In voice-over commentaries adapted from Austen's juvenilia, she both comments on the family and reads extracts from the fiction she is writing. In the 1983 *Mansfield Park* miniseries, her letters to her brother William were used as a pretext for voice-overs that provided continuity and information; Rozema's adaptation of this adaptation injects independence into the figure and elides the episodes in the novel that convey Fanny's lonely struggle with her conscience and desires.

In constructing her film, Rozema drew on the postcolonial critique of the novel that had become dominant in the last decades of the twentieth century. Fundamental to this critique is the view that the Bertrams' estate of Mansfield Park draws its wealth and prosperity from the indefensible practice of slavery on its holdings in Antigua. "We all live off the profits, Fanny," Edmund reluctantly tells her while the two are out riding. Sir Thomas is drawn as a lascivious, tyrannical figure, the typically ruthless planter; Lady Bertram, as an indolent and drug-addicted planter's wife; their eldest son, Tom, as a rebel against his father's iniquities. In an important scene (episode 8, "Sir Thomas's Return" in the DVD's prefatory list), the moment in the novel when Fanny asks Sir Thomas about the slave trade and the silence that follows is reconceptualized in the Rozema film. Edmund and Fanny, who has read Thomas Clarkson's *History of the Slave-Trade*, speak for a modern audience after Sir Thomas reveals his shamelessly racist (and sexist) attitudes. Students might be asked to compare the sketchy moment set in the East Room in the novel, in which Fanny reminds Edmund that she asked a question about the slave trade, with its full dramatization in the film.

Previous literary critical readings of *Mansfield Park* ignored the implications of the family's holdings in Antigua, often treating the novel as a conservative portrayal of the English country house ethos, in which Fanny is a redemptive figure whose presence and influence in the house ultimately restores its moral authority. In contrast, Rozema's film underlines Fanny's hatred of the slave trade and depicts her struggle not to integrate herself into Sir Thomas's family but to attain independence.

An interesting scene in the Rozema film that might be discussed in class occurs when Henry Crawford, taking the volume from Fanny's hands, reads a passage from Sterne's *Sentimental Journey* to Fanny. It includes the moment that *Mansfield Park* alludes to in Maria's expressive declaration before the iron gate at Sotherton: "I cannot get out, as the starling said" (116; vol. 1, ch. 10). In a transmutation of another episode from the novel—Henry's acting of Shakespeare's *Henry VIII*—his reading of Sterne arrests and moves Fanny. This quiet scene in the library, sunlight falling on the two figures, the diffused photography of Fanny's responses suggesting her enthrallment, is a telling example of the process of transpositional reworking that is one of the most fascinating aspects of film adaptation. The implication here is that if Maria, who spies on the pair through a narrow opening, like a cage, is trapped, so in a sense is Fanny. But she will not, as she tells Edmund, "be sold off like one of your father's slaves." This statement is made in the film, not in the novel.

A number of exotic caged birds have been seen in the drawing room in which the Bertram family assembles. One of the film's most daring and visually compelling scenes takes place against the grim background of the Price home in Portsmouth, where a spectacular display of fireworks gives way to the amazing release from a wicker cage of many white pigeons or doves, which circle and fly off into the sky. The boy who is in charge of the display mumbles something about "starlings flying," and Fanny understands—perhaps that it is as much about Henry's capability for lavish expenditure as it is about his declaration of love. This metaphoric chain culminates in the movie's closing sequence. Now Fanny is on the way to becoming a published author, and the camera, filming high above the characters in a swinging movement that imitates a bird's flight, completes this cinematic arc of meaning: Fanny is now free. Treating the original text of *Mansfield Park* as raw material, the filmmaker has made her own distinctive narrative. The film closes in a celebration of Fanny's independence and creativity—a creativity that the writer of the film has claimed for herself.

In the ending, Rozema's distinctive narrative clashes with the novel's narrative trajectory. The happy ending that installs Fanny as the true daughter in the patriarchal edifice, an edifice implicated in the slave trade, blurs the film's ideology. Rozema's narrative is strained by its reliance on the plot of the novel, because in the novel Fanny does not attain independence at the end: she becomes the wife of an Anglican clergyman who owes his living to the patronage of Mansfield Park. The film's ending offers opportunity for lively classroom debate, and that opportunity might be considered with the closing speculations of Paula Loscocco's essay in this volume.

The television play of 2007 is an example of another interesting feature of Austen adaptations: this adaptation is influenced by its predecessors almost as much as by the novel. At the same time, like the earlier adaptations, it strives to distinguish itself. The emphasis on Fanny's physical attractiveness, her energy and mobility, is similar to that emphasis in Rozema's film, but the scenes that show Fanny romping with children take a hint from Emma Thompson's *Sense and Sensibility*. Fanny's brother William, absent from the earlier movie, is made an important figure in the telefilm. Mansfield Park, in Rozema's film an abandoned and decaying mansion, is restored as a beautiful Regency building. In this respect, as in others, the television play is a return to the traditional treatment of Austen novels in productions for a television audience.

That Fanny's return to her home in Portsmouth is omitted means that the last chapters of *Mansfield Park* must be reinvented. Fanny is thus present when Tom is carried home desperately ill. The scenes of her nursing Tom plausibly endear her to both brothers and begin to turn Edmund's thoughts toward his cousin. Mary Crawford arrives, and her true nature is revealed more decisively when she says in the telefilm, "I never bribed a physician in my life," directly and tactlessly to Fanny instead of slipping these words into a letter from London (501; vol. 3, ch.14). The last dialogue between Mary and Edmund, only reported in the novel, occurs in the drawing room, and the Mansfield interior makes Mary's London attitudes seem starkly unacceptable. Edmund is convincingly shocked. The makers of the telefilm may be coping with the difficulties we discuss in "The Last Chapter" in our "Backgrounds and Issues" essay, in trying to make Fanny and Edmund's union romantically believable. The Rozema film explains their union by having Edmund admire Fanny's spirit. The changes both films made in her character might have been to overcome what the filmmakers regarded as problems: the problem of making a compelling film with such a heroine, the problem of Edmund's abrupt courtship of her. In any case, the comparisons make for interesting classroom discussion.

The greatest challenge for a visual interpretation of *Mansfield Park* must lie in those episodes in which Fanny's psychological life is represented in some of Austen's most original and searching prose—when Fanny watches Edmund and Mary out riding or struggles with her conscience and her jealousy in the East Room. These passages are discussed in Brown's and Emsley's contributions to this volume. Their essays make clear that earlier critical treatments of Fanny that find her unpleasantly virtuous ignore her jealousy, her battle with her own passion, and her anger. Of course, it would be difficult to evoke these psychologically complex episodes cinematically. The result is that Fanny Price is constructed as a simpler, and perhaps more appealing, heroine in all three films.

Digital Resources

There is a vast and growing body of digital resources for Austen's novels and for related study that can help teachers and students. The essays in this volume by Carroll and Lynn Voskuil contain specific suggestions for incorporating digital resources into teaching *Mansfield Park*, and Voskuil's essay even suggests how a hybrid course might use certain digital materials and maps online.

www.jasna.org/persuasions/on-line/index.html

Persuasions On-line is a journal of essays about Austen and her writing. The journal is peer-reviewed, and the essays are of excellent quality. It appears twice a year, and its index takes users to past issues. Through the JASNA Web site (jasna.org), teachers can access the tables of contents of issues of the journal, which makes full texts available. Access is free. (Through the Web site, teachers can see contents for the printed journal, *Persuasions*, but not complete essays.)

http://austenonly.com

Austenonly is a blog written by a single person, Julie Wakefield, a Janeite and historian. She does meticulous research and offers essays on specific aspects of the novels. See, for example, her post on the theatricals in *Mansfield Park*: http://austenonly.com/2010/06/06/jane-austen-fanny-price-and-private-theatricals/. Access is free.

http://www.pemberley.com/janeinfo/janeinfo.html

Jane Austen Information Page, perhaps the most familiar of the Austen Web sites, is a vast collection of Austen texts, academic articles, Austen's letters, juvenilia, selections, and modern takeoffs and spin-offs. Austen readers post comments, argue, debate, and comment on one another's comments here, and it is probably the best place to survey the "Fanny Wars" that Kay Souter mentions in her essay. Access is free.

http://ebooks.adelaide.edu.au/a/austen/jane/a93m/

Librivox has free, public-domain audio recordings of books to download. Access is free. There is a recording of *Mansfield Park* (http://librivox.org/mansfield -park-by-jane-austen/) and also one of *Lovers' Vows* (http://librivox.org/lovers -vows-by-august-von-kotzebue/).

http://victorian.lang.nagoya-u.ac.jp/concordance/austen/

A Hyper-Concordance to the Works of Jane Austen is written in C++, a program that scans and displays lines in response to commands entered by the user. The main advantage of the program is that it identifies not only the concordance lines but the words occurring to the left and the right of the word or phrase searched. It also reports the total number of text lines, the total word count, and the number of occurrences of the word or phrase searched. The full text of the Austen book is displayed in a box at the bottom of the screen. Each line of the text is numbered, and the line number and the term or phrase searched provide a link to the full text. Access is free.

http://www.jstor.org/

With more than a thousand academic journals and over 1 million images, letters, and other primary sources, *JSTOR* is one of the world's best sources for academic content. Users may search its list by academic discipline. Access is not free: libraries must subscribe.

http://www.oed.com/

The *Oxford English Dictionary* is the world's most comprehensive dictionary of the English language. It covers words from across the English-speaking world and traces the development of English from the earliest records to the present day. An unsurpassed guide to the meaning, history, and pronunciation of over 600,000 words, it traces the usage of words through three million quotations from a wide range of international English language sources, from classic literature to film scripts and cookery books. Access is not free. In this volume, the essay by Regulus Allen suggests ways that students might use the *OED* to inform class discussions.

http://universitypublishingonline.org/cambridge/companions/

Cambridge Companions Online contains *The Cambridge Companions to Literature and Classics,* a collection that offers over two thousand comprehensive and well-written essays on major authors, periods, and genres, written by experts and designed for student readers. Writers are placed in literary and historical context; their works are analyzed and their influence on later writers assessed. There are two editions of *The Cambridge Companion to Jane Austen,* both edited by Copeland and McMaster (1997, 2011), and each has different essays regarding *Mansfield Park.* Access is not free.

janeausten.ac.uk

Although *Jane Austen's Fiction Manuscripts* includes no material from *Mansfield Park,* it gathers together some 1,100 pages of writing in Jane Austen's hand. Through the site's display of the manuscripts, one can trace Austen's development as a writer from her childhood to the year of her death. Transcriptions of the manuscripts, including their corrections, are also viewable. This is a unique and fascinating resource for all Austen readers. Access is free.

Part Two

APPROACHES

Introduction

The Historical and Naval Background

For more than two decades, from 1793, when Republican France declared war on Great Britain, until Napoleon's final defeat at the battle of Waterloo in June 1815, Britain was engaged in conflict with France and its allies. These years saw the resumption of earlier warfare between the rival imperial powers and ended with Britain's consolidating its position as dominant world power throughout the nineteenth century.

During this time, Britain's army and navy were massively expanded. The navy grew nearly fivefold in size during Jane Austen's lifetime, from 30,000 men in the early 1790s to 140,000 men in 1810. The great increase in manpower was accompanied by an exponential rise in the building of naval vessels. By far the most important site for the construction of ships for the British navy was Portsmouth, a highly fortified city on the south coast of England, protected from enemy action at sea, and from attack by an invading army on land, by a series of ramparts.

Opposite Portsmouth lies the Isle of Wight (Fanny Price's *"the Island"* [20; vol. 1, ch. 1), visible on a clear day and providing natural protection for ships entering the harbor. Watchtowers on the coast kept a vigilant eye out for enemy ships; entry to the city, which is built on an island, was only through manned gateways. Portsmouth's dockyards, where vessels were built and repaired, were the largest and busiest in the world, and its port, from which fighting ships departed to the Atlantic and Indian Oceans as well as to the Mediterranean, was vital to British sea power. (It was from the George Inn on the high street, for instance, that Nelson had departed to his famous victory over the French fleet at the Battle of Trafalgar in 1805.) In addition, thousands of soldiers were barracked on the Isle of Wight, so it is not an exaggeration to say that this area was the heart and engine of British imperial power.

Portsmouth is mentioned early in *Mansfield Park* (8) but only as the place from which Fanny must make her journey northward, via London, to the midlands of England. It seems likely that Austen's original readers were expected to pick up on the significance of the name of Portsmouth (and understood that the Bertram sisters' mockery of Fanny's focus on "the island" only exposes their own ignorance of the importance of that city and island). The setting of the first two volumes of the novel is the Park itself, a secluded country estate to which no town seems close. The unevenly distributed prosperity brought to England by the war, and by overseas holdings, may lie in the background, but the Bertram family, apart from Sir Thomas and possibly Tom, is depicted as insular, complacent, and indifferent to world affairs.

The national background, however, asserts its presence in a number of oblique ways. Soon after Fanny arrives at Mansfield, her brother William decides to make the navy his career, and the two children, aged eleven and twelve, spend a last holiday together at Mansfield before he goes to sea. Fanny's love for William, as well as his life at sea, is kept before the reader once again when in chapter 4—Fanny now just eighteen—the Crawfords arrive at Mansfield. Mary's humorous reference to her brother's short letters allows the novel to enter the information that "Miss Price has a brother at sea" and that William and Fanny have continued to write to each other over the seven years he has been away. "At sea, has she?—In the King's service of course," is Mary's immediate response. That William is serving in the Royal Navy and that Fanny mentions "the foreign stations" he has visited are tiny but telling indications of the wide reach of the campaign against Napoleon's fleets. But "[o]f the [navy's] inferior ranks," Mary Crawford announces, "with an air of grandeur" (perhaps intended to throw a shade of irony over her snobbery), "we know very little" (70). Henry and Mary Crawford have lived with Admiral Crawford, in Hill Street, Mayfair, about the smartest address in London at the time. Mary's talk is of admirals retired and rich from prize money. As far as interest in the progress of the naval war is concerned, the younger Crawfords seem as indifferent as the Bertrams.

Whether Austen is indifferent to the larger historical context of her narrative is a question that students might consider. "Poor William" is much in Fanny's thoughts and mentioned at regular intervals, as when in the midst of a discussion about the clergy Fanny can't but help voice her concern for him (129; vol. 1, ch. 11). Her inner life is hinted at in these glimpses of her preoccupation with William's whereabouts and the dangers she imagines in his life, in her interest in travel literature, her animation in speaking of "the foreign stations he had been on" and her tears when mentioning "the number of years he had been absent" (70). When she is most troubled by the conflict between her various "duties," amid the domestic tensions that develop in volume 1, the reader is reminded again of William Price by the sad little "sketch of a ship sent four years ago from the Mediterranean . . . with H. M. S. Antwerp at the bottom, in letters as tall as the mainmast" that Fanny has pinned up in her East Room (179; vol. 1, ch. 16).

Sir Thomas Bertram returns, and later that year Maria and Rushworth marry; life at Mansfield, in a mild winter, settles down to a quiet routine. Then Henry Crawford comes back for a fortnight's stay and decides to amuse himself by making "a small hole in Fanny Price's heart" (267; vol. 2, ch. 6). Soon after, in the same chapter, William, "the so long absent and dearly loved brother," sends a letter from Portsmouth that makes Fanny tremble with joy at the prospect of seeing him again at Mansfield (270). From this point on, the narrative of Henry's courtship, or perhaps attempted seduction, of Fanny becomes intertwined with her love for her brother. With William, naval matters inevitably come to the surface of the novel again, and the war against Napoleon impinges more and more on the domestic scene at Mansfield.

A good passage to discuss with a class appears when William entertains the assembled family with his adventures:

William was often called on by his uncle to be the talker. . . . Young as he was, William had already seen a great deal. He had been in the Mediterranean—in the West Indies—in the Mediterranean again—had been often taken on shore by the favour of his Captain, and in the course of seven years had known every variety of danger, which sea and war together could offer. With such means in his power he had a right to be listened to; and though Mrs. Norris could fidget about the room, and disturb every body in quest of two needlefulls of thread or a second hand shirt button in the midst of her nephew's account of a shipwreck or an engagement, every body else was attentive; and even Lady Bertram could not hear of such horrors unmoved, or without sometimes lifting her eyes from her work to say, "Dear me! how disagreeable.—I wonder any body can ever go to sea."   (275)

Though William's experiences are convincingly implied to be thrilling, it is interesting that they are not in fact shown in the novel, only characterized by quick reference to the immense distances across the Atlantic and back—"in the Mediterranean—in the West Indies—in the Mediterranean again"—that William has sailed. Even though his accounts include a "shipwreck or an engagement," they are presented in such general terms as "every variety of danger" or "such horrors." In contrast, the narrative gives its attention to the domestic scene, specifying, and rhythmically mimicking, Mrs. Norris's interfering activity, at once self-important and parsimonious, and ending the elaborate sentence that generalizes William's narratives in a return to rueful comedy with Lady Bertram's fatuous contribution. Does this scene confirm the view that Austen's interest is exclusively on domestic life rather than on the political dramas and world events that surround it? Almost certainly not: the very delight in the domestic comedy here exposes the family's insularity, in Lady Bertram taken to an absurd extreme, and ignorance. Austen is dexterous enough both to acknowledge the wider world and to focus on the insular one. Here she captures the difficulty those at home have imagining the circumstances of William's life at sea.

The narrative turns to another in the listening circle—Henry Crawford. Austen has been describing the reciprocal love of Fanny and William through his eyes, a picture that he has "moral taste enough to value" (274). Listening to William's seafaring accounts, Crawford wishes he were an independent and self-made man like the young and courageous midshipman, but reality comically cuts into this "reverie of retrospection and regret" when he finds it "as well to be at once with horses and grooms at his command" (276) so that he can loan William a hunter for the next day's fox hunt and thus insinuate himself into Fanny's affections—and put her in his debt.

In her essay in this volume, Dorice Williams Elliott brings out the importance to *Mansfield Park* of gift relationships. She suggests that Fanny is the recipient of intangible gifts, among them education and the prospect of marriage into the gentry's higher ranks—gifts that come with strings attached and that she can reciprocate only with gratitude, obedience, and submission. The Bertrams, congratulating themselves on the benevolence of their scheme to adopt Fanny in the first chapter, are, however, innocent of any specific design to exploit her. Later in the novel, when Mrs. Norris reminds her that she is a dependent and ought to do as she is told, everyone in the room is shocked at this moral black-mail (173; vol. 1, ch. 15). Nevertheless, as Elliott explains, Fanny is confronted with a series of moral crises in which her strongly ingrained sense of obligation toward her adoptive family painfully conflicts with her instinctive feelings.

Austen makes another, more sinister variation on gift relationships. From the outset of his campaign, Henry Crawford lays siege to Fanny through the manipulation of affective ties and especially of her love for William. The loan of the hunter is only the first of his attempts to make her feel indebted to him. The lead-up to Fanny's coming-out ball, arranged by Sir Thomas, who himself has ulterior as well as generous motives, gives Crawford another opportunity. He has Mary persuade Fanny to accept a necklace from him. By means of this necklace, he can compel her, without his confronting her, to accept this token of his affection and, as Elliott notes, to recognize his intention to possess her. This gift is more like a trap. But it is through William's ambition to rise in the navy that Crawford finds the most persuasive means to exert leverage over Fanny's feelings. The navy and its imbrication in the British social system and politics come most plainly into the novel here.

William is a spirited young man who makes no secret of his frustration at being stuck in the rank of midshipman. He needs a commission as an officer if he is to begin to climb the ladder of promotion, which, with luck, will take him to the captainship of a vessel and the prize money that might, again with luck, result. When Crawford overhears Fanny say that she is sure Sir Thomas "will do every thing in his power to get [her brother] made" ("made" means promoted to the rank of an officer) (290; vol. 2, ch. 7), he sees (as a reader must understand in retrospect) another opportunity to increase her affection for him and demon-strate the genuineness of his feelings for her. The complexity of the judgments the novel asks the reader to make, which Peter Graham emphasizes in his essay, is demonstrated here. It is only because Crawford urgently loves Fanny that he pursues his secret plan, but at the same time, that plan is a form of exploitation, because it targets what he has seen are her tenderest feelings.

Crawford's scheme demonstrates how the British system of patronage and interest—mutual obligations and favors among the powerful—works. William's frustration is historically accurate: there were far more young men aspiring to promotion than there were officer positions for them to fill. Through Crawford's relationship with his uncle the admiral, and through Sir Charles, the admiral's friend, William obtains what many would wait years to obtain. Austen exposes the system in one brilliant satirical paragraph (346; vol. 2, ch. 13). Fanny under-stands that Crawford has "been conferring an obligation," that "[y]our kindness to William makes me more obliged to you than words can express" (349), but the obligation is not enough to make her accept his proposal, which—coming hard on the heels of the news of William's promotion—causes her great distress. Her suffering on the very day that she rejoices in William's promotion is an eloquent testimony to the cruelty of such manipulation of the feelings of others, a cruelty not present in other forms of gift relationship but one that Crawford habitually practices.

Still more pressure is put on Fanny when she is sent home to Portsmouth with William. Passing "the Drawbridge," they enter the town and, guided by William's "powerful voice," arrive at the Price family dwelling, off the high street, a rented house, apparently not the one Fanny left when she was ten. At this point in the novel two dramas meet and clash: her private story and the broader social and political story whose center at this moment is William. Fanny has been longing to return to her birth family, imagining that there she will be at peace: instead she is scarcely noticed, and her distress and disappointment are keen. But cutting across this, and providing (contrapuntally) a wild comedy, is the whole family's excitement that William's new ship, the *Thrush*, is leaving her berth and going out of harbor. In fact each time a member of the family appears, they burst in with a variant of the announcement that "[t]he Thrush went out of harbour this morning" (435–40; vol. 3, ch. 7)—more than six times.

William changes into his new lieutenant's uniform, "looking and moving all the taller, firmer, and more graceful for it"—the proof of his being confirmed in "the King's service"—and Fanny is overcome with the mixed emotions of pleasure and loss (444). Since William is now an officer on the *Thrush*, he must make all speed to join her at anchor with other ships in the squadron waiting for orders to sail, so Fanny will lose days with her brother. The naval war and its imperatives have been thrust into the novel. William must set off on a voyage to serve his country, a voyage from which he may never return. Fanny's pride in his lieutenant's uniform and tears at his impending departure register her awareness of how high the stakes are in his profession. History and the wider world have intersected her inner life and its affections.

Public or political history, then, "real solemn history," as Catherine Morland calls it in *Northanger Abbey* (109; vol. 1, ch. 14), is not directly shown in *Mansfield Park*, but it is definitely and explicitly acknowledged. Austen later ridiculed a novel that might seek for prestige and seriousness by including "the History of Buonaparte" (Le Faye 203; the letter is dated 4 Feb. 1813), and she certainly did nothing like this. But the war with Napoleon is a constant presence in *Mansfield Park*, certainly more so than slavery in Antigua—the appearance of both, however, shows that Austen is joining the intellectual conversation of her time.

Religion

Austen's father was a clergyman of the Church of England, and two of her brothers also became ministers. The influence of Christian values is everywhere in her work, but *Mansfield Park* is the novel in which religion is most important.

Critics, including Lionel Trilling, have frequently described Fanny Price, for example, as a "Christian heroine" (though Trilling does not elaborate ["*Mansfield Park*" 427]). Many earlier critics, misled by a remark in one of Austen's letters, argued that ordination was the central concern of the novel. It is true that in the first half of *Mansfield Park*, the impending ordination of Edmund Bertram is the occasion for a number of vigorous discussions among Mary, Fanny, and him, as well as for the occasion of teasing, by Henry Crawford, about his first sermon (265; vol. 2, ch. 5) and of a "little harangue"—actually a lengthy speech—about the duties of a parish priest, from Sir Thomas (288; ch. 6). Despite Edmund's attraction to Mary, there is never any doubt about the firmness of his resolution and his sense of his vocation. With vigor and cogency he defends his proposed profession in chapter 9 of the first volume, following Mary's discovery that he is to be ordained; in the continuation of his dispute with her in chapter 11; and, more lightheartedly, in Mrs. Grant's shrubbery in chapter 4 of the second volume. The attention of the novel is rather on the possibility that Mary's love for Edmund will overcome her London habits and objections both to his future as a minister and to the prospect of life in the countryside. More important, religion is pervasive in *Mansfield Park* because the values and attitudes of the Church of England underpin the dramatic action throughout.

The Church of England (called the Anglican Church in North America) is a largely Protestant formation, the result of King Henry VIII's defiance of the pope's authority in 1531–34. Supreme spiritual authority became invested in the monarch, so that the Church of England, with its pragmatic origins, is to some extent a political and even social institution as much as a religious one. As in other Protestant denominations, however, the doctrines and prayers of the Church of England emphasize the individual's conscience and piety rather than deference to a priest or obedience to a church hierarchy. *Priest* is a title that confers unique spiritual power, but Edmund is ordained as a minister, meaning that he is the servant of his parish and administers to its needs, having no special access to the divine. Over the centuries, the Church of England became increasingly embedded in English society, and its clergy, who often owed their livings, or appointments, to influential patrons or landowners (such as Sir Thomas Bertram), were, like Dr. Grant, members of the genteel or leisured classes. Their pastoral work—attending the sick and poor, consoling the bereaved—was left to notoriously poorly paid curates.

In Austen's time, the role of a minister in his parish was widely discussed, largely because of the emergence in the church in the latter part of the eighteenth century of a group later to be called Evangelicals, led by the charismatic politician William Wilberforce, whose campaigning was vigorously carried on by Hannah More, a prolific writer. The influence of Evangelicalism on *Mansfield Park* is the subject of disagreement by scholars and critics, but it would be fair to say that Austen, like all devout Anglicans of her day, was aware of Evangelicalism and its ideology and was to some extent touched by the new tone of earnestness that was pervading English genteel life. It's also reasonable to suggest that the influence of evangelical thought on *Mansfield Park* is present if indirect.

Disturbed by the laxity of morals among the ruling classes and by the casual attitudes of many of the clergy, the Evangelicals set about the reform of English society. This had been the project of the Methodists earlier in the eighteenth century, but they had worked mainly with the working classes, while the Evangelicals addressed those in power, those with influence and money, and were therefore more effective in promoting social change. Many of the clergy held several livings in different parishes, were lax in their duties, and set very bad examples. The best saw themselves as pastoral educators and moral teachers (the role Edmund defends in volume 1, chapter 9) rather than as mediators between God and man. Because of the laxity of the clergy, the Evangelicals argued, the poor remained in a state of wickedness and barbarity. The Evangelicals set about to remedy this situation by calls to the clergy to remember the seriousness of their calling. "Serious" as opposed to "nominal" clergy were distinguished in Evangelical writings, though, less by their devotion to pastoral duties than by their conception of what it was to be a Christian. That the word *serious* occurs many times in *Mansfield Park* need not imply allegiance to Evangelical theology, but its usage certainly appears colored by its currency in Evangelical writing.

To be serious, in Evangelical terms, was to have undergone a conversion experience, to have received an inner conviction of one's salvation through Christ. His message could reach even the most hardened sinners and bring them to repentance, and then they would be saved from the punishment of divine wrath. This conversion was at heart emotional, even mystical. It rescued people from the natural wickedness of humankind and inspired them to rescue others—most notably the upper classes, the fashionable world—from sin and vice. As for the poor, since, for the Evangelicals, the cause of social evils was infidelity, it was more important that they be pious than that their living conditions be improved. The Methodists, in contrast, had created schools for the poor all over the country.

The prestige and influence of the Evangelicals was immensely increased by their success in getting resolutions for the abolition of the slave trade passed by Parliament in 1807. Though Wilberforce was the front man in this effort, much arduous and dangerous research was carried out by Thomas Clarkson, whose book on the campaign (1808) was read and admired by Austen, if a letter of 1813 is any guide (Le Faye 198). Following her literary mentors, Samuel Johnson and William Cowper, Austen, like most humane and educated people of her time, was very likely appalled by the trade and very likely rejoiced in its abolition. By the time *Mansfield Park* was being written (1812–13), evangelical convictions had permeated society: non-Evangelical gentry and clergy, like Sir Thomas and Edmund Bertram, began to take their moral responsibilities seriously.

This seriousness is evident in the attention the novel gives to Edmund's defense of his profession during the visit to Sotherton (107–09; vol. 1, ch. 9). Edmund is clearly responding to the Evangelicals' calls for increased commitment from the Anglican clergy when, in the face of Mary's scathing view of London clergy, he outlines his conception of manners. *Thoughts on the Importance of the Manners of the Great to General Society* was the title of an influential volume published by More in 1788, and Edmund's speech sounds almost as if he had it at his fingertips: "The *manners* I speak of, might rather be called *conduct*, perhaps, the result of good principles; the effect, in short, of those doctrines which it is their duty to teach and recommend; and it will, I believe, be every where found, that as the clergy are, or are not what they ought to be, so are the rest of the nation" (109). This is a general position that no Evangelical would dispute, but modeling good conduct is a very different matter from bringing Christ's message to the heart. When Mary Crawford, toward the end of her relationship with Edmund derides his converting an old woman, she is ignorantly confusing his Anglican earnestness with Evangelical mission (457; vol. 3, ch. 9).

All the same, the presence of Christianity, specifically of a Protestant Christianity, is profound in *Mansfield Park*. When the narrator says that Henry Crawford perceives that Fanny is "well principled and religious" (341; vol. 2, ch. 12), the phrasing is too vague to convey much. Fanny never drops on her knees in praise of God, as an Evangelical heroine might. When in a moment of desperation she seeks the relief of "fervent prayers" for Edmund's happiness (307; ch. 9), the theological status of these prayers is obscure. Yet what "well principled and religious" means is amply demonstrated, if not through Edmund's manners or conduct, in the novel's presentation of her lonely struggles with questions of loyalty and passion in the East Room.

In one of her letters, Austen writes of the poet Alexander Pope, "[T]here has been one infallible Pope in the World" (Le Faye 245). It is the offhand quality of this remark that suggests how much she lived in a culture of Anglican mistrust of what was conceived as Catholic authoritarianism and dogma. In a letter to Francis Austen, which incidentally includes a postscript about *Mansfield Park*, she writes of her respect for Sweden, a country "so zealous as it was for Protestantism!" (215). The protest of Protestantism is against the imperative to obey the interpretations and edicts of the pope. The denial of the need for a mediator between God and man, the doctrine often called the priesthood of all believers, is crucial to Protestantism. More largely, the core of Protestant Christianity might be described as a conviction of the authority of the individual witness. It is within the private self that moral questions must be posed and answers sought.

The locating of moral value in the individual conscience is connected in Austen's novels with their focus on the heroine's complexity of thought. Fanny's increasing isolation is the precondition for her development of an inner moral world. *Mansfield Park* charts her struggles against self-pity and envy by tracing her feelings, both acknowledged and hidden, that begin, perhaps, with her sight of Mary on Edmund's horse (vol. 1, ch. 7), continue with her self-searching meditations in the East Room after Mrs. Norris's attack (ch. 16), and reach a climax in her desperate attempts to regain some kind of calm or to do "her duty" when Edmund tells her, in effect, that he is in love with Mary (307; vol. 2, ch. 9). In the course of these inner conflicts, Fanny is seen to develop an ethical life that owes almost nothing to her mentor, Edmund, whose betrayal of her over Henry Crawford's marriage proposal finally confirms that she is on her own.

The reader is shown Fanny's thoughts and feelings through free indirect speech, a novelistic technique that represents a character's inner life through unspoken words but also gives the narrative the freedom to intercept them or color them with an ironic filter. By relaying Fanny's anguish and conflict in her own inner words, Austen develops a prose that not only captures Fanny's thoughts but simultaneously renders her desires, even when these emerge despite her conscious control. The influence of Protestant culture is manifest in this portrayal. Fanny, troubled, even tormented, by the imperatives of her conscience, must resist the authority of Sir Thomas Bertram, who besides standing to her in the position of a parent is also a powerful figure in the world at large: he is a baronet, an important landowner, and a member of Parliament. Having witnessed events others never noticed and having understood what they passed over, she must refuse to conform to his and his united family's wishes. The narrative of *Mansfield Park*, then, is formed around the struggle between conscience and authority. It is not through her Christian beliefs as such that Fanny is a heroine. More profoundly, she is a heroine because the trauma of her early upheaval and arrival into a cold and uncaring family promotes the development of an inner world of independence and self-realization.

The Christian elements in the novel may be developed in another way, through the portrait of Mrs. Norris, the novel's other dependent, marginalized, and troubled female. She is the antithesis to Fanny Price, however, because her inner life is so stunted as to be nonexistent. "Perhaps she might so little know herself," comments the narrator in the first chapter, "as to walk home . . . in the happy belief" of her own generosity (9; ch. 1). Aunt Norris has a repertoire of self-promoting, self-pitying verbal gestures that effectively shield her from self-knowledge: "Is not she a sister's child? and could I bear to see her want, while I had a bit of bread to give her? My dear Sir Thomas, with all my faults I have a warm heart: and poor as I am, would rather deny myself the necessaries of life than do an ungenerous thing" (8). Such speeches present Mrs. Norris to the world as generous to a fault, while simultaneously smuggling in the message that she herself is a victim, threatened, however remotely, with penury. The combination of self-importance and self-pity that runs through almost all her dealings hides from her, but suggests to the reader, a powerful, unappeased ego.

Mrs. Norris, who is the wife and later the widow of a clergyman of the Church of England, might be read as a figure of inauthentic Christianity. She might also be seen as an oblique commentary on the currency of sanctimony brought about by Evangelicalism's success. Her humility and charity are as false as her benevolence. In the first chapter of the novel, she promotes the project of adoption, without the slightest intention, as the narrator says, of going to any expense or suffering any inconvenience on its account. But she is not, in the normal sense, a hypocrite. Her condition is more banal; she merely lives a life devoid of self-understanding, sealed off from the truths of her rage and jealousy by postures and phrases, many of them derived from the Bible, that confirm her view of herself and by actions, like her dealings with servants such as the old coachman (222; vol. 2, ch. 2), that disguise self-promotion as charity. The figure is greatly illuminated by Kay Souter's analysis in this volume. It is a comic but also deeply suggestive moment when, as one of her last actions in the novel, the minister's widow fails to send the gift of a prayer book, containing the liturgy of the Church, to her godchild.

Mansfield Park is suffused with Anglican or Protestant values, which it carries through and recreates in the realm, and through the opportunities, of novelistic prose. The extensive examination of inner lives is crucial to this enterprise. Mrs. Norris has no interior life in the text, not because she is a simple or one-dimensional figure but because she has no interiority to herself. When we do glimpse her mind, when the whole house of cards she has built around herself collapses, she has become "an altered creature, quiet, stupefied" (518; vol. 3, ch. 16). By contrast, Fanny, whose outward demeanor is reserved, is developed as a figure whose private observations, thoughts, and feelings are the site of exemplary moral, and implicitly Christian, value.

The Slave Trade

The passing of the bill to abolish the slave trade by Parliament did not abolish slavery itself, which continued in the British Empire, including Antigua, until 1833. For many years after the passing of the act, ships of the Royal Navy patrolled the Atlantic Ocean to intercept and disrupt the continuing slave trade of other nations, including Napoleonic France.

Part of the Bertram family's income, probably a substantial part, is drawn from sugar estates in the West Indian island of Antigua, which would have been worked by slaves. This income source was not unusual at the time among the landed and genteel classes; Austen's own family had connections with estates in the West Indies. It is "[t]he necessity of the measure in a pecuniary light" that takes Sir Thomas to Antigua during most of the novel's action in the first volume (36; vol. 1, ch. 3), though what circumstances there made his voyage necessary and extended his stay by a year are not divulged—scholars have offered different reasons.

On his return, two years later, Sir Thomas is changed. He seems kinder to her than before, when he left her with a reprimand. He asks, "But where is Fanny?—Why do I not see my little Fanny?" (208; vol. 2, ch. 1) before he sees her, so it isn't just that she now has a more womanly appearance. The narrative suggests that the hardships of travel and of his responsibilities in Antigua have softened his heart and made him more appreciative of everything and everyone in the home that he has missed. He is "communicative and chatty in a very unusual degree" (209). Two chapters later, a moment occurs that has been extensively discussed in modern criticism of *Mansfield Park*. The context is Edmund's encouraging of Fanny to shake off her shyness:

> "But I do talk to him more than I used. I am sure I do. Did not you hear me ask him about the slave-trade last night?"
>
> "I did—and was in hopes the question would be followed up by others. It would have pleased your uncle to be inquired of farther."
>
> "And I longed to do it—but there was such a dead silence! And while my cousins were sitting by without speaking a word, or seeming at all interested in the subject, I did not like—I thought it would appear as if I wanted to set myself off at their expense. . . ."   (231–32; vol. 2, ch. 3)

Discussion has turned on the significance of the phrase "there was such a dead silence!," and different readings of the phrase have been given. Brian Southam's essay, provocatively titled "The Silence of the Bertrams" (1995), has been so influential that many have repeated its argument as if the argument were unequivocally true, but the essay misleads in several ways. With a title that echoes the 1991 film *The Silence of the Lambs*, it suggests hidden abuse and horror. Southam developed this idea in his portrayal of Sir Thomas as a member of the colonizing planter class. He writes, for example, that "the 'dead silence' hints that [Sir Thomas's] loquacity may have dried up at the mention of slaves" ("Silence" [*Mansfield Park*] 495). But Sir Thomas has responded to Fanny's question, because Edmund says that he "was in hopes the question would be followed up by others. It would have pleased your uncle to be inquired of farther." It seems clear that neither Edmund nor his father would be embarrassed by discussion of the slave trade. (It is even possible that Sir Thomas, like some other planters, was in favor of its abolition.) The silence follows his reply, not Fanny's question. There is no indication that Tom Bertram is present, and no one expects Lady Bertram to ask questions.

The silence mainly indicates Maria's and Julia's lack of intellectual curiosity, as well as their restraint in front of their father. Fanny feels that to ask more questions of her uncle would make it "appear as if I wanted to set myself off at their expense, by shewing a curiosity and pleasure in his information which he must wish his own daughters to feel" (232). It is the Bertram daughters who are not interested in understanding more about Antigua or the slave trade. To read this moment as metonymically revealing the whole novel's silence about the colonial slavery on which Mansfield Park's wealth, order, and propriety rest requires that the critic remove the moment from its context. To some critics the Bertrams are guilty, and the moral values that the novel itself seems to espouse are compromised, or contaminated, by the guilty secret on which they rest.

This challenging view has introduced new political issues into the discussion of *Mansfield Park*, which in the past was often read, rather simplistically, as a celebration of conservative moral and social values. But critics who accept that slavery is central to the novel are divided as to whether Austen accepts income from colonial slavery as a given of the genteel world she depicts, and is therefore to some degree in collusion with slavery, or whether the novel is actually an attack on slavery and moral compromise in all its forms.

The principal focus of many of these postcolonial readings of *Mansfield Park* has been on Fanny Price. Edward Said—in "Jane Austen and Empire," a section of his *Culture and Imperialism* (1993), which has been even more influential than Southam's essay—argued that Fanny's uprooting and removal to Mansfield is a metonymy for or reminder of the brutal uprooting and removals of the slave trade. The novel thus enacts global issues in the small compass of the genteel home. According to this reading, Sir Thomas displays the autocratic style of a slave owner and treats his daughters and ward as chattels to be disposed of in the marriage market to his own advantage or, more precisely, for the advancement of the family. Other writers have suggested that he, like many slave owners, sexually exploited his slaves in Antigua. (This idea was given wider currency by Patricia Rozema's film version of *Mansfield Park* in 1999.) Fanny, in turn, is read as a virtual slave: brought against her will to Mansfield, she is treated badly by the family, unpaid, looked upon with contempt, made to do needlework or odd jobs at every opportunity, and finally cruelly punished by being returned to Portsmouth when she disobeys her master by refusing to marry to advantage.

Accounts of the novel both passionate and ingenious have been given along such lines, and students tend to find them exciting, so to debate the novel in the light of these accounts can be a helpful teaching tool. Is Sir Thomas a tyrant? He certainly is guilty of overseeing the marriage of Maria to Rushworth to further his own ambitions, but students will also recognize the role that Maria plays in the transaction. Her sense that it is "her evident duty to marry Mr. Rushworth if she [can]" (44; vol. 1, ch. 4) does reflect the explicit values of her father, mother, and Aunt Norris, but the narrative presents as her own her decision to marry Mr. Rushworth even though she dislikes him. A. J. Downie's "Rehabilitating Sir Thomas Bertram" provides a convincing riposte to the feminist and postcolonial estimates of the character.

Is Fanny a slave? The critics who have seen her as one observe that she is transported to Mansfield and ill-used by Mrs. Norris, and some claim that Norris is the name of a notorious apologist for slavery. But do Fanny's conditions amount to those of slavery? The rhetoric of antislavery was appropriated in this period by campaigners for the liberation of women. Mrs. Norris echoes it when she asks Fanny to work on the costumes for the theatricals. "I want you here.—I have been slaving myself till I can hardly stand" (195; vol. 1, ch. 18). Utterly commonplace, the phrase might pass unnoticed, but it acquires significance in the context of readings of *Mansfield Park* that emphasize the slave trade. Austen is exposing the falsity that equates the conditions of genteel women with those of West Indian slaves. Moreover, the book insists on individual responsibility and gives to Fanny an eloquent speech defending her right to make her own choices (408; vol. 3, ch. 4).

But an important critical principle lies behind this issue: What are appropriate questions to put to a novel? When we fill its silences, its spaces or absences, with our own information or speculations, are we responding responsibly to guides or prompts in the text? It is possible to read Fanny as a slave, Mrs. Norris as an overseer, Sir Thomas as a tyrannical slave owner, and Lady Bertram as a typically indolent planter's wife (all of which have been argued by several critics), but only through a critical approach that assumes that the text is working metonymically. This approach in turn rests on the assumption that slavery or colonialism is a main, if implicit, concern of the novel.

The section in this volume headed "Teaching *Mansfield Park* in the Broader Postcolonial Context" contains three essays that comment on and carry further several of the issues discussed here. Lynn Voskuil, Lisa Kasmer, and Paula Loscocco all offer sophisticated commentary on the postcolonial criticism of the novel and will give teachers ideas about ways of introducing these issues into class discussions. Another question that teachers must weigh is, What other political and social concerns of the novel are displaced or distorted by bringing slavery and the slave trade to the fore of interpretation?

Introspection

Mansfield Park is unique among Austen's novels in that it discloses the inner life of several characters. In her other novels, the heroine's consciousness controls the narrative focus, and access is allowed only to one other person's private thoughts—Marianne Dashwood's, Darcy's, Knightley's, Wentworth's. *Mansfield Park* reveals, even if briefly, the thoughts, plans, and views of Tom Bertram, Sir Thomas, Maria Bertram, Edmund Bertram, and the two Crawford siblings. Students might be asked to look for these moments when the narrative shifts into recording the consciousness of a character who is not Fanny.

Inner lives are not always presented in the same way, but a common thread runs through most of the techniques that Austen uses, beginning with the narrator's comment on Mrs. Norris's belief in her own benevolence: "[P]erhaps she might so little know herself, as to walk home to the Parsonage . . . in the happy belief of being the most liberal-minded sister and aunt in the world" (9; vol. 1, ch. 1). In embryo here is a concept that will play a large role in the novel: people who are capable or incapable of knowing themselves. Knowing oneself is suggested as a key index of moral virtue. The various modes through which characters allow their inclinations and desires to override their better judgments are represented by equally varied techniques.

Mrs. Norris's lack of self-inquiry is echoed in the responses of her favorite, Maria, to the attractive Mr. Crawford: "Maria's notions on the subject were more confused and indistinct. She did not want to see or understand. 'There could be no harm in her liking an agreeable man—every body knew her situation—Mr. Crawford must take care of himself'" (52; vol. 1, ch. 5). As an engaged woman, Maria ought not to be encouraging the attentions of another man. By putting the words in quotation marks, Austen indicates that these are conscious self-defenses, which cannot be lingered over lest their flimsiness becomes clear. The person whose objections she is warding off and the person doing the warding off are both she. All the same, the narrator implies that there is, or might be, an incipient knowledge in Maria to which Maria ought to respond.

The technique of representation differs, but Mary Crawford's thoughts about Edmund Bertram are similar: "There was a charm, perhaps, in his sincerity, his steadiness, his integrity, which Miss Crawford might be equal to feel, though not equal to discuss with herself. She did not think very much about it, however; he pleased her for the present; she liked to have him near her; it was enough" (77; vol. 1, ch. 7). It is interesting that the narrator here uses the provisional, tentative "might," as she does in her account of Mrs. Norris's thoughts: "perhaps she might so little know herself." The addition of "perhaps" in both passages is worth pondering: these are moments in which the author reminds the reader of recesses in her characters that it is difficult to probe.

The presentation of Mary's failure to "discuss with herself'" or examine her feelings for Edmund is developed in these comments on Henry's feelings for Fanny:

> Henry Crawford had too much sense not to feel the worth of good principles in a wife, though he was too little accustomed to serious reflection to know them by their proper name; but when he talked of her having such a steadiness and regularity of conduct, such a high notion of honour, and such an observance of decorum as might warrant any man in the fullest dependence on her faith and integrity, he expressed what was inspired by the knowledge of her being well principled and religious.
>
> (341; vol. 2, ch. 12)

This is the passage of the novel in which an underlying ethical framework is most explicitly expressed, and the word "serious" here has a distinctly evangelical coloring. The narrator's commentary links the capacity for reflection to access to an appropriate vocabulary. You cannot think effectively, she is suggesting, unless you possess the language for it. Henry is thinking that Fanny's honor, faith, and integrity ensure that as a wife she will remain—in the still current phrase—faithful. The words have a wholly social or secular weight, and behind his thinking is the experienced man of the world's cynicism about women. He does not recognize this cynicism in himself, and his failure to understand it reveals how far he is from understanding Fanny.

Austen does not describe Edmund's feelings about Mary in the same mode. Instead, with Fanny as spectator, his falling in love with Mary, and the possible compromise with his principles this love might involve, is conveyed in a series of actions: his four days of riding with Mary, his wandering off with her at Sotherton, his visits to the Parsonage to see and hear her play the harp. It is especially amusing that, when Edmund is standing by the window looking out at the stars with Fanny and Mary is with the others singing at the piano on the opposite side of the room, his promise to stay with Fanny is broken as soon as his attention is drawn to Mary:

> The glee began. "We will stay till this is finished, Fanny," said he, turning his back on the window; and as it advanced, she had the mortification of seeing him advance too, moving forward by gentle degrees towards the instrument, and when it ceased, he was close by the singers, among the most urgent in requesting to hear the glee again. (132–33; vol. 1, ch. 11)

This is sexual attraction represented mimetically. The wavering of Edmund "between love and consistency" (191; ch. 17) is figured in spatial terms. He is not inconsistent, however, in his commitment to his vocation, and as the time of his ordination draws near, Austen affords him three paragraphs in which his plans for the future and his doubts about the strength of Mary's feelings for him are expressed in a largely detached and balanced prose that transcribes lucid thought. Edmund "[knows] his own mind" at this point, and the narrative accords him this respect (296–98; vol. 2, ch. 8).

Sir Thomas Bertram is introduced into the novel as a man of "principle as well as pride" (4; vol. 1, ch. 1), and Austen's finely calibrated rendering of his inner life shows these two sides of his nature, the ethical and the worldly. The sequence in which he speaks to Maria about her proposed marriage to Rushworth is rich with possibilities for class discussion (234–36; vol. 2, ch. 3). His reported speech is kind and firm: he offers to get her out of the difficulties and embarrassments of a broken engagement. But when he meets her calm and absolute affirmation, he is "satisfied, too glad to be satisfied perhaps to urge the matter quite so far as his judgment might have dictated to others" (234). Yet the self-comforting and self-justifying reasonings that follow are akin to his daughter's reasonings about her attraction to Henry Crawford. Like her, he is ready to deceive himself.

The presentation of Sir Thomas's encouragement of Henry's courtship of Fanny registers with great subtlety the intricate pathways such self-deception can take:

> [T]hough infinitely above scheming or contriving for any the most advantageous matrimonial establishment that could be among the apparent possibilities of any one most dear to him, and disdaining even as a littleness the being quick-sighted on such points, he could not avoid perceiving in a grand and careless way that Mr. Crawford was somewhat distinguishing

> his niece—nor perhaps refrain (though unconsciously) from giving a
> more willing assent to invitations on that account.   (277; vol. 2, ch. 7)

The complex sentence allows for the possibility that its first phrases belong to Sir Thomas's conception of himself, which holds worldliness at a distance. Sir Thomas puts what he is thinking at a distance from that self-conception, which, in other words, is a fantasy or idealized construct. He does not allow himself to know what he is thinking. But, as with his failure with Maria, it is the real self that actually, or unconsciously, governs his actions.

The refusal or inability of Sir Thomas, Maria, Mary, and Henry to acknowledge or inquire into their feelings form the context for *Mansfield Park*'s extraordinary and groundbreaking presentation of Fanny's conscience. As Kathryn Sutherland has put it, "One of Jane Austen's greatest contributions to the novel as fiction and epic is her deployment, deepened from novel to novel, of a narrative method inflected by the personal subjectivity of a self-conversing heroine" ("Jane Austen" 254). In two major examples—in the East Room after Mrs. Norris's attack in the first volume (176–79; ch. 16) and after Edmund's virtual declaration of his love for Mary in the second (306–08; ch. 9)—Austen presents "the conversation of the self with itself" (Sutherland, "Jane Austen" 254) as Fanny questions herself, putting the worst construction on her motives, or confronts herself with her desires, so that she can manage them. She seeks to understand what her duty is. *Duty* might mean just her responsibility to repay the family that has adopted her, but the term comes to include her responsibility to herself. (It is unclear whether *duty* includes her obligation to God.) Julia Prewitt Brown offers an illuminating discussion in this volume of how Fanny's emotions color her perceptions of objects in her East Room refuge. Here we examine the second of the passages of free indirect speech in which Fanny's responses to crisis are reported.

Before discussing these passages with a class, however, it is helpful to call attention to two stylistic features of Austen's rendering of private thoughts. "There could be no harm in her liking an agreeable man—every body knew her situation—Mr. Crawford must take care of himself": the dashes among Maria's ideas have a remarkable function. They signal slight hesitations in the run of thought, hesitations that betray more complexity of feeling than can be easily put into words. This effect reproduces what we recognize as a common feature of spoken language, that hesitation in a person's eloquence can suggest the pressure, or at least the presence, of a movement of thought or feeling contrary to the one being expressed.

Austen often uses the dash in conjunction with another device, repetition. Because she is a precise as well as a concise writer, repetition of sentiments, phrases, or words is uncommon in the narrative passages of her novels. But they appear more often in her characters' thoughts. The rational prose that represents Edmund's thinking about his future, for example, betrays his anxieties whenever repetition and dashes appear:

There were points on which they did not quite agree, there were moments in which she did not seem propitious, and though trusting altogether to her affection, so far as to be resolved (almost resolved) on bringing it to a decision within a very short time, as soon as the variety of business before him were arranged, and he knew what he had to offer her—he had many anxious feelings, many doubting hours as to the result.

(297; vol. 2, ch. 8)

Together, these two stylistic devices produce the effect of a complex self in which the dominant thought or feeling may contend with others. Such contending suggests intensity of emotion, as in Fanny's thoughts when Edmund, departing and meaning to be kind, has told her that she is "one of his two dearest," the other being Mary Crawford:

She was one of his two dearest—that must support her. But the other!— the first! She had never heard him speak so openly before, and though it told her no more than what she had long perceived, it was a stab;—for it told of his own convictions and views. They were decided. He would marry Miss Crawford. It was a stab, in spite of every long-standing expectation; and she was obliged to repeat again and again that she was one of his two dearest, before the words gave her any sensation. Could she believe Miss Crawford to deserve him, it would be—Oh, how different would it be—how far more tolerable!   (306–07; vol. 2, ch. 9)

It is unusual for Austen to use repeated exclamation marks to convey emotion. Fanny struggles with herself to find equilibrium, seeking different paths, one after the other, to deal with her disappointment and distress. None of them works, as the repetition of the graphic phrase "it was a stab" indicates.

There follows a passage, introduced by a sober sentence from the narrator, in which Fanny investigates her feelings more closely:

It was her intention, as she felt it to be her duty, to try to overcome all that was excessive, all that bordered on selfishness in her affection for Edmund. To call or to fancy it a loss, a disappointment, would be a presumption; for which she had not words strong enough to satisfy her own humility. To think of him as Miss Crawford might be justified in thinking, would in her be insanity. To her, he could be nothing under any circumstances—nothing dearer than a friend. Why did such an idea occur to her even enough to be reprobated and forbidden? It ought not to have touched on the confines of her imagination. She would endeavour to be rational. . . .   (307)

The dash and repetition in "To her, he could be nothing under any circumstances—nothing dearer than a friend" proclaim the effort needed to repress desires, but at the same time a dash is the space in which those desires push themselves forward. Because "the idea" does occur to her, even though it is "insanity," because it ought not to have "touched on the confines of her imagination," her self must be disciplined: it has called into being language and concepts that make it multiple, pluralistic, unruly. The rhythmic momentum of "To call or fancy it a loss. . . . To think of him. . . . To her, he could be nothing" bespeaks, however vainly, the summoning of another agency or faculty of the self, the determined will. The next paragraph resumes the narrator's commentary and tells us that Fanny has "all the heroism of principle" (307). Her principle is given real substance; it is no mere token of Evangelical piety.

In neither of these introspective passages is Fanny's struggle resolved. In the first, Edmund's tap on the door arouses Fanny in "the attempt to find her way to her duty" (180; vol. 1, ch. 16); in the second, the contest is abandoned as she seizes the fragment of his letter (307). At this point the narrator's commentary segues into an amused, even maternal, tenderness for the character's frailty. That Fanny's intense conflicts are broken off or relinquished has the effect of underlining the intractability of her moral dilemmas, an intractability that continues to the end of the novel. Arguing that *Mansfield Park* is not as Christian a novel "as the vocation of its hero would lead one to believe," Ruth Yeazell argues that its stress is not on "salvation or final ends" ("Boundaries" 147). Precisely: Fanny's conflicts lead not to resolution but to the reader's awareness of the difficulty of satisfying complex human needs.

In these passages, Austen translates Protestantism into the secular realm, and perhaps there is no better demonstration in the English novel of this translation. It is the Protestant insistence that the individual self must confront its own passions and conflicts and work toward its own salvation that gives rise to Austen's various narrative techniques. Fanny finds herself alone, isolated, and independent: Edmund has failed her, and there is no priest to whom she can turn for guidance or advice. Neither can she draw, as an Evangelical heroine might, on an infallible inner voice. She has been trained into obedience and self-doubt yet summons the strength to think for herself. She seeks to overcome her selfishness and pursue the difficult path between contending impulses, without the assurance that she will reach a salvation promised by either the Catholic or the Evangelical version of Christianity.

The sad irony in both passages is that Fanny—at least to a modern reader—is wrong. Of course she should not give in to the pressure of her aunt and cousins to act when she disapproves of the play and dislikes the thought of acting; of course she should fully acknowledge her feelings for Edmund and not try to deny them! But the author's own imagination is constrained, by temperament, upbringing, and inheritance; to stand outside these influences is an impossible Romantic ideal. Even so, Austen convincingly shows that Fanny is not any the less, especially against the background of the other confused lovers in the novel, a heroine.

Fanny Price

There is difference of opinion, however, often in the classroom but in the criticism of *Mansfield Park* too, about Fanny. She has been misunderstood in several ways.

It has been common for critics, even the most distinguished, to disparage Fanny's physical condition. Marilyn Butler notes her "feebleness" ("*Mansfield Park*" 248); for Tony Tanner Fanny is "weak and sickly" ("sickly" being the word Elizabeth Bennet used to describe Miss Anne de Bourgh [Austen, *Pride* [ed. Rogers] 180]) and "debilitated" ("Quiet Thing" 171). Such negative treatment may be qualified: Butler, for instance, says that the "real significance of [Fanny's] character is not its weakness but its strength" ("*Mansfield Park*" 180). But the idea of Fanny's physical weakness has a tendency to suggest weakness in her nature and moral character. Nina Auerbach remarked, in a much-reprinted article, that "there is something horrible about [Fanny], that compels . . . toward the deformed and dispossessed" ("Jane Austen's Dangerous Charm" 447).

Auerbach also calls Fanny "a pauper" (451), and although *pauper* is a term more of abuse than assessment, it does point to an important aspect of the character. Fanny is the only Austen heroine whose childhood is portrayed in the novel, and it is a childhood of deprivation. Her family lives in near poverty. Though Fanny's mother, Frances Price, had a dowry of £7,000, which invested at five percent would yield £350 a year, she has ten children and an out-of-work husband, on half pay of no more than £50 a year "but not the less equal to company and good liquor" (5; vol. 1, ch. 1). As Mrs. Price says, they have "a very small income to supply their wants," which is the main reason that she approaches her rich relations for help (5). When her sisters decide to take Fanny to live with them, Mrs. Price warns them that her daughter is "somewhat delicate and puny" (12). She seems to let Fanny go without a qualm, and her surprise that a girl is chosen rather than a boy is confirmed when much later in the novel the narrator writes, "Her daughters had never been much to her" (450; vol. 3, ch. 8). Her daughter Mary actually dies (446; ch. 7).

In the chronically disorganized Price household, where the six boys are favored over the girls, Fanny is likely to have suffered from a poor and inadequate diet. At ten, she is "small of her age, with no glow of complexion" (13; vol. 1, ch. 2)—signs, if we would read them, of malnourishment. Austen seems to have known that the damage done to a child who gets inadequate nutrition up to age ten cannot be corrected by an adequate diet later. Fanny's frail condition is not an aspect of her personality; rather, as Austen makes clear, it is a consequence of the failings of her parents; it is also an indicator of her social class, because Fanny occupies the lowest rung of gentility. She is not sickly in the ordinary sense of the word, although there is one scene in which she retreats to the sofa with a headache, gets up quickly when criticized for it, and the specific reasons for her indisposition are given (83–84; vol. 1, ch. 7). Anne Mallory's essay in this volume thoughtfully examines this scene.

Fanny's physical condition is contrasted with that of the Bertrams, a "remarkably fine family, the sons very well looking, the daughters decidedly handsome, and all of them well-grown and forward of their age," so that there is "as striking a difference between the cousins in person as education had given to their address" (14; vol. 1, ch. 2). Their good health, upright carriage, and confidence are the result of the family's wealth, just as initially Fanny's shyness and lack of self-confidence are the result of her childhood in poverty. But as she matures, her figure fills out, and by the time she catches Crawford's eye, it is quite clear that she has become an attractive young woman. The moment before the ball when she practices her dancing steps is touching partly because it expresses a newfound delight in her physical well-being (317; vol. 2, ch. 19).

Austen chose as her heroine a child and young woman who is fragile, not debilitated, and she dared construct a plot around this perceptive, conflicted, and misunderstood young woman. As several essays in this volume demonstrate, Fanny finds herself in a situation that places extraordinary and conflicting demands on her. In Portsmouth, she was considered inferior to her brothers; in Mansfield Park, under Mrs. Norris, she is repeatedly reminded that she is a beneficiary of the Bertrams' charity and therefore must be grateful and submissive. She is neither in nor out of the family. She is neither a servant, having received a lady's education, nor merely a lady's companion, though she is required to fulfill both these roles as needed. Shy and self-doubting by nature, but also by training, she is gradually confronted with a cumulating series of situations that demand she make difficult decisions on her own.

Tanner voices a complaint often still heard in the classroom: that Fanny is too passive. "Fanny is timid, silent, unassertive, shrinking, and excessively vulnerable," he wrote. "[W]e expect heroes and heroines to be active, rising to opposition, resisting coercion, asserting their own energy; but Fanny is almost totally passive" ("Quiet Thing" 143). That she is passive is often connected to her physical weakness, as when the feminists Sandra Gilbert and Susan Gubar speak of her "invalid passivity" (167). Sometimes her passivity is linked with her supposed stillness and inflected positively, as when Butler contrasts Fanny's stillness with the "bustle" of Mrs. Norris and Mrs. Price in Portsmouth ("*Mansfield Park*" 180), and Tanner writes, "She suffers in her stillness. For Righteousness's sake" ("Quiet Thing" 171–72).

Fanny is definitely quiet in her overall demeanor, but she is not silent, as Mallory demonstrates in her essay in this volume. For example, Fanny contests Edmund's optimism about her proposed removal to Mrs. Norris's, and though she doubts herself, she is in the right. After Henry Crawford's seductive remarks to Maria Bertram in the grounds of Sotherton and his invitation to her to get around the locked gate, with his assistance, Fanny, "feeling all this to be wrong, could not help making an effort to prevent it. 'You will hurt yourself, Miss Bertram,' she cried, 'you will certainly hurt yourself against those spikes—you will tear your gown—you will be in danger of slipping into the ha-ha. You had better not go'" (116; vol. 1, ch. 20). Her awareness of Henry's flirtatious innuendos, of Maria's helplessness at his hands, and of the disloyalty of both to Rushworth, who has been sent off to fetch the key, produces an alarmed intervention that is all the more courageous for coming from a social inferior. The couple seem to regard Fanny's overhearing of their saucy banter as insignificant as a servant's would be.

Fanny takes an active part in the disagreements in the next chapter over Edmund's ensuing ordination. When Edmund seems to concede a point to Mary—"We cannot attempt to defend Dr. Grant" (130)—Fanny steps in with several sentences of reasoned argument in defense of Dr. Grant's choice of profession. Mary's response, tart and witty, effectively curtails the argument, but Fanny here engages in discussion and intervention, as she is to do a minute or two later when she draws Edmund's attention to the beauty of the night sky. Sarah Emsley, in her essay in this volume, discusses a passage in which a beleaguered Fanny mounts a long, cogent defense of herself and of women's right to choose their own marriage partners (408; vol. 3, ch. 4). This impressive speech might have come from Elizabeth Bennet if she were more embattled than she is by the first two proposals she receives. Throughout the second half of the novel, the central action concerns the protracted attempts of Henry Crawford, Sir Thomas, Lady Bertram, Mary Crawford, and even Edmund (all of them with differing motives) to persuade Fanny to accept Henry. Fanny resists their pressures, even though—so complex is her character—she feels shame at doing so (Folsom, "Power").

So there are few grounds for finding Fanny silent, and none at all for holding her quietness against her. Nor is she particularly still, and in fact the attribution to her of stillness is less the result of careful reading of *Mansfield Park* than an aspect of readings that interprets the novel as religious and Fanny as the "Christian heroine" that Trilling in 1955 ("*Mansfield Park*" [*Moral Obligation*] 298), and Butler in 1975 (*Jane Austen* 222) pronounced her. T. S. Eliot's reiterated line "At the still point of the turning world" in *Burnt Norton*, the first of *Four Quartets*, published in 1935, which invested stillness with immense spiritual significance, may have influenced these critics (119). Reading the novel symbolically or allegorically was a route to redeeming a character that they perceived as a failure in realist terms. Such interpretations work only if the extended passages in which Fanny wrestles with her conflicting feelings—which one of *Mansfield Park*'s early critics, Richard Whately, correctly identified as "restlessness and jealousy" (329)—are simplified or ignored.

Trilling's famous remark that no one "has ever found it possible to like the heroine of *Mansfield Park*" is often reiterated ("*Mansfield Park*" [*Moral Obligation*] 296). Tanner goes one further: "Nobody [that is, no reader] falls in love with Fanny Price" ("Quiet Thing" 143). Auerbach goes further still: "[N]one of the characters within the novel falls in love with her either" (451). Not even Henry Crawford, apparently, whose pursuit of her is most interesting if it is the result of genuine love, as almost all readers assume. Edmund loves Fanny, as he tells her, and so ultimately do both Lady Bertram and even Sir Thomas. But, despite Trilling's magisterial manner, deciding whether a reader can fall in love with a character is no way to assess the heroine of a novel.

In *The Hidden Jane Austen*, John Wiltshire shows that Fanny's wrenching displacement as a ten-year-old is a key issue in her psychology. He notes that Austen chooses unusually explicit language for the suffering of the little girl, who is "as unhappy as possible" (14; vol. 1, ch. 2) and who ends "every day's sorrows by sobbing herself to sleep" (16). As Wiltshire explains, once a reader fully registers the consequences of Fanny's abrupt uprooting, her demeanor and her psychological struggles take on new significance.

First-Cousin Marriage

It is not uncommon for students to express unease or displeasure with the conclusion of the novel, when Fanny and Edmund are married. Cousin marriage is a topic that tends to arouse heated and often ill-informed debate, but some historical and political background may help put the matter in perspective. In earlier centuries, the Roman Catholic Church prohibited first-cousin marriage, but both Luther and Calvin, key figures in the Reformation of the sixteenth century, viewed the ban as an expression of church rather than divine law and brought about its abolition in Protestant communions. Accordingly, the Church of England, as instituted under Henry VIII in the 1530s, permits marriage between first cousins. There is little genetic evidence to support barring cousin marriage (see Bennett et al.), and in the Western world today the only such bans are in the United States. In other parts of the world, marriage between first cousins, for better or worse, is frequent.

For Austen and English society in general of her time, marriage between first cousins was perfectly acceptable and even encouraged. It is possible that among families with strong allegiances to the Anglican Church, like the Austens, marriage between members of the same extended family was seen as a vindication of their Protestantism. The practice was frequent in Austen's family and among her connections. The tone of the concluding paragraphs of *Mansfield Park* makes clear the author's warm endorsement of Fanny and Edmund's union: "With so much true merit and true love, and no want of fortune and friends, the happiness of the married cousins must appear as secure as earthly happiness can be" (547; vol. 3, ch. 17).

But for some modern readers, the marriage of Edmund and Fanny raises the specter of incest. When Fanny, alone in the East Room, attempts to conquer her feelings for Edmund, the intensity of the language may mislead them: "To think of him as Miss Crawford might be justified in thinking, would in her be insanity. To her, he could be nothing under any circumstances—nothing dearer than a friend. Why did such an idea occur to her even enough to be reprobated and forbidden? It ought not to have touched on the confines of her imagination." Fanny's vehemence, approaching horror, might suggest to these readers that she is warding off the thought of sexual attachment to her cousin because of the taint of incest. But this is a misinterpretation. A clue is given in the preceding phrase, "she had not words strong enough to satisfy her own humility." It is not because he is her cousin that she castigates herself for dreaming of his love but because he is the son of a baronet and she is the daughter of a marine on half pay. The shame is of trespassing the boundaries of social class, not of consanguinity.

Students can be reminded of "the distinction proper" that, in the novel's first chapter, Sir Thomas announces must be made between the poor ward and her cousins. "[T]hey cannot be equals. Their rank, fortune, rights, and expectations, will always be different" (11–12). By temperament modest, Fanny does not need Mrs. Norris's constant reminders that she "must be lowest and last" (258; vol. 2, ch. 5). Her early recognition of and acquiescence in her status is evident in the smallest details. "Do you know," says one of her cousins to her aunt, "she says she does not want to learn either music or drawing." Mrs. Norris replies that this is "very stupid indeed" but is pleased by the little girl's reluctance. Fanny, who is intelligent and, as the novel shows, interested in many things, has accepted that the accomplishments of a marriageable young lady are not for her (21; vol. 1, ch. 2). Conscious of the different expectations that she must hold of life, she knows that marriage into a baronet's family is not one of the possibilities.

The specter of incest in *Mansfield Park* is raised also by the fact that Fanny, brought up among her cousins, is sometimes referred to as Edmund's sister. Yet she often calls him cousin, a formality that perhaps reflects her awareness that an appropriate distance between them should be maintained. The most memorable moment when Edmund declares that she is his sister occurs after Maria's and Julia's betrayal of the family and his arrival to bring Fanny back from Portsmouth:

> The idea of immediately seeing him, with the knowledge of what he must be suffering, brought back all her own first feelings. He so near her, and in misery. She was ready to sink, as she entered the parlour. He was alone, and met her instantly; and she found herself pressed to his heart with only these words, just articulate, "My Fanny—my only sister—my only comfort now." She could say nothing; nor for some minutes could he say more.   (514–15; vol. 3, ch. 15)

Students might be invited to perceive the irony in this emotional crisis: that Edmund thinks of her as a sister, and nothing more, is brought home to Fanny once again.

Several places in the novel indicate that Edmund does not feel physical attraction to Fanny. A small example, both amusing and sad, occurs on the occasion of her first formal invitation to dine at the Parsonage in the gathering dusk: "'Now I must look at you, Fanny,' said Edmund, with the kind smile of an affectionate brother, 'and tell you how I like you; and as well as I can judge by this light, you look very nicely indeed. What have you got on?'" Fanny explains that she is wearing the dress her uncle gave her on Maria's marriage. She hopes Edmund doesn't think it too fine. He says, "A woman can never be too fine when she is all in white. No, I see no finery about you; nothing but what is perfectly proper. Your gown seems very pretty. I like those glossy spots. Has not Miss Crawford a gown something the same?" (259; vol. 2, ch. 5).

He has never commented on her dress before, so this is a special moment for her. The pleasure she must receive quickly turns to something else, as it becomes clear that he is actually thinking about Mary. The comedy of male indifference to female dress ("[W]oman is fine for her own satisfaction alone," comments the narrator of *Northanger Abbey* [ed. Benedict and Le Faye] [71]) and of Edmund's preoccupation remains, but the reader is left to wonder how Fanny must feel in the face of his gaucherie. "The kind smile of an affectionate brother" underlines, like so many touches in the novel, the chasm that lies between her desire and his behavior.

The central psychological tension of *Mansfield Park* is between Fanny's need for Edmund's love and his obliviousness to her feelings. Even before Fanny becomes aware of her love for Edmund, he is oblivious, as Mallory shows in her essay in this volume. Fanny's love for Edmund grows with her jealousy of Mary Crawford, which becomes clear as Fanny watches him coach Mary on horseback. The jealousy is indicated in numerous ways. But from Edmund there is a complete absence of anything but protective and brotherly feeling for Fanny. He fails to pick up on any of the clues, which sometimes are not so obvious to the reader either, when they reside in Fanny's silences—silences sometimes indistinguishable from the text's own silence.

When Mary excuses her selfish behavior with the epigram that it "must always be forgiven you know, because there is no hope of a cure," the text merely says, "Fanny's answer was extremely civil" (80; vol. 1, ch. 7). In her essay in this volume, Monica Cohen analyzes the power of such maxims to silence listeners. But what has happened here to Fanny? Has her jealousy dissipated so quickly under Mary's conquering wit? The text doesn't tell us. Mary comes to Fanny "with looks of gaiety" during the play rehearsals, when Fanny is plainly so "full of jealousy and agitation" that she can barely manage a reply (187; vol. 1, ch. 17). She lets no evidence of jealousy escape her lips. She may be an intense person, but her situation in life demands caution and deference. It is perhaps because her deepest feelings must be kept secret that she has such an unyielding view of the behavior of others. And she keeps her secret until the very end of the novel.

The changed response of Edmund to Fanny's physical presence, faintly though it is sketched in the last chapter, does indicate that he finds a new attractiveness in her. He slowly begins to suspect that Fanny was becoming "as dear, as important to him in all her smiles and all her ways as Mary Crawford had ever been." He learns "to prefer soft light eyes to sparking dark ones" (543–44, 544); Fanny's smiles, her ways, her eyes finally become present to him.

But the narrator's emphasis is on the inner qualities that inspire Edmund's change of heart: Fanny's "mind, disposition, opinions, and habits," and indeed her "mental superiority." As in Austen's other novels, even in *Pride and Prejudice*, emphasis is finally on the lovers' mental and emotional affinity, an affinity that the novel's action works out fully. True passion is Fanny's alone, giving her a "happiness" that "no description can reach" (545).

The Last Chapter

In both *Pride and Prejudice* and *Emma*—published, respectively, right before and right after *Mansfield Park*—Austen wrote extended and satisfying debriefing chapters after the romantic climax that show how the heroine and her lover come to understand the past and each other. Expecting a similar resolution, students may be disappointed at the last chapter of *Mansfield Park* and Austen's decision not to dramatize either Edmund's discovery of his love for Fanny or her revelation to him of her long-hidden love. Other features of the chapter may displease them too, not least the author's opening announcement of her intentions.

The chapter is unusual in many ways. One unusual feature is its handling of time. A new time scheme is introduced in the second paragraph with the narrator's announcement, "My Fanny indeed at this very time, I have the satisfaction of knowing, must have been happy in spite of every thing" (533). "[T]his very time" must mean immediately after the "wet Sunday evening" in the chapter before (524), when Edmund finally tells Fanny the story of his last meeting with Mary Crawford. But after that scene, the precise time scheme, which has been consistently maintained throughout the novel, is dropped.

As the chapter unfolds, there is mention of "all the summer evenings" of Edmund's "wandering about and sitting under trees with Fanny"; of Sir Thomas's reviewing of the past, a past that Sir Thomas "gradually grew to feel" had been marked by "grievous mismanagement"; of the Grants' absence "for some months purposely lengthened" and at last made permanent by a removal to London; of Edmund's transfer of affections from Mary to Fanny at "exactly the time when it was quite natural that it should be so"; and, after their marriage, presumably about a year later, of the time that the death of Dr. Grant allows Edmund and Fanny to move to the Mansfield parsonage (535, 542, 544). All in all, this one chapter covers almost as much time as the whole preceding novel does after the fifth chapter of the first volume.

Another unusual feature is the relative absence of attention to the interior life of the characters, which until now was so important a technical achievement of *Mansfield Park*. The exception is Sir Thomas, whose soul-searching, anguish, and eventual relief are analyzed by the narrator in nine of the chapter's thirty paragraphs. So forceful and decisive is the prose that represents his thinking that it is easy for students and critics to assume that they are reading not a transcription of his reflections and conclusions but the narrator's own account:

> Something must have been wanting *within*, or time would have worn away much of its ill effect. He feared that principle, active principle, had been wanting, that [his children] had never been properly taught to govern their inclinations and tempers, by that sense of duty which can alone suffice. They had been instructed theoretically in their religion, but never required to bring it into daily practice.   (535–36; vol. 3, ch. 17)

There might even be a touch of Evangelical propaganda in the emphasis on something within. The phrase "that sense of duty which can alone suffice" is readable as the narrator's words or at least as an endorsement of Sir Thomas's thoughts, especially as "that sense of duty" can sound like a reference to the development of Fanny's moral life. But it is equally possible, and probably more accurate, to read these sentiments, in all their insistent, unsparing emphasis, as signs of Sir Thomas's self-castigation. His recognition that he failed as a parent is put in unequivocal language and highlighted by being given a paragraph to itself:

> Bitterly did he deplore a deficiency which now he could scarcely comprehend to have been possible. Wretchedly did he feel, that with all the cost and care of an anxious and expensive education, he had brought up his daughters, without their understanding their first duties, or his being acquainted with their character and temper.   (536)

In keeping with the narrator's promise in her opening words to the chapter to bestow "tolerable comfort" (533), Sir Thomas is allowed some slight consolation for the behavior of Julia and Tom. Good questions to ask a class are, Do Sir Thomas's moral failings make him wholly responsible for the novel's tragic outcomes? Do they invalidate his commitment to principle? And what exactly is the tone of "Sir Thomas, poor Sir Thomas" (533)?

A feature of the last chapter that students might miss is the recurrent use of provisional tenses and phrases. The first instance occurs in the second paragraph: "My Fanny indeed at this very time, I have the satisfaction of knowing, must have been happy in spite of every thing. She must have been a happy creature in spite of all that she felt, or thought she felt, for the distress of those around her. She had sources of delight that must force their way . . ." (533). Students might be asked what the intention or effect is of "must have been" instead of "was" here. One interpretation is that Austen is now using her imagination and that what she suggests is one possibility among many. If this is a tentative mode of representing her characters' futures, is the narrator now withdrawing her endorsement of these possibilities? Phrases like "it may reasonably be supposed," "it is probable that," "we may fairly consider," and "[Mrs. Grant] must have gone with some regret" are used as the chapter proceeds (538, 540, 542, 543). Are they a sign, on the contrary, of the narrator's full commitment to the outcomes that she now, however briefly, predicts for her characters?

Most students will be interested to learn that Austen's interest in her characters did not cease when she completed their story in her novels. Her seeking Elizabeth Bennet's portrait at an exhibition in London is an example: when she couldn't find it, she wrote, "I can only imagine that Mr. D prizes any Picture of her too much to like it should be exposed to the public eye" (Le Faye 213; the letter was written 24 May 1813). Austen was able to tell readers of *Emma* that "the Knightleys' exclusion from Donwell was ended by the death of Mr. Woodhouse in two years' time" (*Emma* [Cronin and McMillan] 600n3). One might read the tentative or provisional futures the narrator suggests in this chapter in a similar way. She has been so close to her characters throughout the writing of the book that she has known their thoughts, feelings, hesitations, and passions; but now it is as though they have moved away from her, and she must speculate about their feelings, must relinquish her control over their fate, as when she entreats readers to set their own timetable for Edmund's ceasing to care about Mary Crawford (544).

There is another, perhaps more interesting, way of reading this provisionality. Throughout *Mansfield Park*, Austen kept open the possibility that Edmund and Mary would reconcile their differences and that Henry would reform himself sufficiently to overcome Fanny's reluctance to take his courtship seriously. One of *Mansfield Park*'s first readers, Austen's brother Henry, apparently perceived these competing narratives as he read and reported his thoughts to his sister (and as she reported in a letter to Cassandra): "Henry has this moment said that he likes my M. P. better & better; he is in the 3d vol. I beleive *now* that he has changed his mind as to foreseeing the end; he said yesterday at least, that he defied anybody to say whether H[enry]. C[rawford]. would be reformed, or would forget Fanny in a fortnight" (Le Faye 258; the letter was written 5 Mar. 1814). Austen seemed pleased that her brother could not decide how Henry Crawford would turn out. In the last chapter, the narrator confirms the possibility of another ending: "Would he have persevered, and uprightly, Fanny must have been his reward—and a reward very voluntarily bestowed—within a reasonable period from Edmund's marrying Mary" (540). That Fanny's consent would be "very voluntarily bestowed" is surprising and underlines the author's openness to her tale's taking quite a different turn.

Austen intends her characters to be complex creations capable of choice—in other words, their fates should not be predetermined by their author. "Her influence over him had already given him some influence over her" (540) succinctly conveys the way Henry's changed behavior in Portsmouth, for example, has unsettled Fanny's opinion of him. The next paragraph, about Henry, culminates with, "Had he done as he intended, and as he knew he ought, by going down to Everingham after his return from Portsmouth, he might have been deciding his own happy destiny." The clause "as he knew he ought" indicates a mental debate: Henry could have decided not to stay in London, where he would see Mrs. Rushworth again. Instead, the author follows his fate in some of the most unambigious writing in the chapter:

> He saw Mrs. Rushworth, was received by her with a coldness which ought to have been repulsive, and have established apparent indifference between them for ever; but he was mortified, he could not bear to be thrown off by the woman whose smiles had been so wholly at his command; he must exert himself to subdue so proud a display of resentment; it was anger on Fanny's account; he must get the better of it, and make Mrs. Rushworth Maria Bertram again in her treatment of himself.   (541)

"He must," here repeated, has none of the provisional or subjunctive quality of the other parts of the chapter; instead, in combination with the rhythm of this sentence, it represents the urgency of Henry's need to exert control over women, which amounts almost to a mental illness. There follows a passage in which Henry is trapped by his temperament and Maria's unappeased passion:

> In this spirit he began the attack; and by animated perseverance had soon re-established the sort of familiar intercourse—of gallantry—of flirtation which bounded his views, but in triumphing over the discretion, which, though beginning in anger, might have saved them both, he had put himself in the power of feelings on her side, more strong than he had supposed.—She loved him; there was no withdrawing attentions, avowedly dear to her.   (541)

Familiar intercourse, gallantry, flirtation: the casual summary (echoing the style of a man of the world) gives way to the analysis, even shocking in its force and clarity, of Maria's vulnerability. Moreover, writing that Henry is "entangled by his own vanity . . . without the smallest inconstancy of mind" toward Fanny (541) and thus recognizing that Henry's inner life, being complex, offers unrealized possibilities, Austen remains true to the psychological realism that has been so marked throughout the novel.

The treatment of Edmund's change of heart away from Mary and toward Fanny is less convincing to most readers:

> I purposely abstain from dates on this occasion, that every one may be at liberty to fix their own, aware that the cure of unconquerable passions and the transfer of unchanging attachments must vary much as to time in different people.—I only intreat every body to believe that exactly at the time when it was natural that it should be so, and not a week earlier,

Edmund did cease to care about Miss Crawford, and become as anxious
to marry Fanny, as Fanny herself could desire.   (544)

The humor of "the cure of unconquerable passions" and "not a week earlier"
seems odd in the context of what must be the most crucial process of decision
making in the novel. However, as Karyn Lehner posits in her essay in this volume, Austen may be drawing an implicit contrast between the overtly seductive strategies of Henry Crawford, and also, to a lesser extent, of his sister, in
this suggestion of the gradual and inevitable dawn of adult love between her
hero and heroine. That there is no extended treatment of the realized love between them, as there is between the couples in *Pride and Prejudice* and *Emma*,
supports Lehner's idea. In her essay in this volume, Sarah Emsley offers another reason why Edmund's courtship is so briefly rendered: the action that
Austen saw as the heart of this novel is not the courtship of Edmund and Fanny
but Fanny's struggle to resist the pressures to accept the proposal of Henry
Crawford.

   There is a significant difference between the romantic conclusion of *Mansfield Park* and the two works on either side of it in Austen's publishing life. In
Pride and Prejudice and *Emma*, the male figure is in love with the female but
must bide his time until events cause her to recognize her feelings for him. In
Mansfield Park, it is the reverse: the male increasingly feels esteem and liking
for the female, but his sentiments seem far from passionate. It is Fanny whose
intensity of feeling, from early in the novel, demand a return of Edmund's love;
it is Fanny who must guard these feelings—in this case dangerously subversive, as she believes—until the actions of other people bring about a complete
change. The attribution of intense, intransigent, jealous, and abiding love to
the woman is one of the many reasons why *Mansfield Park* is a revolution in
the novel. That this love has been secret and transgressive makes it even more
extraordinary.

Gifts Always Come with Strings Attached: Teaching *Mansfield Park* in the Context of Gift Theory

Dorice Williams Elliott

Many critics, teachers, and readers, ranging from the postcolonial scholar Edward Said ("Jane Austen" [*Culture*]) to the commercial filmmaker Patricia Rozema (*Mansfield Park* [1999]), have focused on the novel's implication in the nascent capitalist global economy of late eighteenth- and early nineteenth-century England. Others have focused on its involvement in a rural agrarian economy symbolized by the country house tradition. Another way to contextualize *Mansfield Park*, however, is in the framework of gift economy. According to theorists of the gift, when a gift is given, whether money, objects, time, or education, the recipient is obligated to reciprocate. Recipients unable to reciprocate must "repay" the gift by demonstrating gratitude, deference, and obedience. Indeed, a paternalist economy relies on gifts that cannot be reciprocated, including patronage and charity, to reinforce the social ties that bind the different ranks and classes together. In *Mansfield Park*, more than in any of her other novels, Austen examines the dynamics of a gift economy. Fanny Price, a "poor relation" with little ability to give gifts to anyone, is the recipient of many of them—from Sir Thomas's large gift of a lady's private education and a decade or so of physical support to Henry Crawford's disguised gift of a necklace for her coming-out ball. Fanny is dutifully grateful for the gifts she receives but also hesitant about accepting them, because she knows from bitter experience that gifts always come with "strings attached"—obligations she may not want to accept.

Teaching student readers of *Mansfield Park* the basic theory of gift giving and asking them to identify both the various gifts exchanged or given one-sidedly in the novel and the obligations attached to those gifts show them another way to think about Fanny and how she responds to the often complex situations into which she is forced by others. She tries to evade obligations to people she does not trust or love and to carve out some autonomy for herself within her very circumscribed position at Mansfield Park. Since she tends to be an unpopular heroine for some students, reading her in this context may help them understand why Austen portrays her as meek, cautious, and suspicious instead of open and confident, like some of the heroines of her other novels. It certainly helps students see just how difficult the position of a female poor relation is to navigate and may encourage them to sympathize with Fanny more and even to admire her courage and intelligence.

In teaching *Mansfield Park*, I introduce the students to gift theory near the beginning of our reading of the novel. I point out that the first paragraph describes the marriage market as a capitalistic exchange where a young woman is a commodity with a quantifiable price: when Miss Maria Ward marries Sir Thomas Bertram, her "uncle, the lawyer, himself, allowed her to be at least three thousand pounds short of any equitable claim" to be "raised to the rank of a baronet's lady, with all the comforts of and consequences of an handsome house and large income" (3). Only a few pages later, however, Sir Thomas and Mrs. Norris, his sister-in-law, have decided to undertake a project of "benevolence" by adopting their young niece Fanny Price (6). Mrs. Norris explains the grounds of gift economy to the new arrival: she "had been talking to [Fanny] the whole way from Northampton of her wonderful good fortune, and the extraordinary degree of gratitude and good behaviour which it ought to produce, and [Fanny's] consciousness of misery was therefore increased by the idea of its being a wicked thing for her not to be happy" (14; vol. 1, ch. 2). Mrs. Norris here makes plain that in a gift economy there is no question of an exact sum that one can exchange for a commodity, as in a capitalist economy. The only way Fanny can pay for "her wonderful good fortune" is with an unspecified but "extraordinary" payment of "gratitude and good behaviour." In Mrs. Norris's opinion, in fact, Fanny can never repay her debt and must always be grateful and well-behaved—presumably for the rest of her life.

Although it is not a tangible object, what Fanny has received from her uncle, Sir Thomas, is, as Mrs. Norris makes clear, a valuable gift. In an era when even institutional education was costly, Fanny is to receive the benefits of learning to be a lady from a private governess, alongside her two wealthy female cousins, and she is to live a life of relative ease in a wealthy baronet's country seat. Besides receiving an education befitting a lady, she also receives her room and board, clothing, sundry presents of toys and small amounts of money, and the use of the books in the family's library, another expensive luxury. Perhaps most important, she is given the chance to associate intimately with people of a higher social rank and hence develop the manners and bearing that qualify her for good society, and, by being known as Sir Thomas's niece, she receives the credit accruing to his name and title.

The giving of gifts, large and small, to those lower on the social scale was central to the preindustrial economy (though it has by no means disappeared from contemporary culture). As the anthropologist Marcel Mauss theorized, there are three central elements of gift giving: the giving of a gift, the necessity of receiving the gift proffered, and the obligation to reciprocate. Gifts, as Mauss makes clear, may include goods or property—even women and children—but also less tangible things such as courtesies, entertainments, military assistance, or education and patronage (3). Some cultures routinely practiced gift-giving customs like potlatch, where huge feasts with expensive gifts for all the guests were given by one family or tribe, followed by a return feast of equal or greater magnitude. Leaders or tribes used this lavish gift giving to display their wealth and to establish political alliances. In all gift economies, however, when a person or group who receives a gift cannot reciprocate by giving back an equal or greater gift, that recipient must repay instead with gratitude and deference, as well as with submission and obedience.

Hence giving gifts is a way to establish power and superiority (Blau 108–09). Sir Thomas makes it clear from the beginning that Fanny is "not a *Miss Bertram*" and that she and his daughters "cannot be equals" (12; vol. 1, ch. 1); she is a gift recipient who must continually show her gratitude by submitting her will and her wishes to theirs. Gifts, even when they seem to be freely given, always include some benefit for the giver, whether it is religious salvation, power, social superiority, or merely self-satisfaction.[1] Both Sir Thomas and Mrs. Norris feel "the pleasures of so benevolent a scheme" even before Fanny has been invited to Mansfield Park (8). Fanny, however, feels the miseries of being the recipient of a major gift even before she arrives in the coach.

After introducing the basic concepts of gift theory, I invite students to discuss their own experiences of gift giving and receiving, having them think particularly about the obligations that gifts create and the way that the cycle of giving gifts tends to regenerate itself. To demonstrate these points, I sometimes share a personal story about when I visited the Philippines. The family with whom I stayed for several days treated me and my family royally, and they also gave us several tangible gifts. When we returned to the United States, I puzzled about what I could send them that would be an adequate expression of my gratitude. I settled on a nice (and relatively expensive) piece of local artwork that I found in a museum shop and sent it with an effusive letter of thanks. I imagined that, though I certainly hadn't matched their gifts and was still in their debt, I had at least reciprocated in an appropriate way. A few weeks later, however, a package arrived in the mail—another gift from them in response to my gift. At this point, I realized that canceling my debt would be impossible, so I sent another letter—offering them return hospitality if they should ever visit Lawrence, Kansas—and reconciled myself to remaining hopelessly in arrears to these very kind people. My students have always responded enthusiastically and thoughtfully with insightful examples of their own to this discussion of how a gift economy still functions, especially in the affective sphere of personal relations, alongside the capitalist one in which we participate.

Though the basic obligations and effects identified by theorists of the gift apply to virtually any exchange of gifts, different types of gift economies generate different kinds of power relations. Another way to describe Sir Thomas's adoption of Fanny, for instance, is in terms of patronage. The system of patronage, a form of gift economy that was central in Austen's time, involves the giving of position or influence to those below one in the social and economic hierarchy, usually in order to obtain a job or position for the recipient. The concept of patronage may be less familiar to students than the idea of giving gifts or presents, but this form of gift economy is evident in *Mansfield Park*. Fanny is, of course, a major recipient of patronage in the novel; by providing her the manners and education of a lady, as well as a publicly acknowledged connection with a baronet, Sir Thomas and Mrs. Norris expect that Fanny will attract a suitable husband and a "creditable establishment" when she arrives at maturity (7; vol. 1, ch. 1). Likewise, her brother William is indebted to Sir Thomas for his naval appointment and later to Henry Crawford for his promotion. Jenny Davidson points out that such patronage necessarily engenders hypocrisy in its recipients and suggests that "Austen defends those forms of insincerity that dependency produces" in Fanny (246). Fanny's dependent position as a poor female relation in receipt of patronage from her uncle's family renders it necessary for Fanny to disguise her real feelings and remain silent on many occasions, argues Davidson, which goes a long way toward explaining why Fanny is quiet and submissive on the outside while often tartly critical in her thoughts.

The system of patronage was a specific form that gift economy took in Austen's time, before the concept of attaining position by merit took hold in the late nineteenth century, though, as we all know, patronage still exists in our culture. I point out to students that both patronage and, another form of gift economy, charitable giving were essential parts of the paternalist society that preceded and coexisted with industrial capitalism in eighteenth- and early-nineteenth-century England. Based on a well-defined hierarchy of social ranks and status, society in Austen's time depended on various types of gift giving as the glue that held the classes together. Those of the upper ranks of society provided patronage, usually to people slightly beneath them on the social and economic scale, such as poorer relatives, friends, or protégés. Charity or philanthropy, on the other hand, was the name for the kind of gift giving directed to the lower classes. Charity included material gifts, education in charity schools, and support in old age, and it was considered an obligation of the landowning class to their servants, employees, laborers, and the local poor—given in return, of course, for the homage, loyalty, and obedience of those lower on the social scale.[2] Farmers who were tenants of rich landowners were even expected to vote for the candidates their landlords favored. Since voting was done in public—not by secret ballot—those who failed to do their duty by voting with their landlords could be in real danger of losing the leases on the land they farmed. As the daughter of a clergyman and the sister of a landed gentleman, Austen herself was a charitable visitor to the poor in her neighborhood, as she mentions in several of her letters.[3]

Such charitable contacts reinforced the existing political system; if the rich —or at least relatively well-off—gave gifts and support to the poor, especially in times of trouble, and the poor were in turn bound to their betters by the obligations such gifts engendered, large-scale governmental involvement in social welfare was unnecessary. The burgeoning industrial capitalist economy, by contrast, defined the relation between the poor and the rich as a contractual one centered on the cash nexus of wages paid for labor, which worked eventually to create the modern sense of class. According to capitalist ideology, as Karl Marx and his followers pointed out, people's primary loyalties are not to those above them on the social scale but to those who, in their same class, share their interests. In *Mansfield Park*, the poorest people we see are the Prices, Fanny's birth family. They look to their wealthy relatives for gifts and patronage instead of expecting assistance from their peers or the government. Mrs. Price's nine children will be unable to find work and success through their own merit alone.

Another form that gift economy can take is what I call affective gift exchange. Most students are likely to be familiar with it: the exchange of gifts between people who are social equals for the purpose of creating or reinforcing bonds of affection, love, or appreciation. My experience with the Philippine family is an example of an affective gift exchange, as is the exchange of gifts for holidays, birthdays, or other special occasions. On the surface, an affective gift exchange is not about establishing power or superiority, though power relations are never entirely absent in it. Parents who believe they are giving gifts to their children freely and from love, for instance, may also be subtly reinforcing their position of authority over their children, as teenagers and young adults will certainly recognize. One of the funniest moments in *Mansfield Park* is an example of affective gift exchange. When Lady Bertram hears that Mr. Crawford has proposed to Fanny, she declares, "And I will tell you what, Fanny—which is more than I did for Maria—the next time pug has a litter you shall have a puppy" (385; vol. 3, ch. 2). Her proffered gift is a token of her affection for Fanny, but it is also her languid way of putting pressure on Fanny to accept the proposal. The allusion to Maria adds an element of economics to the affectionate nature of the gift.

With this background, we come to the specific text of *Mansfield Park*. I ask students, as they read, to watch for examples of gift exchanges or of the obligations associated with gifts. Invariably they notice many in the novel. In order to understand Fanny, they must recognize how strongly she feels the obligations inherent in her position as recipient of both patronage and material gifts at Mansfield Park. For instance, when Sir Thomas leaves Mansfield Park on his voyage to look over his estates in Antigua, she cries "bitterly," causing her cousins, "on seeing her with red eyes," to "set her down as a hypocrite," since they know that, like themselves, she feels constrained and subdued by his presence (38; vol. 1, ch. 3).[4] The narrator tells us that her response is more complicated than that; she does, like her cousins, feel "relief" at Sir Thomas's leaving, but "a more tender nature suggested that her feelings were ungrateful, and she really grieved because she could not grieve" (37). Castigating herself for insufficient gratitude might seem excessive to modern readers, but in the context of the novel—especially given Mrs. Norris's frequent reminders of how much Fanny owes the Bertrams—this emotion is natural enough.

Mrs. Norris, herself the recipient of many gifts from the Bertrams, including much of her food and all her entertainment, is the one who actively enforces Fanny's sense of the gratitude and deference due to her benefactors. Since Mrs. Norris is so obviously an obnoxious character—she would be one of Austen's best comic side characters if the effects of her obsessions were not so harmful to Fanny—students may wonder why Fanny doesn't just ignore her or return tit for tat (as she does in the Rozema film version). But it is because much of what Mrs. Norris says about Fanny's duty is actually true in the context of gift economy that Fanny cannot ignore her or fight back. When Fanny refuses to act in the home theatrical, for instance, Mrs. Norris bitterly upbraids her: "What a piece of work here is about nothing,—I am quite ashamed of you, Fanny, to make such a difficulty of obliging your cousins in a trifle of this sort,—So kind as they are to you!" When Edmund defends Fanny, Mrs. Norris even more explicitly reminds Fanny of her dependent position: ". . . I shall think her a very obstinate, ungrateful girl, if she does not do what her aunt and cousins wish her—very ungrateful indeed, considering who and what she is" (172; vol. 1, ch. 15). Mrs. Norris's reproach is so frank that the other listeners find it embarrassing and rude, but Fanny makes no response. Though Edmund and Mary Crawford try to support and comfort her, she feels the force of Mrs. Norris's argument so keenly that it completely silences her—just how keenly is evident in the next chapter, when she reflects on the difficulty of her position (176; ch. 16). That Fanny holds to her principles, despite such public embarrassment and the more sensitive but hence more powerful urgings of her cousins, shows her not to be the wimp she is often supposed to be. She is shy about displaying herself in front of others, but it should not be difficult to see why, after the public scolding she has just received from Mrs. Norris when she ventured for once to assert herself. Her unwillingness to participate in the play also stems from her sense of obligation to Sir Thomas, who, as both she and Edmund recognize, would disapprove of the play, so in effect she is showing her gratitude to Sir Thomas by refusing to gratify his children and sister-in-law. Mrs. Norris manages to keep Fanny's debt constantly in her niece's mind, but the older woman may do this in order to disguise her own position as an indebted gift recipient. In fact, when Sir Thomas returns, he sees that Fanny has shown due gratitude to him, while Mrs. Norris has not (220–21; vol. 2, ch. 2).

Besides the ironically "generous present of some of their least valued toys" that Maria and Julia give to Fanny on her first day at Mansfield Park, which only serves to increase her sense of overwhelming obligation, the first tangible gifts that Fanny receives are paper, writing materials, and the franking (free postage) for a letter to William, given to her by Edmund—along with the intangible gift of his attention and kindness (15, 18; vol. 1, ch. 2). For the first time, she feels pleasure in receiving a gift at Mansfield: ". . . her countenance and a few artless words fully conveyed all her gratitude and delight" (18). Edmund, following the logic of reciprocation, "began to find her an interesting object" and becomes her friend and mentor; Fanny, again making a return, "loved him better than any body in the world except William" (25). Two important features of gift theory suggest themselves here. One is that how a gift is bestowed has significance. Edmund gives tangible objects, but they are especially valued because they are given with apparent altruism and lack of self-interest.[5] The other key aspect of his gifts to Fanny is that, because they are given in a friendly, nonpatronizing way, they create an affective bond that, though not devoid of power relations, emphasizes affection rather than dominance. While Fanny is definitely submissive in her relations with Edmund, her submission is voluntary and itself more like a return gift than is her more forced deference to Sir Thomas, Mrs. Norris, and the rest of the family at Mansfield. Mrs. Norris may believe she is the "most liberal-minded . . . aunt in the world," but Fanny feels no love for her, having "never received kindness from her aunt" (9; vol. 1, ch. 1; 28; ch. 3).

Although Fanny clearly recognizes her debt of gratitude to Sir Thomas, his beneficence to her does not create love for him. She refuses to feel obligated to Mary Crawford, suspecting that she is befriending her only to ingratiate herself with Edmund or to fill in when Fanny's cousins are away from Mansfield: "Fanny went to her every two or three days . . . yet it was without loving her, without ever thinking like her, *without any sense of obligation* for being sought after now when nobody else was to be had . . ." (242; vol. 2, ch. 4; my emphasis). Although Mary definitely gives gifts to Fanny, including companionship, harp playing (for Fanny alone), and dinner invitations, as well as the necklace (which actually comes from Henry), Fanny is able in this case to accept the gifts without repaying Mary with affection, because she believes that Mary is being repaid for her gifts in other ways—with the love of Edmund, above all. Fanny feels "obliged" to Miss Crawford, in the sense of being grateful (173; vol. 1, ch. 15), but feels no obligation in terms of owing loyalty or love. Her relationship with Henry, however, is more complicated.

One of the key affective bonds that gift giving and receiving can cement, of course, is romantic or sexual love. Students of a previous generation would have understood that a boy paying for a date with a girl could expect a goodnight kiss and that a woman should not accept a gift more personal than flowers or candy from a man she was not engaged to because of the implied sexual obligation. Even now, students may recognize that one of the main reasons for a woman to pay her own way on a date is that then she has a choice about whether she wants to engage in any kind of sexual contact or continue the acquaintance. Discussing such customs may serve as an effective prelude to considering the precarious situation in which Henry puts Fanny when he arranges for the promotion of William by appealing to the patronage of his uncle the admiral—something even Sir Thomas cannot do for Fanny's brother. Such a gift, though Fanny is not at first aware of its romantic implications, puts her in a position toward Henry that is parallel to her position as a dependent of Sir Thomas. Accustomed as she is to this position and its accompanying obligations, she cannot but feel uncomfortable about refusing Henry's advances, even though she has seen firsthand how he manipulates and plays with women. When Sir Thomas approves of these advances and pressures her to accept Henry's proposal with reminders of her obligations to both Henry and himself, Fanny finds herself in an untenable situation. In a time when marriages were contracted more often for convenience than for love, it is only her prior attachment to Edmund that can justify her refusal, even to herself. But note that her love for Edmund has also been generated within the economics of a gift exchange: his kindness and mentorship have been repaid by her love and devotion, even though he is not aware of her feelings. Thus in the novel the affective exchange trumps even a double dose of patronage.

Perhaps the most obvious of *Mansfield Park*'s gift exchanges involves the necklace that Fanny receives, in parts, from the three most important young men in her life. The most time is spent on Henry Crawford's duplicitous gift of a golden necklace on which to wear the "very pretty amber cross which William had brought her from Sicily" (295; vol. 2, ch. 8).[6] Again, the method of presenting the gift is crucial. Henry needs to avoid the appearance of initiating a sexual transaction, while still allowing himself to feel the gratification of anticipating such a transaction in the future, so he has his sister present the gift to Fanny without any direct indication that it comes from him. Although Mary kindly urges Fanny to take one of what she presents as her own chains "to keep for her [Mary's] sake," she intimates that the necklace actually comes from her brother by playfully suggesting that Fanny suspects "a confederacy between us, and that what I am now doing is with his knowledge and at his desire." Fanny responds even to the idea of a friendly gift from Mary with such "scruples" that she "start[s] back at first with a look of horror at the proposal," so it is not surprising that she rejects "with the deepest blushes" this hint that Henry might be involved with the proffered necklace (300–01; vol. 2, ch. 8). She thus tries to reject any tangible gift that might be construed as the acceptance of an affective tie with either Mary or Henry. Since Mary's hint is less than subtle, though, it is difficult to believe that Fanny does not suspect Henry's involvement, and, indeed, the more Mary insists that Fanny take the necklace, the more uncomfortable Fanny becomes. Yet one of the tenets of gift economy is the obligation to receive, and Fanny reaches the point where she "dared not make any further opposition; and with renewed but less happy thanks accepted the necklace" (302). "Less happy" surely indicates her doubts about whether there might in fact be an implied consent to a sexual exchange, especially since the rest of the chapter details her dawning awareness of Henry's attraction to her.

When Fanny returns to her room to deposit her newly acquired gold chain, itself a symbol of a woman's dependent relation to a husband or lover, she finds Edmund waiting for her with his own gift of a necklace. Her feelings now are pleasurable, but not because of his motives, at least not conscious motives, in giving. Although it is perfectly acceptable both socially and personally for her to receive a gift from Edmund, a cousin who has been like a brother to her, this time she entertains the secret pleasures of an imagined romantic-sexual exchange. Edmund in fact comments that her "thanks are far beyond the occasion," not knowing the complicated reasons for her gratitude (304; vol. 2, ch. 9). Next Fanny begins to worry about offending any of the parties by wearing one or the other of the two gifts; her dilemma is solved only by her discovering that the necklace of Mary and Henry is too large for the hole in the cross. This discovery makes her so happy that she is willing to wear both, thus indulging both Henry's and her own fantasies of sexual-romantic gratification. Only the cross, given to her by William, her real brother, can be worn without the sexual implications of a gift exchange between a man and a woman.

Thus there are many anxieties attendant on Fanny's reception of gifts of different types from various characters in the novel. It is only when Fanny becomes the giver rather than the receiver that she thoroughly enjoys the process of gift exchange. In the Portsmouth section of the novel, she gives her first tangible gift to someone else: a silver knife to her little sister Betsey, which solves a long-standing quarrel between Betsey and Susan, her other sister. The narrator points out that Fanny "was so wholly unused to confer favours, except on the very poor, so unpractised in removing evils, or bestowing kindnesses among her equals, and so fearful of appearing to elevate herself as a great lady at home, that it took some time to determine that it would not be unbecoming in her to make such a present" (459; vol. 3, ch. 9).[7] The gift not only solves the quarrel but also gives Fanny "influence" and "an office of authority" over Susan (459), who now is the one who must render gratitude and practice submission. Susan does so willingly, and Fanny is able to teach her better manners. This results eventually in Fanny's also becoming a patron: when Fanny leaves to marry Edmund, she is able to establish Susan in her former place as Lady Bertram's companion and as the recipient of Sir Thomas's beneficence. Finding herself in the position of giver is the final step for Fanny in terms of the gift economy: dispensing a gift is a sign of the power she has gained through the course of the novel. Her elevation should bring a sense of satisfaction to students who have come to understand the implications of her position and the ways that she has managed to negotiate them despite the abject powerlessness with which she began the novel.

It is particularly significant that Austen represents the wooing of Fanny by Henry Crawford through the lens of gift economy instead of the market economy invoked on the first page of the novel. Fanny, as a dependent poor relation with no dowry to bring to a marriage settlement, has no price affixed to her, whereas Lady Bertram had a price affixed to her when she was Miss Maria

Ward. Although Sir Thomas is certainly aware of the financial advantages for Fanny in marrying a rich man like Henry, Henry does not offer himself to her as an income or an estate, as Mr. Rushworth does to Maria Bertram. The novel's insistence on embedding its heroine in a gift economy rather than a marriage market is a rejection of the notion that people—women and, by implication, workers—are commodities with fixed or negotiable prices. This rejection of the market might seem to ally Austen with a conservative paternalism, but it actually leads in a different direction—toward the domestic economy of separate spheres that preserved affective values in the home, where women presided, and freed men to indulge market values where such values were thought to belong: in the world of commerce. *Mansfield Park* may seem to reject a capitalist economy in favor of a gift economy, but in fact it uses a gift economy to clear the path for modern capitalism. That modest Fanny Price is, in a sense, the only woman left standing at the end of the novel demonstrates that the affective ties generated through a gift exchange can be extremely powerful, even in the context of a capitalist economy.

NOTES

[1] On the spiritual motivation for gift giving, see Davis (11–17). Jacques Derrida argues that a true gift is impossible, because the very notion of a gift presumes no return, but even the thought of giving a gift presupposes some reward (15).

[2] On education as a gift in a charitable gift economy, see Elliott.

[3] See, for instance, the letters dated Monday 24–Wednesday 26 December 1798 (24); Sunday 29–Monday 30 November 1812 (132); and Sunday 24 January 1813 (135) in Austen, *Selected Letters*.

[4] Davidson also discusses this incident (253).

[5] Many modern gift theorists have debated whether true altruism is possible in gift-giving. See, for example, Schrift; Osteen.

[6] Lynn Festa also comments on the obligations of Mary and Henry's gift, though without invoking gift economy per se (445).

[7] This is one of the rare mentions in Austen of the charitable gift economy, in which even Fanny has participated as a benefactor. Charitable giving is mentioned at more length in *Emma* (*Emma* [Parrish] 57).

Mansfield Park: Austen's Most Teachable Novel

Pamela Bromberg

Mansfield Park may not be the favorite Austen novel for some students, perhaps not for some professors either, but I do think that it is the most teachable. For a variety of reasons, students often initially express disappointment in the novel, especially after they have read only the first volume. In my experience, however, teaching *Mansfield Park* invariably leads to deeply considered conversation about Austen's skillful narrative development of a cast of diverse and psychologically complex characters, about the elegant patterns traced by contrasting groups of characters in richly realized settings, about her acute interest in the way that socioeconomic factors shape her characters' lives, and finally about the novel's plot and uneasy resolution.

When I teach *Mansfield Park* as the culminating text in my course on the development of the English novel, our earlier reading of such eighteenth-century works as *Tom Jones*, *Millenium Hall*, *The Castle of Otranto*, and *Evelina* provides historical and narrative contexts in which to consider tensions between the land-based wealth of the aristocracy and country gentry and the emerging mercantile, professional, and industrial class centered in London. Recognizing that Austen stages ideological friction between the more socially liberal London world of the Crawfords and the conservative values of Mansfield Park helps students contextualize their appreciation for Mary's wit and Henry's flirting. While the novel's conclusion certainly privileges the conservative view, readers are left to reflect on the Crawfords' London attitudes, the democratizing role of the British navy and merchant fleet, the importance of the Caribbean slave economy in early-nineteenth-century England, and the centrality of marriage as the institution determining women's socioeconomic realities. Beyond this wealth of historical and thematic material, *Mansfield Park* supplies nuanced characterization, a formal design that is both clearly structured and detailed, and language so resonant that every rereading leads to new discoveries. *Mansfield Park* is Austen's most teachable novel because it can be approached from so many different angles, because of its seriousness and depth, and because of the various strains in its plot and characterization that elicit from students lively responses and animated debate.

For many students, however, one of the biggest barriers to appreciating *Mansfield Park* is Fanny Price, especially when they have recently read *Pride and Prejudice*. When I position *Mansfield Park* as the grand finale in my course on the development of the English novel, students readily express admiration for Austen's narrative craft, the complexity of her design, and the psychological depth of her protagonist. But in more Austen-intensive courses, where chronology dictates that *Mansfield Park* follow *Pride and Prejudice* on the syllabus, I often encounter resistance. Students generally begin the novel with sympathy for the ten-year-old girl uprooted from her family and deposited in the cold world of the Bertrams. Tone in the opening chapters is governed by the voice of an omniscient narrator who invites the reader's sympathy with Fanny's traumatic losses, tender nature, and feelings of insignificance.

But when Mary Crawford enters the novel as the lively, beautiful, witty, and athletic foil to Fanny, Fanny tends to fall in the estimation of students. Mary, with her love of activity, her high spirits, her elegant musicianship, and her natural gifts of "strength and courage" (81; vol. 1, ch. 7), brings new energy to the cast of characters and appears at first the true heir to Elizabeth Bennet. The episode in which she appropriates Fanny's horse and shows a talent for riding (vol. 1, ch. 7) serves as the first extended dramatization of these contrasted characters and provides rich material for exploration of their opposing qualities and of Austen's complex portrait of Fanny's intense emotions as Mary charms Edmund Bertram (and some readers of *Mansfield Park*). Austen explains why Mary's first outing quickly leads to repeated rides. A descriptive passage emphasizes Mary's strength, pleasure in exercise, and prowess and suggests the beginning of her sexual attraction to Edmund. Close reading of this passage can show students how Austen carefully stages these paired characters, and it will prepare them to appreciate future dramatic instances of Fanny's secret pain and Mary's blithe pleasure:

> Miss Crawford's enjoyment of riding was such, that she did not know how to leave off. Active and fearless, and, though rather small, strongly made, she seemed formed for a horsewoman; and to the pure genuine pleasure of the exercise, something was probably added in Edmund's attendance and instructions. (78)

The other characters, including the old coachman and Fanny's cousins, join in admiration of Mary and participate in a series of enjoyable excursions from which Fanny is excluded. After five days without her horse and Edmund's company, Fanny, who has been relegated to the sidelines, is pained by feelings of neglect. She struggles against "discontent and envy" (87). Students certainly respond to Fanny's hurt feelings and self-reproach, but admiration for Mary's energy, enthusiasm, and good humor can outweigh their sympathy for Fanny. Fanny rides for her health; Mary rides for pleasure. Fanny is weak, frail, prone to headaches, Mary strong and athletic. Fanny is quiet, timid, and earnest, Mary exuberant and witty. Mary's "energy of character" (81) is charismatic, making Edmund forget his fraternal solicitude for Fanny's health and well-being. While Austen has clearly established Fanny as the protagonist, students who have fallen in love with *Pride and Prejudice* and its Elizabeth typically see in Mary a more appealing candidate for the role of heroine. Fanny appears to be the opposite not only of Mary but also of Elizabeth; in fact, she may even remind students of the sickly Anne de Bourgh.

One way to deal positively with this tension is to focus on it, asking the class to consider and debate how readers respond to Fanny and Mary, who are viewed as friends by other characters yet become rivals in Fanny's secret inner world. Fanny is treated by her relatives more as a servant than a full-fledged member of the family. Valued too little to have her own story in the Mansfield household, she is an onlooker in the first volume, providing us instead with an outsider's view of the courtship and marriage stories of her cousins. But Austen's narrative voice establishes the novel's moral and emotional center in Fanny's acute ethical perception and sensitive feelings. Recent critics have argued that Austen does not present Fanny as a paragon of virtue (Waldron, "Frailties"; Wiltshire, *Jane Austen*). Although the monstrous Mrs. Norris and the supremely lazy Lady Bertram tend to cast Fanny as victim, a languishing Cinderella, careful attention to Austen's dramatization of her inner thoughts and forbidden feelings for Edmund allows students to perceive that Fanny is struggling secretly with ethical dilemmas. Close reading of the horseback riding episode helps students appreciate the psychological complexity of Austen's treatment of Fanny and also reflect on their own responses to Fanny as the novel's protagonist.

But moving students from their identification with Mary toward sympathetic understanding of Fanny remains a central challenge in teaching *Mansfield Park*. It is useful to remind them of Austen's development as a writer and suggest the importance of biographical context for both *Mansfield Park* and *Pride and Prejudice*. *Pride and Prejudice*, the Austen novel most frequently taught in college literature courses, is a youthful work: it was begun in 1796, when its author was not yet twenty, completed when she was twenty-one, then revised and published finally in 1813. It embodies and transmits the optimism and energy of a young woman with wit and prospects, and young adult readers find it a kind of romantic master plot. Its extraordinary current popularity as source material for endless spinoffs reflects the appetite for Elizabeth and Darcy as readers' alter egos. *Mansfield Park*, on the other hand, written after the author spent ten unsettled and later nomadic years, years in which she completed no fiction, is, in Claudia L. Johnson's words, "an ambitious and difficult novel, the first composed and published exclusively in [her] adulthood" ("Introduction" xi). Austen herself later remarked about *Pride and Prejudice*, to her sister, Cassandra, that it is "too light & bright & sparkling; it wants shade" (Le Faye 203; the letter was written 4 Feb. 1813). *Mansfield Park*, begun in 1812, after Austen had revised her earlier works, is indeed a novel that has shadow: the worth of its heroine is appreciated by her adoptive family only after richly deserved catastrophe befalls them. With its retiring protagonist, dense prose, and somber register, *Mansfield Park* makes demands on the reader.

Hearing Fanny

A discussion of *Mansfield Park* that begins with a focus on Mary and Fanny as foils for each other and on the psychological depth of Austen's portrayal of Fanny in the early chapters provides a good foundation for students to follow

Fanny's development and the plot of her secret rivalry with Mary. But Fanny may be considered another way, not in comparison with Austen's earlier heroines but in the light of the history of the English novel: a new kind of heroine, she anticipates the Victorian fiction of Charlotte Brontë and Charles Dickens, with their stories of orphans who must find their way in a hostile world. Austen carefully establishes Fanny's lower-middle-class status in the opening chapter. The marriages of the three Ward sisters determine their stations in life, ranging from the "comforts and consequences" Miss Maria enjoys as the wife of a baronet at Mansfield Park (3), to the comfortable economies of Mrs. Norris's establishment, down to the "very small income" (5) afforded Mrs. Price and her nine children by her husband, a disabled and hard-drinking marine lieutenant. Fanny arrives at *Mansfield Park* as the poor relation, lacking in her cousins' "rank, fortune, rights, and expectations" (12). In addition to her lower status in the family, she is small, shy, lonely, sensitive, and generally misunderstood. Austen's call for sympathy implies a relationship of reader to protagonist that differs profoundly from those of her first three novels. From the buoyant irony of *Pride and Prejudice* and *Northanger Abbey* (and *Emma*), the narrative register is more partisan, aligning readers with the mistreated Fanny and against the adults who mistreat her. The momentum of the plot derives less from the heroine's growth in knowledge of self and others than from the shortcomings of her various foster parent figures and their overprivileged children.

I tell students that the novel was originally published in three volumes and ask them how Austen exploits this partitioning to trace Fanny's change from quiet victim to soft-spoken but resolute moral authority. Furthermore, as Fanny develops the ability to assert and articulate her feelings and views in conversation with Edmund, Sir Thomas, and Henry Crawford, Austen presents dialogues with increasing depth and subtlety of moral vision.

As students continue to read the novel, I invite them to consider the movement of Fanny from bystander to the center of the action and to consider also the development of her voice and agency as she is presented with new opportunities and choices. Austen's narrative technique in *Mansfield Park* shifts away from the dramatic dialogue of *Northanger Abbey* and *Pride and Prejudice* toward fuller use of a third-person, authorial voice. There's still plenty of dialogue, though Fanny is rarely heard directly in volume 1, and then usually in brief replies to questions. The reader learns of her feelings and thoughts almost exclusively through the words of the sympathetic narrator and occasional use of free indirect discourse. The lack of dialogue is in fact a direct consequence of the prevailing lack of regard for her views or feelings. Although Fanny, in the words of the narrator, "was never a great talker" (426; vol. 3, ch. 6), her lack of status in the Bertram family is a critical factor in her lack of voice. Only when she is with Edmund and, later in volume 1, with Edmund and Mary, does she find listeners willing to hear her thoughts. For example, in chapter 11, the reader learns that Fanny appreciates "the sublimity of Nature" (132) and has the confidence to mount a spirited and well-argued defense of the clergy against Mary's use of

Dr. Grant, Mary's brother-in-law, as a prime example of the moral indolence Mary considers characteristic of the profession (130). Fanny also demonstrates her ability to form independent judgments and resist the demands of others when she refuses to take a part in the play, a decision that elicits lively discussion from students as they weigh the dangers of role-playing for this group of young, romantically interested characters.

With the return of Sir Thomas, Fanny begins to be appreciated for her beauty and "improvement" (267; vol. 2, ch. 6). In this middle section of the novel, a wider variety of points of view is included as the other characters take notice of her. She gradually becomes important in other characters' plots, especially those of the Crawfords and her uncle. In response to this new attention and elevation in her status in the household, the meek Fanny of volume 1 begins to speak at greater length and with more frequency, though always with humility. To Edmund she voices her "opinion" about her uncle's desire for "quietness" and "repose" at home, and she asks Sir Thomas about the slave trade, a subject that notably silences her shallow cousins (230; vol. 2, ch. 3). The departure of the Bertram sisters produces a further increase in her "consequence" and "value," both at home and at the Parsonage (239; ch. 4). Having become "a welcome, an invited guest" at the Parsonage, she expresses to Mary her wonderment at the growth and beauty of Mrs. Grant's shrubbery and at "the operations of time, and the changes of the human mind!" (239, 243). Though Fanny responds initially to Henry Crawford's happy memories of the theatricals with "silent indignation," she soon shows anger and "daring" in reproving his disappointment at their termination (263; ch. 5). The ball in chapter 10 establishes the full extent of her ascent at Mansfield Park; though she is uncomfortable, even "frightened" at the great "distinction" (320–21) of leading the first dance, this occasion registers her new status: "[T]here were few persons present that were not disposed to praise her. She was attractive, she was modest, she was Sir Thomas's niece, and she was said to be admired by Mr. Crawford" (321). In the eyes of society, Henry's admiration bestows value on Fanny, but in his ardent praise of Fanny to his sister, he values Fanny more for her character than for her beauty, good manners, or sweetness (343; ch. 12).

In the first two volumes, Fanny plays an essentially passive role in society, as she wholly lacks status and power in the Bertram household. She is grateful for kindness and eager to oblige others. In the third volume, now the protagonist in what has developed into a central courtship plot, she becomes the focus of everyone's attention. Desired and vigorously courted by Henry but steadfast in her love of Edmund and her disapproval of Henry's conduct, she suddenly discovers and exercises the power to refuse. The other characters, accustomed to her earlier compliance, are shocked. Her newly elevated status as the object of Henry's affection affords her new opportunities for expression; she becomes increasingly articulate and even resourceful as she engages in sustained conversation with the three men who seek to determine her future—Henry, Sir Thomas, and Edmund—and with Mary. Volume 3 deepens the novel's emotional and moral territory with exchanges about character and marriage and more insight into the depth of Fanny's feeling for Edmund, especially in chapter 5, where Fanny reluctantly engages in intimate conversation with Mary, who nostalgically recalls the rehearsal of *Lovers' Vows*.

These dialogues provide rich material for analysis of language, character, and dramatic technique. My students and I look closely at the first chapter of volume 3, where they appreciate the multiple layers of dramatic irony as Sir Thomas confronts Fanny with his disappointment at her refusal of Henry's offer. Her decision not to defend herself by betraying her cousins' inappropriate flirtations with Henry shows her integrity. Readers, sharing her knowledge of the misbehavior of her cousins and her suitor in volume 1, wince as Sir Thomas unleashes his patriarchal wrath against the innocent Fanny: "I had thought you peculiarly free from wilfulness of temper, self-conceit, and every tendency to that independence of spirit, which prevails so much in modern days, even in young women, and which in young women is offensive and disgusting beyond all common offence" (367). But readers also feel the shock of Sir Thomas's surprise at Fanny's rejection of Henry, whom he believes to be "a young man of sense, of character, of temper, of manners, and of fortune, exceedingly attached to you, and seeking your hand in the most handsome and disinterested way." The ironies deepen when Sir Thomas pays his greatest compliment to Crawford: "Gladly would I have bestowed either of my own daughters on him" (368). Readers have the satisfaction of knowing that in fact both Sir Thomas's daughters would have been glad for the offer of marriage that Fanny, whom they despise, has refused. Readers may also savor the further irony that Fanny's hidden love for Edmund does in fact constitute "that independence of spirit" of which Sir Thomas so disapproves.

In chapter 4 of the third volume, Fanny expresses her position in a conversation with Edmund that takes the novel's exploration of marriage to a new depth. In response to her polite assertion that she and Henry are too dissimilar to "ever be tolerably happy together," Edmund articulates a case for their compatibility based on their common tastes, their warm hearts, and differing but complementary temperaments (403). Fanny, recognizing that Edmund's discourse really reflects his thoughts of marrying Mary Crawford, is emboldened to state the real ground of her objection:

> I must say, cousin, that I cannot approve his character. I have not thought well of him from the time of the play. I then saw him behaving, as it appeared to me, so very improperly and unfeelingly, . . . so improperly by poor Mr. Rushworth, not seeming to care how he exposed or hurt him, and paying attentions to my cousin Maria which . . . will never be got over.
> (404)

This summary condemnation of Henry's character presents the novel's most critical view of his heartless flirtations with Julia and Maria. Edmund's reply that Henry's choice of Fanny "has raised [Henry] inconceivably in my opin-ion" (405) offers a counterview that will be developed by the narrative until the point when Fanny learns from Mary's letter that Henry has eloped with Mrs. Rushworth.

Henry Crawford: (Reformed?) Rake

Austen's characterization of Henry Crawford is one of the most intriguing and puzzling aspects of *Mansfield Park*. Is he just another of her many philanderers, momentarily baffled by Fanny's lack of response to his attentions and moti-vated by the challenge she presents to pursue her, or does he genuinely learn and change, developing moral intelligence under her guidance? But if he has changed, how can we account for his elopement with Maria? In the first half of *Mansfield Park*, Henry is a man of taste and wit, whose libertine upbring-ing has made him a careless and unprincipled flirt. Students in my eighteenth-century novel course recognize him as a descendant of the rakes they encoun-tered earlier in the semester in the amatory fiction of Aphra Behn and Eliza Haywood and in the character of Willoughby in Fanny Burney's *Evelina*. The authorial censure of his "idle vanity" guides readers' judgments: "thoughtless and selfish from prosperity and bad example, he would not look beyond the present moment" (135; vol. 1, ch. 12). While readers may feel that the Bertram sisters deserve his callous treatment of them, we cringe when he tells Mary that he plans to "amuse [himself]" by making Fanny fall in love with him (267; vol. 2, ch. 6).

Yet Henry undergoes a moral awakening, educated by Fanny's conduct to a new appreciation of her "good principles." Although he has yet to find a vo-cabulary with which to articulate this awakening, those principles have begun to reform him:

> Henry Crawford had too much sense not to feel the worth of good prin-ciples in a wife, though he was too little accustomed to serious reflection to know them by their proper name; but when he talked of her having such a steadiness and regularity of conduct, such a high notion of honour, and such an observance of decorum as might warrant any man in the full-est dependence on her faith and integrity, he expressed what was inspired by the knowledge of her being well principled and religious.
>
> (341; vol. 2, ch. 12)

The language in this passage repays careful reading. Henry thinks in secular and social terms, using the phrases "regularity of conduct," "honour," and "ob-servance of decorum" as he struggles to put Fanny's principles into words. Per-haps his inability to find a more serious language is a sign of his ultimate lack of the "active principle" (536; vol. 3, ch. 17) that should have guided his conduct.

Even so, in this passage he takes on a new and unexpected role in the novel, giving the most complete and profound expression of Fanny's worth as a woman of integrity, honor, and "goodness of heart." He speaks intimately and honestly with his sister, appreciating "the gentleness, modesty, and sweetness" of Fanny's character, the "warmth" of her love for her brother William, and the excellence of her "understanding" and "manners" (340–41; vol. 2, ch. 12). This passage represents a turning point in the story of Fanny's ascent: it's the first time another character fully appreciates her worth.

I invite the class to consider the question of whether Austen's portrait of Henry as a confirmed flirt whose moral intelligence is briefly improved by Fanny's company is believable. His appreciation of her character in volume 3 is difficult to reconcile with his actions in the novel's final chapters. There's strong textual support for the reading that he remains at heart "thoughtless and self-ish." Students cite passages expressing both Fanny's and the narrator's criticism of his behavior. Students see his determined pursuit of her as motivated by his enjoyment of the challenge, point out that such a natural actor may confuse the role of reformed rake with his true nature, and cite the irrefutable evidence of his elopement with Maria. Yet there's material in support of the view that Henry really changes. His language and behavior in the second and third volumes raise the possibility that *Mansfield Park* inverts the central plot of *Pride and Prejudice*, in which Elizabeth grows in feeling and self-knowledge: Fanny educates not only Henry but her uncle and cousin Edmund as well.

Henry makes every effort to woo Fanny through the demonstration of his good character. His acting and reading skills are confirmed by the "truly dramatic" reading of speeches from Shakespeare's *Henry VIII* (390; vol. 3, ch. 3), to which Fanny responds with reluctant enjoyment. In the conversation that follows, he defers to her dislike of the theatricals, asserting that there will never be a theater at Everingham (392). "The subject of reading aloud" leads to discussion about reading the liturgy in which Henry questions Edmund with "friendly interest" and appropriate "seriousness" for this "serious" subject, interrupting his own comments to explain his earlier inattentiveness in church, which he guesses displeased Fanny (392–93). Despite his strenuous efforts to present himself as a reformed and appreciative advocate for "the eloquence of the pulpit," he stumbles when he qualifies his professed interest in preaching by insisting on an educated "London audience" and by acknowledging that he would not like to preach on a regular basis: "it would not do for a constancy" (394–95), *constancy* being another of those resonant words that Austen emphasizes through repetition. Alert to Fanny's involuntary shake of her head, he rushes to her side to entreat her to explain the meaning of this gesture. After intense conversation, he tells her that he understands her poor opinion of him and that he will try to change her mind not by "protestations" but by his conduct:

> My conduct shall speak for me—absence, distance, time shall speak for
> me.—*They* shall prove, that as far as you can be deserved by any body, I do

deserve you.—You are infinitely my superior in merit, all *that* I know. . . .
It is he who sees and worships your merit the strongest, who loves you
most devotedly, that has the best right to a return.   (397–98)

No character in the novel shows higher esteem for Fanny. And Henry follows
these ardent, eloquent words with his promised conduct, continuing to learn by
following her "good principles."

When he visits her in Portsmouth, he demonstrates exquisite tact in his interactions with her family and unfailing concern for her welfare. He impresses
her with an account of his successful efforts on behalf of a "large and . . . indus-
trious family" who live on his Norfolk estates. He considerately spares her the
embarrassment of joining their family dinner party, expresses anxiety about her
health and prolonged absence from Mansfield, and offers to escort her back
there (472; vol. 3, ch. 10; 475–78; ch. 11). After his departure, Fanny, though
"tolerably secure of not seeing Mr. Crawford again," is "very low" nonetheless,
which suggests that she does not know her own mind at this point in the novel.
She expects to feel relief now that her rejected suitor has left but instead misses
his company. "[Q]uite persuaded of his being astonishingly more gentle, and
regardful of others, than formerly," she takes comfort in this "wonderful improvement" in him (479). Henry Crawford now appears both to the reader and
to Fanny as a man who has grown and changed.

Although he disappears from the novel's main stage, Fanny regards him with
increasing warmth. In the following weeks, Tom Bertram falls ill and Fanny's
exile in Portsmouth continues, then suddenly word comes of Maria Rushworth's
adulterous elopement with Henry, and the novel rushes toward its denouement. Readers may conclude that Henry, without Fanny's presence to guide
him, reverted to his old ways. Similarly, the removal of Mary from Edmund's
good influence appears to have made her more vulnerable to London amoral-
ity (vol. 3, ch. 16). In discussion about the end of the novel, students have offered alternative explanations. One suggestion they made is that the emerging
complexity of Henry's character and the plot of his improvement by Fanny are
sacrificed in the end to the need to bring Edmund and Fanny together and in-
stall her as the real daughter to a chastened Bertram family. Many students are
disappointed by the third-person account of Edmund's belated interest in marrying his cousin, especially after the detailed dramatization of Henry's patient,
respectful, and devoted wooing of Fanny. The ending neatly eliminates all the
threats to the world of the Bertrams and presents Fanny's elevation as the happy
resolution to all their earlier moral failures. I acknowledge these strains in the
plot and even inconsistencies in the treatment of certain characters, particularly
the Crawfords and Sir Thomas, but argue that *Mansfield Park* achieves a depth
and complexity beyond those of Austen's earlier work.

The final chapter presents other problems. One is the sudden intrusion of the
author in the opening lines, a metafictional moment some students find unsettling. Another is the characterization of Sir Thomas Bertram. He is arguably

Austen's most nuanced portrait of a self-aware father. Austen expresses sympathy for his suffering as "a parent, and conscious of errors in his own conduct as a parent" when he reflects back on "the motives of selfishness and worldly wisdom" that led him to condone Maria's marriage (533–34). In an extended passage of free indirect discourse, he rues the mistake of countering Mrs. Norris's "excessive indulgence and flattery" with his own "severity," holding himself responsible for his failure to educate his daughters' moral principles (535). This passage presents an interesting opportunity for comparison with Mr. Bennet's brief moment of parental contrition in *Pride and Prejudice* (vol. 2, ch. 7). *Mansfield Park* closes by endorsing the value of "early hardship and discipline" and Fanny's "consciousness of being born to struggle and endure," emphasizing the moral trajectory that moves its protagonist from the obscure sidelines to the happy center of a reformed Bertram family (547). The class is left to continue the conversation about the ideology and values embedded in this novel.

Mansfield Park's Textual Metamorphoses

Laura Carroll

Textual scholarship, the study and interpretation of textual transmission and the physical states of a text, is generally regarded as a field best entered when a student's educational career is well advanced. It seems to require a sophisticated grasp of literary theory as well as a thorough knowledge of literary history (see Greetham 22–26). It seems to demand a minute attention to tiny, almost molecular differences of language, punctuation, and presentation, which readers may be willing to grant only when they become convinced that the text really does carry significance at this level. Yet it is just the combining of a broad and imaginative set of disciplinary tools with attention to the smallest textual details that makes a textual scholarship approach so suitable for teaching *Mansfield Park*.

It is widely considered the most challenging and demanding text of Jane Austen, but it was not always so highly valued. The elevation of this novel was not simply a matter of delicate critical winnowing and burnishing; it is also traceable to the influence of generations of publishing professionals who actively shaped the text. Studying *Mansfield Park*'s past and present physical forms, with the aid of real books and facsimiles, produces a practical understanding of how canon formation works. Comparing and evaluating different versions of the text and textual apparatuses reveal the roles played by editors, illustrators, designers, and publishers in creating and maintaining influential assumptions about the nature of this novel.

Bringing a textual scholarship approach to *Mansfield Park* provides ways for students to learn about the novel's reception history, evaluate received critical notions, explore controversies, imagine the circumstances of the novel's composition, and think critically about the various frames through which the novel is presented to them. It gives students the means to weigh the textual bases of controversial and debated interpretations of the novel. Best of all, textual scholarship stimulates students to pay close attention to the rhythms and flows of its sentences and to think about the depths of meaning encoded in its language. In this essay I discuss strategies and techniques for using illustrations and other adornments, scholarly apparatuses, early edition texts, and electronic editions to teach *Mansfield Park* in university classrooms, to diverse student cohorts, and in other spaces of learning. I take into consideration that instructors may not all have access to the same materials.

I introduce the textual history of *Mansfield Park* in my teaching in two kinds of literature courses, using different aspects of that history to open up different issues and problems for students. Illustrations are a fabulous tool for engaging students of the visual generation and for rapidly conveying to them a sense of the novel's textual history. In a large first-year survey, where *Mansfield Park* is the only nineteenth-century novel taught and we assume no prior knowledge of Austen's work, I begin my lectures on the novel with a slide show presenting many illustrations from nineteenth- and twentieth-century editions, using these to highlight changing ideas of what Austen's novel is about, who it is for, and how it is to be valued. I explain that book illustration, like film adaptation and critical commentary, is an interpretative act that emerges from a complex encounter among the text, the reader, and the historical moment: thus these pictures reveal both what a particular reader made of the novel and how that reader sought to present it to the book-consuming public of that age.

Beginning with the first illustrated English edition, published by Bentley in 1833, the illustrative tradition returns repeatedly to certain moments in *Mansfield Park*: Fanny receiving and adorning herself with Mary's and Edmund's gifts of necklaces, Tom Bertram relishing the sight of his bewildered father coming upon Mr. Yates, who is in full and marvelous rant on the stage of the makeshift theater. Seeing serial illustrations of these scenes crystallizes and highlights for students the enduring fascination of readers with the story of Fanny's "improvement," or passage into adult sexuality and their enduring enjoyment of the novel's richly comic, and probing, attention to theatricality and role-playing.

I also talk about how three significant illustrated editions reveal period-specific interpretations and judgments that have influenced understandings of this novel but that readers today are unlikely to recognize or share. Hugh Thomson's drawings for the 1894 Macmillan edition of *Mansfield Park*, in an example that always surprises and unsettles student readers, unequivocally portray Mrs. Norris as a deliciously, if grotesquely, comic figure: she has a lumpy body, large hands that are always active, and a big ugly nose and downward turn to her mouth, like a Punch and Judy figure. Seven of Thomson's forty illustrations center on her. Instructors might compare the enjoyment of seeing Mrs. Norris in these drawings with references to her in the "Opinions of *Mansfield Park*," compiled by Austen in 1814–15: several among the novelist's friends and family are "delighted" with Mrs. Norris, "enjoyed" her, and are "amused" by her. Anna Harwood is "delighted with Mrs. Norris & the green Curtain" (433).

Thomson's drawings are regularly reprinted in inexpensive editions, as are the delicately tinted watercolor sketches made by C. E. Brock for J. M. Dent's deluxe edition of 1908. Brock draws Fanny as a blonde and fluffy niminy-piminy little chick, shoulder height to each man she stands beside, the lines of her body entirely hidden by her gowns and her eyes always cast down with irritating submissiveness. The demure, faded prettiness of these pictures, their elaborately drawn borders of ribbons, urns, and scrolls, their hand-lettered copperplate captions, and the insipidity of the faces and figures they contain represent for many students the despised Austen of the popular imagination who is "dated, saccharine and irrelevant" (Carroll and Wiltshire 75), "expressing the gentler virtues of a civilized social order" (Harding 346).

I like to show students one of the sources in visual form of this off-putting idea of the gentle Jane. Inviting them to critique Brock's drawings of Fanny is an excellent way to focus on the text for actual data about her embodiment, her vitality, her gestures, looks, and gazes. Students might compare these pictures of Fanny with Fanny in the text "watching in the hall, in the lobby, on the stairs" for William to arrive (272; vol. 2, ch. 6), "actually practising her steps about the drawing-room" (317; ch. 10), or sitting with her eyes "fixed on Crawford, fixed on him for minutes" (390; ch. 3). The third illustrated edition of *Mansfield Park* I discuss is R. W. Chapman's Oxford edition, volume 3 of *The Novels of Jane Austen*, first published in 1923 and much reprinted since. Chapman's edition contains nine illustrations; the most significant thing about them—and in fact an innovation—is that all were taken from historical sources and therefore show the types of images Austen and her readers would have been familiar with. Unlike the Thomson and Brock pictures, and unlike those in the illustrated editions of the novel preceding Chapman's,[1] these are not imaginative renderings of the scenes narrated in *Mansfield Park*. They are a pair of country estate views by Humphry Repton; a fashion plate; drawings of Portsmouth scenes and naval uniforms; a number of pictures connected with *Lovers' Vows*; and, interestingly, a facsimile of the title page of the first edition, which is typographic rather than pictorial. Useful as some of these images undoubtedly are for providing historical background, they are not equivalent to the other scholarly materials included in the volume. They serve the additional purpose of decorating the text and connoting the expensiveness of the edition. Thomson's and Brock's illustrations also had this function, but in Chapman's edition the effect aimed at is the luxuriance of historical correctness, authenticity, and the antique—the genuine article.[2]

Illustrations are an efficient means for drawing student attention to the changes in *Mansfield Park*'s reception history, especially when other aspects of the novel clamor to be given classroom time. But if I teach *Mansfield Park* in an upper-level course devoted only to Austen's writings, I find it useful to look at illustrations with students in a wider discussion about the significance of the many different packagings of the text throughout its publication history. We talk about the book features that Gérard Genette names "the publisher's peritext" (front cover artwork, back cover blurbs, formats, book construction and materials, typesetting) and about the introductions, footnotes, notes on the text, and critical or historical documents that make up the apparatus in scholarly editions (16). All these elements shape the meaning of the novel for readers yet are not the work of the novelist.

I have given up trying to make students purchase and use a single recommended edition when old copies of the novel are everywhere to be had for a fraction of the outlay. Thus, when my students come to class, they typically bring among them at least ten different editions of the novel, a motley assortment in various stages of decay, which I supplement with a few editions from my own collection and the university library. Trying as this variety is when we need to locate a passage to read together, it lends itself to studying a text's physical states.[3]

Study editions with extensive compilations of research material included are not readily available in Australia, and my students have generally not worked with either the Norton or the Broadview edition of *Mansfield Park* before I bring copies of these out, organize the class into two groups, and give each group one of these books to examine and describe collaboratively. (A critical comparison of these two editions makes a valuable writing assignment.) One cannot predict what features of an edition students will regard as noteworthy, but with judicious questioning instructors may lead them to think critically about how packaging affects readers' perceptions of the novel.

Claudia L. Johnson's 1998 Norton Critical Edition of *Mansfield Park* reproduces on the cover the so-called Rice Portrait, a full-length painting of a confident-looking adolescent girl with cropped hair and glowing brown eyes, in a loose white muslin Empire gown, smiling at the spectator. As is noted in the blurb on the back cover, the portrait was once alleged to be of Austen herself, but authenticity is not offered as the reason for its use: "the gown depicted here, with its glossy spots, brings Fanny Price to mind." June Sturrock's 2001 Broadview Literary Texts edition is decorated with a circa 1900 black-and-white studio photograph of an adolescent girl in a corseted Edwardian dress, gangly, with troubled eyes, posed stiffly before a painted garden backdrop. In both pictures the girl holds a folded parasol in her right hand, a coincidence that instructors can point to as a means of highlighting the otherwise significantly different semiotics of the images.

These pictorial choices, of course, align with familiar positions in the debate over how Fanny ought to be thought of and understood. The girl on the Norton cover externalizes Fanny's inner resistance to the pressures of class and gender and conflates her—wishfully, in my opinion—with the subversive wit and confident charisma displayed in Austen's juvenilia, producing a hybrid creature related to the rebellious, unchained Fanny in Patricia Rozema's 1999 film adaptation of *Mansfield Park*. The girl on the Broadview cover, in her uncanny, awkward posture, speaks to those assessments of the novel that see Fanny as a heroine defined by stillness, whether the stillness is viewed positively as stoicism and advocating tradition and stability or negatively as a diminished self, constricted and intimidated by the abuse and neglect she has suffered from her adoptive family.

Choosing to dress the cover of *Mansfield Park* with a photograph or with a painting is analogous to the more material interpretative issue of whether the novel is to be viewed through the historicist lens of contextual documents or whether it is better understood as a starting point, throwing light outward from the imagination. The novel's relation to the script of *Lovers' Vows* (Elizabeth Inchbald's version of August von Kotzebue's play *Das Kind der Liebe* ["The Love Child"]) seems a particularly acute question to address here, since the novel gives its twenty-first-century readers no clear instructions about whether they need to be acquainted with the play in order to appreciate the use being made of it. Here too textual scholarship offers a lateral approach to a subject more usually examined by studying the text, because from Chapman's edition onward, the frequent inclusion of the entire script as part of the text's scholarly apparatus has effectively determined readers' choices for them. Working with the Norton and Broadview editions, instructors might ask students to look at the contextual materials provided in the back of each volume and engage critically with how they invite, or direct, readers to approach the novel. The Norton edition reprints excerpts from contemporary essays, poems, sermons, debates, and pamphlets, which are sequenced to correspond roughly with the order in which the subject matter appears in the novel; parts of nine late-twentieth-century critical essays; and the entire script of *Lovers' Vows*. The Broadview edition contains no critical selections, only excerpts from a wide range of historical materials, grouped thematically. *Lovers' Vows* is excerpted and accorded no greater prominence than other items. Instructors might ask students how the inclusions of different selections of *Lovers' Vows* shape their understanding of those passages in Austen's novel where roles, scenes, and speeches are alluded to and mentioned.

In *Mansfield Park*, important social and ethical consequences follow from how the characters interpret and act *Lovers' Vows*, but the play's script is not made available to the novel's audience. Instead, the novel produces multiple accounts of it, refracted and implied, in the pointedly partial uses it is put to by nine separate personalities. As with so much in Austen's writing, a sort of verbal prestidigitation has readers wondering exactly what is so fascinating about that text or event screened off at one side of the domestic narrative. They may also suspect that the real engine of the fiction is how the characters respond to things not displayed to us.

The fame (or notoriety) of Inchbald's play suggests that Austen expected her contemporaries to apply their knowledge of *Lovers' Vows* to *Mansfield Park*, but the play has now dropped off the radar for all readers but students, specialists, and enthusiasts, and the issue now, since the novel appears to work perfectly well without knowledge of the play, is to what extent readers can exercise choice in their approach. Readers of *Mansfield Park* may become acquainted with *Lovers' Vows* and use it to fill in certain gaps in the novel (gaps that may have been designed not to be filled, functioning instead as negative space), or they may ignore the play altogether and draw their conclusions by weighing one character's conduct against another's.

A simple textual scholarship exercise for alerting students to the effect on interpretation of the growing bulk and complexity of the scholarly apparatus produced by editors of *Mansfield Park* involves discussion about the increasing use of explanatory notes in editions over time. An instructor might gather a late-nineteenth- or early-twentieth-century edition, the Oxford edition edited by Chapman, a recent student paperback edition, and the 2005 Cambridge edition edited by John Wiltshire. From each, the instructor makes a set of photocopies of the same passage of text and distributes them among class members, whose first task is to find the explanatory note markers in the passage. The Cambridge edition will contain as many as eight or ten, the student edition two or three, and the oldest edition and the Oxford will contain no markers at all—the Oxford edition has explanatory notes, but readers must identify the obscure word and turn to the end of the book hoping to find a note to correspond. Next, students with the unmarked states of the text look for and circle words or phrases that they think call for explication, and students working with the annotated editions speculate on how the marked words and phrases will be explained in the endnotes. Then, as a group, class members can literally compare notes, commenting on why language presented as self-explanatory in the edition of one decade requires heavy annotation in another.

For this exercise to work effectively, the passage selected should involve matters that are unfamiliar to modern readers: the dinner table discussion about estate improvement is an example (281–84; vol. 2, ch. 7), as is the conversation between Edmund and Henry Crawford about "the eloquence of the pulpit" (394; vol. 3, ch. 3). I have used several versions of Mrs. Norris's speech cataloguing the triumphs and spoils of her day at Sotherton to demonstrate changing editorial purposes and interventions:

> "Nothing would satisfy that good old Mrs. Whitaker, but my taking one of the cheeses. I stood out as long as I could, till the tears almost came into her eyes, and I knew it was just the sort that my sister would be delighted with. That Mrs. Whitaker is a treasure! She was quite shocked when I asked her whether wine was allowed at the second table, and she has turned away two housemaids for wearing white gowns. Take care of the cheese, Fanny. Now I can manage the other parcel and the basket very well."
>
> "What else have you been spunging?" said Maria, half pleased that Sotherton should be so complimented. (123; vol. 1, ch. 10)

Wiltshire's edition provides three explanatory notes to this passage: for "second table," "white gowns," and "spunging." *Spunging* is English slang, which this editor assumes may not be in the lexicon of all readers (although my Australian students do know what it means). Sturrock's Broadview edition also explicates "spunging," but Chapman's edition and the recent student editions from the British editors Kathryn Sutherland (Penguin, 1996) and Jane Stabler (Oxford World's Classics, 2003) do not. Such subtle variation in editorial decisions about notes can draw attention to how different states of the novel encode different constructions of the people reading it. Likewise, the decision to annotate or not annotate terms having to do with housekeeping techniques and dynamics of class among the servants of the large Sotherton household reveals much about what editors consider either common knowledge or necessary for fully understanding this passage of the novel.

That Chapman's Oxford edition provides no annotation for these phrases raises questions. Does this absence imply that Chapman assumes his (educated,

English, leisured) readers of 1923 are familiar enough with the workings of great English houses to know that "the second table" overseen by the house-keeper is where the upper servants dined secluded from the lower and that housemaids "wearing white gowns" are seen by Mrs. Whitaker and Mrs. Norris as aping the fine ladies to whom they ought always to appear inferior? Or does it imply that such details are stage decorations from the past and have little significance in the greater scheme of the novel's webs of meaning? There are no right or wrong answers to these questions (though there are, perhaps, generous and ungenerous answers), but students must reflect on what the narrative here reveals about Mrs. Norris's grasping meanness, her obsessive identification with servants, and her equation of good management with withholding comfort and pushing people down.

The approaches I have discussed so far lend themselves to teaching other novels by Austen, but *Mansfield Park*'s early textual history is unique. It was her first novel to be entirely planned and written after the family settled at Chawton in 1809. It is pivotal in her professional career: she changed publishers in 1815, between the 1814 edition of *Mansfield Park* published by Thomas Egerton and the 1816 edition brought out by John Murray, a publisher of considerable lit-erary prestige and influence. The 1816 text— Austen had some input into its preparation for publication—corrects many obvious printing errors in the 1814 text (and, inevitably, introduces new ones), makes a small number of substantive changes to the wording of the novel, and is punctuated differently throughout.

We know from studying materials such as the canceled chapters of *Persua-sion* that the accidentals, as they are called, that Austen wrote in her manu-script were changed by compositors as they set up the type: the compositors took out or toned down the use of long dashes, italics, and initially capitalized words; altered comma placement and semicolon use to conform to house styles; and in general thought it unnecessary to reproduce every textual quirk of the manuscripts from which they worked. The punctuation of 1814 is sometimes idiosyncratic—ungrammatical perhaps—but as Sutherland has convincingly argued, the nonstandard disposition of commas and dashes often conveys valu-able traces of the emphasis belonging to a speaking female voice, which she connects to Austen's fresh and "uncounselled" authorial judgments before the interventions of male publishers and editors (*Jane Austen's Textual Lives* 266–313). Many of the changes introduced in the 1816 text bring it closer to con-forming to a standard grammatical style, and Chapman and almost all editors after him have preferred it as the text revised and corrected by Austen and thus nearest to her final intentions, which must be assumed to include producing a text linguistically acceptable to readers within and without the publishing indus-try. It has also been preferred on aesthetic grounds: Wiltshire writes that "the punctuation of 1816 arguably produces a more incisive text, as well as generat-ing effects absent in 1814" ("Commentary" 635).

The variations between the texts printed in these two early editions are sub-tle, but their implications are profound and fascinating and have given rise to editorial debate, extensive and teachable, about which edition is to be preferred as the basis for a copy text.

The best place to begin a classroom study of the differences between the 1814 and 1816 texts, and what those differences imply, is by comparing substantive variants in volume 3, chapter 7. In this long speech made to William Price by his father about the ship on which William is shortly to sail from Portsmouth, a passage that demonstrates Mr. Price's disconcerting failure to speak of people and places and in language intelligible to Fanny or to allow her into the gabbled conversation, six significant changes have been made to the gossip and jargon used. Here are both texts in full:

[1814]
With a friendly shake of his son's hand, and an eager voice, he instantly began—"Ha! welcome back, my boy. Glad to see you. Have you heard the news? The Thrush went out of harbour this morning. Alert is the word, you see. By G—, you are just in time. The doctor has been here enquiring for you; he has got one of the boats, and is to be off for Spithead by six, so you had better go with him. I have been to Turner's about your things, it is all in a way to be done. I should not wonder if you had your orders to-morrow; but you cannot sail with this wind, if you are to cruize to the westward; and Captain Walsh thinks you will certainly have a cruize to the westward, with the Elephant. By G—, I wish you may. But old Scholey was saying just now, that he thought you would be sent first to the Texel. Well, well, we are ready, whatever happens. But by G—, you lost a fine sight by not being here in the morning to see the Thrush go out of harbour. I would not have been out of the way for a thousand pounds. Old Scholey ran in at breakfast time, to say she was under weigh. I jumped up, and made but two steps to the point. If ever there was a perfect beauty afloat, she is one; and there she lays at Spithead, and anybody in England would take her for an eight-and-twenty. I was upon the platform two hours this afternoon, looking at her. She lays just astern of the Endymion, with the Cleopatra to larboard."

"Ha!" cried William, "*that's* just where I should have put her myself. But here is my sister, Sir, here is Fanny;" turning and leading her forward;— "it is so dark you do not see her."

[1816]
With a friendly shake of his son's hand, and an eager voice, he instantly began—"Ha! welcome back, my boy. Glad to see you. Have you heard the news? The Thrush went out of harbour this morning. Sharp is the word, you see. By G—, you are just in time. The doctor has been here enquiring for you; he has got one of the boats, and is to be off for Spithead by six, so you had better go with him. I have been to Turner's about your mess; it is all in a way to be done. I should not wonder if you had your orders

to-morrow; but you cannot sail with this wind, if you are to cruize to the westward; and Captain Walsh thinks you will certainly have a cruize to the westward, with the Elephant. By G—, I wish you may. But old Scholey was saying just now, that he thought you would be sent first to the Texel. Well, well, we are ready, whatever happens. But by G—, you lost a fine sight by not being here in the morning to see the Thrush go out of harbour. I would not have been out of the way for a thousand pounds. Old Scholey ran in at breakfast time, to say she had slipped her moorings and was coming out. I jumped up, and made but two steps to the platform. If ever there was a perfect beauty afloat, she is one; and there she lays at Spithead, and anybody in England would take her for an eight-and-twenty. I was upon the platform two hours this afternoon, looking at her. She lays close to the Endymion, between her and the Cleopatra, just to the eastward of the sheer hulk."

"Ha!" cried William, "*that's* just where I should have put her myself. It's the best birth at Spithead. But here is my sister, Sir, here is Fanny;" turning and leading her forward;—"it is so dark you do not see her."[4]

The class might read through these passages and locate the six variants, and perhaps consult the notes of a scholarly edition to clarify some of the more obscure phrases and learn about the real world correlates of the names of ships and places mentioned—for the places named are real sites in Portsmouth and in the broader theater of war. Although there has never been a ship named *Thrush* in the Royal Navy, *Endymion*, *Cleopatra*, and *Canopus* are the names of actual ships on which Austen's brothers Francis and Charles had served.

Then the instructor might ask class members to talk over a set of linked issues. First, what is the dramatic effect of these changes? They render Mr. Price's talk more alienating. To the already heavily technical drift of his language in the 1814 text, the 1816 text adds an element of territorial disorientation. Reading 1814's "She lays just astern of the Endymion, with the Cleopatra to larboard" and 1816's "She lays close to the Endymion, between her and the Cleopatra, just to the eastward of the sheer hulk," a nonsailor will recognize "astern" and "larboard" as nautical terms describing spatial relations but not feel the need to understand their precise meanings. But "to the eastward of the sheer hulk" calls not only on technical knowledge—Chapman's note to this phrase explains that a sheer hulk "is a kind of movable dockyard" (549)—but also on precise local knowledge about the placement of the hulk and the two ships in the harbor at Spithead, and indeed about the relation of the whole scene to Mr. Price's lookouts from "the point" (1814) or "the platform" (1816). Mr. Price's more marked habit, in the 1816 text, of referring to locations strange to both Fanny and the reader works to further trouble her longed-for homecoming. But the change from "Alert is the word" to "Sharp is the word" perhaps signals little to modern readers, and Austen's intention must remain opaque. I think this is an important point to discuss with students: it shows that interpretation always has its limits.

Students will come to see that nobody involved in readying the 1816 edition for publication could have made these revisions but the author herself. It is important, then, to ask where Austen could have obtained the knowledge underwriting the changes—most editors think her brothers the likely source. The class can debate the implications of this for Austen's authority over the 1816 text. Students may decide in favor of the first version as representing her independent authorship; or they may prefer the revised version as including information that she decided served her novel better even though it came from other people. Or they may resist preferring one edition over the other. What matters is the intensive engagement with the logic of the novel and the ultimate recognition that the texts by which we know *Mansfield Park* reach us through the active choices and interventions of editors.

Scholars wishing to study the first- and second-edition texts of *Mansfield Park* had until recently only two options: use a reconstructed edition such as the Cambridge (ed. Wiltshire), which reprints the text of 1816 with 1814's variants listed at the foot of the page, or turn to the rare-books section of a major institutional library. With the advent of *Google Books* in the past five years, access to facsimiles of the first two editions is now open to anybody with a computer and an Internet connection.[5] Google has made digital facsimiles of 1814 and 1816 three-volume editions of *Mansfield Park* held in libraries at Oxford and Harvard, and these are freely available through *Google Books*. The nineteenth-century printings are, of course, out of copyright in all legal jurisdictions. Because the facsimiles can be viewed online or downloaded in portable document format (PDF), we may now largely bypass the critically edited text, which, however meticulously prepared, necessarily "emerges from active editorial choices among variant readings" (Sutherland, *Jane Austen's Textual Lives* 328) as well as from the interventions of publishers and printers. Students and instructors can now read exactly what was printed in the two editions of *Mansfield Park* that appeared in the author's lifetime and see exactly how those texts looked on the page.

Readers who have grown up in an age of digital textuality are not accustomed to thinking of the texts of classic novels as shifting and changeable. A novel for them is a thing that can be frictionlessly decanted from one neutral container to another—be it printed page, electronic screen, or digital file—without gain or loss. Students studying literature at a university have often been exposed to the notion that the texts of Shakespeare's plays vary widely from one edition to the next or that Emily Dickinson's poems have been published in profoundly editorialized forms, but they do not know that the novels of Austen are equally mutable.

Austen's canonical status supports the idea that readings and interpretations of her novels may diverge, but the texts themselves are fixed. Austen is an author valued for the entrancing quality of crisp precision in the language of her texts. D. A. Miller has written of his pleasure on first discovering Austen the stylist: "[N]o extraneous static encumbered the dictation of a grammar that completed, and an art that finished, every crystalline sentence" (*Jane Austen*

2). Sutherland, who alone among recent editors champions the less polished 1814 text, notes that Austen's "is a reputation founded on conformity. Nowhere is this more evident than in the critical attention paid throughout the twentieth century to the surface texture of her novels, to their finished achievement as a matter of style" (*Jane Austen's Textual Lives* 268–69). Comparing *Mansfield Park's* 1814 and 1816 texts or comparing one of them with the text of a later edition where spelling and punctuation have been invisibly regularized is a way of drawing attention to the subtlety of Austen's style, in particular to the expressive functions of punctuation, which shift in different versions of the text.

Reading aloud in the classroom will be most meaningful when joined to some discussion of how to interpret commas, periods, semicolons, and dashes and transmit them vocally. Of course, passages should be selected that touch on aspects of the novel that students are interested in. The significance of the punctuation of the early editions is best appreciated when it is contrasted with an overzealously corrected text of the kind published by Routledge, Dent, and Little, Brown in the late nineteenth century. Such books are now antiques and not easy to come by, but instructors and students have ready access—possibly too ready—to a suitably compromised text of *Mansfield Park* thanks to the *Project Gutenberg* digital file, which is in the public domain and forms the textual basis of a very wide array of low-cost electronic editions formatted for Kindle, Kobo, iPad, Nook, and other e-book readers. These devices are beginning to appear in my classroom, bringing with them new pedagogical challenges and opportunities. One advantage of foregrounding the concerns of textual scholarship in relation to *Mansfield Park* is that students learn to critically evaluate texts of doubtful origin.

The passage in which Sir Thomas Bertram hesitates over whether to bring Fanny to Mansfield, identically punctuated in 1814 and 1816 but radically altered in the 2010 *Project Gutenberg* edition, is an instance of what happens when a characteristically Austenian use of semicolons and dashes is changed. The 1816 edition reads:

> Sir Thomas could not give so instantaneous and unqualified a consent. He debated and hesitated;—it was a serious charge;—a girl so brought up must be adequately provided for, or there would be cruelty instead of kindness in taking her from her family. He thought of his own four children—of his two sons—of cousins in love, &c.;—but no sooner had he deliberately begun to state his objections, than Mrs. Norris interrupted him with a reply to them all whether stated or not.   (7; vol. 1, ch. 1)

The *Project Gutenberg* edition emends the punctuation thus:

> Sir Thomas could not give so instantaneous and unqualified a consent. He debated and hesitated;—it was a serious charge;—a girl so brought up must be adequately provided for, or there would be cruelty instead

of kindness in taking her from her family. He thought of his own four children, of his two sons, of cousins in love, etc.;—but no sooner had he deliberately begun to state his objections than Mrs. Norris interrupted him with a reply to them all, whether stated or not.

The punctuation of 1816 is used with the precision of musical notation and has a similar role in creating the psychological coloration of the text. The five pauses in Sir Thomas's deliberations, marked with long dashes, are rhythmic rests. He pauses longest when pondering, and speaking of, the financial commitment: "He debated and hesitated;—it was a serious charge;—a girl so brought up must be adequately provided for," and the text marks this pause with a semi-colon and dash combined. When he thinks of the potential affective consequences, "of his own four children—of his two sons—of cousins in love, &c.," his hesitations are briefer, marked by a dash only, which perhaps signals that while he is not thinking of "cousins in love" with any pleasure, it worries him less than the prospect of undertaking a financially irresponsible work of charity, and this important distinction is subtly figured at the beginning of the novel. By contrast, in the *Project Gutenberg* text's punctuation, interpolated commas have Sir Thomas hurrying precipitately through the thought "of his own four children, of his two sons, of cousins in love." The introduction of a comma to the final clause—"no sooner had he deliberately begun to state his objections than Mrs. Norris interrupted him with a reply to them all, whether stated or not"— is more grammatically conventional but at the expense of destroying the 1816 text's implication that Mrs. Norris's interruptions are precipitate and intrusive. Breathless herself, she cannot allow others time to breathe. A corrupt text can have value in the learning environment: adding a punctuation mark where none should be throws light on an important meaning of the text that would otherwise remain unarticulated.

Johnson reminds us that even as we "squeeze a lot of nuance" from punctuation and other artifacts of textual presentation, we must not neglect the role of compositors "not simply in the transmission [of Austen's text] but also in the very formation of our sense of Austen's artistry" ("Introduction" xix). Printers, publishers, and editors, whether they are scrupulous professional scholars or entrepreneurial repackagers, all make a contribution to our sense of what a novel means and our understanding of how it arrives at those meanings. Readers who are guided to an awareness of the complex textual metamorphoses of *Mansfield Park* will gain a deeper appreciation of the rich linguistic operations that make this novel so involving and so alive.

NOTES

[1] An exception is the lavish 1912 Oxford edition of *Pride and Prejudice*, edited by Katharine Metcalfe, who would later marry R. W. Chapman and collaborate extensively

with him on the complete Oxford edition of the novels. See Sutherland, *Jane Austen's Textual Lives* 36–37.

[2] Both the Thomson and C. E. Brock illustrations to *Mansfield Park* are out of copyright and thus readily available in cheap modern reprint editions or on the Internet. A selection of them can be found reproduced in Carroll and Wiltshire; Sutherland, *Jane Austen's Textual Lives*; and Gilson, "Later Publishing History."

[3] A simple exercise to warm up the group is to put all the books together on a table and organize them. Students, for example, can be asked to place the books in order of most to least expensive-looking or most to least tasteful-looking. This activity translates the nonverbal messages sent by book packaging about consumption and taste into open and sometimes hilarious discussion, which process is of course the whole point. I also ask students to rank the books according to which covers they think are the best and worst matches for the novel inside.

[4] These quotations are taken from facsimiles of *Mansfield Park*, 1814 and 1816, provided by *Google Books*: 1814 (149–51; vol. 3, ch. 7), 1816 (149–51; vol. 3, ch. 7).

[5] *Google Books* does not currently provide stable URLs for digital texts in its collection. To locate facsimiles of the 1814 and 1816 editions of *Mansfield Park*, which are of course each divided among three individual volumes, one must search using specific terms such as "Mansfield Park 1814 volume 1." Alternatively, I have compiled a bookshelf in *Google Books* titled "Facsimiles of 1st and 2nd Editions of *Mansfield Park*," which can be accessed at http://bit.ly/9J1uEy. It should be noted that *Google* facsimiles are made using scanning devices that process up to a thousand pages per hour, and the resulting images are not always high-quality.

Suggestions of Desire in Horse Riding, Foxhunting, and Music Making in *Mansfield Park*

Karyn Lehner

In *Mansfield Park*, Jane Austen explores feelings of sexual desire and their expression in socially acceptable forms. The metaphoric resonance of these forms; their use as a map of both the subconscious and conscious aspects of desire; and the ability of these forms to represent an inexpressible truth, uninhibited by social constraints of decorum, are revealed, I suggest, in the ways that characters in this novel engage in pleasurable activities. Although firmly placed in the background, the motifs of horses, foxhunting, and recreational riding as well as music and musical accomplishments that recur throughout *Mansfield Park* demonstrate the subtlety of Austen's disclosure of erotic feeling in ordinary and, at least for the gentlefolk of this novel, everyday activities.

The topic of horse riding is introduced early, in a conversation between Fanny Price and Edmund in chapter 3, when she is "about fifteen" (26). Her initial experiences of riding are instigated by Sir Thomas, but it is probable that Edmund coached her:

> Yes, dear old grey poney. Ah! cousin, when I remember how much I used to dread riding, what terrors it gave me to hear it talked of as likely to do me good;—(Oh! how I have trembled at my uncle's opening his lips if horses were talked of) and then think of the kind pains you took to reason and persuade me out of my fears, and convince me that I should like it after a little while. . . . (31)

Her acquired pleasure in riding is bound together with her memories of Edmund's kindness and attention to her. It is interesting to note the language used to describe the class of horse and mode of riding deemed suitable for her. Her original mount is an "old grey poney"; when she rides out, she is always accompanied by the "steady old coachman" (78; vol. 1, ch. 7). The general perception at Mansfield Park is that she requires a practical, utilitarian style of horse, as the riding she engages in is remedial rather than social, that she should be in the company of a servant rather than in the company of her cousins "as they [take] their cheerful rides" (41; ch. 4), and that she is less motivated by a desire for pleasure. For Fanny, riding is an important means of "exercise" (42).

Given this early history of her participation in equestrian activities, we should consider the means by which, after the death of her first mount, the "old grey poney," Fanny comes to acquire a new horse. Edmund, disgusted at his mother's and Mrs. Norris's indifference to Fanny's need for exercise, exchanges a "useful road-horse" for "one that his cousin might ride," which "with a very little trouble . . . became exactly calculated for the purpose" (42–43). Although not directly stated by Austen, it is implied that as this is Edmund's scheme, it is Edmund who undertakes this "little trouble" of training the mare to the purpose of being a "regular lady's horse, of [Fanny's] own, in the style of her cousins" (42). Mrs. Norris claims that this change is "improper," as well as "adding to the great expenses of [Sir Thomas's] stable" (42). Although this assertion seems punitively motivated, her suggestion that a "steady old thing" should be found clearly suggests her real objection is to the horse's symbolic status rather than to its purchase price (41). Fanny's acquiring of "a regular lady's horse" has many implications.

In "Learning to Ride at Mansfield Park," Donna Landry notes that nineteenth-century female equestrian pursuits were flavored with "self-promotional and erotic exhibitionist qualities" and that riding carried an association with "wealth and position as well as health" (62). Lord Osborne's carelessly snobbish declaration in *The Watsons* is an example: "A woman never looks better than on horseback –. . . if they knew how much it became them they would all have the inclination" (Austen, *Later Manuscripts* 115). Landry argues that the choice of a mount suitable for a lady was based on criteria designed to show off a woman to best advantage, criteria that included her beauty, her sensitivity as a rider, and her knowledge of paces that were enjoyable and attractive (64). Students might consider these remarks when thinking about Edmund's motives in selecting a horse for his cousin. He asserts that Fanny "must have a horse" (42), perhaps thinking of her health first and foremost, but since he produces a true lady's horse, whether or not he does so consciously, he is also acknowledging Fanny's sexual maturity by giving her the means to appear as an object of desire.

Fanny derives a dual pleasure from the gift. The mare provides her with an experience "far beyond any former pleasure of the sort," even though she thought that nothing "could ever suit her like her old grey poney," a mount probably accustomed to the clumsy fumbling of a novice rider. It is not only the physical pleasure of riding a well-trained and well-bred horse that Fanny enjoys: "[H]er delight in Edmund's mare was far beyond any former pleasure of the sort; and the addition it was ever receiving in the consideration of that kindness from which her pleasure sprung, was beyond all her words to express" (43). This feeling, latent in the verb "sprung," suggests the deep roots of her emotion: she is like a plant newly flourishing in the soil of her cousin's long-established kindness. This change in her experience of pleasure derives from her awareness of the change in Edmund's perception and acknowledgment of her as a grown-up who is sexually attractive in the "style of her cousins" (42).

In his introduction to *Sense and Sensibility*, Tony Tanner discusses Austen's representation of the veiled aspects of emotion and passion in ways that are also relevant to *Mansfield Park*: "There is a much more important kind of secrecy that Austen makes us aware of—the secrecy of everything the heart may not enforce with the hand, display with the face, or express with the voice; that is the secrecy of those things within, which are struggling to get out and meet with different kinds of restraints or expressions" ("Original Penguin Classics Introduction" 359). Despite Edmund's friendship, Fanny is a particularly solitary heroine, and Austen employs complex means to represent the "secrecy of those things within." Part of the secrecy of this internal space is the imaginative quality inherent in human emotion and the difficulty of truthfully and accurately representing it. Chapter 7, when Fanny is forced outside and views Mary's riding lesson from a distance, is an especially subtle representation of secret feelings, in which we can discern the intersection of truth, imagination, and desire in Fanny's thoughts:

> [B]y walking fifty yards from the hall door, she could look down the park, and command a view of the parsonage and all its demesnes, gently rising beyond the village road; and in Dr. Grant's meadow she immediately saw the group—Edmund and Miss Crawford both on horseback, riding side by side, Dr. and Mrs. Grant, and Mr. Crawford, with two or three grooms, standing about and looking on. A happy party it appeared to her—all interested in one object—cheerful beyond a doubt, for the sound of merriment ascended even to her. It was a sound that did not make *her* cheerful; she wondered that Edmund should forget her, and felt a pang. She could not turn her eyes from the meadow, she could not help watching all that passed. At first Miss Crawford and her companion made the circuit of the field, which was not small, at a foot's pace; then, at *her* apparent suggestion, they rose into a canter; and to Fanny's timid nature it was most astonishing to see how well she sat. After a few minutes, they stopt entirely, Edmund was close to her, he was speaking to her, he was evidently directing her management of the bridle, he had hold of her hand; she saw it, or the imagination supplied what the eye could not reach. She must not wonder at all this; what could be more natural than that Edmund should be making himself useful, and proving his good-nature by any one?   (78–79)

As Fanny views the distant lesson, she watches Mary and comes to the realization that Mary experiences riding as a "pure genuine pleasure," though no doubt enhanced by Edmund's "attendance and instructions" (78). In particular she notes Mary's lack of fear, which reflects on Fanny's "timid nature." Fanny registers the "merriment" of the group of onlookers, notices with surprise how well Mary sits to the canter, but feels most keenly the "pang" that Edmund should forget her. Although she experiences a feeling of exclusion, represented spatially by the distance between herself and the group, her main concern is that Edmund has forgotten her. Mary has taken her place on the mare so carefully selected by Edmund as an ideal mount for a now adult Fanny. Fanny perceives, though she resists fully understanding it, that horsemanship in a woman is erotically attractive, and she is dismayed that Edmund finds this truth demonstrated more by Mary than by herself.

At the conclusion of the lesson, Edmund and Mary stop, and he apparently instructs her in the "management of the bridle." It is unclear how much of this part of the lesson Fanny can actually see and how much is imagined, but the rhythm of the sentence suggests, at the very least, an increasing intensity of focus: "[T]hey stopt entirely, Edmund was close to her, he was speaking to her, he was evidently directing her management of the bridle, he had hold of her hand." The step-by-step increments of physical proximity reveal an unconscious excitement. As Fanny watches Mary receive instruction that otherwise Fanny would have received from Edmund, she may be attributing a past experience of her own to Mary. If so, "the management of the bridle" becomes especially telling.

Landry discusses in detail the role of the rider's hands. A woman rider's ability to use her hands effectively is linked to an "exquisite sensibility and power of adaptation" to the horse (68). There are many methods of communicating an instruction to a horse, among them a whip or spurs. In traditional English equestrianism these are considered artificial aids: although providing an external stimulus to drive a horse forward, they do not require the skill of the rider's hands to respond to the horse. A typical English bridle is composed of leather strapping that gently encases a horse's head; the strapping is designed to hold the metal bit in the correct position in the horse's mouth. When fitted and managed correctly, a bridle allows for a nuanced communication between the rider's hand and the horse's mouth. There is an intimacy and trust associated with this mode of instruction, because a bridle gives the rider access to a soft internal place with which to communicate with the horse. Fanny's guess that "he was *evidently* directing her management of the bridle" (my emphasis) thus fuses her memories of Edmund's instruction with a recognition of intimacy.

This partly imagined scene between Edmund and Mary is evidence that equestrian activities have a quasi-erotic nature or at least are a source of intimate pleasure sanctioned by genteel custom. In Fanny's imagination, the intimacy between horse and rider becomes a metaphor for that between Edmund and Mary. This connection is beyond the easy description of words, in much the same way that the complicated change in Fanny's feelings for Edmund defies her ability to articulate it. She makes two attempts at definition. "What could be more natural than Edmund making himself useful?" reflects her realization that it is only natural that Edmund should offer his kindness to Mary, the attractive newcomer. Her second attempt is a transfer of sympathy to the "poor mare," which has the "double duty" of carrying both riders in the same day (79). Perhaps Fanny also recognizes the mare's dual role of carrying the hopes and desires of both women.

This episode gains in significance when we consider that a common activity in the background of the novel is hunting, specifically foxhunting on horseback. When Henry Crawford returns to Mansfield and finds Fanny and Edmund at the Grants, there is "so much" conversation "between the two young men about hunting" (260; vol. 2, ch. 5) that Fanny can remain silent, and soon Dr. Grant's suggestion of Henry's "sending for his hunters from Norfolk" is supported by everyone else present, except Fanny (261). During William's visit ten days later (presumably after Henry's horses have arrived), Edmund and Henry make plans to hunt, and William expresses a keen interest. In the card game, Speculation, Henry recalls to Edmund an incident on the hunting field where his horse lost a shoe, which leads to his discussion of a "scheme" in which he would take over the rent of Thornton Lacey to allow for his presence in Mansfield beyond the hunting season and also provide adequate accommodation for his hunters (280, 286; ch. 7). The frequency and casualness with which foxhunting is mentioned in *Mansfield Park* suggests its ingrained nature in upper-class country life. Hunting would have featured prominently at Austen's girlhood home, Steventon Parsonage, situated in one of the "best portions of the Vine Hunt" (Austen-Leigh 18); Austen's brothers hunted to hounds from an early age (37). At the heart of foxhunting, usually an all-male activity, is the pleasure of pursuit, and almost every male character of marriageable age in *Mansfield Park* engages in the sport. Tom Bertram, Edmund, and Henry all own horses called hunters, bred for power and speed.

Pursuit and capture—central to the English tradition of foxhunting—is the theme of the courtship narrative at the center of *Mansfield Park*. When Henry decides to stay on at Mansfield and pursue Fanny, he sends for his hunters. He claims he has "grown too old to go out more than three times a week" and says that on the days he doesn't hunt he will need to find a similar source of stimulation. Riding out and walking with Mary are not sufficient; such activities "would be exercise only to [his] body"—they will not satisfy his need for excitement in the pursuit of a prey. His plan is to make Fanny fall in love with him. That he "cannot be satisfied . . . without making a small hole in Fanny Price's heart" (267; vol. 2, ch. 6) echoes the ritualized aspects of hunting. He sees the pursuit of her as a way to derive pleasure similar to that of chasing a fox across country on a powerful horse.

The sadistic aspect of this pursuit of Fanny is highlighted when Henry takes William hunting. Fanny is rightly afraid for her brother, aware of the dangers of an inexperienced rider on a "high-fed hunter in an English fox-chase." The intention of Henry that Fanny feel obliged to him for this kindness to William is tinged with a more sinister motive. Her fear that William will experience "accident or discredit" comes from her understanding of the pleasure Henry derives in playing with people's emotions (276). Even Mary acknowledges this predatory aspect of Henry when she tells him that he should be "satisfied with her two cousins" (267). Whether his plan is to ingratiate himself with Fanny or to elevate his masculine status by discrediting the man she most loves, he is motivated by the desire to capture her.

If hunting is a male pleasure, music is in many ways its female correspondent. A sort of music is present in the pleasure of the hunt, as Wordsworth suggests in his idealized references to hunting in "Simon Lee" (1798):

> And still there's something in the world
> At which his heart rejoices;

> For when the chiming hounds are out,
> He dearly loves their voices.

Hounds were bred for beauty and tone of cry, and their "full cry" signaled the climax of the fox hunt (Carr 30). The sound is as primal as sexual desire, resonating with that indefinable space of human emotion that Austen conveys in writing.

If men are lured to the hunt by the hound's cries, women lure men by their music. Both have a quasi-erotic effect. The image of Mary Crawford playing her harp at the window, framed by the beauty of the summer garden, is considered "enough to catch any man's heart." Though the word is the narrator's, not Mary's, "catch" implies pursuit, and pleasure and power mingle in the exercise of capturing a prey. Mary seems carefully "placed" in front of the window to appear at best advantage against the "rich foliage of summer" (76; vol. 1, ch. 6). The harp, a highly crafted and beautiful instrument, also has the allure of the exotic in this setting of rural England. Note that although Mary said, "I shall be most happy to play to you both [Edmund and Fanny]" (69), the eventual invitation is extended only to Edmund, as the narrator later states that Fanny would be glad to hear the harp "uninvited and unnoticed" (77; ch. 7).

This scene is similar to Mary's riding lesson, in that the harp playing, a pleasurable pursuit that offers an environment of intimacy, is also a socially acceptable way for a woman to display her body. Juliette Wells argues that the physical nature of harp playing, with the "active use of extended limbs," means that "Mary can in propriety command Edmund's attention to her body" (108). This strategy was widely understood at the time. Walter Scott, in *Marmion* (1809), wrote of a woman playing the harp:

> Fair was her rounded arm, as o'er
> The strings her fingers flew;
> And as she touched, and tuned them all,
> Ever her bosom's rise and fall,
> Was plainer given to view. (Austen, *Mansfield Park* [Wiltshire] 657–58n1)

Austen expresses the same idea in regard to Mary's harp playing when she writes that it "added to her beauty, wit, and good humour" and also notes that Edmund's closeness was gratifying to Mary—"she liked to have him near her; it was enough" (76, 77; vol.1, ch. 7). When Mary has Fanny stay to hear one more piece, "your cousin Edmund's prime favourite," Fanny is forced to imagine Edmund "sitting in that room again and again, perhaps in the very spot where she sat now, listening with constant delight to the favourite air, played, as it appeared to her, with superior tone and expression," just as she imagined Edmund in close physical contact with Mary during the riding lesson. Austen leaves it to the reader to understand why Fanny is "sincerely impatient" to depart after the harp playing (242; vol. 2, ch. 4).

The relation of Fanny to music is made clear when she admires the view out the window at twilight in the company of Edmund and Mary Crawford (132; vol. 1, ch. 11). She is aware of the competition she faces from Mary. When the Miss Bertrams invite Mary to take part in a glee at the piano, Fanny is described as having the "pleasure of seeing [Edmund] continue at the window, in spite of the expected glee." As Edmund remains beside her, she attempts to gain his attention by contemplating the sublime aspects of the beauty of the starry sky, and its superiority over "painting . . . music . . . poetry" to "lift the heart to rapture." She comments on the inability of these forms to adequately express the more pure and true nature of pleasure and harmony. But as the singing "advanced," she has "the mortification of seeing [Edmund] advance too, moving forward by gentle degrees towards the instrument, and when it ceased, he was close by the singers" (133). This gradual drawing of Edmund to the group registers physically the capture of him by desire. Fanny is left alone, excluded from the group both by her reluctance to take part and by her belief that true pleasure lies not in the manufactured world of exhibitionism and performance but in the simpler beauty of the night sky.

A focus on *Mansfield Park*'s attention to horse riding and music as socially sanctioned occasions for the expression of desire throws a new light on Fanny. Her desire, revealed only in her love of nature, is for close connection; it has no need to lure, to entrance. What she seeks in Edmund is the intimacy of the rider's hand and horse's mouth, the knowing and understanding one has of the soft space inside another. Men who follow the full cry of the hounds and women who employ the siren call enact sexual desire by imitating the staged chase. Fanny, attuned to the innate and natural rhythms of desire, understands that it gradually springs up "after [one wanders] about and [sits] under trees . . . all the summer evenings" and that it comes to fruition only at "exactly a time when it was quite natural that it should be so" (535, 544; vol. 3, ch. 17).

The Price of a Maxim:
Plausibility in Fanny's Happy Ending

Monica F. Cohen

Having appropriated Fanny's needful time on Edmund's horse, Mary Crawford flashes a maxim that is meant to pass as an apology: "Selfishness must always be forgiven you know, because there's no hope of a cure" (80; vol. 1, ch.7). Mary, as the novel's infamous rival heroine—the saucy seductress figure who nevertheless speaks the witty language of Austen's more beloved heroines—emerges here as the character who also generates most of the novel's maxims: "Every body is taken in at some period or other" (53; vol. 1, ch. 5), "every thing is to be got with money" (69; ch. 6), ". . . where the natural taste is equal, the player must always be best off, for she is gratified in more ways than one" (69) are some examples. To begin a discussion of the role of ironic style in the novel, I ask students to focus on this localized instance of wit, Mary's justification of selfishness at the moment in which her status as Fanny's sexual rival first crystallizes. The phrase opens a discussion of three important features of Austen's writing style: irony, generalization, and wit.

The first question is, With what values is Mary associated? Urban and urbane, worldly and witty, she is a figure of playfulness, movement, humor, ambition, and courage. She comprehends the social semiotics of gestures and gift giving, of being "out" and "not out" (56–60; vol. 1, ch. 5), of conversation's gradations where "never" means "not often" (107; ch. 9). In characters like Emma Woodhouse and Elizabeth Bennet, these are positive qualities. Why does readerly sympathy then exclude Mary Crawford, and what is she doing in Fanny Price's story?

One answer emerges in the language Mary employs. What, for example, is her apology intended to do? Does it stand in a descriptive or prescriptive relation to the culture of the novel and its more overt ideological commitments? In what position does it place Fanny? In what position does it place the reader? Useful here is Robert Donovan's distinction between Austen's "destructive irony" and her "morally committed irony" (Weinsheimer 113). "Destructive irony" pivots on a disparity between a professed motivation and a real motivation in order to criticize pretense without any obvious or deep moral condemnation; "morally committed" irony, by contrast, turns on the disparity between a communally sanctioned ideal and a subject's departure from it. Donovan's example of the latter is the narrator's sly remark that Tom writes to the gamekeeper first and then to Edmund (134; vol. 1, ch. 12): the order illustrates Tom's obliviousness to the family duties that are respected in Edmund's and Fanny's codes of conduct. We might ask here what kind of irony informs Mary's axiomatic wit.

Here and elsewhere, Mary's speech appears characterized by generalizations. As Howard Babb has pointed out, however, her generalizations are always inflected by her self-interest; whether aligning her with the fashionable world and its ideology or projecting her personal desires as universal truths, "there remains a touch of the self-regarding in all her feelings" (156–57). Tinted as they are by a self and that self's singular experiences, Mary's generalizations receive authorial sanction neither ethically nor even epistemologically: her view of all clergymen, as Babb astutely notes, is confined to the personal experience of one clergyman, her brother-in-law, Dr. Grant (158). In this way, the novel makes it clear that Mary's generalization cannot serve as an appropriate foundation for right conduct or right feeling.

Certainly Mary's sententious style can be seen in contrast to Austen's use of generalizations elsewhere. I often ask students to identify such counterexamples. Edmund's speech provides a provocative point of departure. Although Edmund claims that "there is not the least wit in my nature" (109; vol. 1, ch. 9), his phrases, particularly when arguing (and, significantly, flirting) with Mary, nevertheless betray an unexpected artfulness. In their argument over compulsory chapel prayers for the household at Rushworth's estate, for example, he asks rhetorically, "Do you think the minds which . . . are indulged in wanderings in a chapel, would be more collected in a closet?" (102). Yoked by the governing subject, indulged minds, the chapel and the closet form an elegant, alliterative, even Palladian setting for his generalization that attending church is not in fact boring. Interestingly, however, his argument aims at convincing Mary not only of the good in compulsory chapel prayers but also of the good in the clergy as a profession, and hence, ultimately, of the desirability of one clergyman, Edmund, as her future husband. Do his generalizations gain ethically and aesthetically from the fact that his personal desires happen to coincide with a communally sanctioned good? Students often see his generalizations as morally grounded in principles external to his private desires. Mary attempts to ironize this coinciding of principles and desires with the remark, "It is fortunate that your inclination and your father's convenience should accord so well" (127; ch. 11), but students generally feel, and I agree with them, that her cynicism remains unendorsed by the novel as a whole.

The apparent contrast between these types of generalizations illuminates two (if not more) Austens: the Austen of a morally grounded style and the Austen whose wit mocks—if not subverts (and again, that is a classroom question: Is mockery necessarily subversive?)—things conventionally understood as sacred. Hence the shock—and the pleasure—that rippled through a recent audience at the Morgan Library in New York City when people heard a notorious line from one of Austen's letters to Cassandra: "Mrs. Hall, of Sherborne, was brought to bed yesterday of a dead child, some weeks before she expected, owing to a fright. I suppose she happened unawares to look at her husband" (*Jane Austen's Letters* 17; 27 Oct. 1798). Conspicuously absent here is any sign of the tactful aunt laboring over her legendary piece-of-ivory propriety.

What distinguishes Mary's generalization from those of the other characters, including Edmund's, is her wit, which is a little more difficult to define in class.

This wit gives her generalizations a sparkle and an edge that tend to appeal to today's college students. In this sense, her maxims register as less generalizations, less gnomic truths, than eighteenth-century salon bons mots and repartees. What is especially unsettling about her remark defending selfishness, and about maxims generally, is that there can be no objection, no response, no exchange. Mary's words are followed only by Fanny's silence. That Mary's maxim silences is disturbing in a novel concerned with tyranny, because it illustrates the potential of wit to emerge as autocratic speech. Most students feel that at the same time that her wit silences Fanny, however, it also distances the reader by exemplifying Mary's cavalier disregard for others—a casualness that serves as her dispositive sin when she loses Edmund's love through the linguistic crime of wrong naming: she calls adultery mere "folly" (526; vol. 3, ch. 16).

When Mary employs a maxim to silence Fanny over the use of Edmund's horse—a moment that clearly signals their romantic rivalry— she contributes to an accumulation of speech acts to which Fanny can give no answer other than what is dictated to her, dictated not by impersonal civic principles but by the self-interest of others. As Claudia L. Johnson has noted (*Jane Austen* 102), Tom Bertram unwittingly describes the tyranny that language can impose when he bridles at being asked to play whist in such a way as to leave him "no possibility of refusing"; railing at the "pretence" of being given a choice (141; vol. 1, ch. 12), he identifies language that cannot be answered, that precludes choice, that also happens to be the language of sociability in all its inexorable power. The narrator even remarks on that power during the evening at the Grants. After the whist table is made up, Mrs. Grant and her sister find that there are enough guests left for a round game, and "everybody being as perfectly complying and without a choice as on such occasions they always are, Speculation was decided on almost as soon as Whist" (278; vol. 2, ch. 7). Although the novel makes the coercive nature of paternalistic discourse explicit when Sir Thomas advises Fanny to go to bed despite her inclination ("but it was the advice of absolute power" [326; ch. 10]), we can see that such tyranny is not limited to the novel's representation of paternalism. In Mary's use of a maxim, we see the absolute power of the language of sociability.

Silence as a marker of coercion occurs in two other significant places and provides a gateway into the novel's nuanced exploration of speech, tyranny, protest, and gender. Toward the beginning of volume 3, Lady Bertram gives the "only piece of advice, which Fanny had ever received from her aunt," in reference to Henry Crawford's offer of marriage: "[I]t is every young woman's duty to accept such a very unexceptionable offer as this" (384; ch. 2). The advice, like Sir Thomas's bedtime dictation, silences Fanny and inscribes her in a long tradition of innocent daughters who are sacrificed in the name of patriarchal ideals— whether for the family to rise socioeconomically through marriage or whether, Iphigenia-like, for the ships to be able to set sail for Troy. The most infamous silence of the novel occurs in response to Fanny's words, the "dead silence" in the middle of the novel, when Fanny asks her uncle about the slave trade in Antigua (231; vol. 2, ch. 3). These three instances differ in many ways but all illustrate how in the relation between autocratic speech and silence hidden structures of power achieve representation, not least of which is Fanny's moral superiority.

I have found it useful to discuss the maxim as a type of speech act by contextualizing it through François de La Rochefoucauld ("Our virtues are often but vices in disguise," "If we had no faults, we should not take so much pleasure in noting those of others," "The refusal of praise is actually the wish to be praised twice") and sometimes through Benjamin Franklin ("God helps those who help themselves," "Remember that time is money," "Early to bed and early to rise makes a man healthy, wealthy and wise," "There never was a good war or a bad peace"), who provides a nice Protestant Anglo-American twist on the French salon-type of worldliness.[1] I put some maxims up on the board, and we talk about the maxim as a kind of speech in which prescriptive cultural norms are articulated, in which an ideology emerges. We also talk about the tone of a maxim: instructive but playful. Students will often identify the maxim as linguistic theater insofar as it is intended to be noninteractive, appreciated, and applauded. Students may be invited to think of other kinds of autocratic speech in the novel, especially Henry Crawford's reading of *Henry VIII* and his advice about sermon giving (vol., ch. 34). Both Crawford siblings apprehend language as an instrument of performance. One might ask how this usage contrasts with Fanny's quotations from Cowper (66; vol. 1, ch. 6). To what end does Austen juxtapose the authority of wit and stagecraft with the authority of poetry? Most of my students are thorough romantics and believe wholeheartedly in poetry and its correlative, the private self. To them, the wit of social life is mere artifice, not the tool of an ethics whereby psychic integration rests on social foundations.

Most students where I teach will have read *Pride and Prejudice*, and so they immediately associate Mary's speech to that novel's opening line, the most famous maxim in all Austen's novels: "It is a truth universally acknowledged that a single man in possession of a good fortune must be in want of a wife." This truth universally acknowledged not only composes the sociolect of *Pride and Prejudice* but also expresses the worldview of none other than Mrs. Bennet, thus ironically enthroning the middle-class housewife as an agent for and, in a sense, author of the story line. For, as students know, men in possession of good fortunes do indeed come to marry her daughters. *Pride and Prejudice* offers a convenient illustration of how a maxim can govern plot construction. And whatever ideological position cowers in the witty maxim, so ironically and so humorously inviting us to disregard it, we are ultimately happy to embrace such a truth, because Elizabeth Bennet, on the strength of her own wit and good judgment, is so deserving.

Is there a maxim that governs the marriage of *Mansfield Park*? Although many readers imagine a neoclassical principle—Virtue Rewarded—hovering around the title page, how does that principle compare with a maxim? Perhaps we should think about Fanny and Mary as representing two different plot structures, the principle-governed and the maxim-governed. The tension between the plots would place their juxtaposition on the fault line between the eighteenth and nineteenth centuries—and by definition, a fault line is where tremors are bound to occur. The dialogic confrontation between the two plots emerges most dramatically when Fanny speaks up to defend her rejection of Henry Crawford's offer of marriage: "Let him have all the perfections in the world," she answers Edmund, "I think it ought not to be set down as certain, that a man must be acceptable to every woman he may happen to like himself" (408; vol. 3, ch. 4). In a moment worthy of Elizabeth Bennet, she repudiates the reigning consensus about women in the marriage market with language that echoes *Pride and Prejudice*'s famous line about what a man "must be." The consensus in *Pride and Prejudice* is that a single, wealthy man "must be in want of a wife"; here the phrasing is negative ("it ought not to be set down as certain"), and the perspective shifts, the "must be" followed this time by "acceptable to every woman he happens to like himself," from representing a consensus about male desire to repudiating a consensus about female desire.

Fanny, finding her voice here, not only articulates a personal opinion but also, again ironically, uses language that resembles a maxim, even if only to reject it. This almost quippy remark is not at all characteristic of her speech elsewhere: it requires great "recollection" and "exertion" (408); it departs from the generally anguished reports of her thoughts and feelings. And it is designed specifically to take down Mary, whose disapproval of Fanny's refusal Edmund has just come to relate. Fanny's language is pitched to Mary's own style of speech in its use of pithy and edgy generalizations, but the universal truth it sketches refers to how women should feel rather than to a social consensus about the ways of the world: "I *should* have thought," Fanny retorts, ". . . that every woman must have felt the possibility of a man's not being approved, not being loved by some one of her sex, at least, let him be ever so generally agreeable" (408). In other words, the world is wrong and Mary insufficiently feminine in her refusal of a sisterhood whereby feelings ("every woman must have *felt*" [my emphasis])— and specifically feminist sympathy (what every woman must feel about "some one of her sex, at least")—take precedence over social consensus. We might argue that her statement synthesizes the two plot structures (the one governed by principle, the other governed by maxims) in the forging of an ideology that valorizes female feeling as itself a universal truth. This reading meshes with what Nancy Armstrong has proposed, in *Desire and Domestic Fiction*, about Austen's fiction generally.

I would also suggest that the speech marks the emergence of Fanny as the novel's heroine. Until this moment, she has figured as its long-suffering subject. Now she wins (at least among my students) readerly sympathy if not Edmund's love. But how the novel moves from crafting our desires for Fanny's happy-ending marriage to gratifying those desires raises many questions. Indeed students often complain that the conclusion, Fanny's reward of marriage to a man who has spent most of the novel professing mad love for another, is unconvincing.

The inadequacy of narrative resolution comes up a lot in nineteenth-century novel classes, and *Mansfield Park* is no exception. The disparity between Mrs. Norris's assurance that "cousins in love, &c." (6; vol. 1, ch. 1) would be im-possible—a statement that propels the novel's opening action—and the novel's concluding account of exactly that "et cetera" is enormous. In many ways, this move from the beginning to the end exploits the ambiguity residing in the verb used to describe patriarchal consent to the marriage: "It was a match which Sir Thomas's wishes had even forestalled" (545; vol. 3, ch. 17). *Forestall* can mean both "prevent" and "anticipate." It can also mean to buy (goods) up privately with a view to enhance the price, that is, to hold privately in order to raise a price, an idea that reflects perversely the novel's project as a whole—the raising, in every sense, of a Price. Here students often apply Edward Said's postcolonial reading of *Mansfield Park* (*Culture* 84–97) and see the adoption of Fanny, her education in the mores of English estate life (an education that is so successful that she emerges as the rightful caretaker of that inheritance), as analogous to the Europeanization of colonial subjects in the cultural imagination of many nineteenth-century novels. That the concluding marriage occurs through the cagey term of *forestallment* suggests that the fashioning of her subjectivity rests on some labile boundary between desire and taboo.

This enactment of what the book initially told us is impossible raises the ques-tion of plausibility. Is Fanny's story plausible? Is it believable? Many students understand the conclusion's hyperbole and evasiveness as signs that under-mine the fairy-tale ending ("the happiness of the married cousins must appear as secure as earthly happiness can be" [547; vol. 3, ch. 17], "Let other pens dwell" [533]). It is significant that the assurance of implausibility comes from Mrs. Norris, who served as the presiding genius of Fanny's adoption in the first place. Named after a notorious slave trader, Mrs. Norris suffers the overthrow of her own plan when Fanny does indeed land the hero. Students often see this ironic evolution—the disparity between what Mrs. Norris authoritatively says will happen and what actually does—as marking the heroine's radical departure from the normative culture as it first appears in the beginning of the novel.

This glimpse of cultural transformation as a precondition of Fanny's marriage brings us back to the maxim. Nancy K. Miller has identified implausibility in women's fiction as a function of cultural expectation: what we accept as believ-able in fiction is determined by our beliefs about how things should be rather than about how they sometimes happen; maxims encode cultural norms about how those things should be and thus exclude fictional subjects who depart from those norms (36). That Fanny's marriage poses questions about narrative plau-sibility implies a culture whose norms are not stable enough to generate max-ims that apply. By giving maxims to Fanny's rival rather than to Fanny, Austen invents a heroine whose own speech and narrative representation must develop in other directions. This choice opens up new possibilities, both fraught and exciting, for women's fiction.

NOTE

[1] The quotations of La Rochefoucauld are from *Collected Maxims* 3 ("Our virtues . . ."), 43 ("A refusal of praise . . .") and *Maximes* 48 ("If we had no faults . . ."); the quotations of Franklin are from Bartlett 347–48.

Speculation in *Mansfield Park*

Regulus Allen

Students are often slow to warm to *Mansfield Park*. Many are familiar with the "light & bright & sparkling" tone of *Pride and Prejudice* (Le Faye 203; 4 Feb. 1813, to Cassandra) and find the mood of Austen's maturer novel too serious. I like to infuse a sense of play in my treatment of the text by demonstrating its characterizations and themes through the card game Speculation. As a popular pastime of the leisure classes, card games appear in all of Austen's novels. With their suits arranged in strict social hierarchies, with careful dynamics of concealing and revealing, and with fortunes at stake, such games become apt symbols for the situations of her characters. The playing of Speculation in *Mansfield Park* provides an especially good example because Austen's narrator explicitly links what the characters do in the plot to what they do at the card table. The scene allows many to reveal their motives through the activities of organizing the game, teaching or learning the rules, and playing altruistically or aggressively. The game of Speculation takes place in the seventh chapter of the second volume, precisely at the middle of the book, and fittingly, the scene concerns some of the novel's central issues: the improvement of estates, decisions about courtship and marriage, the relationship of a clergyman to his parishioners, and the tension between diversion and duty.

Several critics have explored the importance of games in Austen's writing. David Selwyn places the development of her novels in the context of the puns, riddles, and other literary diversions that Austen often created for her family's amusement ("Games"). He also traces, in his book *Jane Austen and Leisure*, the symbolic value of these pastimes throughout her writing ("Toys"). Scholars tend to agree that the games allow Austen to express the social realities of her day, the subtle motivations of her characters, and the major concerns of her works. Also, most concur that she does this more fully in the Speculation scene in *Mansfield Park* than she does in any other novel. Selwyn contends, "Nowhere else in the novels is a card game used with the skill and subtlety that Jane Austen shows in this scene; indeed, she had never used any game in such a virtuosic and highly developed manner" ("Toys" 275). Katrin Ristkok Burlin says of *Mansfield Park*, "Austen limits its card-table scenes but develops them fully for maximum moral relevance" (180). Alistair Duckworth acknowledges that the game of Speculation "serves as a symbolic synecdoche of the novel's characterization and the themes. . . . It is a subtle and complex chapter in which the motif of card-playing is more fully integrated into the fictional fabric than ever before" ("'Spillikins'" 289–90).

It is not surprising that Austen would choose Speculation for her fullest literary treatment. As her correspondence reveals, the game was one for which she felt a particular affection. In a letter to her sister Cassandra dated 24 October

1808, she describes how she has been attempting to console her two young nephews George and Edward a few weeks after the death of their mother and her sister-in-law, Elizabeth Bridges Knight, and that games were a welcome distraction to the boys. Continuing with the events of 25 October, she writes, "Our evening was equally agreeable in its way; I introduced *speculation*, and it was so much approved that we hardly knew how to leave off" (Le Faye 152). Later hearing that Speculation was supplanted by the card game Brag, she playfully writes to Cassandra on 10 January:

> [I]t mortifies me deeply, because Speculation was under my patronage;—& after all, what is there so delightful in a pair-royal of Braggers? it is but three nines, or three Knaves, or a mixture of them.—When one comes to reason upon it, it cannot stand its' ground against Speculation—of which I hope Edward is now convinced. Give my Love to him, if he is.   (163–64)

On 17 January, after learning that Brag had also fallen out of favor with the boys, she pretends that she has "just received some verses in an unknown hand" and was asked to forward them to her nephew Edward:

> "Alas! poor Brag, thou boastful Game! What now avails thine empty name?—
> Where now thy more distinguish'd fame?—My day is o'er, & Thine the same.—
> For thou like me art thrown aside, At Godmersham, this Christmas Tide;
> And now across the Table wide, Each Game save Brag or Spec: is tried."—
> Such is the mild Ejaculation, Of tender hearted Speculation.—   (167)

The personification of Speculation as tenderhearted emphasizes the soft spot the game holds in Austen's heart because of its association with her beloved nephews, and she singled out the card game for special attention when she began composing *Mansfield Park* a few years later.

The importance of Speculation to Austen critics and the author herself suggests that looking closely at the scene in *Mansfield Park* where characters play this game will reward student readers. I usually teach the novel in three two-hour classes, devoting a session to each volume. To prepare for the first class, I ask students to keep a chart of the major characters, their relationships to one another, and some of their defining features. I also ask students to note what they see as recurring issues in volume 1. In the first class, the students share their impressions of the characters, and there is usually much debate about Fanny Price and Henry Crawford. Many students admire Fanny's sensitivity, but some find her too mild-mannered. On the other hand, students know that they are supposed to dislike the irresponsible Henry, and yet some find themselves drawn in by his bad-boy appeal. We examine some of the volume's major themes. Subjects on which students often focus include debates about improvement, choices about courtship and marriage, the role of the clergy, and the balance between diversion and duty. In the second class, we analyze how the game Speculation can deepen our understanding of the novel's characters and concerns. In preparation for this discussion, I distribute a simplified version of the game's rules (see the appendix to this essay). I adapted these rules from *Hoyle's Games*; the book first included Speculation in the 1800 London edition. The *OED*'s first recorded usage of *speculation* as a name for a card game was in 1804, in another of Austen's works, her unfinished novel *The Watsons* (def. 10). I ask the class to contemplate the significance of *speculation* by looking up other definitions of the word in the *OED*. The definitions in the dictionary's second edition correspond to those available through the *OED Online*. Last, I ask students to consider, as they read the scene, each character's way of playing the game.

I begin the next class by breaking students into small groups to play a few rounds of Speculation. To add an element of authenticity, I provide facsimile playing cards from the era, which are inexpensive and can be purchased from gaming companies on the Internet. (I bought my cards from MacGregor Historic Games.) One potential challenge of these cards is that they do not feature numbers or letters in the corners, such as K for king, and some students have trouble distinguishing between the jacks and the kings. This difficulty, however, can demonstrate a point about how Austen's society was more attuned than ours to the distinction of rank. In fact, the 10 January 1809 letter quoted above shows that the cards now called jacks were then called knaves. The older name signified a servant, a status that players in Austen's society would see as antithetical to the royal king. To approximate the fish-shaped counters used for gambling in Austen's day, I use fish-shaped crackers or candy. The game hinges on the buying and selling of trump cards; the player possessing the highest trump wins the pot. Most people find the game easy to learn and highly entertaining. After a few rounds, the students are ready to compare their own approaches to the game with those of Austen's players and analyze what the different styles of playing reveal about the characters.

I start our discussion by asking students to consider which characters are chosen to play Speculation and why. The narrator relates that after dinner "it was found, according to the predetermination of Mrs. Grant and her sister, that after making up the Whist table there would remain sufficient for a round game, and . . . Speculation was decided on" (278; vol. 2, ch. 7). Whist can be played only by two sets of partners, but a round game does not require partners, so any number of people can play. Students may argue that the divide between those with and without partners can reflect the courtship plots that are always included in Austen's fiction. This observation might lead to the expectation that Whist will be played by the two married couples, the Bertrams and the Grants, and Speculation by the remaining six single people. Yet Lady Bertram cannot choose between the games and asks her husband which would amuse her more: "Sir Thomas, after a moment's thought, recommended Speculation. He was a Whist player himself, and perhaps might feel that it would not much amuse him to have her for a partner" (278). The matrimonial analogy is still useful, however, because students can easily see that Sir Thomas would not enjoy having to explain the rules of Whist to his wife and would find it more entertaining to have as a partner someone who at least knew the game. Mrs. Norris's willingness to be Sir Thomas's Whist partner indicates her eagerness to assume a place of authority in the Bertram household.

Students can link each character's particular approach to Speculation with his or her portrayal earlier in the novel. Lady Bertram does not know how to play the game, but she casually declares, "'Fanny must teach me'" (279), making her typical assumption that her niece will do everything for her. Because Fanny is also a first-time player, Henry Crawford volunteers to teach both ladies, but his task with Lady Bertram proves comically difficult. Characteristically obtuse, she cannot understand the game and is too indolent to learn. When her husband asks how she likes it, she calls it "[v]ery entertaining indeed. A very odd game. I do not know what it is all about. I am never to see my cards; and Mr. Crawford does all the rest" (280). One of the first rules of the game is that players cannot initially look at their cards, since they are supposed to speculate whether a turned up card is higher or lower than what is in their hand. Henry's dialogue is peppered by such exclamations as, "Excuse me, your ladyship must not see your cards. There, let them lie just before you" (283). Readers who know how to play Speculation will be amused by Lady Bertram's inability to understand even this basic rule. Henry plays her hand as well as his own while coaching Fanny. He approaches everything with "playful impudence" (279), and students often note that he is an expert player, not only at cards and as an actor in the young people's ill-advised attempt to perform the racy play *Lovers' Vows* but also a player in the modern sense of having dalliances with women. His managing three hands at once points to the love triangle that he previously sparked with the Bertrams' two daughters, and he has now set his sights on making their cousin Fanny fall for him as well.

Fanny's approach to Speculation highlights her intelligence and selflessness. She quickly picks up Henry's instructions on the game but not his competitive nature: "[T]hough it was impossible for Fanny not to feel herself mistress of the rules of the game in three minutes, [Henry] had yet to inspirit her play, sharpen her avarice, and harden her heart, which, especially in any competition with William, was a work of some difficulty" (279). Her easy mastery of the game supports Henry's later praise of her to Mary: "[H]er understanding was beyond every suspicion, quick and clear" (340; vol. 2, ch. 12). Students find that her lack of ambition to win the game accords with her character. Some point to a want of spirit in her play as well as in her personality, but others admire her unselfish and considerate nature. She is especially softhearted toward her brother, and at a point when the game will be hers, her cousin Edmund notes, "Fanny had much rather it were William's. . . . Poor Fanny! not allowed to cheat herself as she wishes!" William is a capable but less altruistic player of the game, attempting to buy a queen from his sister without offering "half her value" (284; vol. 2, ch. 7) and selling a knave to Mary Crawford "at an exorbitant rate" (282). Although William appears only intermittently in the novel, the feature that students remember about him is his desire to rise from poverty through the ranks of the navy. His manner of mercilessly playing the game to win the most money aligns with that ambition. Students will recall this scene when they read in the final volume how after William is made second lieutenant, all his thoughts are on his ship, including "conjectures how she would be employed, schemes for an action with some superior force, which (supposing the first lieutenant out of the way—and William was not very merciful to the first lieutenant) was to give himself the next step as soon as possible, or speculations upon prize money" (433; ch. 7). Students who have played Speculation and read volume 2 will notice the use of "speculations" about William's schemes for the future.

Mary Crawford, also ambitious, is a foil for Fanny. Students will observe how the opposition between the two characters comes through in Mary's manner of card playing. After risking everything to buy a single card, she exclaims, "There, I will stake my last like a woman of spirit. No cold prudence for me. I am not born to sit still and do nothing. If I lose the game, it shall not be from not striving for it" (282; vol. 2, ch. 7). Students may criticize Mary for her recklessness or admire her for her spirit (much as they both criticized and admired Fanny). She is striving to lure Edmund away from his plans of becoming a clergyman and to transform him into a fashionable gentleman and suitable marriage partner for herself. By contrast, Fanny's affection for Edmund is strengthened by his choice of occupation. Of the six at the card table, Edmund is the only one whose approach to the game is not described, and I ask students to account for this omission. The class will usually mention that he is focused more on his upcoming ordination than on the game—just as he, much to Mary's chagrin, places his duties over her desires. His lack of interest in the cards makes a good transition from considering how characters play to considering what the game itself means.

To connect the card playing to the novel's themes, I ask the class how some of the definitions of *speculation* they found in the *OED* apply to both the game and the novel. One meaning is an "undertaking of an enterprising nature, esp. one involving considerable financial risk on the chance of unusual profit" (def. 9). Students observe that a game centered on gambling echoes several elements of the narrative that involve economic risk. The threat to Sir Thomas's fortune comes from "some recent losses on his West India Estate" (27; vol. 1, ch. 3). His Antiguan sugar plantation may have become a shakier investment when Britain abolished the slave trade in 1807. Another kind of questionable venture that the novel explores is the improvement of estates, which became a fashionable but costly endeavor for the era's landed gentry. Henry Crawford's proposals to renovate Edmund's property at Thornton Lacey are debated over the cards. Henry declares, "The farm-yard must be cleared away entirely, and planted up to shut out the blacksmith's shop. The house must be turned to front the east instead of the north—the entrance and principal rooms, I mean, must be on that side, where the view is really very pretty" (281; vol. 2, ch. 7). The young man's idea, which involves nothing less than reorienting the whole house, would be a ruinous investment even for someone with a more comfortable income than a clergyman. Edmund responds, "I have two or three ideas also . . . and one of them is that very little of your plan for Thornton Lacey will ever be put in practice. . . . I think the house and premises may be made comfortable, and given the air of a gentleman's residence without any very heavy expense, and that must suffice me" (282). A final economic venture that the Speculation scene highlights is the marriage market. The card party is the first time that Sir Thomas notices Henry's attentions to Fanny: "[I]t was in the course of that very visit, that [Sir Thomas] first began to think, that any one in the habit of such idle observations *would have thought* that Mr. Crawford was the admirer of Fanny Price" (278). Although he is careful to separate himself from those who make such observations, the sentence's syntax parallels his thoughts with theirs, and the italics emphasize the connection. Sir Thomas seems to be engaging in a little speculation of his own when he contemplates the wealthy man's attentions to his niece, but his thoughts on the matter are couched once again in the language of self-deception:

> [T]hough infinitely above scheming or contriving for any the most advantageous matrimonial establishment that could be among the apparent possibilities of any one most dear to him, and disdaining even as a littleness the being quick-sighted on such points, he could not avoid perceiving in a grand and careless way that Mr. Crawford was somewhat distinguishing his niece—nor perhaps refrain (though unconsciously) from giving a more willing assent to invitations on that account.   (277)

Just two chapters later, Sir Thomas organizes a ball in Fanny's honor, which serves as her formal introduction to society and forces her to participate in what sounds closer to a business venture, "the trade of *coming out*" (309).

Along with its economic definition, *speculation* means "intelligent or comprehending vision" (def. 1), and students note that successful players of the game must pay careful attention. Fanny picks up the game quickly, and in volume 1 of the novel she is the only member of the Bertram household who recognizes the danger in her cousins' plan to act out romantic scenes with the Crawfords; she is the only one who can see through the charming performances of Henry and Mary on and off the stage. This fact will resonate with students when they read the final volume, where Fanny says of Henry's flirtation with the Bertram sisters, "I had not . . . been an inattentive observer of what was passing between him and some part of this family in the summer and the autumn. I was quiet, but I was not blind" (419; ch. 5).

Speculation also refers to "the conjectural anticipation *of* something" (def. 4c), and players hang their hopes on the possibility of a winning card. As the game comes to a close, Mary's "agreeable fancies" of Edmund as a fashionable spouse are upset by the talk of ordination; she is "no longer able, in the picture she had been forming of a future Thornton, to shut out the church, sink the clergyman, and see only the respectable, elegant, modernized, and occasional residence of a man of independent fortune." At this point, the narrator engages in a little game herself, employing wordplay to sum up the situation with a pun: "All the agreeable of *her* speculation was over for that hour" (289; vol. 2, ch. 7).

Lastly, *speculation* means "the contemplation, consideration, or profound study *of* some subject" (def. 4). Although this definition initially seems not to apply to the light entertainment of a card game, when Sir Thomas comes over to observe the round table game, the conversation turns to the serious topic of the responsibilities of a clergyman. The tension between these subjects is captured by Mary's exasperated feeling that "[i]t was time to have done with cards if sermons prevailed" (289). Students, however, will realize that there need not be such a strict divide between light diversions and weighty lessons. The Speculation scene is one of many in the novel that show Austen's ability to use amusing pastimes as a medium to present material of weight.

In our final class, we consider how our observations about the novel's characters and themes play out in the conclusion. Austen begins her last chapter with a switch to first-person narration: "Let other pens dwell on guilt and misery. I quit such odious subjects as soon as I can, impatient to restore every body, not greatly in fault themselves, to tolerable comfort, and to have done with all the rest" (533). While the conclusion can be interpreted as teaching moral duties through the familiar device of poetic justice, the tone is light and playful. In the same way, the card scene can serve readers as serious edification and diverting entertainment. A lesson plan that combines instruction with games is therefore appropriate. Overall, an analysis of the Speculation scene can encompass many of the novel's important issues, and the excitement of cards and wagers will engage even the most recalcitrant student. You can bet on it.

APPENDIX

THE GAME OF SPECULATION

These rules are adapted from the 1800 London edition of *Hoyle's Games Improved*.

The game should be played by small groups (four to eight players works well). Each group should have a deck of cards, and each player should begin with the same number of fish counters (ten is a good number).

Players should take turns dealing. At the start of each game, all players ante one fish into the pot; the dealer antes two. The dealer deals a stack of three cards facedown to each player, including himself or herself. These cards must not yet be revealed. The dealer then turns up the next card in the deck to determine the trump suit (the suit in play). The player with the highest trump (highest card in that suit), with ace ranking highest, will win the pot for that round.

The turn-up card belongs to the dealer; if it is an ace, the dealer automatically wins the pot. If the card is not an ace, it still may end up being the highest trump of that round, since the other cards have not yet been revealed. The other players may "speculate" or offer to buy it with some of their fish counters. The dealer decides if he or she wants to keep this trump card or sell it to the highest bidder.

Afterward, each player, beginning with the one to the left of whoever owns the highest trump card, turns over the card at the top of his or her stack. This continues, omitting the player who holds the highest trump, until someone turns over a higher trump card. That person may then choose to keep that trump or sell it to the highest bidder. The more speculating that takes place, the more exciting the game becomes. Play continues until all cards have been revealed or until someone turns over an ace of the trump suit and automatically wins the pot.

If an ace is turned over, or the game is otherwise won, before all the cards have been revealed, the dealt cards are all turned faceup before they are discarded so that each player can note which cards are no longer in play. A player who can recollect which superior cards of each suit have already appeared will have the advantage of making more informed speculations in future rounds. The deck is then passed to the person on the previous dealer's left, and a new deal begins.

Mansfield Park and the Family: Love, Hate, and Sibling Relations

Kay Souter

The moral landscape of *Mansfield Park* has long been the focus of uneasy critical attention. The novel is often read as a baffling domestic tragedy, with unlikable main characters and even echoes of *King Lear*. The Internet-based Fanny wars provide a contemporary manifestation of this confusion, people exchanging fire over the assessment of Fanny Price—resilient domestic heroine or charmless puritan?—and Mary Crawford—crude adventuress or bright spirit? As the persistence of these debates indicates, the moral-ethical core of *Mansfield Park* continues to resist summation. It seems hard to make up our minds about the characters. The novel's treatment of the social landscape, however, is very clear. The treatment of the social is comic rather than tragic, although it is comedy of the unsettling sort where, as in *The Merchant of Venice*, the good (about whom we have serious reservations) end fairly happily and the bad (with whom we rather sympathize) are punished quite unpleasantly. There is, in short, a tension in *Mansfield Park* between the comic and the tragic, between the morally equivocal on the one hand and precise psychosocial detail on the other.

I suggest that this tension is the effect of Austen's careful elaboration of unhappy multigenerational and multifamily dynamics and their effect on individuals. The main characters in *Mansfield Park* are much more socially embedded and constructed than is usual in the English novel, and they can be fully understood only if read as part of the social and psychological interactions in which they live. *Mansfield Park* is not an aberration in Austen's oeuvre, the sole unsatisfactory novel in a glorious pantheon, but the logical conclusion of one aspect of her work. Family and particularly sibling dynamics are central to the representation of social life in her novels, where, as in her life, interlocking sibships provide the raw material for friendship and marriage, as well their essential intersubjective space and much of their psychological structure.[1] Consideration of the tangled family and sibling dynamics of *Mansfield Park* therefore shines a powerful light on the novel, in terms of both the plot and the main characters.

As if to bear out Leo Tolstoy's maxim that all happy families are alike (1), Austen's family strikingly exemplifies the model of successful sibling interaction proposed by Frank Sulloway in his book *Born to Rebel* (1996). Sulloway argues that sibling interaction is determined by a Darwinian competition for parental interest, first in order to survive childhood and second to win the right to reproduce, either by amassing seductive goods and property, if the sibling is male, or by cultivating ways winning enough to attach a prosperous and attractive admirer, if female. The resulting sibling competitiveness means that siblings must diversify if they are to prosper. That is, children must be sufficiently different from one another to interest their parents and induce them to spread family and matrimonial resources. This goal presents no problem for the firstborn child, who generally fascinates the parents no matter what he or she is like, but the need to diversify grows as the number of offspring increases and parents cease to see the novelty of infancy. But children must claim a share of the parental investment; they need to minimize sibling competition and also therefore sibling rivalry and aggression. In a relatively conventional family structure, firstborns "specialize in strategies designed to subordinate rivals. . . . Firstborns tend to be dominant, aggressive, ambitious, jealous and conservative," an effect very much accentuated in Austen's time by primogeniture and patrilineal inheritance. "Laterborns" must divert parental attention away from the prized firstborn, as well as protect themselves against the older and more powerful sibling, and therefore "often manifest a decided inclination to rebel [but] work hard to improve their lot through good-natured sociability and cooperation" (79).[2] "Middleborns" are often found to be rather quiet and may try to be peacemakers.

   This pattern of sibling relations is familiar to students, many of whom like to discuss the way that birth order works out in their own families. The discussion of sibling relations often illuminates the novel's structure for them.[3] It will also be apparent to readers that the basic pattern of sibling diversification can have both charming and unpleasant consequences: firstborns can be serious or pompous, laterborns adventurous or unreliable, and so on. The main variable that affects the pattern appears to be serious conflict with a parent. Such conflict is likely to reverse the expected behavior, so that firstborns who have unrewarding or conflictual relationships with a parent may become unreliable and unconventional, like Tom Bertram. Abused or neglected laterborns may become conventional rather than adventurous, like Julia Bertram, who is younger but more risk-averse than Maria. In addition, birth order is not always

self-evident in a group of children. Fanny, though cast in the role of downtrod-
den youngest at Mansfield, in fact started life as a serious and reliable oldest
daughter and "secondborn" of many, and she was lovingly twinned with a classic
firstborn son. A further variable is a child's access to unequal family resources,
such as parental preference, an inheritance, and so on. In its basic pattern and
consideration of the variables of family conflict and resources, this model of
sibling dynamics thus provides a powerful and flexible tool to consider the representation of the family.

Although the historical Austen family was a model of cooperative diversification, Austen's novels are concerned with family dynamics that are more or
less destructive. In these works, parental preference or discrimination, particularly the issues that swirl round primogeniture, male inheritance, and marriage,
maximize sibling disharmony. Conflict is based on marriage prospects—in
Darwinian terms, the right to reproduce—which is the major sibling issue in
all Austen's novels. *Mansfield Park* is especially concentrated on the tensions
between sibling love and sibling rivalry, the latter at times escalated to the point
of hatred. The novel begins with a historical account of such a rivalry, smoothed
over by the ironic cadences of the authorial voice describing the prospects of
three pretty sisters, all competing for matrimonial success: "[T]here certainly
are not so many men of large fortune in the world, as there are pretty women
to deserve them" (3; vol. 1, ch. 1). This elegant reformulation and reversal of
the celebrated opening lines of *Pride and Prejudice* ("It is a truth universally acknowledged, that a single man in possession of a good fortune, must be in want
of a wife" [ed. Rogers] [3]) characterizes a more contingent universe, one where
outcomes are unlikely to be wholly satisfactory. The wild card is named in the
novel's first sentence. It is luck, Miss Maria Ward's "good luck" in captivating Sir
Thomas Bertram. This match does not compute for the neighbors: her fortune
is "at least three thousand pounds short," and her sisters "quite as handsome."

The unexpected development (in Darwinian terms, it is a huge input of unequal resources) throws the Ward sibling organization into permanent disarray:
both sisters marry in reaction to Miss Maria's unexpected luck. Miss Ward finds
herself "obliged to be attached" to a friend of Sir Thomas, becoming Mrs. Norris, and Miss Frances goes the other way, marrying "to disoblige her family" (3),
becoming Mrs. Price. The play on the word "oblige" emphasizes the extent to
which the oldest and youngest sister are locked into sibling reactivity, closely
conforming to Sulloway's scheme, in that the middleborn's astonishing trajectory
into gentry heaven forces the oldest sibling into a conformist and the youngest
into a rebellious path. None of the sisters is well served by this turn of events.
The first chapter of *Mansfield Park* gives us a brisk overview of the ten or fifteen
years following Miss Maria's lucky break, during which time success paralyzes
Lady Bertram into fashionable torpor, Mrs. Norris's firstborn dominance cur-
dles into bullying and antilibidinal hyperactivity, and youngest sister rebellious-
ness crushes Mrs. Price under the weight of all the children that result from
her erotic acting out. Like all Austen heroines, Fanny, the future Mrs. Edmund

Bertram, is a secondborn child.[4] This is the family position that is most associated with tact and thoughtfulness but also carries awareness of a subordinate position in the family. Miss Maria's luck disrupts the usual sibling structure, and she becomes a sleepy caricature of the diplomatic and agreeable middleborn.

The central consequence of the Bertram marriage is that the Ward sisters and their resulting families become locked together for the next twenty or thirty years. If the sisters had all made similar marriages, it is easy to imagine them simply busying themselves with their own lives and seeing little of one another. Instead, the families become enmeshed, particularly through the hostile preoccupations of the humiliated oldest sister, Mrs. Norris. Her apparently random proposal to sponsor a Price girl to be reared at Mansfield Park is the most significant result of this hostility. Childless and chronically angry (and nothing makes her angrier than Mrs. Price's fertility [5]), Mrs. Norris startles the Bertram family by suggesting the adoption. No real reason is given, but her responses provide a clue. When the matter is discussed, she acts under more than usual pressure, constantly interrupting Sir Thomas, dismissing his objections out of hand, and weaseling out of actual responsibility for the child when the crunch comes. Her ostensible motive, benevolence, is unconvincing. A more likely reason can be found in the aspect of the offer that strikes both Sir Thomas and Mrs. Price as odd, the wish to adopt a girl rather than a boy. The adoption touches Mrs. Norris's deepest and presumably unconscious motivations. The unknown niece is "the one whose name just happens to be the same as her mother's," as William Deresiewicz notes ("*Mansfield Park*" 63). She provides an outlet for Mrs. Norris's wounded sense of firstborn superiority: another oldest daughter whom the aunt can despise and subjugate, in an attempt to relieve her rage at the outcome of her own demeaning marriage and unsatisfactory life. In getting Fanny under her control, Mrs. Norris can symbolically continue the punishment and domination of the socially successful middle sister and the younger sister who, though poor, married a dashing hero and had heaps of children as fast as possible in a provoking display of erotic self-indulgence. Mrs. Norris simultaneously tries to protect her sense of worth by idealizing Maria and Julia as ideal selves and oldest sisters (Souter 211). By the time the present of the novel gets under way, Fanny has been established as the nexus of several sets of sibling difficulties, all focused on marriage and courtship: her mother's and aunts', her cousins', and eventually the Crawfords'. The families become a sort of superfamily with multiple resentful, unhappy, and improper connections. Fanny's position at the center of this complex is bound to be uncomfortable.

Three sets of siblings, then, the Bertrams, the Prices, and the Crawfords, have become entangled as a result of the sibling passions of the previous generation. The Bertram family exemplifies the problems of primogeniture very clearly. In a Darwinian world, siblings compete for parental investment, but under primogeniture there is no need for competition, as parental investment in the eldest son is already placed and at the maximum. Mary Crawford's initial decision to be (that is, like Mrs. Norris, Mary is ready to consider herself "obliged to be") attracted to Tom because he is the heir acknowledges the system. We see the same dynamic at work in Maria's engagement to Mr. Rushworth. Perhaps this is why Tom Bertram shows little sign of firstborn conscientiousness: primogeniture ensures his success no matter how he behaves, and his difficult relationship with his father would further decrease his firstborn traits. Tom does, however, score high in terms of his firstborn-like wish to subordinate his siblings, particularly his brother, the spare heir: Sulloway observes that in certain sorts of families, particularly aristocratic ones, oldest children expect the younger to act as their servants (*Born* 67) and actively attempt to dispossess them. This is certainly the case in *Mansfield Park*, where Tom "rob[s]" Edmund for ten, twenty, thirty years, perhaps for life, of more than half the income which ought to be his" and quickly falls back on "cheerful selfishness" as comfort (27; vol. 1, ch. 3). Indeed, the novel shows that the system of patriarchal primogeniture cannot work for younger brothers, as it does not work for women. Mary Crawford insists that the fashionable world recognizes a descending order of prestige, with inherited title and wealth at the top, then "an uncle or a grandfather to leave a fortune to the second son" (107; ch. 9), followed by the professions in order of éclat: the forces, the law, and finally, hopelessly unstylish, the church. Edmund Bertram has to make up for his lack of dominance with goodness, kindness, and common sense. In doing so, he establishes himself as possessing an entirely new measure of sexual attractiveness.

Primogeniture affects the Bertram girls differently. As neither of them stands to gain much from the family save elegant clothes and a fashionable education satirized as a waste of gold paper (16; ch. 2), they have little interest in constructive sibling diversification. Their only way of ensuring their future welfare is through marriage, as a commodity in the trade between patriarchal father and patriarchal groom. Maria has an older sibling's edge over the "less flattered, and less spoilt" Julia (539; vol. 3, ch. 17); Henry Crawford finds Maria "the handsomest and . . . the most agreeable" (52; vol. 1, ch. 5), and without doubt she is the more headstrong sister. The world does not seem to discriminate between them, however: they are both docilely preparing for the "duty" of a marriage "as soon as they can do it to advantage" (44, 50; ch. 4), as Mary Crawford puts it; and ideally they will marry in order of age. Mary Crawford's long interrogation of Edmund on the question of whether Fanny is "out" or not makes plain how unseemly it would be in this milieu for the younger daughter to be married first: "Poor Miss Sneyd! Though I have no younger sister, I feel for her. To be neglected before one's time, must be very vexatious" (59; ch. 5). Julia therefore has no problem with Maria's engagement to a man whose only attraction is his immense wealth, as it does not damage her own prospects at that point and might even improve them. When the sisters discover a matrimonial resource of a different sort—the phenomenal sexual attractiveness of Henry Crawford— they launch into unrestrained sibling rivalry over the gentleman's favors.

Mansfield Park is populated by sisters furiously competing for assets. The hostile exchanges between Susan Price and Betsey Price over the knife (which itself signifies violence) willed to Susan by "little sister Mary" (446; vol. 3, ch. 7) provide the most uncomplicated example of such contention. Because the Price girls have little in the way of material goods, as is demonstrated by Mrs. Price's long complaint about the stinginess of Betsey's godmother, Aunt Norris, the pathetic deathbed gift is correspondingly precious. Mrs. Price, "a partial, ill-judging parent" (451; ch. 8), intensifies the rivalry in the attempt to spread the meager resources of her children to the advantage of her favorite. While the little girls fight over a silver knife, grown-up sisters compete most intensely for matrimonial and sexual resources: initially the Ward sisters, then the Bertrams, then Mary's London friends, of whom Edmund writes:

> I do not like Mrs. Fraser. She is a cold-hearted, vain woman, who has married entirely from convenience, and though evidently unhappy in her marriage, places her disappointment, not to faults of judgement or temper, or disproportion of age, but to her being after all, less affluent than many of her acquaintance, especially than her sister, Lady Stornaway, and is the determined supporter of every thing mercenary and ambitious, provided it be only mercenary and ambitious enough.   (488; ch. 13)

There are other sorts of resources to compete for, too: Mrs. Norris's "spunging" at Sotherton, as Maria calls it (123; vol. 1, ch. 10), and making off with the Bertrams' material goods, ranging from green baize to rose petals, provide the crudest examples of sibling theft.

The family and social system in which the Bertram children have been raised give them virtually no help in their search for adult happiness. Tom's aggressive narcissism is unmoderated until the plot requires a life-changing illness at the end. His sisters have a more explicitly adversarial relation with the patriarchal society that treats them dismissively, in that they are made aware that their only real significance lies in making what Lady Bertram calls an unexceptionable marriage. Each sister directly uses her one opportunity to defy the aspect of the gender-property system that most affects them, Maria by seeking "a larger income than her father's" (44; ch. 4) and Julia by seeking to avoid the "increased dread of her father . . . greater severity and restraint," which she feels is likely in the wake of Maria's transgression (539–40; vol. 3, ch. 17). Only Edmund can reflect on the family system in a way that will help him find his own way to emotional maturity.[5]

The situation of the Price children is different. In this large family, the children separate into groups: William and Fanny, the two eldest, love each other and evince the most favorable outcome of birth order: the firstborn is brave and conscientious and follows in his father's footsteps; the secondborn is loving and cooperative and has an unexpected capacity for firmness of purpose where her affections are challenged. Probably because of her premature removal from the family, where she had "always been important as playfellow, instructress, and nurse" (16; vol. 1, ch. 2), the rest of the Price children do not do well. Mary, who dies during Fanny's absence, is younger than Susan, who survives, and Mary is said to have been "remarkably amiable" (446; vol. 3, ch. 7). With the sibling keystones all removed—the conscientious William, the maternal Fanny, and the amiable Mary—the Price family system degenerates into unrestrained sibling chaos and aggression. Mrs. Price stokes the fires of sibling disharmony by undisguised son preference: "Betsey was the first of her girls whom she had ever much regarded. To her she was most injudiciously indulgent. William was her pride; Betsey, her darling; and John, Richard, Sam, Tom, and Charles, occupied all the rest of her maternal solicitude" (451; ch. 8). Mrs. Price's behavior reflects normal aristocratic practice, though no fortune here follows the preference. This youngest of the Ward sisters resembles the second sister, Lady Bertram, in incompetence and immaturity; Betsey, another youngest daughter, seems likely to turn out similarly.

In the Bertram-Price-Norris extended family, we see the development of the Ward sisters' foundational sibling upheaval. This development, complicated enough in its intergenerational form, becomes much more so when a third set of siblings enters the picture. Mary and Henry Crawford arrive to stay with their half sister, Mrs. Grant, as the result of an unpleasant family emergency. Their guardian, an uncle who is unrelated to Mrs. Grant, installs a mistress after the death of his wife, making it impossible even for a broad-minded girl like Mary to remain there. The complexity of this sibling group is increased by the fact that the brother and sister have a different father, therefore different alliances and values, and in addition Mrs. Grant has not seen Henry and Mary since they were children. Moreover, Dr. Grant's installation at Mansfield parsonage in the first place is owing to what Sir Thomas names an act of sibling robbery, the family imbroglio that required the living to be sold away from Edmund.[6] The plot device, "a stranger comes to town," appears in many of Austen's novels, but here the stranger is part of a sibling set that has preexisting problems and will interact unpredictably with other sibling sets in the neighborhood.[7] In fact, the Crawford siblings, "young people of fortune" as they may be (46; vol. 1, ch. 4), have a good deal in common with the penniless Fanny. Much is made of their uprooted childhood, their living under the care of a warring husband and wife whose morals are questionable and who seem to have used the children as pawns in domestic hostilities, the admiral claiming the boy and his wife claiming the girl. This history has taught the Crawford siblings to think of relationships as a set of strategies: they do not take feelings seriously, and they do not esteem marriage as a social duty.

Fanny does take feelings seriously but, like the Crawfords, refuses to think of marriage as mere social duty—although for different reasons. She prizes emotional ties over alliances. Her childhood was reshaped by the experience of being shipped away from her home for social purposes, and she is not prepared to contemplate it again. Above all, she shares with the Crawfords the experience of being displaced and effectively orphaned (she does not see her parents for eight years) and therefore at the mercy of wealthy relatives who use the adopted child for their own purposes. The adoptive parents are distorted mirror images of each other: Admiral Crawford is worldly and licentious and torments his wife; Sir Thomas Bertram is an Enlightenment gentleman whose wife is a pampered cipher. Fanny and the Crawfords share an outlaw status: they follow their own rules. It is not surprising, then, that the Crawfords and Fanny are drawn to each other. Henry loves Fanny's gentleness and fortitude in her humiliating position as an adopted waif, which must bring to mind his own painful experience at the admiral's house. Fanny, obliged to hold her tongue under the most unkind attacks by Aunt Norris, is drawn to Mary's sassiness, though against her own better judgment: "[S]he could not be easy without going [to see Mary], and yet it was without loving her" (242; vol. 2, ch. 4). When Henry first tells his sister of his intention to marry Fanny, he says, somewhat obscurely, "I could so wholly and absolutely confide in her . . . and *that* is what I want" (341; ch. 12), probably meaning that he can trust her, have confidence in her. Fanny's moral probity and the common experience of being orphaned and transplanted make both Crawfords instinctively feel sure about her. The situation of Henry, whose "unsettled habits" displease his sister and keep him from spending much time in Everingham (136: vol. 1, ch. 12), and of Mary, dependent on a sister she barely knows, parallel that of Fanny, who is caught between two families neither of which seem quite hers. Henry's being drawn to Fanny, and Mary and Fanny's unexpected pleasure in each other's company despite Fanny's jealousy, at first so surprising to readers as well to the characters themselves, are in fact predictable: they are uprooted or orphaned children drawn to each other.

The Crawfords' family history also sheds light on their relationship with the Bertram children. Tom, Maria, and Julia have never given their fate a second thought until illness hits Tom and Henry Crawford befalls the sisters. Tom has "easy manners, excellent spirits . . . the reversion of Mansfield Park and a baronetcy" (55; vol. 1, ch. 5). Maria and Julia are "the belles of the neighbourhood. . . . Their vanity was in such good order, that they seemed to be quite free from it, and gave themselves no airs; while the praises attending such behaviour, secured, and brought round by their aunt, served to strengthen them in believing they had no faults" (40; ch. 4). The Crawfords have not been able to take their lives for granted in this way. Henry and Mary's contemptuous dealings with Tom, Maria, and Julia are in large part the result of their unconscious dislike of the Bertrams' complacency. By contrast, Edmund Bertram must make his way in the world and therefore has a chastened and thoughtful manner that is anything but complacent. As Fanny's gentleness fascinates Henry, Edmund's bluntness and honesty are a welcome antidote to Mary's brittle artifice. In short, the seductive insecurities of the Crawfords are calmed by the wounded sobriety of the two cousins to whom patriarchy has offered little.

Mrs. Grant, Henry, and Mary exemplify many of the traits of birth order that Sulloway describes, modified by a disrupted childhood. Mrs. Grant, the oldest child of an at least partly intact family, is conservative. Henry, the second child of his mother but the first of his father, combines first- and secondborn traits but appears very like a firstborn in his tendency to emulate his foster father, the admiral. He also shows some incipient moral conservatism in his choice of Fanny. Mary, a youngest child, has adventurous tendencies, but as a survivor of family discord eventually shows the reverse pattern and becomes conservative after Edmund rejects her at the end of the novel. Raised by people who use children as ammunition, the Crawfords are bound to be exploitative and dangerous to rich young people who have never had to think about their place in the world. Despite the many examples of sibling love in the novel, the deepest layer of feeling proves to be sibling hatred. Dangerous levels of sibling rivalry grow out of the bloated and enmeshed family system, where the siblings do not seem able to separate their own lives out.

Aunt Norris is the foundational sibling hater whose spitefulness has grown over the years. A typical bully, she turns her hatred away from those with power over her and wages psychological warfare against a child: constant criticism, denial of dignity, denial of pleasure, denial of comforts. No wonder Fanny is nervous growing up. A more openly vicious example of bullying is to be found in Aunt Norris's account of her confrontation with ten-year-old Dick Jackson, the carpenter's child. She spends half a page relishing her triumph:

> . . . who should I see but Dick Jackson making up to the servants' hall door with two bits of deal board in his hand, bringing them to father, you may be sure. . . . I knew what all this meant, for the servants' dinner bell was ringing at that very moment over our heads, and as I hate such encroaching people, (the Jacksons are very encroaching, I have always said so,— just the sort of people to get all they can.) I said to the boy directly—(a great lubberly fellow of ten years old you know, who ought to be ashamed of himself,) *I'll* take the boards to your father, Dick, so get you home again as fast as you can. The boy looked very silly, and turned away without offering a word, for I believe I might speak pretty sharp; and I dare say it will cure him of coming marauding around the house for one while—I hate such greediness. . . .   (166–67; vol. 1, ch. 15)

This passage shows Mrs. Norris at her most brutal, delighted to have humiliated Dick, an even more vulnerable child than Fanny, and to have deprived him of the dignity of the traditional messenger boy's bowl of soup in the kitchen. The terms in which she speaks of him are striking. She has picked on a child who is the age Fanny was when she came to Mansfield, and the terms she uses to abuse him, his encroaching ways, his greediness, show a crude projection of her own marauding, encroachment, and greed. This passage exposes the exact pathology of Mrs. Norris's sadism and hatred: imagining an underprivileged ten-year-old child to be a powerful enemy, "a great lubberly fellow," provides the best fit for the projection of her own misdeeds and bad intentions. The story of Dick Jackson paves the way for Mrs. Norris's coarsest abuse of Fanny: "I shall think her a very obstinate, ungrateful girl, if she does not do what her aunt and cousins wish her—very ungrateful, indeed, considering who and what she is" (172). The two episodes show a woman deformed by sibling resentment, whose mission in life has become to wound and humiliate the vulnerable.

Maria and Julia embody sibling rivalry too but concealed under a surface gentility. As children, the Bertram girls are "entirely deficient in . . . self-knowledge, generosity, and humility" (22; ch. 2), and as young women they think themselves faultless. The older sister, Maria turns out to have "strong passions" that brook no interference when roused (536; vol. 3, ch. 17); Julia has more modest charms and a somewhat more reflective turn of mind. She sometimes remembers her duty, for example, and can give Henry up when she sees that he does not care for her. Under everyday conditions, they are friendly enough, but like their mother and aunts, marital prospects bring out their dark side. At the crucial moment when Henry picks Maria as his leading lady, Julia knows that "Maria could not be happy but at [Julia's] expense" (159; vol. 1, ch. 14). Maria rejoices in vanquishing her sister in Henry's affections, and when Henry eventually leaves, Julia rejoices that "Maria gained him not" (227; vol. 2, ch. 2). Beneath the surface amiability, the Bertram sisters long to displace and humiliate each other.

In the quiet figure of Fanny, sibling love and hatred unexpectedly come together. Against her own wishes, she finds herself catapulted out of lower-middle-class life into a one of aristocratic privilege. Hard and humiliating as her new life is, it gives her a triumph over the brothers and sisters she leaves behind—except William and, much later, Susan, who derive a sort of parallel benefit. William and Fanny end up a class above their siblings, as Fanny discovers with shock when she returns home after eight years. She is now a lady, and William is in the king's service, whereas his father is a mere lieutenant of marines. Fanny's success over her siblings causes negative or neutral feeling in her family of origin: they ignore her. In her foster family, she is likewise ignored. In each family she has one brother who loves her and other siblings who do not. When she becomes entangled with a third sibling group, the Crawfords, there is greater complication. She dislikes the "corrupted mind" of both Henry and Mary Crawford (263; vol. 2, ch. 5); this dislike is strong at first, then weaker, but finally intense. The Crawfords however, admire and love Fanny throughout. Mary considers herself and Fanny sisters; Henry enthuses about Fanny's "ineffable sweetness and patience" (343; ch. 12).

The three families, Prices, Bertrams, and Crawfords, engage in a Darwinian struggle over resources—for money and lovers—with very mixed results. Only Fanny and Edmund are successful in love, but money does seem to follow primogeniture: Tom is more magnificently provided for than his younger siblings, given Maria's fall into social ruin, and the younger Price children must make do with less than the older.

Mansfield Park shows the multigenerational ripple effect of sibling rivalry and explores how members of dysfunctional families are drawn to one another. Edmund and Fanny, marginalized by the dominant members of the various sibships, are the only ones to survive comfortably when the different family systems either implode (the Crawfords, Grants, and Prices) or explode (the Bertrams and Mrs. Norris). In the postcatastrophe world, Fanny, Edmund, and Sir Thomas, along with a few good siblings like William and Susan Price, and perhaps the penitent Tom and Julia Bertram, build a new, well-constructed family system on the ruins of one that is old, overextended, and corrupted. *Mansfield Park* takes the sibling plots of Austen's other novels to their logical extreme. Troublesome families disappear. The shaky superstructure of adoptees, hangers-on, half siblings, cousins, and sibling-like friends is swept away, and an invigorated and much smaller core family is established in its place. In tracing these complicated interactions and resolutions, Austen's work shows a grasp of social relations and their psychologies that is consistent with, and in some ways in advance of, still developing modern models of family and sibling dynamics. Austen understands that sibling interaction is a major engine of psychosocial existence and uses this insight to drive her fiction.

NOTES

[1] In all the novels except *Emma*, a series of romantic entanglements involving three groups of siblings direct the plot (in *Emma* the third group consists of orphans: Frank Churchill, Jane Fairfax, and Harriet Smith, and the Martin siblings are also on the sidelines), and usually one sibling group is more or less undeserving (again, *Emma* is the exception).

[2] The term *firstborn* is Standard English; the useful terms "laterborn" and "middleborn" appear to be Sulloway's coinage ("Birth Order" and *Born*; see also Zajonc and Sulloway).

[3] I have frequently seen this response when giving academic papers on the topic of sibling relations in Austen's work. During discussion, audience members readily discuss interesting family patterns such as multiple births, large age gaps between siblings, adoptions, and so on. Like love stories, the theme of sibling relations provides an intuitive entry to a confusing work.

[4] Catherine Morland in *Northanger Abbey* may not actually be the eldest, but she is the eldest daughter and effectively has just one older sibling in narrative terms, her brother James. In *Sense and Sensibility*, both Elinor and Marianne could be considered secondborns, depending on whether or not you count their half brother John. The same is true of Henry and Mary Crawford. Edmund Bertram is also a secondborn, as are many of the heroes. Mr. Knightley and Mr. Darcy, however, are archetypal firstborns.

[5] Edmund's awareness of his relatively precarious economic position is exactly similar to Colonel Fitzwilliam's, the younger son of an earl and cousin of Mr. Darcy in *Pride and Prejudice*.

[6] The advent of the Grants also rouses Mrs. Norris: deprived of what little social standing she had by widowhood and eviction, she furiously resents the Grants' expansive style of living.

[7] In *Pride and Prejudice*, similarly, the Darcy family comes with various Wickham and Bingley entanglements unknown to the people of Hertfordshire.

Questions of Interiority:
From *Pride and Prejudice* to *Mansfield Park*

Julia Prewitt Brown

The distinguished and diverse criticism *Mansfield Park* has inspired makes it an exciting novel to think about, but it is a humbling novel to teach. In my varied classroom encounters with it, I have come to appreciate the modest aims of Mrs. Goddard, mistress of a school in *Emma*, whose students manage to "scramble themselves into a little education" ([Parrish] 12). The word "scramble" is perhaps a blend of the obsolete word *scramble* ("struggle for") and *cramble* ("crawl"). How do we initiate this struggle or crawl toward knowledge in our students when they first read *Mansfield Park*?

My students, reading Austen for the first time, are hungry for facts about the world of her novels. I have found that Park Honan's biography not only compresses a great deal of relevant background information about the gentry as Austen knew it—the shift from traditional to modern society, the prospects of rising in the navy, and the situation of women—but also contains a superb, psychologically suggestive, and informative chapter on the period in Austen's youth perhaps most relevant to *Mansfield Park*: when, at the sensitive age of twelve, Austen stood watching as her flirtatious cousin Eliza, comtesse de Feuillide, engaged in amateur theatricals with her brothers James and Henry, using rehearsals of a risqué play to make love to them both.[1] Through their reading of the biography, or even just a chapter or two of it, students receive an excellent introduction to the biographical and historical context of *Mansfield Park*.

Turning to the critical tradition of the novel, we encounter strikingly different interpretations. Austen's political vision is variously described as conservative (by Marilyn Butler), radical (by Mary Poovey), and progressive (by Claudia L. Johnson). Her treatment of sexuality and the body is deeply attentive (as John Wiltshire notes) and consciously dismissive (as Susan Morgan notes). In the portrait of Fanny, Austen affirms the tradition of the passive Christian heroine (in the opinion of Lionel Trilling) and replicates colonialist expansion in images of Fanny's movement and rise (in the opinion of Edward Said). If, as Oscar Wilde wrote, "When critics disagree the artist is in accord with himself" (17), then Austen must be having a good time.

One point on which critics generally agree is Fanny's lack of appeal relative to other Austen heroines. Assigning critical readings on the novel is especially instructive in *Mansfield Park* because of the contrast between critical engagement with the challenge Fanny presents to the modern reader and the commercially driven decisions of contemporary directors to suppress her personality altogether in their adaptations. I refer to Patricia Rozema's 1999 film *Mansfield Park* and the third and most recent Masterpiece Theatre adaptation, directed by Iain B. MacDonald in 2007. In neither of these films is the heroine recognizable as the heroine of the novel; the actress is far too assertive in each. In Rozema's transformation, Fanny is reinvented as a writer whose voiceover displays the caustic wit of the triumphant, unassailable narrator of Austen's adolescent parodies. "By representing Fanny in fragments taken only from burlesque," writes Wiltshire, "the film refuses to engage the possibility that Austen in *Mansfield Park* has matured beyond the phase of youthful defensiveness" or that she is now concerned with "the representation of interiority" at a deeper and more conflicted level than any she had explored before (*Recreating* 96–97). Since film adaptations are taken seriously as interpretations of novels (as the inclusion of essays about adaptations in critical editions of novels indicates), we need to encourage students to critique adaptations as interpretations with the same degree of rigor we would expect in analyzing a critical essay. Discussing a film adaptation in class can easily become an escape from the complexity of the novel rather than an examination of when and why the film succeeds or fails to grasp the novel's deepest concerns. For recent adaptations of *Mansfield Park*, it's helpful to ask students to articulate what is so disturbing about Austen's representation of interiority that popular filmmakers are driven to eliminate it. In other words, we might ask whether the supreme value our culture places on assertiveness as the sine qua non of modern womanhood doesn't come with too high price if it demands the sacrifice of inwardness. Isn't this the very problem Austen is exploring in her portrait of the extroverted Mary Crawford? Of Mary's attraction to Edmund the narrator comments, "There was a charm, perhaps, in his sincerity, his steadiness, his integrity, which Miss Crawford might be equal to feel, though not equal to discuss with herself" (77; vol. 1, ch. 7). Fanny's inner life, her power to interrogate her own feelings, is one reason, perhaps *the* reason, she is the heroine.

Austen's first deep entrance into Fanny's subjective life occurs in chapter 16, when Fanny retreats to her room, the old schoolroom, to determine if she should submit to the importunate demands of her cousins to act in the play.[2] When teaching *Mansfield Park*, I devote as much time as possible to the close reading of passages from this chapter. "[W]hat should she do?" Fanny asks herself, trying "to find her way to her duty" (176, 180). The little white attic, where she had slept the night before, proves "incompetent to suggest any reply" (176), but the old schoolroom is more forthcoming. There, surrounded by her books, plants, furnishings (a transparency of Tintern Abbey, Julia's footstool); by treasured objects (her brother's childish sketch of his ship, Edmund's profile); and by guilt-inducing gifts from Maria, Julia, and Tom, the agitated Fanny paces, thinks, and above all observes things in order to determine her duty: "[S]he could scarcely see an object in that room, which had not an interesting remembrance connected with it.— Every thing was a friend, or bore her thoughts to a friend . . ." (178).

Students will appreciate how remarkable this passage is in the Austen oeuvre if they compare it with the way Elizabeth Bennet's inner life is realized in the previous novel, *Pride and Prejudice*. I almost always teach the two novels together for that reason, opening the discussion of chapter 16 of *Mansfield Park* by reading aloud sections of the passage in *Pride and Prejudice* in which Elizabeth reads Darcy's letter. I then ask the students to compare Elizabeth's self-realizations with those of Fanny. The discussion can move in many directions, of course, since Elizabeth's confrontation with another person is central to her growth, whereas Fanny is far more isolated in her development. But focusing on the two passages allows the class to observe in concrete detail the differences between the ways the heroines think. Whereas Elizabeth's consciousness unfolds as Elizabeth reads and thinks over Darcy's letter, Fanny's is revealed in terms of the spatial configuration of the room and of the objects in it: her consciousness is inseparable from the things in her room. Austen creates a new world in this masterful scene, the world of Fanny's circumambient self. In this domestic interior, Fanny is the only genuinely reflective character in a society of the morally obtuse. (Even Edmund deludes himself in the scene that follows the schoolroom passage, when he rationalizes his submission to the urgings of his siblings to perform in the play.) The former schoolroom not only has a personal prehistory; it also alludes to the nation's past in the image of Tintern Abbey, reminding us of Wordsworth's recently published "Lines Composed Five Miles above Tintern Abbey," in which the relations between time and space, past and present, are also meditated in an individual consciousness. In Wordsworth's poem, the medium through which contemplation is conveyed is nature, but in Austen's novel it is a more confined and ambiguous domain. In the descriptive details of the room, which set the scene for Fanny's internal monologue, the narrator's affectionate amusement is registered as well: Tintern Abbey is no more than a commonplace Romantic site turned into a commercial commodity as a transparency, and the subdued comic phrase telling us that it "held its station between a cave in Italy, and a moonlight lake in Cumberland" quietly deflates the whole assemblage of these amateur objets d'art (179).

Fanny's "[finding] her way to her duty" is conceived of as a struggle to see the interior clearly. As Fanny observes the things around her, both the friendly objects associated with her brother and Edmund and the gifts from the other Bertram siblings, "she grew bewildered as to the amount of debt which all these kind remembrances produced" (179–80). The primary purpose of the East Room, which has always been to provide consolation, is destroyed by what nourishes it, for the objects that reassure her also burden her. When the scene is interrupted by Edmund's tapping, Fanny is at an impasse, unable to determine where her obligations lie. As her meditation focuses on material debt, her judgment founders. At the center of her bewilderment is the ambivalent nature of things themselves, their dual capacity as historical-economical objects and as repositories of memory.

The hierarchy of things in the passage moves from collected objects (plants and books) to objects cast off by other members of the family and treasured by Fanny (transparencies, Julia's footstool, family profiles) to objects given as gifts, beginning with her brother's sketch and ending with "present upon present" from her cousins. On a descending scale, the highest value is placed on the conscious choice reflected in collected objects, the lowest on objects bestowed by those with too much to give, whose gifts are actually a form of trash, as the allusion to objects "thought unworthy to be anywhere else" suggests (179). Austen, not Fanny, constructs this hierarchy, for Fanny is too immersed in the world of the East Room to make these distinctions. With "affliction" and "affection" "now so blended together," she cannot extricate herself from the debt without violating the duty that she decides to perform (178–80). For her, both debt and duty merge irrevocably in the objects themselves.

The contrast with Elizabeth Bennet is striking: the struggle of Elizabeth takes place while she is contemplating words; Fanny's is a matter of physical observation. When invited to come up with a metaphor describing the consciousness of each heroine, students give suggestive answers. One student once remarked that Elizabeth's mind is like a vessel, in which input from Darcy alters already formed conceptions, such as her opinion of her father, whereas Fanny's consciousness is far more porous, more like a field or space without boundaries that determine an inside and outside.

At this point in the discussion I suggest to students that the historical context might help explain the importance Austen gives to domestic space in this new conception of consciousness. What changes were taking place in society at this period regarding attention to location? Here again comparison with *Pride and Prejudice* is useful, for while Pemberley is crucial to the novel, Darcy's estate is an idealized space, a symbol of preindustrial tradition in harmony with nature. The portraits of Mansfield Park and Sotherton suggest the disruption of that ideal. In the visit to Sotherton, in which the prospective bride's, Maria Bertram's, approach from afar and tour of the estate's impressive house and grounds seem almost to parody Elizabeth's visit to Pemberley, we are reminded that Darcy's estate exists in relation to its past, whereas at Sotherton traditions have been abandoned. Mr. Rushworth, the proprietor of Sotherton, is a buffoon whose inability to memorize his lines in the play is emblematic of his failure to represent his estate, a symbol of cultural continuity secured in part through memory. The graceful integration of interior and exterior space at Pemberley is negatively reproduced in the way the "wilderness" at Sotherton (105; vol. 1, ch. 9), the godless exterior space that unleashes the seductive energies of Henry Crawford onto Maria, is abetted by the vacated chapel within. Comparing the two estates (in discussion or in a paper) offers students the opportunity to consider the concrete manifestation of social change in Austen's world and then relate it back to chapter 16. For it is in Fanny's lonely room there that Austen follows her investigation of the historical shift from traditional to modern society to its logical conclusion: the isolation of the individual.

In short: when I teach the novel, I move from discussions of Fanny's character, focusing on her inwardness, to the social-historical circumstances Austen places Fanny in, the very circumstances that have created that inwardness. Fanny's visit to the city of Portsmouth is central to this idea and the subject of a later class on the novel. What happens in Portsmouth? At her natural family's home, Fanny is surprised to discover what was already made clear in chapter 16: she is profoundly dependent on things, both in their material aspect, for the comfort they provide, and in their emotional importance as embodiments of memory. Austen uses the urban context of Portsmouth to explore the dissolution of "the ties of blood," which Fanny discovers are "little more than nothing" (496; vol. 3, ch. 13) in the new money-driven society, as well as to expose bourgeois nostalgia for the rural past.[3] Fanny now longs for and idealizes the place that had made her miserable. In writing about *Mansfield Park* in another context, I have emphasized its "dialectical intractability" (Brown 54), the way the novel refuses to resolve the problems it poses, and this intractability may be found at every level, from the novel's portrait of the ambiguity of social change (we feel nothing of the resounding optimism of the final chapter of *Pride and Prejudice*) to its imagination of a heroine whose resistance to change is presented as a virtue (see Brown 54–59).

The critical assessment of *Mansfield Park* is therefore more diverse than that of other Austen novels. Having students review the criticism makes them aware of just how difficult it is to locate any single line of inquiry or interpretation. In this essay I have outlined my approach to teaching *Mansfield Park*, but I also tell students that I find it more difficult to grasp than any other Austen novel. When I first studied Austen in graduate school, at the beginning of the class on *Mansfield Park* my teacher, Michael Wood, posed the question of whether it wasn't a "more honest" novel than *Pride and Prejudice*. In *Pride and Prejudice*, he said, all the most attractive and charming characters are also the most virtuous, but this isn't always true in real life. Imagine Austen's deciding to reverse the formulas of *Pride and Prejudice* and write a novel in which the most virtuous characters (Fanny and Edmund) are less appealing than the lively, amoral characters (Henry and Mary Crawford). To this honesty we might add the portrait of social change: the rise of democratic individualism is not a delightful process—a young woman's declaration of her right to be happy and to live for herself ultimately leads, through her marriage to the responsible Mr. Darcy, to the revitalization of English tradition—but as one in which a morally sensitive woman must defend herself against the predatory individualism of others by seeking protection in traditions that are threatened with decay. To be sure, Edmund will be a more responsible clergyman at Thornton Lacey than Dr. Grant was at Mansfield, but on the last page of the novel he acquires the Mansfield living as well when Dr. Grant dies. Earlier in the novel, Sir Thomas inveighed against the evils of multiple incumbency, insisting that the clergyman who does not live among his parishioners does very little good, and Austen leaves it open as to whether Edmund's "increase of income" is gained at the expense of the community at Thornton Lacey (547; vol. 3, ch. 17).

There is no nostalgia in the conclusion of *Mansfield Park*. We have already seen the influence that wealth and comfort have had on Fanny; we know that she was offended by the dirt and disliked the discomfort of her natural home in

Portsmouth, and we learn that she might have succumbed to Henry Crawford's efforts to win her over. When she returns to Mansfield in springtime, she returns to a house of illness and melancholy. The question I like to pose in the final class on *Mansfield Park* is whether the society described at the conclusion of the novel represents any moral advance over the society described on the first page. We return to chapter 1 and do a close reading of the opening paragraphs. Once again, the comparison with *Pride and Prejudice* is telling, for in the earlier novel's opening a local truth is humorously offered as universal truth, and the neighborhood that abides by the hyperbole is satirized: "However little known the feelings or views of such a man may be on his first entering a neighborhood, this truth is so well fixed in the minds of the surrounding families, that he is considered as the rightful property of some one or other of their daughters" ([ed. Gray] 3). In the opening of *Mansfield Park*, the voice speaking is that of the neighborhood itself, and the irony at work is the kind of smug irony the neighborhood enjoys: "But there certainly are not so many men of large fortune in the world, as there are pretty women to deserve them." If the opening of *Pride and Prejudice* invites us to delight in the comic psychology of a neighborhood that aims to perpetuate itself through marriage, the opening of *Mansfield Park*, which recounts the fates of the three Ward sisters, is about money in the crudest sense: "All Huntington exclaimed on the greatness of the match [between Sir Thomas and Maria Ward] and her uncle, the lawyer, himself, allowed her to be at least three thousand pounds short of any equitable claim to it" (3).

In E. M. Forster's *Howards End*, Margaret Schlegel describes money as "the warp of the world." When asked, "Then what's the woof?" she replies, "Very much what one chooses. . . . It's something that isn't money—one can't say more" (102). If the opening of *Mansfield Park* is about money, the warp of the world, where do we find the woof in *Mansfield Park*? What will serve to counter the money values enshrined in the unregenerate voice of the neighborhood if not Fanny's consciousness, the depth of her inner life, and her capacity to question herself? In the editor's introduction to the Norton Critical Edition of *Mansfield Park*, Claudia L. Johnson introduces the subject of dollar-pound money equivalences by stating, "Few subjects fascinate students reading Austen for the first time more than money. . . ." Anyone who teaches Austen knows this to be true—yet why is it the case? According to Johnson, the reason has to do with Austen: "Austen's characters themselves are both extremely interested in their neighbors' annual incomes and extremely well-informed about them" (xiii–xiv). Perhaps another reason has to do with the students. Their fascination with the subject of money may say as much about them and their generation as it does about Austen. They quickly recognize that few writers understand the "warp of the world" better than Austen, and in their eagerness to learn, for example, what the three-thousand-pound bounty on Maria Ward's beauty would be in today's dollars, they accept without reflection the wall of material facts that Austen constructs between the warp and the woof. Her attention to money is an obstacle meant to challenge us and one that students reading her for the first time must struggle to overcome. As a teacher, I set the stage for that struggle through questions and hints, as my teachers did for me, since, as Austen well knew, even "a little education" is something they must "scramble themselves into." No one else can do it for them.

NOTES

[1] Chapter 4 of Honan's biography, "The Lady from France," suggests that Eliza is the original for both Crawfords (42–55).

[2] In the ensuing discussion of the novel, I draw on my book, *The Bourgeois Interior*, entitled "Fanny's Room" (40–59). See also C. Johnson, "Jane Austen's Relics."

[3] Perry discusses how the novel stages Fanny's return to Portsmouth "to dramatize the dissolution of her ties with her family of origin" (*Novel Relations* 230).

Understanding Fanny Price:
Close Reading Early Scenes

Anne Mallory

As we begin our study of *Mansfield Park*, my students offer a range of opinions concerning Fanny Price. Moved by her suffering and powers of endurance, some find her immediately sympathetic. Yet more often than not, a portion of the class expresses disappointment and irritation. What troubles them is not just that Fanny lacks the spirit and independence of an Elizabeth Bennet but also that she appears unreasonably timid, obliging, and passive. Accustomed to strong-willed heroines, some find her unworthy of serious attention.

This tendency to dismiss Fanny out of hand can be frustrating to a teacher, and it doesn't necessarily dissipate on its own. I have found that students are more likely to overcome their resistance when we work closely in class with a set of scenes from volume 1: Fanny's dialogue with Edmund about her proposed removal from Mansfield to the White House, the evening on which Fanny reveals her presence on a sofa at the opposite end of the drawing room, and her conversation with Edmund and Mary in the Sotherton chapel (these scenes are located in chapters 3, 7, and 9, respectively).

The approach of emphasizing early scenes allows for a thorough discussion of Fanny's circumstances at Mansfield Park. The scenes depict Fanny at her most vulnerable. In each, she has been or is about to be sent away or left behind. Confronted with evidence of her social and economic dependency, students see that her survival depends on her willingness to oblige and readiness to yield. They appreciate how little opportunity she has to act, to express her views, or to influence those around her. These scenes reveal Fanny's emotional needs as well. They dramatize a conflict between her need to feel "important"— that she matters—and the domestic, economic, and social arrangements that render her insignificant and powerless (16; vol. 1, ch. 2). Students cite passages from these scenes as evidence of Fanny's feebleness or passivity, but when they have a chance to discuss the scenes in detail, many come to see Fanny as more active, engaged, and effective than they initially thought. When her position is most precarious, and her ability to maintain it most in doubt, students glimpse a heroine who, while vulnerable, is determined and resilient. Despite her straitened circumstances, she tries and occasionally succeeds in her efforts to establish her importance, demonstrate her potential, and communicate her beliefs.

Each of the three scenes may be taught on its own, but there are advantages to reading them together. As Bruce Stovel argues, volume 1 constitutes "a self-contained prologue to the main action" (1). Fanny's early trials and small victories prepare the class for events to come. The most revealing and climactic episodes—those in which Fanny refuses to act the part of Cottager's Wife and refuses to marry Henry Crawford—strike students as more comprehensible and resonant when understood as part of a pattern of characterization and as variations on familiar themes.

Before we turn to our first scene, I ask students to review Austen's account of Fanny's painful transition from Portsmouth to Mansfield. When Fanny arrives at the great house, she brings with her a history of economic and emotional privation. As the eldest daughter of a disabled father and a harried mother unable to manage the household, she acted as surrogate parent to an ever-expanding brood of siblings. Mrs. Price had little affection to spare for her daughters; Fanny's brother, William, served as an "advocate" with her mother "in every distress" (17; vol. 1, ch. 2).

Austen's refusal to sentimentalize Portsmouth makes her depictions of Fanny's homesickness at Mansfield all the more poignant. Separated from everyone and everything, Fanny longs "for the home she had left," as any ten-year-old would. One paragraph provides a springboard for discussion; it elaborates on her loneliness and adds to our understanding of the full extent of her losses. Noting that she is "as unhappy as possible," and "[a]fraid of every body, and ashamed of herself" (14), the narrator lists characters who inspire Fanny's fear and mortification, ranging from the elder Bertrams, her cousins, and Miss Lee down to the maidservants who "sneered at her clothes." Adding to her misery, we learn, is the thought "of the brothers and sisters among whom she had always been important as playfellow, instructress, and nurse" (16).

Fanny has lost not only her siblings but also her sense of importance. When asked how the word "important" functions in this passage, students generally note that Fanny, like anyone else, needs to feel that she has value, whether in the eyes of another person or in the context of a group. This understanding helps them distinguish the need to feel important from the need to feel superior (a need we can attribute to Mrs. Norris). Fanny yearns not to stand above but to find a place within a relationship, family, or household.

Many factors contribute to her isolation and insignificance at Mansfield. She is disadvantaged as a dependent and further disadvantaged on account of her class, age, gender, temperament, and physical size. Neither a family member nor a servant, she is at once easily forgotten and open to attack from all sides. Life at Portsmouth was hard, but she knew who she was and what she could do: as "playfellow, instructress, and nurse" as well as sister, she earned appreciation and found a way, amid the chaos, to feel important. At Mansfield, her only function, as a poor relation, is to make others feel important by comparison. Initially, she fails even at this; she sobs inconsolably on arrival and later is "little struck with the duet [Maria and Julia] were so good as to play" (15).

Fanny derives what satisfaction she can from being useful. With Maria and Julia, she serves in the capacity of a "third." She waits on Lady Bertram. But only Edmund offers kindness and practical assistance. Taking her on as his pupil, he shows her a way to be important; she will never be a Miss Bertram, but she can be a force for good. Fanny comes to rely on him; subsequent scenes demonstrate how much she needs to belong, how hard she looks for ways to be important, to him and to the family as a whole. But she is repeatedly reminded of her insignificance, and as entropy threatens to take over, even Edmund lets her down.

We next consider the scene in chapter 3, which takes place after five years of relative contentment for Fanny. When Reverand Norris dies, Sir Thomas expects Mrs. Norris to assume responsibility for Fanny's support. Fanny learns of this from Lady Bertram, who casually announces, "So, Fanny, you are going to leave us and live with my sister." Shocked by this news, Fanny approaches Edmund, only to learn that he believes the plan to be "an excellent one" (29). Although Fanny is only to be moved across the park, the prospect of being moved at all evokes memories of abandonment and implies a repetition of her traumatic displacement from Portsmouth to Mansfield. Also, she knows that as Mrs. Norris's sole companion she will be subject to relentless bullying with no possibility of protection or escape.

Students often recall the ensuing dialogue as one in which Fanny defers meekly and completely to Edmund's authority. Reading it for the first time, they have often focused on its content without much regard for context or tone. This scene provides an excellent opportunity for dramatic reading. I divide the class into pairs and ask students to discuss and annotate the dialogue as though it were a script. Like professional actors preparing to perform, they make and justify decisions about tone, pacing, and emphasis. When it comes time to read portions of the scene aloud, the performances lead to productive discussion. Generally, the conversation reflects students' growing awareness both of how little control Fanny has over her circumstances and how determined and resourceful she is in her efforts to convince Edmund that she ought not be sent away.

Her opening speech is surprisingly bold. It reminds us that she and Edmund have disagreed before and that, as his pupil, she has some room in which to express her views. He presents a measured, intellectual argument. She counters with strong expressions of feeling. In response to his hope that the proposed plan doesn't distress her very much, she asserts, "Indeed it does. I cannot like it. I love this house and every thing in it. I shall love nothing there" (29; vol. 1, ch. 3). As her short sentences transform negative claims ("I do not like") into positive assertions ("I love"), her verbs intensify in parallel grammatical structures: she progresses from "like" ("I do not like," "I cannot like it") to "love" ("I love this house and everything in it. I shall love nothing there").

Austen captures, with gentle irony, the speech patterns of an unworldly fifteen-year-old. At the same time, Fanny's assertions represent the beginnings of an argument, and this argument, combined with her emotional intensity, throws into relief the detached, analytic nature of Edmund's approach. When I ask the class which character they would ask to join their debate team, many choose Fanny, impressed by her warmth but also by her rhetorical flexibility. Whereas Edmund elaborates a single argument, Fanny shifts tone and tactics several times. Early in the dialogue, she appeals to Edmund directly, as though trying to shift his focus from the realm of the ideal to the concrete and from the impersonal to the personal: "You know how uncomfortable I feel with her" (29).

When Edmund introduces the word "important," Fanny's tone shifts again: "I can never be important to any one," she replies (29). At first, student readers may cringe. Taken out of context, this claim connotes self-pity and may even appear disingenuous. But when we recall how much Fanny yearns to be important, this resonant word reminds us of the extent of her hurt and disappointment. Indeed, she takes a risk; her words fairly invite the response that she wants to hear but that is not forthcoming: "You will always be important to me."

This dialogue reveals Fanny's strength but also one of Edmund's limitations. Edmund means well by Fanny but is unaware of the horror with which she views the proposed move. Although she cannot alter his opinion, her words clearly affect him. We may gauge her rhetorical power through an analysis of his responses. As the scene progresses, his manner becomes increasingly rigid. When Fanny alludes to her "foolishness" and "awkwardness," he frames his response as a lesson on false modesty and linguistic propriety: "[Y]ou never have a shadow of either, but in using the words so improperly." He praises her, yet in doing so he turns an intimate, awkward moment into a lesson on proper speech. Then he addresses her in a manner he has actively discouraged in others, reminding her that she is not just a pupil but also a poor relation: "You have good sense, and a sweet temper, and I am sure you have a grateful heart, that could never receive kindness without wishing to return it" (30).

In Edmund's compliment, the reader hears an echo of Fanny's recent conversation with her aunt Bertram, and Fanny, so attuned to questions of gratitude, surely does as well. A comment from Lady Bertram as to how comfortable a life Fanny has led up to now prompted Fanny to say, "I hope I am not ungrateful, aunt." To this the older woman responded with characteristic incomprehension, "No, my dear; I hope not" (28). This layer of dramatic irony adds to the poignancy of Fanny's response to Edmund: "'You are too kind,' said Fanny, colouring at such praise; 'how shall I ever thank you as I ought for thinking so well of me? Oh! cousin, if I am to go away, I shall remember your goodness, to the last moment of my life'" (30). Coming from Edmund, any implication of ingratitude is one that Fanny will take seriously; she hears "praise," perhaps, but also reproach.

Fanny has plenty of reason to feel angry but expertly channels anger into self-reproach. That she begins the speech with a stilted, conventional phrase, "You are too kind," suggests that she requires a moment in which to collect herself. At once devastated and grateful, she articulates the terms of internal conflict in a substantial and moving speech:

> Fanny sighed, and said, "I cannot see things as you do; but I ought to believe you to be right rather than myself, and I am very much obliged to you for trying to reconcile me to what must be. If I could suppose my aunt to really care for me, it would be delightful to feel myself of conse-

quence to any body! —*Here*, I know I am of none, and yet I love the place
so well." (30–31)

In this heartbreaking address to the only person in the household whom she
loves and trusts, she exhibits deep feeling and remarkable poise. Adopting his
vocabulary ("ought," "obliged") and echoing his figures of speech, she conveys
her readiness to accept his teaching but stops well short of agreement. An instructor might point to this speech as an example of the delicate and intricate
verbal patterning characteristic of the dialogue as a whole. Fanny's "*Here*"
echoes Edmund's earlier antithesis: "*Here*, there are too many, whom you can
hide behind, but with *her* you will be forced to speak for yourself" (30). Austen
buries in Fanny's concession speech a concise expression of what Fanny has
recognized from the beginning as the fundamental flaw in Edmund's argument:
Mrs. Norris doesn't love her. Although Edmund ignores this crucial point, Austen vindicates Fanny a few lines later: "So ended their discourse, which, for any
very appropriate service it could render Fanny, might as well have been spared,
for Mrs. Norris had not the smallest intention of taking her" (31).

Annotating, performing, and discussing this dialogue in class help students
discover the subtlety with which Austen shows that what Fanny says and what
she feels are not always the same and that she is capable of rhetorical force and
exceptional self-control. Most important, perhaps, they see that Fanny, even
when powerless, can maintain an independent perspective.

From a scene composed mainly of dialogue, we turn to one in which Fanny
says little: the sofa scene, near the end of chapter 7. Knowing that Fanny is shy
and physically frail, the class may at first see nothing surprising in her having
passed part of an evening hiding on a sofa. But when we work through the
scene, focusing on its dramatic qualities and, more specifically, on the implications of spatial positioning, physical gestures, and shifts in narrative perspective,
her disappearance and return acquire multiple levels of meaning.

This scene reminds us again of Fanny's precarious position in the household.
Now eighteen, Fanny has not been sent away, but since Mary Crawford's arrival,
Edmund seems barely to notice her. Austen asks us to imagine much of the
scene in spatial terms; even as she sets it up, she associates social importance
with freedom of movement and command of space. When Mary wants to ride
the mare farther than usual, Edmund obtains Fanny's permission. But one excursion leads to another, and by the time Fanny retreats to the sofa, the young
people have spent four consecutive mornings on horseback, leaving her confined, in hot weather, to the house, the grounds, and the company of the aunts.
Images of Fanny's physical confinement and later references to back-and-forth
walks between houses literalize her condition at Mansfield: circumscribed by
her obligations as a dependent and wishing to avoid the appearance of ingratitude, Fanny is boxed in.

Starting with the paragraph that begins, "Between ten and eleven," I ask the
class to visualize the scene as it unfolds (83). Returning from the Parsonage,

Edmund and Julia enter the drawing room, where they converse with Maria, Lady Bertram, and Mrs. Norris. It is Edmund who notices Fanny's absence:

> . . . when the first pause came, Edmund, looking around, said, "But where is Fanny?—Is she gone to bed?"
>
> "No, not that I know of," replied Mrs. Norris; "she was here a moment ago."
>
> Her own gentle voice speaking from the other end of the room, which was a very long one, told them that she was on the sofa.   (83)

Austen arranges for her readers to share in the assembled characters' surprise; she has described aspects of the scene in detail but without mentioning Fanny's presence. The unexpected intimacy of the moment is affecting. Fanny has almost disappeared for want of attention; Edmund's question, by establishing her importance, brings her back.

Austen creates the impression that Fanny is present, but just barely. Her "voice," though audible, is "gentle" to the degree that the narrator must confirm it is "her own." Breaking with the dialogue to which we have grown accustomed, Austen adds to the illusion that Fanny is at once present and absent. She enters the scene as a "voice": her "voice . . . told them that she was on the sofa." The characters hear her words, but we do not.

While the length of the room may at first seem unimportant, much of the scene's effect depends on it. Fanny speaks from "the other end of the room, which was a very long one." The comment closely resembles a stage direction. It asks us to visualize the action in spatial terms and, as we do so, to reflect on what Fanny has done. Imagining the scene as it might appear on a stage, we picture all the characters except Fanny gathered at or near a table toward one end of the long room. Given the late hour, between "ten and eleven," which Edmund and Julia confirm with their discussion of a detail Austen reinforces by having Edmund and Julia refer to starry skies, the table must be illuminated, perhaps by candles or an oil lamp. Fanny's voice originates in the room's shadowy outer reaches. As Fanny returns to the table (a journey Austen doesn't describe), she moves from relative darkness into the light.

As these events unfold, the question arises: how did Fanny end up on the sofa? Conversation reveals that earlier that evening, when no one was paying attention, she left the table where she was sewing, walked across the room, and settled on a sofa at its edge. Students recognize the location's metaphorical significance: her position in the room reflects her status in the household: she is both family member and outsider, neither fully in nor out. She feels at home in the margin. But it is one thing to rest there silently and another to speak and then emerge.

The class may now appreciate multiple ironies. Fanny, who takes such pains to remain unobtrusive, resembles an actress making an entrance. Her absence proves more influential than her presence ever has. Her disembodied voice suggests a haunting, a return of the repressed: the Bertrams must acknowledge a figure whom they all (except for Edmund) would prefer to forget.

To work out the scene's implications more fully, I point to the tonal shift that occurs once Fanny, now a physical presence, has returned and characters try to account for her behavior. While Mrs. Norris dismisses her action as a "foolish trick," Edmund, after looking at her "attentively," decides she has a headache (84). From this point on, as she and her headache become the subject of general conversation, romantic intimacy gives way to an awkwardly public (and very funny) denouement during which Edmund pieces together the story of a day Fanny spent cutting roses and walking, twice, to Mrs. Norris's house and back. The climax comes when, in a speech nominally addressed to his mother but meant for Mrs. Norris's ears as well, he expresses his dismay: "Upon my word, ma'am, it has been a very ill-managed business" (85). Reminded by Mrs. Norris of his role in this debacle—he has treated Fanny as though she were of no importance—he resolves to "check a pleasure of Miss Crawford's" so that Fanny may resume riding (87).

Austen might have ended the scene and chapter on this gratifying note—a paragraph detailing Edmund's self-reproaches. But the final paragraph, strongly colored by Fanny's perspective, reveals that Edmund's explanation is incomplete: her retreat to the sofa resulted less from physical weakness than from the strength of her feelings. She had been "feeling neglected, and been struggling against discontent and envy for some days past. As she leant on the sofa, to which she had retreated that she might not be seen, the pain of her mind had been much beyond the pain in her head" (87). Fanny left the table when she was no longer able to suppress or conceal "discontent and envy"—feelings she considers inappropriate and against which she had been "struggling for days." Students should compare Fanny's and Maria's behavior in this scene. Upset at having been excluded from dinner at the Grants', Maria struggles to conceal her vexation in public; at home, however, she enacts it freely, albeit indirectly, by "throw[ing] as great a gloom as possible over . . . dinner and dessert" (83). Fanny suffers daily from the effects of exclusion but can't afford, even at home, to act as Maria does, in a manner we might now label passive-aggressive. When Fanny can no longer conceal her feelings, she conceals herself.

By presenting Fanny's perspective at the end of the chapter, Austen prompts us to revisit the scene from the beginning. From this vantage, Fanny's retreat appears less as a retreat than as an episode in an ongoing struggle not just to control her feelings for Edmund but to maintain a sense of self. Driven by feeling and circumstance to act, a heroine who can do almost nothing manages to do just enough. When Edmund's question presents her with an opportunity to speak, she responds as if on cue.

Asked why Fanny didn't simply go to bed, as Edmund first assumes, students often volunteer that she is waiting up for him, hoping to hear him return. This explanation might lead to further reflection: Fanny seeks privacy but not exclusion. Too upset to remain at the table, she will not leave the room, since to remove herself entirely would be to accept the position in which she has been, to accept her unimportance. When she speaks from the sofa she reveals more than her location. She has made a place for herself that she conceals and reveals on her own terms. Without jeopardizing her position as poor relation, she brings about a small, but significant change. It is change of precisely the sort that someone who has been struggling for days with feelings of neglect and envy might want: Edmund pays attention, the aunts suffer a rebuke, and Mary is deprived of a pleasure. The last words of chapter 7—"the sudden change which Edmund's kindness had . . . occasioned, made her hardly know how to support herself"—describe the intense emotional transformation Fanny's small actions set in motion (87). After the structural pause of the chapter break, the first sentence of chapter 8 is blunt in noting the practical effect of her return from absence: "Fanny's rides recommenced the very next day" (88).

Scenes from chapters 3 and 7 depict Fanny's efforts to retain a place in the household and in Edmund's field of attention. In chapter 7, intense feeling, accompanied by minimal action, generates concrete change. Indirectly and inadvertently, Fanny reveals how poorly she has been treated. Austen, through Edmund's rebuke ("it has been a very ill-managed business"), links her treatment to the theme of domestic disorder and mismanagement.

The third scene we discuss, which is set in the chapel of another great house, demonstrates what happens when Fanny tries, at this early stage of the novel, to intervene directly in personal and social affairs. Her attempt to influence those around her fails, but Austen uses the scene to suggest that Fanny now has the knowledge and confidence to reform the household, were anyone willing to listen.

Austen introduces the idea of the Sotherton trip in chapter 8, directly after the sofa scene. Another crisis of exclusion looms—Mrs. Norris wants to leave Fanny at home—but Edmund, newly resolved to look out for Fanny's interests, insists that Fanny be permitted to go. She has looked forward to the visit and to sharing the experience with him. But when they arrive, he seems distracted; when she speaks to him "in a low voice," disappointed that the chapel is so plain, he reminds her, somewhat dismissively, that it is of relatively recent construction (100; ch. 9).

Always careful in her arrangement of characters, Austen positions Edmund, Mary, and Fanny in a "cluster." Having just heard Mrs. Rushworth explain that the chapel is no longer in use, Mary responds first, "with a smile, to Edmund," "every generation has its improvements." Then Fanny, the least important member of the trio, addresses not just Edmund but Mary as well:

> "It is a pity," cried Fanny, "that the custom should have been discontinued. It was a valuable part of former times. There is something in a chapel and chaplain so much in character with a great house, with one's ideas of

what such a household should be! A whole family assembling regularly for the purpose of prayer, is fine!"   (101)

Rarely, if ever, does Fanny speak so forcefully as to cry anything. Her outburst raises the question of what prompts her to speak in this way, at this moment, and in this place. One factor might be setting: Sotherton is relatively neutral territory. Away from Mansfield, Fanny may feel slightly less like a poor relation. As Edmund's protégée, she understands the ideals behind the tradition of the great house. Confident in her own view, she attempts to improve Mary's.

Although Mary laughs it off, Fanny's speech in the chapel as to what the character of a great house should be marks an essential step in her gradual emergence as one who will someday be important to the Bertrams, as Fanny was to her siblings at Portsmouth. Mary's levity jars Fanny's seriousness, but Mary's reference to "improvements" offends in part because Fanny increasingly sees her role at Mansfield as that of a quiet, cautious improver (101). One might hope to hear more from Fanny, but Austen demands patience of her readers, and Fanny's tiredness allows Edmund and Mary to leave her alone on a bench while they proceed with their ramble. Left behind, Fanny tries to control her feelings, but she also tries to intervene—warning Maria, for example, not to circumvent the gate. Maria laughs, as Mary did, but Fanny has developed to the point where she is confident enough to try to correct what she understands, more clearly than anyone, to be a deteriorating moral situation that will, in time, ruin Maria's reputation and jeopardize that of the family.

Having worked through these early scenes, students recognize Fanny as a complex creation—one that now inhabits the classroom as a compelling fictional presence. When, at the end of volume 1, we reach the theatricals, students appreciate her dilemma more fully. They hear greater resonance in her declaration, "No, indeed, I cannot act," recognizing that she is not just saying that she cannot perform, or even that she cannot feign, but—this is just one of many layers of meaning—that her situation allows her to do very little (171; ch. 15). Most important, they see that when she is asked to perform the role of Cottager's Wife, what Tom Bertram refers to as "a nothing of a part, a mere nothing," adding that "it will not much signify if nobody hears a word you say," she is being asked—and for as long as possible refuses—to perform her unimportance (171).

Ambiguities of the Crawfords

Peter W. Graham

Henry and Mary Crawford, arguably Jane Austen's most controversial sibling pair, have exerted a strong appeal on readers all the way back to the author's time, when her favorite brother, Henry, hoped his charming namesake would gain the hand of the heroine in the novel his sister was writing. Readerly resistance to the ordained marital outcome has persisted up to the present day, in the classroom and beyond. The endurance of this errant response suggests that twenty-first-century dislike of the union that ends *Mansfield Park* is not simply because a later audience endorses manners, morals, and relationships between the sexes that are freer than and radically different from those of Austen's day or because it disapproves of first-cousin marriage more than people in her milieu generally did. It's also true—and, I would argue, crucial—that many readers, then and now, fell and still fall for the lively, healthy, humorous Crawfords rather than for the restrained and self-effacing Fanny Price and Edmund Bertram and find the Crawfords better complements to Fanny and Edmund than the cousins are to each other.

The better such resistant readers know the Austen canon, the likelier they may be to believe that both Crawfords, quite apart from their personal accomplishments, pass Austen's crucial test for marrying one of her heroines or heroes, which is that they appreciate and continue to love that heroine or hero in the face of discouraging circumstances. Granted, the Crawfords don't love Fanny and Edmund unselfishly. But despite the evidence of worldly self-interest and despite Fanny's and Edmund's deficiency of charm, the Crawfords form an attachment that does not diminish in the course of the novel. For Henry especially, it takes what some would see an unconvincing manipulation of plot to cause the lapse that results in his losing the chance to win and wed the admirable, principled heroine he loves.

When I teach Austen's novels, *Mansfield Park* invariably proves to be the one in which the most students wish that the marital outcome had turned out another way, with Fanny and Edmund married to Crawfords rather than to each other. What makes the Crawfords so compelling notwithstanding the serious moral reservations careful readers must have about them? I account for this response through attention to character development, tone, and ethical principles in a remarkably provisional narrative, where the seldom voiced yet ever-evident possibilities of an alternate, equally plausible outcome are seductive.[1]

The attractiveness of the Crawfords doesn't mean that Fanny, the novel's ethical center, lacks supporters, particularly among those readers who take Austen most seriously as a writer concerned with moral philosophy. Alasdair McIntyre sees constancy as the keynote to Fanny's nature and argues that Fanny "has only the virtues, the genuine virtues, to protect her" (242). Henry and Mary Crawford notably lack her constant virtue and virtuous constancy. Instead, they possess a parallel but not necessarily opposing pair of qualities: mobility and charm. Charm, in contrast to virtue, is a matter of style rather than substance, a simulacrum rather than the real thing, though a charming exterior may have virtue underneath. Wit, energy, and empathy (within the limits of their moral imaginations) contribute to the Crawfords' charm; and each of these qualities, though good in many ways, can and sometimes does go offtrack in the narrative. Mobility, which at first glance seems even more different from constancy than charm seems from virtue, is a natural, not a cultivated trait. It involves being true to an ever-changing self and thus is the kind of constancy that is possible when human nature is seen as dynamic rather than static and when truths are seen as subjective and contingent rather than universally acknowledged and transcendent. Mobility promotes qualities—openness, flexibility, playfulness—that are different from those constancy encourages and that all have both positive and negative potential.

The Crawfords are characterized by an interplay of temperamental mobility, stirrings of nobility, flawed nurture, and close dependence on each other. These traits delight readers and charm many of the characters in *Mansfield Park*. They also doom the Crawfords to fail in their pursuit of Fanny and Edmund, the partners who could, above all others, unite with them in mutually beneficial ways. The critical question: does Austen stack the deck against Henry and Mary? It is easy for partisans of the Crawfords to feel that she does. But I suspect the author knew that many of her readers would fall for the Crawfords, even meant them to, and accordingly laid out her novel with a plausible counterscenario that shadows the scenario actually set before us. In such a work, the outcome will be determined less by authorial intent, however overt that seems in the concluding pages of *Mansfield Park*, than by the contingencies of choice, chance, and character.

Just who are these Crawfords anyway? Austen typically introduces novelty in one of two ways: her heroines encounter new people and situations by moving to or visiting new places, or their established country neighborhoods change by dint of newcomers. The Crawfords enliven Mansfield Park as newcomers. Their older half sister is Mrs. Grant, whose clerical husband has bought a life incumbency of the parish living from Sir Thomas Bertram. Orphans raised in fashionable Mayfair by their uncle Admiral Crawford and his recently deceased wife, Henry and Mary come to Mansfield because the widowed admiral brought his mistress under his roof: for propriety's sake Mary must live elsewhere. Her personal fortune is 20,000 pounds. Henry, educated at Westminster School and Cambridge, has an annual income of 4,000 pounds and a Norfolk estate, Everingham. The siblings' ages and birth order are not disclosed, but we can infer that Mary is some years beyond minimally marriageable age, and we soon learn that Henry is over twenty-one (he says that at that age he had completely carried out his youthful plans for improving Everingham) but still young enough for what Sir Thomas calls an early marriage (366; vol. 3, ch. 1).

Personally, the Crawfords are small, dark, and lively; Mary is "extremely pretty" (74; vol. 1, ch. 7), and Henry, though not handsome, is so charismatic as to be exceedingly attractive. The Crawfords are sophisticated cosmopolites. Henry can't stay settled on his estate even to give his sister a home; Mary is suf- ficiently out of touch with country ways to be surprised that in the midst of hay harvest there's not a horse-drawn "waggon or cart" to transport her harp (68; ch. 6); and French words are associated with them throughout the novel. Mary even observes of Henry, "If you can persuade Henry to marry, you must have the address of a Frenchwoman. All that English abilities can do, has been tried already" (49; ch. 4).

Although Henry's asserted and demonstrated proclivity is to flirt and evade marriage whereas "[m]atrimony was [Mary's] object, provided she could marry well" (48), the two are very much on the same wavelength. Well-bonded sibling pairs are rare in Austen's work, but it is perhaps unique that the personalities of the Crawfords are similar, not complementary. Both unite playfulness with keen intelligence—an intoxicating combination that seldom fails to charm read- ers or the denizens of Mansfield Park, Fanny excepted. However edgy the wit- ticisms, such as Mary's quip on admirals, "Of *Rears*, and *Vices*, I saw enough" (71; ch. 6), most readers are likely to concur with Edmund in thinking a lively mind "seizing whatever may contribute to its own amusement or that of others; perfectly allowable, when untinctured by ill humour or roughness" (75; ch. 7). But some of what pleases in the Crawfords raises, however subtly, a red flag. In Austen's novels, a London connection does not bode well, unless the Londoner is originally from the country and still attached to it. Cosmopolitan associations stand against Englishness, which connotes soundness. And verbal play, though engaging, is dangerous—even in heroines but especially in men. Austen's other fictional Henry, Tilney of *Northanger Abbey*, is the only male wit who marries one of her heroines.

In the first phase of acquaintance with the worldly Crawfords—the brother idly aiming to make the Bertram ladies like him, the sister deploying her charms to more practical purpose, but neither contemplating what could be called crime by any stretch of the moral imagination—readers are given many rea- sons to be suspicious of them. The narrator sometimes explicitly and sometimes implicitly points to their calculating natures. Henry, for example, "did not want [the Bertram sisters] to die of love; but with sense and temper which ought to have made him judge and feel better, he allowed himself great latitude on such points" (52; ch. 5). Mary's point of view on the superior appeal of Tom the heir over Edmund the younger son is similarly assessed: "She had felt an early pre- sentiment that she *should* like the eldest best. She knew it was her way" (55). It is important that Fanny, early established as the novel's most reliable judge of morals, distrusts both Crawfords.

Mary's practical preference for elder sons and Fanny's own apprehensions aside, Edmund soon falls in love with Miss Crawford, "and to the credit of the lady it may be added, that without his being a man of the world or an elder brother, without any of the arts of flattery or the gaieties of small talk, he be- gan to be agreeable to her" (76–77; ch. 7). The situation precipitating this rapprochement is, says the narrator, a formula for love: "A young woman, pretty, lively, with a harp as elegant as herself; and both placed near a window, cut down to the ground, and opening on a little lawn, surrounded by shrubs in the rich foliage of summer, was enough to catch any man's heart" (76). Whether she seems an angel in the house or a siren luring men to destruction, the contriver of this romantic *tableau vivant* is the harpist herself, an avowedly worldly husband hunter who yet is disinterestedly attracted to a man seriously worth admiring—a woman who might be able to "feel" the charm of "his sincerity, his steadiness, his integrity . . . though not equal to discuss with herself" these attributes or her feeling (77). Does an ambiguously characterized attachment of this sort suggest that Miss Crawford plays with the angels or the sirens?

That she is meant to be seen as on the tempter's side, like her brother, becomes clearer in the Sotherton episode, which mingles several major themes of the novel: ordination, the "improvement" of estates (62; ch. 6), nature versus artifice. On the road to Sotherton, the seat of the Rushworths and thus Maria Bertram's future home but also Henry's momentary candidate for an extreme, avenue-abolishing makeover, Mary and Fanny differ "in every thing but a value for Edmund. . . . She [Mary] had none of Fanny's delicacy of taste, of mind, of feeling; she saw nature, inanimate nature, with little observation; her attention was all for men and women, her talents for the light and lively" (94; ch. 8). The contrast emerges still more dramatically in Sotherton's chapel, where Mary's wry comment on the leaving off of family prayers, "Every generation has its improvements," both inspires Fanny's earnest defense of the institution as "a valuable part of former times" (101; ch. 9) and blows up in her own face when, "almost aghast" (104), she learns that Edmund is destined to be a clergyman.

Mary sees her offense as a matter of manners, not morals, and it is important to note that this kind of transgression is typical. It sometimes surprises my students to realize that whether we consider her a bad girl or not, Mary Crawford never actually does anything that could be termed immoral. Her offenses are verbal. If we assume that Mary's words literally externalize her feelings and values, as Fanny's words externalize hers, they manifest what Edmund calls "a corrupted, vitiated mind" (528; vol. 3, ch. 16). If we assume that words reflect values and that momentary thoughts are consistent with inner principles, then even when Mary behaves properly we may conclude that it is because she's following the dictates of etiquette, not a moral code—or, as Kierkegaard in *Either/Or* might put it, because she is a creature of the aesthetic realm, not the realm of ethics. Her brother, of course, behaves culpably at Sotherton in trifling with the engaged Maria Bertram and thereby troubling her dim fiancé. But whether we are inclined to consider Henry's flirtation and Mary's free speech as sins or indiscretions, the rhetorical and narrative details of the Sotherton episode consistently imply and occasionally assert the moral sketchiness of both siblings. An aura of corruption progressively intensifies around them, especially if we accept the narrator's and Fanny's views as valid.

Having already been tainted by traits generally suspect in Austen's novels—a taste for capricious improvement of estates in Henry's case, mockery of the clergy in Mary's—both Crawfords are cast in the role of tempters by the fact that a key part of the exploration of Sotherton takes place in what is called the "wilderness" (105; vol. 1, ch. 9) This artfully uncultivated landscape, set off by iron fencing and a ha-ha, provides the backdrop as Henry lures Maria, who compares herself to the imprisoned starling in Sterne's *Sentimental Journey*, to escape from her actual and figurative restraints by squeezing through the hedge beside the locked gate with him while her fiancé goes for the keys and the admonitory Fanny sits like a guardian spirit at Eden's portal. This quasi-natural spot is also where Edmund, walking with Fanny and Mary (his good and bad angels) on either arm and following what is significantly described as a "very serpentine course" (110), hears Mary's further disparagement of the clergy and her preference that men be more ambitious. At this point he stands his ground, decisively disagreeing with Mary. She assumes that London clergy of her acquaintance are typical because "[t]he metropolis, I imagine, is a pretty fair sample of the rest," to which he replies "Not, I should hope, of the proportion of virtue to vice" (108). If his sister Maria figures as an Eve tempted by the flexibly serpentine Henry, Edmund's situation here more closely resembles Christ's temptation in the wilderness, with the metropolitan coquette's arguing the satanic case that excellent men should seek to distinguish themselves, not simply perform the obscure duties to which they are called.

It's clear that the *Lovers' Vows* episode is set up to be a moral litmus test in *Mansfield Park*, so students are sometimes surprised when I claim that it seems inappropriate for this test to be applied to the Crawfords. The chief problem facing the Bertram household is that by staging the play in Sir Thomas's absence and transforming his sanctum into their green room, they are going against his patriarchal values, a loosely biblical sort of failing. The Crawfords, new to the neighborhood, can hardly be expected to know how to respect the rules and feelings of a man they have never met. Yet they are judged along with the household. The narrator's metaphors for the theatricals—"an itch for acting," a "bewitching" prospect—are negative from the start (143; ch. 13). The narrator's over-the-top language makes Henry's enthusiasm seem a sinister sensuality: "Henry Crawford, to whom, in all the riot of his gratifications it was yet an untasted pleasure, was quite alive at the idea" (144–45). Henry goes on accurately to describe his own mobility in similar hyperbole: "I could be fool enough at this moment to undertake any character that ever was written, from Shylock or Richard III. down to the singing hero of a farce in his scarlet coat and cocked hat. I feel as if I could be any thing or every thing . . ." (145). And so he can, as he later demonstrates in the extemporized reading from *Henry VIII* that allows him to gain ground in Fanny's esteem by showing his intelligent empathy to advantage: "[H]e could always light, at will, on the best scene, or best speeches of each; and whether it were dignity or pride, or tenderness or remorse, or whatever were to be expressed, he could do it with equal beauty. . . . His acting had first taught Fanny what pleasure a play might give, and his reading brought all his acting before her again" (390; vol. 3, ch. 3).

As this passage shows, even Fanny has no moral objections to plays and acting in and of themselves. But staging *Lovers' Vows* at Mansfield Park with the roles cast as they are allows Henry and Maria, as Frederick and Agatha, to make otherwise inappropriate expressions of love, while Mary as Amelia can be saucy and forward to Edmund playing Anhalt, the young chaplain of Amelia's fancy. The moral problem of the Crawfords is their inclination to blend acting in one sense (feigning a feeling or character) with acting in another (translating one's feelings and character into words or deeds). Whatever the degree of individual culpability, the *Lovers' Vows* episode emphasizes the differences between Fanny's constancy and the Crawfords' mobility, between acting out one's unchanging essence and empathically acting many roles. The Crawfords, harpist sister and thespian brother, are performers. However superbly they may "act," they can't "act" in the one way Fanny can—so even if the specific moral litmus test of *Lovers' Vows* is not entirely relevant to them, they fall short of an important ethical standard.

The ambiguities of the Crawfords become yet more striking at the midpoint and hinge of the narrative, as Henry, with the Bertram sisters off in London, resolves on "making a small hole in Fanny Price's heart" (267; vol. 2, ch. 6) but ends up losing his own heart to her and proposing marriage. His initial, facetiously expressed resolution that for a fortnight Fanny should give him smiles and blushes, save a chair for him, be animated in his company, "think as I think, be interested in all my possessions and pleasures, try to keep me longer at Mansfield, and feel when I go away that she shall be never happy again," causes Mary archly to reply, "Moderation itself!" (269). Readers may feel more scruples than she does about his professed goal, though it is difficult to be totally clear as to how one should respond. Should Henry's flirting with shy, naive, but sound-principled Fanny strike us as worse than the same behavior was with her more polished, socially confident, but morally ungrounded cousins, whose hearts indeed were punctured in the process? Is treating other people as objects, as idle flirtation does, always wrong? Furthermore, where is the boundary between irony and sincerity in Henry's articulation of his seductive project and Mary's response to it? The Crawfords' ever-morphing blend of levity and sincerity and their shared penchant for verbal wit makes it difficult to judge the nature of their intentions or to know if these goals are single-minded and fixed or mixed and fluid even when the brother and sister are speaking in candid confidence to each other. Austen's narrator often glosses the Crawfords' conversations, but she too cannot always be read straightforwardly.

Moral and motivational ambiguity complicate the symbol-rich scene where the prettily worked necklace that Mary at her brother's unacknowledged behest gives Fanny for the ball contrasts with the plain gold chain Edmund offers, and the necklace proves unable to carry William Price's brotherly gift of a cross that Fanny hopes to wear to the ball in her honor. Mary's presentation of the

necklace blends generosity, consideration, duplicity, and perseverance in remarkably subtle ways. Her "affectionate earnestness" in offering a gift of friendship (300; vol. 2, ch. 8) is partly that; partly a loyal sister's serving her brother's
purposes without candid disclosure; and partly the shrewd creation of a theatrical effect, Mary's way of demonstrating benevolent generosity for Edmund
to see and value, as indeed he does when "gratified by their coincidence of
conduct" in providing for Fanny's accessorization (305; ch. 9). How far, readers
may ask, does the self-interest of an act compromise its generosity—and how
compromised does the Austen narrator mean us to judge that act to be?

Similarly, how does a frivolous impulse that eventually results in a wise decision or an admirable feeling color a reader's view of the action and the feeling?
When Henry Crawford finds that it is not Fanny's but his own heart that has a
small hole in it, proposes, and perseveres in wooing her and when Mary continues to hope to marry Edmund although his clerical life to be is at odds with
her worldly preferences, the Crawfords are displaying admirable feelings and
(even if in spite of themselves) commendable values. Some students feel that
the novel's concluding union of Edmund and Fanny is arbitrarily fictive rather
than emotionally convincing—as typified by the narrator's "I only intreat every
body to believe that exactly at the time when it was quite natural that it should
be so, and not a week earlier, Edmund did cease to care about Miss Crawford,
and become as anxious to marry Fanny, as Fanny herself could desire" (544;
vol. 3, ch. 17). Such readers argue that the Crawfords, who have grown and
deepened during their time at Mansfield, are flattened out to puppet libertines
to justify their dismissal and promote the ordained union of the virtuous first
cousins.

Chapter 12 of volume 2, containing Henry's admission of his intention to pro-
pose to Fanny and Mary's warm approval of the gesture, shows both Crawfords
to best advantage. Henry, whose attention to Fanny started with what Mary
mockingly calls his "wicked project upon her peace" and intensified when he
found Fanny more unusual and worthy a target than he had first supposed, now
truly loves her—and for exemplary reasons, totally ignoring her lack of fortune.
When he dwells on her charms, the narrator's direct report of his encomium
first mentions "Fanny's beauty of face and figure, Fanny's graces of manner and
goodness of heart" (341). He proceeds from these amiable qualities to her estimable traits of mind and manner and then beyond, deeper:

> Nor was this all. Henry Crawford had too much sense not to feel the
> worth of good principles in a wife, though he was too little accustomed
> to serious reflection to know them by their proper name; but when he
> talked of her having such steadiness and regularity of conduct, such a
> high notion of honour, and such an observation of decorum as might war-
> rant any man in the fullest dependence on her faith and integrity, he ex-
> pressed what was inspired by the knowledge of her being well principled
> and religious.

When his last words on Fanny are directly transcribed, he says, "I could so wholly and absolutely confide in her . . . and *that* is what I want" (341).

Even if we believe that Henry has not reflected on what to call some of the virtues he cherishes in Fanny, these are commendable traits to seek and value in a marriage partner in the world of Austen's novels. Mary, to her credit, can recognize all the good in his choice and endorse it without reservation: "I approve your choice from my soul, and foresee your happiness as heartily as I wish and desire it" (338). Fully alive to Fanny's luck in such a match and not exactly disinterested in welcoming such a connection for herself to the Bertram family, Mary is nonetheless wise enough to see how such a marriage will be good for Henry.

Her comment to Edmund after the "*fracas*" (509; vol. 3, ch. 15) that has ended both Maria's marriage to Rushworth and Henry's chances of winning Fanny is also wise and disinterested. "He has thrown away," Edmund reports Mary as having said, "such a woman as he will never see again. She would have fixed him, she would have made him happy for ever." This observation, a mobile character's endorsement of constancy, is a moment of penetrating insight in an interpretation that otherwise reveals Mary's wrongheadedness and, more important, wrong-heartedness, to Edmund. For her, the adulterous elopement of Henry and Maria has been "folly," not sin: as Edmund explains, "it was the detection, not the offence which she reprobated" (526; 16). In describing his last interview with Mary to Fanny, he at last recognizes that "I had never understood her before, and that, as far as related to mind, it had been the creature of my own imagination, not Miss Crawford, that I had been too apt to dwell on for many months past" (529–30). He judges her guilty of "faults of principle," not "faults of temper"—"of blunted delicacy and a corrupted, vitiated mind" (527–28).

The vitiated mind and cold heart had been long suspected by Fanny and directly revealed to her before Edmund's avowal, in a letter that strains narrative credibility. Just nine paragraphs after Fanny, though generally optimistic about her seriously ill cousin Tom's chances of recovery, has been musing that "Miss Crawford gave her the idea of being the child of good luck, and to her selfishness and vanity it would be good luck to have Edmund the only son" (498; ch. 14), Mary sends a letter in which commonplace expressions of sympathy for Tom and his family give way to callous humor: "Fanny, Fanny, I see you smile, and look cunning, but upon my honour, I never bribed a physician in my life. Poor young man!—If he is to die, there will be *two* poor young men less in the world; and with a fearless face and bold voice would I say to any one, that wealth and consequence could fall into no hands more deserving of them" (502). Coldly connecting an end of Tom to an eventual Sir Edmund at Mansfield Park is conceivable as a worldly woman's private, momentary thought. But it strains credibility that the perceptive Mary would put that thought in writing and imagine that earnest, loyal Fanny would "smile" and "look cunning" on reading it. Fanny's report of this selfish fantasy to Edmund puts the final nail, a superfluous one, in the coffin of Miss Crawford's chances with him. Nonetheless some readers may conclude that Mary has been set up to fail and feel some lingering regret at how she does. Unlike Edmund, who discovers he's loved a self-created illusion, Mary loved him for who he is, despite the religious vocation she doesn't understand and the principles her "corrupted" mind can't fathom.

If Edmund is provided with good and bad angels in Fanny and Mary, the Crawfords seem to be variously attracted by the moral gravity of good and bad places. The final fall of Mary involves, like her earlier sins, words, not deeds, but she reverts to her old self fairly soon after returning to the metropolis. Henry takes longer to lose the good influence of Mansfield Park, largely because of how and where he spends his time on leaving its orbit. Hopeful of winning Fanny, he first goes to Everingham and does what he imagines she would want: he tends to practical affairs, rides herd on his agent, improves things for some tenants. Then he visits Portsmouth, where he reports these activities to Fanny, who is gratified by more than these good deeds and his altered manner. In the naval city of Portsmouth she has been kept mindful of all he has done to further her brother William's career, and she appreciates by palpable contrast the blessings she took for granted in country house life, blessings she would be able as mistress of Everingham to confer on her promising younger sister Susan. In the way of a true gentleman, Henry brings out the best in both her parents and, the opposite of a worldly snob, takes what pleasure he can in her family circle, makes things easier for Fanny in that uncongenial environment, and tactfully evades the domestic encounters that would embarrass her.

Having persevered in his wooing despite Fanny's total lack of encouragement and despite having seen how far beneath him and the Bertrams the Price family is situated, Henry leaves for London still meaning to win Fanny and intending to return directly to Everingham. So why does he linger in the London suburbs for a mere party? On encountering Maria Rushworth and experiencing her coolness, why try to reinsinuate himself into her affections, a sign of inconstancy that in itself would be enough to lose Fanny, who reads the report of his flirtation as evidence "that he was not capable of being steadily attached to any one woman" (507; vol. 3, ch. 15)? When flirting with Maria evokes feelings more powerful than he'd imagined her to hold, why not withdraw his attentions instead of eloping? Fanny's hypothesis—"*his* unsettled affections, wavering with his vanity, *Maria's* decided attachment, and no sufficient principle on either side" (511)—half coincides with the narrator's explanation:

> He was entangled by his own vanity, with as little excuse of love as possible, and without the smallest inconstancy of mind towards her cousin. . . . All that followed was a result of her [Maria's] imprudence, and he went off with her at last, because he could not help it, regretting Fanny, even at the moment, but regretting her infinitely more, when all the bustle of the intrigue was over, and a very few months had taught him, by the force of

contrast, to place a yet higher value on the sweetness of her temper, the purity of her mind, and the excellence of her principles.

(541–42; ch. 17)

After the adulterers part, Henry's penalty is said to be the poignant self-punishment a man of sense would feel in his heart and head: "[N]o small portion of vexation and regret—vexation that must rise sometimes to self-reproach, and regret to wretchedness—in having so requited hospitality, so injured family peace, so forfeited his best, most estimable and endeared acquaintance, and so lost the woman whom he had rationally, as well as passionately loved" (542).

Nowhere else in the Austen canon does a love both rational and passionate turn out this way. And, the narrator tells us in the concise reportage of the tie-things-up-regarding-Henry-Crawford paragraphs concluded by the lines just quoted, the rational and passionate lover would have been well on his way to winning a wife were it not that he had, "ruined by early independence and bad domestic example, indulged in the freaks of a cold-blooded vanity a little too long" (540). The allegation of "cold-blooded vanity" is a curious charge to make against a true lover. How, if Henry both rationally and passionately loved Fanny, could the man of mobility's desire to be liked or loved by every passing woman have trumped the persevering lover's need to earn and win Fanny? Just how close he'd come the narrator goes on to say, subtly emphasizing the conditional nature of the outcome by interweaving indicative and subjunctive verbs:

> Her influence over him had already given him some influence over her. Would he have deserved more, there can be no doubt that more would have been obtained; especially when that marriage had taken place, which would have given him the assistance of her conscience in subduing her first inclination, and brought them very often together. Would he have persevered, and uprightly, Fanny must have been his reward—and a reward very voluntarily bestowed—within a reasonable period from Edmund's marrying Mary. (540)

The final chapter of *Mansfield Park* starts with an announcement that what has gone before has been but a fiction, a verbal contrivance the author could have taken in whatever direction she wished: "Let other pens dwell on guilt and misery. I quit such odious subjects as soon as I can, impatient to restore every body, not greatly in fault themselves, to tolerable comfort, and to have done with all the rest" (533). The ironist of these sentences has more often been an earnest moralist in *Mansfield Park*, but here she reminds her readers that she has invented these characters, events, and circumstances, not watched them unfold and judged them according to her principles. This foregrounding of fictionality encourages readers to ask why Austen tells the story this way, and posing this question is how I tend to conclude classroom discussions of *Mansfield*

Park. Why have Fanny Price be the heroine of a familiar Pygmalion plot—a mentor falls in love with the being he has shaped, whether before or after she falls in love with him—instead of the heroine of a plot that is even more popular with novel readers, that featuring a rake reformed by loving a good woman, whether he comes to deserve her before or after winning her heart? Why not finish the novel with Fanny as the mistress of her own country house and the wife of a man she will shape for the good rather than as the wife of a clergyman who is already good and in addition the very cousin who helped her develop the principles to which she is constant and whose eventual parish is tied to the great house where they both grew up?

The ethical answer to these questions is straightforward. The two young people constant to their principles unite, and either would be ill matched if joined to Mary or Henry, who are inconstant in their principles however constant their affections for Edmund and Fanny may be. A related pragmatic answer might follow the argument by William Deresiewicz and others that the novel is about educating readerly desire and retrospectively redirecting it away from an alliance with the charming Crawfords ("*Mansfield Park*" 85). For a contextually literary explanation, we might turn from contingencies of plot to those of oeuvre; recognize that Austen, a writer both constant and mobile, always varies her pattern; and remember that revising and publishing *Pride and Prejudice* (where Elizabeth Bennet combines Fanny's sound principles with Mary's sparkling liveliness, rejects her clerical first cousin's proposal, and eventually marries a social superior who makes her mistress of an estate distant from her home) immediately preceded the composing of *Mansfield Park*. But whatever her reasons for ending *Mansfield Park* as she did, Austen does not seem to deny the potential of what waited down the road not taken. Thanks to the fascinating ambiguities of the Crawfords, even if Fanny is kept from falling for Henry and Edmund is saved from Mary, the moral and narratological contingencies of *Mansfield Park* allow readers to imagine another, radically different conclusion.

NOTE

[1] The argument given here on the provisional nature of the *Mansfield Park* plot and the Crawfords' role in that plot is a condensed form of my essay "Falling for the Crawfords: Character, Contingency, and Narrative," *ELH* 77.4 (2010): 867–91.

Reading with *Mansfield Park*'s Readers

Susan Allen Ford

Readers of Jane Austen's novels meet readers in those novels. While Catherine Morland, in *Northanger Abbey*, is probably the most obvious example of a character whose reading affects—and effects—the novel's plot and shapes her view of the world, the books read by the characters of *Mansfield Park* operate in ways more complex. Fanny's moral seriousness and even her interiority are defined through her habits of reading. Her "fondness for reading" is one of the qualities that Edmund values, and their shared reading is central to their relationship: "[H]e recommended the books which charmed her leisure hours, he encouraged her taste, and corrected her judgment; he made reading useful by talking to her of what she read, and heightened its attraction by judicious praise" (25; vol. 1, ch. 2). Throughout the novel she is revealed to be a reader of poetry, essays, travel, drama. Her cousins and Henry Crawford, though not depicted in the kind of solitary reading in which she engages, have an acquaintance with drama that erupts into the rehearsals of *Lovers' Vows* and the seductive reading of speeches from *Henry VIII*.[1]

Many of the references to the texts that *Mansfield Park*'s characters read mean little to students beyond whatever information an edition's footnotes might provide. Setting students to explore these texts, then, can involve them in Austen's novel on a number of levels. They become engaged in an analysis of her tactics of characterization as well as of her interest in genre and her concern with gender. The cited texts offer another means of understanding the novel's historical context and can stimulate consideration of how readers read and how Austen's readers might have read, specifically, how references to other plots and other characters might have shaped readerly expectations of the plot and characters of *Mansfield Park*.

The works cited in the novel provide many avenues for student exploration. *Lovers' Vows* and *Henry VIII*, the plays that define the dramatic sections of the novel, present character types and narrative trajectories against which Austen's characters might be measured or might measure themselves. The many other plays mentioned provide thematic and generic contexts through which to understand her narrative choices. The poetry Fanny cites (particularly the lines from Cowper's *The Task* and Scott's *The Lay of the Last Minstrel*) or reads (Crabbe's *Tales*) suggests something of the color of her mind and imagination as well as something about contemporary social issues (Cowper, Crabbe) and the taste for romance (Scott, Crabbe). The prose Fanny is engaged with (an account of Macartney's embassy, Johnson's *Idler* essays) opens up a range of thematic and cultural connections.

It's often difficult for students to understand all the fuss about the novel's most visible intertext, the play chosen by the young people to while away the time before Sir Thomas's return from Antigua: Elizabeth Inchbald's *Lovers' Vows*, a 1798 adaptation of August von Kotzebue's 1790 play *Das Kind der Liebe*. The obvious interpretation for students—attributing an antitheatrical prejudice to Austen so that the very idea of playacting is condemned—is simplistic, given the Austen family's home theatricals and Austen's theatergoing in London and Bath. Specific knowledge of the play chosen is helpful, and in fact *Mansfield Park* assumes readers' knowledge of *Lovers' Vows*.[2]

Constructing with students a chart that defines the roles and the casting helps them discover how characters and character types are distributed. Status defined the distribution of parts at Ecclesford (vol. 1, ch. 13), but at Mansfield the heir to the estate chooses only small comic roles for himself.

DRAMATIS PERSONAE	**CASTING**		
	Ecclesford	**Mansfield**	**Rehearsal**
Baron Wildenhaim	Lord Ravenscroft	Mr. Yates	Fanny
Count Cassel	Mr. Yates	Mr. Rushworth	Fanny
Anhalt	Sir Henry?	Edmund Bertram	Fanny
Frederick	the duke	Henry Crawford	Fanny as prompter
Verdun the Butler		Tom Bertram	
Landlord		probably Tom Bertram	
Cottager		Tom Bertram	
Farmer			
Countryman			
Agatha Friburg	Lady Ravenscroft	Maria Bertram	Fanny as prompter
Amelia Wildenhaim	an "inimitable" lady	Mary Crawford	Fanny, almost
Cottager's Wife	the governess	Mrs. Grant	Fanny
Country Girl			

Students observe that the relations between actors and their roles are unexpected: Maria and Rushworth, the engaged couple, in contrast to Lord and Lady Ravenscroft, have no scenes together; Maria and Julia Bertram compete for the role of mother to Frederick (Henry Crawford), who has no romantic role in the play; Mr. Yates wants Julia to play his daughter, Amelia. (The erotic interests here turn oddly intergenerational.) In addition, the task Fanny has in helping the characters rehearse means that, despite her protestations against acting, she not only comes to know the play very well (as Maria, for example, recognizes) but also, as prompter and rehearsal partner, actually must speak much of it.

Recruiting students to run segments of act 1, scene 1, in which Frederick discovers his debilitated mother at the side of a road and then learns that he is illegitimate, and act 3, scene 2, in which Reverend Anhalt teaches his pupil Amelia about the good and bad of matrimony while she discloses her love for him, can provide a vivid sense of the language of sentimental drama that begins to pervade Fanny's consciousness, of the dangerous attraction of these two scenes, and of their complex implications.

A segment from act 1, scene 1, beginning with Frederick's entrance and ending just after Agatha reveals the name of her seducer takes about fourteen minutes to play. It makes palpable the emotional physicality of the sentimental stage, the dangers for Maria (and Henry), the reason for Mr. Rushworth's displeasure and Fanny's concern, and Mary's careless enjoyment of the flirtation. During this scene, as students will notice, the stage directions instruct Agatha and Frederick to embrace or touch five times; the actors might reasonably add physical contact in at least five more instances. The scene explores the dangerous relation between the courtship and seduction plots (the untrustworthiness of lovers' vows); warns of the importance of female chastity; finds the cause of Agatha's sexual fall in her vanity and her susceptibility to physical pleasure; and recounts her punishment, exclusion from society and even from her parents' household. All these issues, of course, are echoed in *Mansfield Park*.

The section of act 3, scene 2, that Mary and Edmund presumably rehearse before Fanny—from the beginning until the entrance of the rhyming butler—can be run in about nine minutes. While the turgid, overblown language of act 1, scene 1, is difficult for actors to present compellingly, act 3, scene 2, creates a charming contrast between the whimsical flirtatiousness of Amelia and the embarrassed stolidity of Anhalt. The role of Amelia, of course, is the subject of particular controversy both inside and outside the novel. Julia calls her an "odious, little, pert, unnatural, impudent girl" (160; vol. 1, ch. 14). Anne Plumptre, a competing translator of the play, argued that Inchbald had converted Kotzebue's Amelia from an "artless innocent Child of nature" into "a forward Country Hoyden" (v). The *Star*'s description of the actress who played Amelia evokes Edmund's image of Mary Crawford: she is "so fascinating in her air and smile—her coquetry is so playful that even her errors please us. . . .

[S]he plays the hoyden with so much grace, that we almost wish her to continue to trespass on truth, and please us by being wrong" (qtd. in Pedley 307).

As these descriptions suggest, act 3, scene 2, serves as a pointer to the ways womanhood is constructed on stage and in *Mansfield Park*. What qualities are valued? What behaviors are off-limits? This scene clarifies for those students who are more sympathetic to Fanny the charms of Mary Crawford. In addition to allowing Mary to say to Edmund what she cannot say otherwise, it also illuminates Fanny's character and highlights her limitation as a reader. Fanny has "read, and read the scene again" (196; ch. 18) but sees it only as an opportunity for Mary to declare her love for Edmund and Edmund to reciprocate. She doesn't see her own connection to Amelia: a young woman in love with her tutor, a love partly motivated by gratitude, a love that bridges the divide of class or status. Adding a third actor, a student who plays Fanny forced to watch Edmund and Mary playing Anhalt and Amelia, underscores the complex theatricality of Austen's scene.

Another strategy for helping students understand Austen's use of *Lovers' Vows* is to assign the entire play. The Mansfield players focus only on its seduction and courtship plots, but other elements open up fruitful discussion. Anhalt, the role that no one wants and that Edmund must be persuaded to take, is a clergyman, the voice of conscience in the play. The comparison between Anhalt's effectiveness and Edmund's ineffectiveness in the role is telling. Kotzebue's play also shows how relationships between parents and children can inhibit moral action and distort identity, an idea that looks forward to the generational tension of *Mansfield Park* and specifically to the conflict between Fanny and Sir Thomas. The baron's desertion of Agatha is a concession to maternal pressure; paternal power in *Lovers' Vows* is chastised but ultimately reformed and reinstated. A reading of *Lovers' Vows*, then, might lead students to consider how Austen's politics in her "condition of England" novel compare with Kotzebue's.

The other play that impinges on the plot of *Mansfield Park* is *Henry VIII*, which Fanny reads to Lady Bertram before Henry Crawford takes up the book. *Henry VIII: All Is True*, a play with which students are usually unfamiliar, is an anomaly among Shakespeare's plays, a historical pageant that forgoes both tragedy's plotted move toward anagnorisis and romance's sudden and total renewals. Henry's Crawford's reading invokes the dramatic expression of many characters and is disconnected from the temporal definitions of plot:

> The King, the Queen, Buckingham, Wolsey, Cromwell, all were given in turn; for with the happiest knack, the happiest power of jumping and guessing, he could always light, at will, on the best scene, or the best speeches of each; and whether it were dignity or pride, or tenderness or remorse, or whatever were to be expressed, he could do it with equal beauty.—It was truly dramatic.

Shakespeare is, he asserts, "part of an Englishman's constitution" (389–91; vol. 3, ch. 3)—*constitution* a word that simultaneously invokes the fundamental principles of government and society, the composition of the mind, the vitality of the body. His language is telling.

Henry's disclaimer of any special knowledge of the play provides a cue to how it might be incorporated into student projects and classroom presentation:

> . . . I do not think I have had a volume of Shakespeare in my hand before, since I was fifteen.—I once saw Henry the 8th acted.—Or I have heard of it from somebody who did—I am not certain which. But Shakespeare one gets acquainted with without knowing how. . . . His thoughts and beauties are so spread abroad that one touches them every where, one is intimate with him by instinct.   (390–91)

Although some editions of Shakespeare marked passages identified as "beauties" for the convenience of the reader, instinct here has probably been assisted by the beauties spread abroad through frequently reprinted anthologies of passages from Shakespeare's plays, such as William Dodd's *The Beauties of Shakespear* (1752 and thereafter); *The Beauties of Shakespeare*, published by Kearsley (1783); and Vicesimus Knox's *Elegant Extracts* (first published in 1783 and designed for use in schools). William Enfield's *The Speaker*, another school text, includes the entire scene between Wolsey and Cromwell beginning with Wolsey's "Farewell, a long farewell to all my greatness!" It seems less likely that Henry Crawford has read or seen *Henry VIII* than that he's encountered it in its fragmented state.

Which passages does he choose to read to Fanny and Lady Bertram? Students with access to a rare-book collection or *Eighteenth Century Collections Online* or *Google Books* might look at the *Beauties of Shakespeare* or *Elegant Extracts*, ranging through the sections on *Henry VIII* with an eye or ear for particularly resonant passages. Such a process encourages close attention to the relation between Shakespeare's language and Austen's. Wolsey's "Farewell, a long farewell"—a speech in which Henry Crawford might play as a repentant rejection of pride—is a favorite with students, especially for its opportunity for him to claim in front of Fanny, "Vain pomp and glory of this world, I hate ye! / I feel my heart new opened" (3.2.366–67).

Fanny has not been reading from a collection of *Beauties* or from *Elegant Extracts*. She is reading the play itself, in which characters both perform their emotional identity and are embedded in an overall action, however vaguely defined. Margaret Kirkham (114–16), Elaine Bander, and Marcia McClintock Folsom ("Part" 69–78) have all examined the relation between *Mansfield Park* and *Henry VIII* in terms of character and theme.[3] Bander points to similarities between Henry Tudor and Henry Crawford, seducers who are masked or engaged in playing roles—a link also traced to their shared absence of constancy (116–17). Both Kirkham and Folsom remark the scenic connection between novel and play, particularly between the scenes in which two men (Henry and Edmund, Wolsey and Campeius) enter a room in which two women are engaged in needlework to exert pressure on one of the women. Bander and Folsom explore similarities between Katherine and Fanny. Katherine is, in her own words, a "most poor woman, and stranger" (2.4.13), "true and humble . . . / At all times to your will conformable" (21–22), characteristics that Fanny might use to describe herself.

In addition to exploring the intertextual relation between Shakespeare's play and Austen's novel, students might want to analyze her technique in incorporating the play. Leaving to the reader's imagination the passages that Henry chooses, Austen describes his performance and its effect on Fanny. Patricia Howell Michaelson, in her study of eighteenth-century protocols of domestic reading, identifies the reader before a group as the figure "in a position of power," able to "censor texts and guide their interpretation" (141–42), a power that certainly has its impact on Henry's listeners. This oral reading adds another dimension to a novel that has already examined the effects of both acting in and watching a play, or at least a rehearsal of a play. As Henry reads, Edmund observes the needlework fall from Fanny's hand, her eyes "turned and fixed on Crawford, fixed on him for minutes, fixed on him in short till the attraction drew Crawford's upon her, and the book was closed, and the charm was broken," and her resulting blushes (390; vol. 3, ch. 3).

Lovers' Vows and *Henry VIII* are not the only plays cited in *Mansfield Park*. Before *Lovers' Vows* is settled on, "[a]ll the best plays were run over in vain. Neither Hamlet, nor Macbeth, nor Othello, nor Douglas, nor the Gamester, presented any thing that could satisfy even the tragedians; and the Rivals, the School for Scandal, Wheel of Fortune, Heir at Law, and a long etcetera, were successively dismissed with yet warmer objections." Rejected as "ranting tragedies," or because they have "[t]oo many characters," or "[n]ot a tolerable woman's part," or "buffoonery from beginning to end," or for "low parts" or being "insipid" (154; vol. 1, ch. 14), these repertory standards are quickly superseded by *Lovers' Vows* in the consciousness of the characters and of Austen's readers. But pausing to investigate those alternatives—perhaps by assigning individual students to consider the resonances of a particular play on the list—could open discussions of character types, thematic issues, and generic pressures.

In accord with the issues that Austen has defined in *Mansfield Park*, many of these plays center on parental authority and the bond between father and son—or sometimes between father and daughter or mother and son. This theme is a driving force in the tragedies, some of which will be familiar to students. *Hamlet* can be read as a play primarily about the vexed relationship between father and son, a play in which paternal authority is figured in the ghost of Old Hamlet and Claudius, the usurping stepfather. *Macbeth* depicts a more nationally defined filial loyalty, violated by the murder of Duncan and usurpation of his throne. And *Othello*, of course, begins with Desdemona's filial disobedience, which—despite her perception of "a divided duty" to husband and father (1.3.182)—is offered as a warning to her husband. In John Home's *Douglas* (1757), the tyrannical patriarch is dead, though the conflict has endured through the next generation; the defining situation of the play is the reunion between mother and long-lost son. Finally, the tragic hero of Edward Moore's *The Gamester* (1753) is Beverley, an improvident husband, brother, and father who gambles away the fortunes of all connected to him, including the expectations of his infant son—certainly a lesson to which Tom Bertram should attend.

Given the basic pattern of comedy, in which lovers meet an obstacle to their happiness that is finally overcome or removed, it's not astonishing that in many of the comedies considered and rejected by the Mansfield players the paternal figures act as comic blocks, improvident or flawed tyrants. In Richard Brinsley Sheridan's *The Rivals* (1775), Sir Anthony Absolute commands Jack to marry, a charge that the hero resists just until he realizes that the wife his father has chosen for him is the very Lydia Languish he's been courting (in disguise) all along. Jack's consequent playing of filial duty—"[I]f I can please you in the matter, 'tis all I desire"—is met with howls of frustration by Sir Anthony until he too is in on the joke (38; act 3, scene 1). Sheridan's *The School for Scandal* provides two patriarchs: one the disguised Oliver Surface, who tests his two nephews to discover which of them is worthy; the other Sir Peter Teazel, in thrall to a young wife and consequently trying to exert his authority over his ward, "whom I ought to have the power of a father over, [but who] is determined to turn rebel too" (240; act 1, scene 2). Surely Austen heard the echoes of this relationship as she inverted it for the more demure but equally resistant Fanny Price.

> *Sir Peter.* Go, perverse and obstinate! But take care, madam; you have never yet known what the authority of a guardian is—don't compel me to inform you of it.
> *Maria.* I can only say, you shall not have *just* reason. 'Tis true, by my father's will, I am for a short period bound to regard you as his substitute, but must cease to think you so, when you would compel me to be miserable. (259; act 3, scene 1)

Whereas Sir Peter's authority is so diminished by Lady Teazel that his threats aren't taken seriously, the authority of Sir Thomas, even though he expresses disappointment rather than threatens, is more than mere bluster, as his exile of Fanny to Portsmouth indicates.

Both Richard Cumberland's *The Wheel of Fortune* (1795) and *The Heir at Law* (1798), by George Colman the Younger, include flawed patriarchs who finally give way to the expected happiness of the younger generation. *The Wheel of Fortune* features an improvident father—a gamester—who has lost the fortune that should have passed to his heroic son, who was off fighting the French. *The Heir at Law*, the play Tom Bertram proposes for "about the fifth time . . . , doubting only whether to prefer Lord Duberley [sic] or Dr. Pangloss for himself" (155; vol. 1, ch. 14), is more comic than *The Wheel of Fortune*, getting its laughs from the farcical elements of class mobility, its drama from fathers who have died and an heir who has been lost at sea. Tom's preferred role in that play is neither the true nor the supposed heir, nor the defender of a sister's honor, but the broader buffoon types, Dr. Pangloss, "L.L.D. and A double S," and Lord Duberly, who realizes he's been "a kind of peer's warming pan" (84; act 5, scene 3), a description also defining Tom's position as regent at Mansfield Park.

It's also worthwhile noting the characters' objections to these plays—specifically the nonavailability of significant roles for women (a problem also with *Lovers' Vows*). The Shakespeare plays in particular are characterized, as Penny Gay has remarked, by "strong roles for male actors" (*Jane Austen* 10). Most of the plays considered define tragedy in terms of the fall of the male hero. From that perspective, tragedies begin, if not in happiness, at least with a sense of the hero's possible control over his destiny; his fall comes usually through his own error. The tragic heroine, by contrast, is (Lady Macbeth excepted) the suffering victim: Ophelia, Desdemona, Lady Randolph, and Mrs. Beverley are defined by a passive acceptance of their status, and all but one (Mrs. Beverley) end up dead. The patterns of female heroism provided by these tragedies suggest the dangers to which Sir Thomas Bertram's daughters are subject.

The options offered by these comedies aren't appealing, particularly for a young lady wanting to sigh and sob as virtue in distress. It's difficult to picture any of Mansfield Park's would-be actresses subsuming herself into Mrs. Malaprop or the assortment of older comic women in *The School for Scandal*. *The Rivals's* Lydia Languish is a witty ingénue, but others are pale versions: Lydia's cousin Julia, though suffering for love, is also somehow simultaneously all-forgiving and sensible; Emily Tempest (of *The Wheel of Fortune*) comes almost as close as Amelia does in *Lovers' Vows* to proposing marriage to the man she loves but lacks Amelia's wit; in *The Heir at Law*, with the plot again in male hands, the female characters have relatively small roles. These plays, and probably those of the "long etcetera" as well, again suggest the narrow range of roles—and of plots—for young women. There's something imprisoning in the choices before the women at Mansfield, and Austen makes that limitation clear through the dramatic roles they're able to consider.

Plays constitute much of what Mansfield's readers read or have read, but Fanny and Edmund are also readers of poetry and nonfiction prose, and they incorporate that reading into their conversation with each other. Kathryn Sutherland defines Cowper, Johnson, and Crabbe as "representing a wholesome programme of edifying family reading" (Introduction xxxviii). But Fanny's reading is also relatively current, and the poets to whom she gravitates mark the cultural shift toward Romanticism.

Plays are more amenable to classroom activity, but other texts to which Fanny and Edmund refer—particularly Scott's *Lay of the Last Minstrel*, Cowper's *The Task*, and accounts of Macartney's embassy to China—can provide valuable insights to students.

Fanny's quotation of *The Lay of the Last Minstrel* suggests her romantic and romanticizing nature. The story itself, most unlike *Mansfield Park*, involves war and the impulse to vengeance, magic, and the supernatural. Scott sets the narrative in a frame that emphasizes the distance between the present and the heroic past, between the past of this "last of all the bards" and an even deeper past about which he sings in his "ancient strain" (11, 15; introd.). Fanny's direct quotation of Scott's poem arises out of her disappointment with the chapel at Sotherton, where she finds only "a mere, spacious, oblong room, . . . with nothing more striking or more solemn than the profusion of mahogany, and the crimson velvet cushions" (100; vol. 1, ch. 9), instead of the midnight scene at Melrose Abbey, in which "Full many a scutcheon and banner, riven, / Shook to the cold night-wind of heaven / Around the screened altar's pale / And there the dying lamps did burn" (49; 2.10).

Cowper's *The Task* plays a more significant role in the novel. Fanny quotes Cowper in the discussion of estate improvement that precipitates so much of the novel's action: "Cut down an avenue! What a pity! Does not it make you think of Cowper? 'Ye fallen avenues, once more I mourn your fate unmerited'" (66; ch. 6). Located somewhere between Milton's *Paradise Lost* and Wordsworth's *The Prelude*, *The Task* is a confessional poem, a spiritual pilgrimage defined by its wandering movement from topic to topic, stance to stance, even—as Joseph Musser suggests—from audience to audience. Cowper looks at his world, both the landscape around Weston Underwood and in the world elsewhere, and his ruminations are by turns comic, nostalgic, celebratory, critical, guilty, angry, philosophic. Books 1 through 3 in particular take up the subjects of natural beauty, the church, London versus the country (especially in terms of virtue), England's connection to the wider world, abolition, adultery, gaming, landscape and its improvement.

The Task inspires much of Fanny's and Edmund's conversation, and it also informs the way Austen's readers understand the day at Sotherton and the stargazing scene. One example will serve as evidence of a larger pattern for investigation. Edmund's arguments about the importance of his chosen profession rely on Cowper, who defines the pulpit as "[t]he most important and effectual guard, / Support and ornament of virtue's cause" (*Poems* 62; bk. 2). In contrast to Mary Crawford's charge that the church is "never chosen" because "[m]en love to distinguish themselves and, . . . a clergyman is nothing" (107; vol. 1, ch. 9), Cowper presents the clergyman as "messenger of truth," "legate of the skies," hero, warrior, teacher:

> By him, the violated law speaks out
> Its thunders, and by him,
> . . . the gospel whispers peace.
> He stablishes the strong, restores the weak,
> Reclaims the wand'rer, binds the broken heart
> And arm'd himself . . . trains . . . to glorious war,
> The sacramental host of God's elect.   (63)

This passage presents the image that Fanny associates with the name Edmund: "a name of heroism and renown—of kings, princes, and knights; [that] seems to breathe the spirit of chivalry and warm affections" (246; vol. 2, ch. 4). Edmund's language is quieter but equally firm on the prime importance of the clergy, "which has the charge of all that is of the first importance to mankind, . . . which has the guardianship of religion and morals, and consequently of the manners which result from their influence" (107–08; vol. 1, ch. 9). Beyond the comparison of language and idea, beyond investigating the construction of character and the thematic issues involved, students might consider how Austen expects her readers to make sense of these connections. Does Cowper sound as a normative voice, or is there irony in Austen's invocation?

Finally, a very different kind of text—a text that Fanny has in her room—plays a role in *Mansfield Park*. When Edmund visits the East Room to tell her he will join the players, he opens a book on her table, remarking, "You . . . will be taking a trip into China, I suppose. How does Lord Macartney go on?" (183; vol. 1, ch. 16). The book Edmund opens might be Lord Macartney's *Journal of the Embassy to China*, published in 1807 as a large portion of the second volume of John Barrow's *Some Account of the Public Life and a Selection from the Unpublished Writings, of the Earl of Macartney*. But Austen does not specify (as she clearly and subtly does when she quotes Inchbald's *Lovers' Vows* instead of another translation), perhaps precisely because she wants to access the contemporary interest in Macartney's embassy and the range of literary texts it produced—a range that offers a more varied insight into Fanny's solitary reading and her connection to the popular taste.[4]

In the years following the return of Macartney's embassy, a number of firsthand accounts by various members of the party were published.[5] These books detail the unsuccessful British attempt to expand trade with China, providing insight into the political negotiations as well as the narrative of a trip through a remote land. The varied accounts of the embassy describe an exotic world both familiar and unfamiliar, a world that invites critical comparison both with England and, for Austen's readers, with Mansfield Park itself. Looking more closely at the accounts of Macartney's embassy enables students not only to recognize Austen as a writer not limited to three or four families in a country village but also to understand how she could depend on—and help construct—a global perspective in her audience, how she built a similar field of vision into the character of her heroine. Through the range of perspectives that these accounts provide and their complex reverberations in the world of *Mansfield Park*, she creates in both Fanny and in her readers an awareness of the intricate ironies of the British imperial project.

The narratives of Macartney's embassy reveal again Austen's elaboration of character through connections to the readers' knowledge of other texts. Aeneas Anderson's and George Staunton's accounts of the pleasures and excitement of world travel, for instance, anticipate moments of narrative interest in *Mansfield Park*. These books provide Fanny—who has "pinned against the wall" in the

East Room "a small sketch of a ship sent four years ago from the Mediterranean by William, with H. M. S. Antwerp at the bottom, in letters as tall as the mainmast" (179; vol. 1, ch. 16)—an opportunity to follow a voyage at sea that her brother's naval life makes peculiarly interesting. Anderson describes in great detail the ceremony of manning the yards as Lord Macartney lands at Madeira (*Narrative* 2–3); in Staunton's account, the voyage—from Portsmouth to Madeira and the Canary Islands to Rio de Janeiro and then around Africa toward China—occupies the entire first volume and is accompanied by foldout maps. Each furnishes local information (Staunton's has an optional volume of plates [*Plates*]) as well as the activities of the British party on shore. These narratives strengthen the readerly sense of the connection between Fanny and William, piecing out his experience for her and for us; they bring readers of Austen's novel, just as they might bring Fanny, into closer contact with the unimagined or with the not yet imagined. The exotic becomes, through the agency of these other writerly voices, familiar.

The accounts of Macartney's embassy cover a range of topics that shed light on what happens within, and without, the view and patronage of Mansfield Park: landscape, theater, slavery, female liberty, the family, duty, and gratitude (particularly as refracted in the exchange of gifts). Students exploring these texts will gain a more comprehensive sense of Austen's real and fictional worlds.

There are dangers for teachers and students in such travels to other texts—not merely to China with Macartney but also into Cowper's England or Scott's Romantic past, or onto the various stages represented in *Mansfield Park* (or even into Dr. Johnson's *Idler* or Crabbe's *Tales*). John Wiltshire has gently cautioned against the "pleasure" of searching for "[a]ssociation, affinity, influence" (*Recreating* 61, 60). It is possible that in such a search students may wander too far from *Mansfield Park*. But, returning, they will bring with them some part of the possessions Austen must have imagined her readers would carry, now better equipped to understand her artistry.

NOTES

[1] Some of the ideas in this essay were previously developed in my "'It Is about Lovers' Vows'" and "Fanny's 'Great Book.'" My thanks to the editorial board of *Persuasions* for permission to use language and ideas from these essays.

[2] Students have access to *Lovers' Vows* through electronic sources (*Eighteenth Century Collections Online, Google Books*) and print: editions of *Mansfield Park* by R. W. Chapman, Claudia L. Johnson, and John Wiltshire include the entire text of Inchbald's adaptation; June Sturrock's Broadview Press edition includes excerpts from Inchbald's introduction and from act 1, scene 1, and act 3, scene 2, the two scenes most significant to the novel.

[3] Bander's essay also connects *Mansfield Park* to the cultural history of *Henry VIII*.

[4] For more on the logic for expanding the reference beyond Macartney's journal, see my "Fanny's 'Great Book.'"

[5]From Aeneas Anderson, Lord Macartney's valet, came *A Narrative of the British Embassy to China* (1795), an account abridged and republished in a cheaper edition that same year by another member of the expedition. Sir George Staunton, the secretary of the embassy, provided *An Authentic Account* (1797), taken from the papers of Macartney, Sir Erasmus Gower (the expedition commander), and others. A volume of *Plates to Staunton's Account* was published in the previous year, 1796. In 1798, Samuel Holmes, a sergeant major in Macartney's guard, published his *Journal*. Barrow, the embassy's comptroller, released his own account in 1804, as *Travels in China*. William Alexander, draftsman to the embassy, was responsible for two illustrated volumes: *The Costume of China* (1805) and *Picturesque Representations of the Dress and Manners of the Chinese* (1814), the latter too late for Austen to have had it in mind but indicative of the continuing interest in Macartney's expedition. See also the British Library's online exhibition *The Lion and the Dragon: Britain's First Embassy to China*, which contains digitized pages from many of the books mentioned here (www.bl.uk/onlinegallery/features/lionanddragon/homepage.html).

Understanding *Mansfield Park* through the Rehearsals for *Lovers' Vows*

Penny Gay

Most readers of *Mansfield Park* come to it after falling in love with *Pride and Prejudice*'s wit and the erotic charge of the romance between Elizabeth and Darcy. Students, in particular, will be even more familiar with the hyperromantic 1995 BBC television adaptation of *Pride and Prejudice*. Its various historical inaccuracies will have been read as normal—Darcy's plunge into the reedy pond, almost fully clothed, being only the most memorable of improprieties involving the bodily behavior of the gentry. How then to convince students that in *Mansfield Park* Austen deliberately wrote an antiromance, that possibly her artistic pride forbade her to repeat the formula of *Pride and Prejudice*? She analyzes the sexual energy of young adults using a different prism: Elizabeth Bennet becomes Mary Crawford; Lydia Bennet becomes Maria Rushworth; Wickham becomes Henry Crawford. And two new character types, having no equivalent in *Pride and Prejudice*, emerge as the antiromantic heroine and hero: Fanny and Edmund, Miss Prude and Mr. Pomposity, as students might nickname them. It's certainly how students view them.

If bodily decorum and indecorum are unreadable to modern students, as teachers we are challenged to come up with situations that will show rather than tell. Modern students can learn about embodiment at a visceral level and through their understanding of spatial semiotics, something they know as "body language." We can also posit that early-nineteenth-century readers of Austen's novels had their own understanding of the semiotics of the body—that is, decorum and indecorum covering dress, gesture and speech, bodily closeness and contact. In the classroom exercise that this essay describes, I used the episodes of the rehearsals for *Lovers' Vows* to attempt to create in twenty-first-century Australian students an early-nineteenth-century understanding of embodiment. My underlying aim, of course, was to win them over to an empathic relationship with Fanny and Edmund. Ultimately I wanted students to agree that Fanny and Edmund were truly the heroine and hero of a complex and challenging novel. The task of my fellow teachers and me was not to brainwash the students but to awaken them to new possibilities in their reading experience.

The Model

The rehearsals for *Lovers' Vows* make up one of the two major narrative events of volume 1 of *Mansfield Park*. Austen uses the rehearsals to raise the reader's consciousness about issues connected with theatricality: fantasy and false representation; allowed transgression; the performance of gender, class, and sexuality; and the unavoidable theatricality of everyday life—how people perform their public selves and how such performance relates to their private knowledge, wishes, and desires (see Gay, *Jane Austen*, ch. 5). Because students are familiar with such ideas from their other studies, a general discussion of them is a good starting point.

Some background is needed for today's students. *Lovers' Vows* was an enormously popular play of the 1790s. By 1814, it was a little old-fashioned but had the advantage of a mix of comic and serious roles and did not require (despite Mrs. Norris's enthusiasm [166]) the elaborate scenery that characterized the new melodramas and other spectaculars of the early nineteenth century. As Mr. Yates's expostulations make clear (163), it's the perfect play for a house party of young people, all of them wanting meaty parts. It also makes a good play for twenty-first-century young people in a classroom.

In preparation for our exercise, an illustrated lecture was given on eighteenth-century acting styles, to provide examples of "attitudes," or postures, that could be utilized as shorthand for emotions. Having students then strike attitudes was a way of freeing them from their physical inhibitions, but we were only partly successful in the short time we had, since the unfamiliarity of the gestural language tended to produce hilarity.

We were not expecting students to be actors but simply asking them to imagine and inhabit the thoughts and emotions of those characters in *Mansfield Park* who are in some way involved in the theatricals. To focus this response, we asked students to read, in preparation, chapters 17 and 18 of volume 1. They were also to look at the following sections of *Lovers' Vows*, which would be rehearsed: act 1, scene 1, from Agatha's first soliloquy ("Oh Providence!") to her line "Where could be found such another son?" (566–74); act 3, scene 2, from the beginning of the scene (Amelia's soliloquy) to Amelia's line "Heaven's blessing will follow" and the interruption by the rhyming butler (590–95).

In terms of classroom work, the first scene, having a bigger cast, was a good icebreaker. The exercise involved not a literal rendition of some passages in Austen's text but a gathering together of all the characters who might have been at a rehearsal at some stage in the feverish proceedings. Actors playing Tom (as Landlord), Henry (as Frederick), and Maria (as Agatha) were called for. If there were no volunteers, the instructor, like an eighteenth-century theatrical manager, would typecast. But after the first run-through, eager volunteers for a second or even third run often came forward. The spur for this enthusiasm was the second element in the casting of our imagining of the rehearsal scene—the members of the Mansfield audience. Lively discussion was guaranteed when the instructor asked, "Who might be present at the rehearsal, and with what feelings?" The remaining students were easily cast. Mr. Rushworth was always the first to be named, then Fanny, Mrs. Norris, Julia, Mary, Edmund, Mrs. Grant, even Lady Bertram (the performer of this role usually opted to doze on a sofa). A breakthrough was made in one early class when someone remembered the almost invisible army of servants that supported the household: Baddeley the butler with his tea tray, and the gossiping underservants thrilled by the possibility of scandal among the great folk and finding a way to pass by and peek into the rehearsal room.

In my first use of this model, the rehearsal of act 1, scene 1, began with the instruction that the actors of Henry and Maria follow Austen's stage directions, explicit and implicit, as well as those of Mrs. Inchbald: for example, Julia notices that "Frederick was listening with looks of devotion to Agatha's narrative, and pressing her hand to his heart" (205; vol. 2, ch.1). At frequent intervals I would stop the rehearsal and ask a member of the audience how he or she reacted, in character, to what was just seen or heard. The words "my seducer" in Agatha's first speech, for example (567), elicited thrilled expressions of shock and scandal from the audience. An instructor might here point out that Austen uses the word nowhere in the novel; her narratorial style generally conforms to Fanny's prudish interior monologue. Stage directions in the opening emotional scene emphasize the physical contact between the two actors of Frederick and Agatha, who are mother and son in the play, but that relationship cannot be replicated on the stage. Directions such as *"Leans her head against his breast"* and *"He embraces her"* (568, 573) describe actions forbidden between an unmarried man and woman, which is, of course, how everyone in the room perceives Henry and Maria. Maria, moreover, is engaged to Mr. Rushworth, whose jealousy at these embraces is noted by Austen (194). The instructor might segue at this point to the extraordinary moment in volume 3 of the novel, when Edmund arrives at Portsmouth to escort Fanny back to Mansfield:

> He was alone, and met her instantly; and she found herself pressed to his heart with only these words, just articulate, "My Fanny—my only sister—my only comfort now." She could say nothing; nor for some minutes could he say more.
> He turned away to recover himself. . . .   (514–15; ch. 15)

In the context of the rehearsal scene just witnessed by the class, this narrative moment takes on an eroticism that few students ever recognize in Fanny and Edmund's relationship. It includes, even, the soupçon of incestuous transgression that features in the play.

Productive discussion can arise from asking all role-playing members of the audience how their character might react to this transgressive scene. Ask the student playing Mrs. Norris about her reaction, and, if the student is astute, the answer will probably be, "She is congratulating herself on the curtains that she has contrived," remembering this passage: "'You had better stay till the curtain is hung,' interposed Mrs. Norris—'the curtain will be hung in a day or two,— there is very little sense in a play without a curtain—and I am much mistaken if you do not find it draw up into very handsome festoons'" (196; vol. 1, ch. 18). Discussion might then progress to her failing in her self-appointed task of guardian of the young people while Sir Thomas is away. It could proceed further to issues at the heart of the novel, parenting and moral authority.

The second scene, the rehearsal of Amelia and Anhalt's discussion of love and marriage by Mary and Edmund before their only audience, the increasingly uncomfortable Fanny, has a very different dynamic and raises a different set of questions. For this exercise, only three students need be cast as actors, and one of them, who plays Fanny, will be silent though not inactive. Students need to be aware that Amelia is a classic eighteenth-century comedy role: the *jeune première*. The actress's main function is to charm all the onstage males as well as the whole audience. It is easy to see how this role is perfect for Mary Crawford—acting such a part is her modus operandi wherever we find her in the novel. Amelia's opening soliloquy would be delivered by Mary very knowingly and would be expected to garner laughs from the audience:

> *Amelia*. Why am I so uneasy; so peevish; who has offended me? I did not mean to come into this room. In the garden I intended to go. [*Going, turns back*.] No, I will not—yes, I will—just go, and look if my auriculas are still in blossom; and if the apple-tree is grown, which Mr. Anhalt planted.—I feel very low-spirited—something must be the matter.— Why do I cry?—Am I not well? (590)

A well-practiced comic start would accompany Anhalt's arrival on the scene. From here on, the scene should have two students who are confident with words and quick to find the appropriate embodiment. It is brilliant writing, a clever, sexy scene reminiscent of the verbal sparring of Elizabeth and Darcy. But even if the students are not stars of the college drama society, the scene will play itself, helped by attention to Inchbald's stage directions: who is standing, who sitting, who turning away, who coming forward. The instructor should ensure that these small moves in the intimate space of Fanny's East Room are accurately observed. Comedy continues, especially in the somewhat indecorous speeches of Amelia and in Anhalt's wonderful "Pshaw!" as he turns away from this Rosalind-like charmer of such a coming-on disposition (594). Comedy completes the scene, as whatever might have happened next—an embrace?—is interrupted by the butler.

In *Mansfield Park*, however, there is an audience of one for this scene as it is rehearsed by Edmund and Mary. Comedy, which often relies on sexual suggestiveness, is not a genre that Fanny likes. She has already registered, on reading the play, that "the language of [Amelia]" was "unfit to be expressed by any woman of modesty" (161; vol. 1, ch. 14), but by the time of the proposed public rehearsal of the first three acts, she has a more ambivalent attitude:

> . . . Edmund and Miss Crawford would then be acting together for the first time;—the third act would bring a scene between them which interested her most particularly, and which she was longing and dreading to see how they would perform. The whole subject of it was love—a mar-

riage of love was to be described by the gentleman, and very little short of a declaration of love be made by the lady.

She had read, and read the scene again with many painful, many wondering emotions, and looked forward to their representation of it as a circumstance almost too interesting. She did not *believe* they had yet rehearsed it, even in private.   (196; ch. 18)

The completely unexpected private rehearsal, then, proposed and imposed first by Mary and then by Edmund, both invading Fanny's virginal East Room, presents a moment of extreme anxiety for Fanny. She is being obliged to watch a representation of lovemaking, verbalized but also embodied by two actors who, in student slang, have the hots for each other. She longs for it, dreads it, finds it "almost too interesting," strong indications not only for the performer of Fanny in this student exercise but also for all the rest of the class to discuss. Once that discussion has taken place—and one of its outcomes should be the recognition that Fanny has sexual feelings and that she knows she has them—the rehearsal can proceed. As in the first scene, the instructor should stop the rehearsal at various moments to ask how Fanny responds. Austen provides a considerably detailed set of stage directions for her:

> She was invested, indeed, with the office of judge and critic, and earnestly desired to exercise it and tell them all their faults; but from doing so every feeling within her shrank, she could not, would not, dared not attempt it; had she been otherwise qualified for criticism, her conscience must have restrained her from venturing at disapprobation. She believed herself to feel too much of it in the aggregate for honesty or safety in particulars. To prompt them must be enough for her; and it was sometimes *more* than enough; for she could not always pay attention to the book. In watching them she forgot herself; and, agitated by the increasing spirit of Edmund's manner, had once closed the page and turned away exactly as he wanted help.   (199–200)

The class might discuss what that last moment was, when Fanny couldn't bear to look and Edmund forgot his words.

If more time is available, I suggest two variations to this exercise to explore the psychological situation among Fanny, Edmund, and Mary. The first would be to have the students act out this whole scene in the novel from the moment of Mary's entry, using Austen's dialogue and descriptions that amount to stage directions, to focus the class's awareness of Fanny's embarrassment and unwilling fascination. The second would be to dramatize the almost equally sexually suggestive scene in which Mary gives Fanny the necklace, acting as deputy for the absent Henry but once again exercising her dangerous charm (vol. 2, ch. 8). (A shortcut might be to show the excellent performances of these scenes in the generally very faithful BBC adaptation of the novel in 1983, starring Sylvestra le Touzel as Fanny and Nicholas Farrell as Edmund. Patricia Rozema's film, with a different feminist agenda, is not much help, and the 2007 ITV adaptation, starring Billie Piper, is a travesty.)

If sufficient time can be given to practical exploration of the dramatic means that Austen has drawn so pointedly to our attention in volume 1, then I venture to suggest there will be many fewer students lacking sympathy for Fanny.

How It Worked in Practice

This class exercise has been twice trialed in the English Department at the University of Sydney, with students in their second and third years of study. In 2008, lectures that were given before *Mansfield Park* was studied included discussion of conduct books for young ladies and an illustrated talk on the theater of the late eighteenth century that Austen was familiar with. In 2010, the lecturer, Nicola Parsons, raised issues about the performance of masculinity and femininity with such topics as "Reading Marianne Dashwood: Sexuality and Sensibility," "Masculinity in *Pride and Prejudice*," and "Darcy on Screen: *Pride and Prejudice*." Issue-based lectures, such as "The Slave Trade and the Colonization of *Mansfield Park*" were given specifically on *Mansfield Park*. The one-hour classes in which the rehearsal exercise took place were taught mostly by postgraduate tutors, few of whom had any dramatic experience. This lack of experience was not, I believe, a disadvantage—rather the opposite, as I encouraged them simply to use the classes as teaching tools, not to attempt to elicit quality acting from the students. The basic advice I gave the tutors was, "Encourage your students to place themselves in the positions of the characters in the novel; they are, after all, of much the same age and have similar interests and aspirations." They all took to the exercise with enthusiasm and reported very positively on it (with the single complaint that much more time was needed to extract all the benefits from the exercise).

In 2008, Deirdre Linkiewicz, a postgraduate student, reported on her five workshops. She observed that the tendency of the students to laugh at themselves by hamming it up somewhat distracted from the desired focus. Tutors needed to be prepared for this and have some means of heading it off. She also noted that when she was able to cast male students in the parts of Frederick and Anhalt, this casting "created a sense of tension. . . . The students in the audience also appeared more attuned to the nuances of gesture in these scenes, their attention riveted by the sexual potential of the scenes." Casting female students in the masculine roles did enable "a willingness to indulge in the physical intimacy of the scenes. . . . However, the lack of tension in these performances resulted in a loss of that which would have been felt amongst the characters in the novel, rendering these performances less effective in approximating the mood of those staged in *Mansfield Park*."

The second tutor in the pioneering year was Katrina Clifford, also a postgraduate student. She reported on the issues raised by the exercise rather than on the mechanics of the exercise itself. I give a summary here, as the issues might be of use as discussion starters:

> The idea of transgression—not just on Sir Thomas's space but also on Fanny's (including her special relationship with Edmund).
>
> The relationships between Henry and Maria, Frederick and Agatha— why would Henry choose Frederick for himself instead of Anhalt? How appropriate is the sexual rendering of the mother-son relationship? What does it suggest?
>
> Edmund's position—to what extent is Edmund aware of Maria's behavior, and how distracted is he by Mary? To what extent can we see his acceptance of Anhalt's role as being gentlemanly and coming to the rescue, and how much is he influenced by his own, perhaps unacknowledged, desires?
>
> To what extent was Austen using the play to echo ideas and events in *Mansfield Park*? What connections between the play and the novel did she expect her readers to make?
>
> If the physical and emotional intensity of the first scene is felt as uncomfortable by modern students, how would it have affected the ordinary people of Austen's day?

The exercise was repeated in 2010, with three new tutors, also postgraduate students.

Meegan Capsopoulos added several variations of her own to the model. First, she asked a student to read aloud a brief extract from Erasmus Darwin's essay on young women performing plays at school (this essay is appended to the Broadview edition of *Mansfield Park*), as a contextualizing exercise. She then asked all the students to "imagine they were on a Regency stage—to try to embody the physical characteristics of each character they were to play" as they played a simple game:

> Students lined up on either side of the stage—on one side were the Agathas, on the other side were the Fredericks. It was made clear to students that, for the time being, they should play the roles of Agatha and Frederick (and not Henry Crawford and Maria Bertram). We began [the scene] with the first pair of students until I called "freeze," at which point each actor would hold the position his or her character had assumed until the next pair jumped in. The new actors would hold the position of the previous pair until I called "action," at which point they would continue the performance until I called "freeze." This continued until around four pairs had had a chance of performing. . . . This activity, and its emphasis on exaggerated performance, created a lot of good energy for the rest of the tutorial.

The final tutor who conducted classes using the model in 2010 was Ailish McKeown. Her report also focused on insights that the exercises offered for discussion. In the first scene, she asked the students how Tom (playing the Landlord) was feeling about Maria's conduct:

> The [female] student playing Tom said that she was actually so preoc-cupied with her own role and her entrance and a prop she had found, and enjoying it, that she hadn't noticed what the other students were do-ing at all. This shed some light on Tom, who seemed to have been [so] preoccupied with his own comic role as to not really notice what was oc-curring. . . .

The boy playing Henry

> said that he was enjoying himself immensely. Both Henry and Maria com-mented that the embrace was not very filial. Henry said that he was enjoy-ing being told that he is loved. (AMcK: I thought that it was interesting the way he picked up that the action is about himself and his vanity rather than being strictly sensual.)

A student playing Maria thought that

> the action presented Agatha as weak and dependent and required her to represent this physically, and that this was demeaning to Maria. She thought that this would also have made Henry feel vain and powerful, as Maria was presented as being helpless and dependent upon him.

Discussion of this point might segue to Maria in the novel's last chapters, that first she is dependent on her lover, then, ironically, locked permanently into the company of the equally morally weak Mrs. Norris.

Edmund's failure of moral authority in the family was of interest to this class: "What Edmund would dislike most was the revelation or publicity." This much more complex view of Edmund, as not only in thrall to lust but having a certain family amour-propre, was reinforced by the students' work in class on the sec-ond scene. McKeown reported on these interesting aspects of the exercise:

> We . . . moved to the back of the hall where the ceiling was lower and the lighting closer, giving the impression of a smaller, more intimate space. . . . [A female student playing Edmund] commented on the way that she had, unconsciously, pulled her chair in close to Mary for the rehearsal and that, looking at the set-up afterwards during the discussion, she noted how that arrangement worked to exclude Fanny. She was very critical of herself as Edmund for not having noticed the way that he was treating Fanny and excluding her in his interest in the rehearsal itself.

McKeown asked the class, in discussion,

> why Fanny needed to be present for the rehearsal, why Edmund and
> Mary, having found each other ready to rehearse, had not gone off to
> rehearse alone once they met each other. . . . Some of the responses were
> that, first of all, Fanny was a sort of "chaperone," again to give legitimacy
> to Edmund's involvement in the play. Her presence made it seem as
> though the rehearsal and Edmund's involvement were countenanced by
> Fanny, and this was very important to Edmund himself as part of his ra-
> tionalization of his behavior. Another felt that Mary had come to Fanny as
> the way to get to know Edmund and to win his approval. . . . A surprising
> number of students felt, when they had watched the rehearsal as Fanny,
> that Mary might suspect Fanny's feelings for Edmund. Even if she didn't,
> they felt that performing before Fanny was a way for Mary to show her
> exercise of power and to enjoy having someone else see it. . . . [A student
> playing] Fanny commented that, listening to the dialogue, she realized
> how much she was like Amelia but how different she was. She wants to be
> Amelia. She feels that Amelia's lines belong to her—Edmund has been
> her tutor, she feels it is her role.

These detailed discussions and speculations were obviously very fruitful for the
students. McKeown noted "the change in response from many of the students
towards Fanny as a result of this part of the exercise" and furthermore that "the
students seemed to become more critical of Edmund as a result of both parts of
the exercise." These students had learned, through discussing their experience
of performance, that to label Edmund merely a pompous killjoy and Fanny a
frightened prude is to ignore the complex psychological drama of which the
Lovers' Vows rehearsals constitute act 1.

Delicately handled, such a participatory technique can get students to dig
deeper in their reading experience of Austen. Austen's imagination works dramatically; she is, like so many of the fine comic (and often female) playwrights
of the late eighteenth century, a mistress of scenes and dialogue. Students will
become more engaged in the novel's themes if they have entered, however
briefly, into her theater.

NOTE

I would like to express my gratitude to the tutors Meegan Capsopolous, Katrina Clifford,
Deirdre Linkiewicz, and Ailish McKeown, for their contributions to this experiment in
teaching and for their permission to quote from the reports that they agreed to write up.
I would also like to thank Nicola Parsons for enthusiastically supporting the repetition
of the exercise.

The Tragic Action of *Mansfield Park*

Sarah Emsley

The ending of *Mansfield Park* often disappoints readers. "Let other pens dwell on guilt and misery," says the narrator at the beginning of the last chapter. "I quit such odious subjects as soon as I can, impatient to restore every body, not greatly in fault themselves, to tolerable comfort, and to have done with all the rest" (533). As in Austen's other major novels, the heroine marries happily in the end, but this time the narrator seems especially impatient to dispense with the fates of all the characters. The hastily narrated ending may seem perfunctory, unsettling, and not romantic enough for those who expect a satisfying and happy union of the kind that rewards Elizabeth Bennet and Mr. Darcy at the end of *Pride and Prejudice*. Despite finding the ending disappointing, most readers continue to think of *Mansfield Park* as a comedy, not simply because Austen's satire is amusing but also because it ends with marriage.

Reading the novel as a tragedy—a tragedy with a happy ending—rather than as a flawed comedy may help us understand it better.[1] Teachers might argue that Austen's interest in this novel lies not in the romance plot but in the tragedy averted by Fanny Price's recognition that marriage to Henry Crawford would be morally disastrous. In the central scenes of the tragic action of the novel, in which Fanny heroically resists pressure from Sir Thomas, from her cousin Edmund, and from Henry himself, Austen uses dialogue to explore moral questions, the details and intensity of which contrast sharply with the briefly narrated summary of the heroine's marriage at the end of the novel.

An earlier scene in which Austen makes extensive use of dialogue, the discussion of which play to perform at Mansfield, can be highlighted in class to help determine the genre of this novel. The narrator says that "[t]here were, in fact, so many things to be attended to, so many people to be pleased, so many best characters required, and above all, such a need that the play should be at once both tragedy and comedy, that there did seem as little chance of a decision, as any thing pursued by youth and zeal could hold out" (153; vol. 1, ch. 14). The desire to find the most pleasing balance between tragedy and comedy leads to the choice of *Lovers' Vows*. Tom Bertram thinks it will be perfect because it has "two capital tragic parts for Yates and Crawford" and a comic part—"the rhyming butler"—for himself (155). Henry Crawford tries to persuade Julia Bertram to play Amelia rather than the more tragic Agatha, even though Maria and Julia both feel they have "the best claim to Agatha" (157): he says to Julia, "Tragedy may be your choice, but it will certainly appear that comedy chooses *you*" (159).[2] *Mansfield Park* itself is "at once both tragedy and comedy," and the combination of the two has led readers to judge it a problem novel, in the way Shakespeare's *Measure for Measure* and *The Winter's Tale*, for example, have been labeled problem plays. Both plays alternate between comedy and tragedy, concluding with the comic ending of marriage rather than with death and sorrow.[3]

The Duke's insistence on marrying off everyone at the end of *Measure for Measure* bears some resemblance to the impatience that Austen's narrator admits to in the last chapter of *Mansfield Park*. In his final speech, the Duke orders, "She, Claudio, that you wronged, look you restore. / Joy to you, Mariana; love her, Angelo" (5.1.523–24), and then he attempts to arrange his own marriage to the virtuous Isabella. Compare this hasty treatment with the brief statement of Julia Bertram's elopement with Mr. Yates: "It had appeared to her the only thing to be done" (540; vol. 3, ch. 17). And, of course, the marriage of Edmund and Fanny: we are asked "to believe that exactly at the time when it was quite natural that it should be so, and not a week earlier, Edmund did cease to care about Miss Crawford, and became as anxious to marry Fanny, as Fanny herself could desire" (544). Joy to you, Fanny; love her, Edmund. Austen, like Shakespeare, wraps up the plot quickly. To many students, her conclusion is strained, yet if we understand the novel as a tragedy, the ending is consistent with the plot.

The last chapter of *Mansfield Park* is narrated quickly, without dialogue, even though it includes the courtship and marriage of the heroine and her hero. Austen's brilliant dialogue is often absent from proposal scenes. In *Emma*, when we are wondering, "What did she say?" in response to Mr. Knightley, we are simply told, "Just what she ought, of course. A lady always does" ([ed. Cronin and McMillan] 470). The original version of Captain Wentworth's proposal in *Persuasion* was silent, but when Austen revised the ending, she replaced the narrated proposal with a letter ([ed. Todd and Blank] 257–58); thus, although we are given the words of the proposal, we do not hear them in dialogue. At the end of *Mansfield Park*, we do not even get an account of the proposal; we are told only that Edmund "was very steadily earnest in the pursuit of the blessing, and it was not possible that encouragement from [Fanny] should be long wanting." Suggesting that it would be impossible to find the right words, Austen says that "there was happiness elsewhere which no description can reach" (545).

The lack of detail in the courtship and marriage of Edmund and Fanny is even more conspicuous than the absence of dialogue in the proposal scenes of Austen's other novels. In *Mansfield Park*, the scene in which Henry Crawford proposes to Fanny is presented in some detail, but there is still very little dialogue. The narrator says that Henry speaks of his *"twofold motives"* (347; vol. 2, ch. 13) in arranging for William Price's promotion, and that in response Fanny is "exceedingly distressed, and for some moments unable to speak" (348). She does exclaim "No, no, no," just as she later cries "[N]ever, never, never," when she is telling Edmund she cannot marry Henry,[4] yet most of the scene is narrated rather than dramatized (349; vol. 2, ch. 13; 402; vol. 3, ch. 4). The reason the marriage between Edmund and Fanny is so hastily described, and the reason Henry's proposal scene is narrated instead of given in dialogue, is that the tragic action of Fanny's resistance to the persuasion of Sir Thomas and Edmund and her rejection of Henry's later offer to rescue her from Portsmouth are more important in this novel than the comic element of a marriage proposal. The scenes in which Fanny refuses to obey Sir Thomas and, secondarily, refuses to be persuaded by Edmund to accept Henry's proposal are both crucial and given in dialogue.

These scenes and the later conversation with Henry in Portsmouth can be illuminated by reference to the elements of tragedy that Aristotle discusses in his *Poetics*. Aristotle says, "A tragedy, then, is a *mimesis* of an action—that is, it is [morally] serious and purposeful, having magnitude." Austen uses dialogue and sometimes what Aristotle calls "heightened language," presents the action "by people acting rather than by narration," shows how the plot is driven by "pity and fear," and eventually, through the action of these scenes, brings about the "purification" of the estate, all of which are central to Aristotle's understanding of tragedy (*Poetics* 69).[5] The estate is purified not through death but through Sir Thomas's new understanding of morality that comes after Maria's elopement with Henry, an understanding that is made possible largely through Fanny's principled resistance to Henry. Students can discover that *Mansfield Park* may be read in Aristotelian terms as an imitation of a morally serious action—that is, of a tragic heroine's resistance to the attempts of authority figures to persuade her to marry a man she believes to be immoral.

Fanny certainly experiences fear when she anticipates the confrontation with Sir Thomas: "She sat some time in a good deal of agitation, listening, trembling, and fearing to be sent for every moment"; she "began to tremble again, at the idea of his coming up to speak to her"; "The terror of his former occasional visits to that room seemed all renewed" (359–60; vol. 3, ch. 1). She is being tested, and it is not a foregone conclusion that she will prevail. When Sir Thomas lists for her the many reasons why she should look favorably on Henry, Fanny "did feel almost ashamed of herself, after such a picture as her uncle had drawn, for not liking Mr. Crawford" (365). Yet she repeatedly tells Sir Thomas she cannot accept Crawford: "I gave him no encouragement yesterday"; "I—I cannot like him, Sir, well enough to marry him"; "His attentions were always what I did not like"; "I am so perfectly convinced that I could never make him happy, and that I should be miserable myself" (363, 364, 369). It is ironic that Sir Thomas repeatedly says there is nothing more he can say, before continuing to berate Fanny for her ingratitude: "Well, there is nothing more to be said" (365); "It is of no use, I perceive, to talk to you" (367).

Fanny tries "to harden and prepare herself against farther questioning" (365), which suggests that she is struggling to preserve her privacy and resist Sir Thomas's control. This struggle even leads her to conceal that she loves someone else: when Sir Thomas begins to say, "[I]t is hardly possible that your affections—," he sees "her lips formed into a *no*, though the sound was inarticulate," and "her face was like scarlet." Interpreting her blush as a sign of innocence rather than of guilt, he chooses to believe that it is "quite impossible" for her to have seen anyone else she could love (365). Although he does not ask her directly, her silent no is tantamount to a lie. Fanny is not a priggish heroine but a complex character who agonizes over moral decisions and struggles to act virtuously. Her resistance to Sir Thomas leads her into a painful—but utterly understandable—betrayal of her real feelings. By reading some of the dialogue aloud, students will perceive the enormous pressure on her. Austen gives the lengthy speeches of Sir Thomas in detail, the effect of which is to build up the strength of the force Fanny must resist. He accuses her of being "wilful and perverse," of "think[ing] only of [her]self," and of, "in a wild fit of folly, throwing away from [her] such an opportunity of being settled in life, eligibly, honourably, nobly settled, as will, probably, never occur to [her] again" (367–68). Her virtuous resolve is strained here, and she bursts into tears, sure that "[t]he past, present, future, every thing was terrible" (370). Although she feels sure that she cannot marry Henry, she is not absolutely certain that she is right to go against the wishes of her uncle and the best interests of her family. She even feels pity for Crawford: "[I]f he really loved her, and were unhappy too!—it was all wretchedness together" (370).

It is a challenge for Fanny to stand up to Sir Thomas's authority; it is even more painful for her to resist Edmund's attempts at persuasion. Edmund says, "[L]et him [Mr. Crawford] succeed at last" (402; ch. 4); "I cannot suppose that you have not the *wish* to love him—the natural wish of gratitude"; "He is lively, you are serious; but so much the better; his spirits will support yours" (403); "He will make you happy, Fanny, I know he will make you happy" (406). In her dialogue with Sir Thomas, Fanny does not speak at length, but she feels more at liberty with her cousin to explain her reasons: "There never were two people more dissimilar. We have not one taste in common. We should be miserable" (403). She goes on to confess, "I must say, cousin, that I cannot approve his character. I have not thought well of him from the time of the play" (404). When Edmund tells her of the surprise both Mary Crawford and Mrs. Grant feel on learning that Fanny has rejected Henry, he calls Fanny's good sense into question: "[Y]ou must prove yourself to be in your senses as soon as you can, by a different conduct; nothing else will satisfy them" (408).

The suggestion that she is not in her senses is too much for Fanny to bear, and her cousin's apparent agreement with Miss Crawford and her sister calls forth her most passionate speech, in which she speaks not only in defense of her own situation but also on behalf of all women and their right to protect themselves from unwanted affections. This long and eloquent defense of her right to reject Henry's addresses is worth reading aloud so that students will appreciate her formidable and unexpected eloquence:

> "I *should* have thought," said Fanny, after a pause of recollection and exertion, "that every woman must have felt the possibility of a man's not being approved, not being loved by some one of her sex, at least, let him be ever so generally agreeable. Let him have all the perfections in the world, I think it ought not to be set down as certain, that a man must be acceptable to every woman he may happen to like himself. But even supposing it is so, allowing Mr. Crawford to have all the claims which his sisters think

he has, how was I to be prepared to meet him with any feeling answerable to his own? He took me wholly by surprise. I had not an idea that his behaviour to me before had any meaning; and surely I was not to be teaching myself to like him only because he was taking, what seemed, very idle notice of me. In my situation, it would have been the extreme of vanity to be forming expectations on Mr. Crawford. I am sure his sisters, rating him as they do, must have thought it so, supposing he had meant nothing. How then was I to be—to be in love with him the moment he said he was with me? How was I to have an attachment at his service, as soon as it was asked for? His sisters should consider me as well as him. The higher his deserts, the more improper for me ever to have thought of him. And, and—we think very differently of the nature of women, if they can imagine a woman so very soon capable of returning an affection as this seems to imply."   (408; vol. 3, ch. 4)

It is extremely unusual for Fanny to speak for so long on any topic to anyone, and it is very difficult for her to stand up to her cousin and mentor as she does here. Edmund, who has been so close to her over many years, ought to be able to recognize that the length and vehemence of her speech are indications that she means what she says, yet he sees only what he wants to in her reply and is blind to her rational assertion that not every woman will love, or even approve of, every man who may wish to pay court to her. Fanny speaks confidently and presents a convincing argument that a woman has the right to love whomever she chooses. To say these things to the man who has guided her education and who is also the one she loves takes immense courage, because it means she is breaking away from his authority.

Her hesitations toward the end of the speech signal just how distraught she is after laying out this argument for her cousin. Like Anne Elliot, who speaks so passionately to Captain Harville in defense of women's constancy, she hesitates slightly when she defends the nature of women's affections to a man who doubts the truth of her argument. Yet unlike Anne, who speaks "with a faltering voice" when she concludes that "[i]t would be too hard indeed" if "woman's feelings" were added to all the "difficulties, and privations, and dangers" that men already endure (*Persuasion* [ed. Todd and Blank] 254), Fanny does not falter. Her hesitation, "And, and—" does not necessarily indicate the kind of unsteadiness that we hear in Anne's voice. It may even imply that she is about to say something else about Henry, perhaps something more damning about his character, or to reveal some aspect of her judgment (and perhaps also her jealousy) of Mary. The hesitation certainly suggests that she could add to her list of reasons why she should not accept a man she does not love or approve of.

The danger of offering the suddenness of Henry's attentions as a reason for being unable to return his love is that Fanny will now be seen as properly modest, the "perfect model of a woman" that Edmund earlier in this scene urged her to be (402). He listens only to the second part of her long speech, decides that he was perfectly justified in telling Miss Crawford and Mrs. Grant that Fanny "could tolerate nothing that [she was] not used to," and enjoys the memory of Miss Crawford's making them laugh by saying it would take ten years of marriage for Henry to find that Fanny would at last accept his addresses (409). Like Mr. Collins, who refuses to believe that Elizabeth Bennet is actually refusing his proposal, sees her protestations as "uniformly charming," and insists that she will think differently with time and the approval of her parents (*Pride* [ed. Rogers] 122), Edmund thinks Fanny is merely being appropriately reserved and that with more time and further persuasion from her friends, she will learn to love her suitor. Fanny sees that in "guarding against one evil," she is "laying herself open to another," and despite her ability to hold fast to her principles, she is "oppressed and wearied" (409–10), worn down by her debates with both Edmund and his father.

These two scenes of intense dialogue about moral questions are at the heart of the plot of *Mansfield Park*. Drama of conversation is provided also in Fanny's response to Henry's offer to take Fanny from Portsmouth to Mansfield, in the debate over which play to produce, and in the discussion of chapels and clergymen at Sotherton.[6] These scenes help us identify Austen's focus and figure out what she is doing with the genre of the comic romance and with the concept of tragic action.

It is useful to introduce the commonly accepted definition of tragedy, which involves disaster. M. H. Abrams says, "The term is broadly applied to literary, and especially to dramatic, representations of serious actions which eventuate in a disastrous conclusion for the protagonist" (321). Abrams goes on to say in his *Glossary of Literary Terms* that readers should be open to definitions of tragedy beyond Aristotle's theories, because in the more than two thousand years since the writing of the *Poetics*, "many new and artistically effective types of serious plots ending in a catastrophe have been developed—types that Aristotle had no way of foreseeing" (322). Abrams attempts to ensure that readers will not find Aristotle's definitions limiting yet does not consider works that Aristotle considered tragedies but that modern readers usually think of as flawed comedies. Ironically, the assumption that the genre has become more inclusive in our time erases the possibility that Aristotle knew more about tragedy than we do. What if a literary work represents a serious, tragic action but does not end in disaster?

The following passages from the *Poetics* are taken from the groundbreaking translation by George Whalley, who emphasizes Aristotle's insistence on the difficult process of the making of poetry. Aristotle describes four kinds of tragic action: one in which the deed is "done with [full] knowledge and understanding," as in Medea's killing of her children in Euripides's *Medea*; one in which a character knowingly "refrain[s] from doing the deed"; one in which the character acts but does "the frightful deed (*deinon*) unwittingly" and later realizes that there was a "blood-relationship," as in Sophocles's *Oedipus the King*; and one in which a character realizes "before committing [the deed]" that it will be fatal, as in Euripides's *Iphigenia in Taurus*. Aristotle's judgment of the relative merit of these four does not privilege the tragic recognition after the fact; instead, perhaps surprisingly, Aristotle says, "But the best is the last [in the list]" (103–05; the words in square brackets are Whalley's addition). Therefore the best form of tragic action may in fact be when a character's recognition of a potential mistake in judgment (*hamartia*) actually forestalls disaster. In addition to the reference to *Iphigenia in Taurus*, Aristotle lists two other examples of this kind of tragedy, but they have not survived: *Cresphontes* and *Helle*.

Whalley terms such plays "tragedies that [have] a prosperous outcome," and in his essay "Jane Austen: Poet," he suggests that *Mansfield Park* might be considered one of them (133).[7] He does not see Austen's language as "poetic" (115), and he is not thinking of the verses she wrote. Instead, invoking the Greek root of the word *poet*, which means "maker,"[8] he talks about Austen as "a maker in words" and as a maker of tragedies as well as comedies. He believes that seeing her as a comic writer may limit our understanding of her (132). Raising questions about the assumption that tragedy must conclude with darkness or disaster, he says that "Aristotle, with his intense concentration on the peculiar configuration of the tragic action and the integrity of it—the single figure the whole play traces—recognized that there were works that traced the specific arc of tragic action under the guidance of stories or plots that were not intrinsically disastrous." Aristotle was not thinking of "'dark' tragedies with a happy ending" simply tacked on, because "for Aristotle the end is always implicit in the beginning" (133). Aristotle says that "the [course of] events—the plot—is the *end* of tragedy, and the end is what matters most of all" (73).[9]

Teachers can use Aristotle's definition of tragedy to show how in the language and action of *Mansfield Park* Austen is making a tragedy, whether of a new or old type. The tragic action of the novel centers on Fanny's temptation to marry Henry. As *Mansfield Park* traces her moral development as a child in a morally unstable household, she learns to make choices about how to act and speak. She is not a passive heroine, virtuous and never tested: she struggles with temptation before she makes her choices.[10] According to Aristotle, the plot or action (*praxis*) is even more important than character.[11] If the final action is rejection by Fanny of a marriage proposal from an immoral suitor—a proposal, moreover, strongly urged by all her friends—her character must develop to the point where she is strong enough to carry out that action.

The pressure to accept Henry continues after Fanny has resisted the persuasions of Sir Thomas and of Edmund, for Sir Thomas sends her to stay with her family in Portsmouth, where she is bitterly unhappy. When Henry visits her there, she begins to see improvements in his character and is reminded of some of the advantages of accepting his proposal. She sees that he is learning to be more kind and attentive, even to his tenants at Everingham, and she is pleased to hear the story of how he has been "the friend of the poor and oppressed" on his estate (469; vol. 3, ch. 10). Revisiting her earlier impressions of him, she is now "willing to allow he might have more good qualities than she had been wont to suppose" (470). Like Elizabeth Bennet, who revises her opinion of Darcy when she hears from his housekeeper that he is an excellent landlord (*Pride* [ed. Rogers] 276), Fanny is touched by an aspect of her suitor's behavior that has been hidden from her. The difference, however, is that Darcy turns out to have been a good landlord all along, whereas Henry has been "making acquaintance with cottages whose very existence, though on his own estate, had been hitherto unknown to him" (469). That he is making an effort impresses Fanny, and she does start "to feel the possibility of his turning out well at last," so that there is some irony in her vehement conviction that "he was and must ever be completely unsuited to her, and ought not to think of her" (470).

Fanny has not been tempted by Henry's property, social position, or personal charms, but she is interested in the possibility of change in his moral character: "[H]e was much more gentle, obliging, and attentive to other people's feelings than he had ever been at Mansfield," and "He was decidedly improved." She thinks of him as almost agreeable but not quite: "[S]he had never seen him so agreeable—so *near* being agreeable" (471–72). It is difficult for her to resist the attempts of Sir Thomas and Edmund to persuade her to marry but even more difficult to resist Henry when she can see for herself that he is becoming a better man. The most important aspect of the temptation she experiences in Portsmouth is his kind offer to take her away from the unpleasantness of life in Portsmouth and convey her home to Mansfield Park, for "Portsmouth was Portsmouth; Mansfield was home" (499; ch. 14).

The story of Henry's kindness to his tenants and the observations Fanny makes about his improved character are described, not dramatized. The offer to take her home and her response to it, however, are made in a conversation between the two in her sister Susan's presence. Henry tells Susan of his concern that Fanny "ought never to be long banished from the free air, and liberty of the country" and assures Fanny of the "ease, and the pleasure" with which he and his sister would "immediately come down, and take you back to Mansfield" (476; ch. 11). She thanks him but tries to laugh off his offer. When he persists, saying that he knows she cannot lie about her health, she is "affected and distressed to a degree that made it impossible for her to say much, or even to be certain of what she ought to say" (477). Her inability to answer him indicates that he has succeeded in wearing down some of her resistance. He takes another tack, asking her advice about how to protect the livelihood of one of his tenants, "an honest man, to whom I have given half a promise already" (478). He expects her to advise him to go home to Everingham at once to attend to this business, that her concern for the well-being of "the poor and oppressed" will induce her to urge him to act and thus further obligate her to him.

Ironically, the stratagem backfires: Fanny tells Henry, "We have all a better guide in ourselves, if we would attend to it, than any other person can be" (478). The efforts of men to make her behave as they think other women should behave serve only to strengthen her adherence to the "better guide" within. After this exchange, she is "very low," and while she is still very much aware of "his being astonishingly more gentle, and regardful of others, than formerly," she retains her hope that if he really is so concerned for her comfort, he will give up trying to persuade her to do something she does not want to do: "[M]ight not it be fairly supposed, that he would not much longer persevere in a suit so distressing to her?" (479–80).

The idea that Henry might be concerned for her well-being prompts Fanny to imagine a situation in which, "had it been possible for her to return [his] regard," she would have a home of her own to which she could invite Susan and thereby rescue her from Portsmouth as well. Now Henry seems "really good-tempered," and she can even "fancy his entering into a plan of that sort, most pleasantly." If he is benevolent to his tenants, he might be helpful to her sister, "a girl so capable of being made every thing good" (486; ch. 12). Austen's painfully specific portrayal of the squalor, dirt, and noise of the Portsmouth household, and of the thoughtlessness of Fanny's parents, makes clear what the stakes are in Fanny's refusal of Henry's proposal. To refuse him means to lose the chance of being "settled in life, eligibly, honourably, nobly settled," in a place of order and comfort.

Her love for Edmund complicates her motives for continuing to refuse Henry, but she also knows that it would be wrong to accept the comforts Henry offers even if she weren't in love with someone else. When Mary Crawford's letter reiterates the invitation for Fanny to travel with her and her brother but also reveals "the sister's feelings—the brother's conduct—*her* cold-hearted ambition—*his* thoughtless vanity" (504–05; ch. 14), Fanny finds that she was right all along to be suspicious of the Crawfords. Mary betrays her interest in seeing Edmund as the heir of Mansfield Park, and Henry is "still the acquaintance, the flirt, perhaps, of Mrs. Rushworth!" With "a decided negative," Fanny declines their offer to take her to Mansfield (505). She gives this answer in a letter, which serves as further confirmation of what she has said to Henry, to Sir Thomas, and to Edmund. When vanity leads Henry from a flirtation with Maria Rushworth to an affair and Fanny learns of their elopement, she recognizes the full weight of the event: "[I]t was too horrible a confusion of guilt, too gross a complication of evil, for human nature, not in a state of utter barbarism, to be capable of!" For a brief hysterical moment, she even wishes that the tragedy of Mansfield Park would end in death: "[I]t appeared to her, that as far as this world alone was concerned, the greatest blessing to every one of kindred with Mrs. Rushworth would be instant annihilation" (511; ch. 15).

But although the story does not end happily for everyone, it ends well, with the recognition that a greater disaster has been averted. The opening of the novel is a brief history of the fortunes of the three Miss Wards, which leads to the arrival of Fanny at Mansfield Park: Miss Maria Ward marries well, and there is reason to expect her two sisters to marry "with almost equal advantage"; however, "there certainly are not so many men of large fortune in the world, as there are pretty women to deserve them" (3; vol. 1, ch. 1). The final chapter is a brief history of what happened to everyone as a result of the tragic action, including the change in Edmund's affections: "I only intreat every body to believe that exactly at the time when it was quite natural that it should be so, and not a week earlier, Edmund did cease to care about Miss Crawford, and became as anxious to marry Fanny, as Fanny herself could desire" (544; vol. 3, ch. 17). Whalley writes that the opening of *Mansfield Park* is "forthright, abrupt," and that it "set[s] the situation as swiftly and emphatically as possible." "[T]he book closes with corresponding despatch, yet with something of the elegiac recognition of sheer necessity" (131). The ending, like the beginning, is simply a framework for the drama in between; the real interest of the plot lies in the middle. Fanny is tempted to marry Henry but averts the mistake in judgment because she recognizes that marriage to him would be disastrous.

The tragic action of *Mansfield Park*, therefore, is consistent with what Aristotle identified as one of the best forms of tragedy, where recognition forestalls catastrophe. The ending is not meant to be a romantic happy ending; instead, it may be better understood as a "prosperous outcome" for the tragic heroine. The beginning and ending are history, the morally serious action of the plot is a tragedy, presented in dialogue rather than narration, and the outcome is prosperous. The last two thousand years may have seen the invention of many new types of tragedy, but we should also be alert to the possibility that even the new may turn out to have ancient precedents. Austen's innovation in the genre may help us refine our definitions of tragedy; the tragedy of *Mansfield Park* can also help illuminate the brief and sometimes cryptic definitions Aristotle offers in his *Poetics*. A number of Greek tragedies with "prosperous outcomes" have been lost, but, fortunately, we have Jane Austen and *Mansfield Park*.

NOTES

This essay is a revised version of my "Tragic Action," which is used in this volume with permission. The argument builds on the reading of *Mansfield Park* in my book *Jane Austen's Philosophy of the Virtues*.

[1] In his *Poetics*, Aristotle describes a kind of tragedy that ends well. Several other writers over the centuries have commented on the idea of the tragedy with a happy ending. The Italian playwright Giraldi Cinthio, for example, discusses two different kinds of tragedy in his *Discourse on the Composition of Romances, Comedies, and Tragedies* (1554): he distinguishes tragedies that end happily from those with sad endings, and he says that the unhappy tragedies work well as "closet dramas," while "happy" tragedies are best for performance. Giovanni Battista Guarini in his *Compendio* (1601) stresses the way tragedies may incorporate aspects of comedy in addition to the happy ending and the way such combinations help the audience find a healthy balance between melancholy and mirth ("Tragicomedy"). According to John Wiltshire, "*Mansfield Park* is a tragedy set (uncomfortably in the end) within the form of the romantic novel" (Introduction lxxxiii). Reading the novel in the light of Aristotle's theory of tragedy, however, suggests that a

tragic action with a prosperous ending may be read as one of the best kinds of tragedy rather than as an uncomfortable kind of romance.

[2]As R. J. Dingley suggests, Henry's position in this scene may allude to Sir Joshua Reynolds's famous portrait *Garrick between Tragedy and Comedy*. Henry is between Maria and Julia at this point, and the way he tells Julia that comedy chooses her also tells her that he chooses Maria.

[3]Shakespeare also weaves comic elements into his greatest tragedies: Mercutio and the Nurse in *Romeo and Juliet*, for instance, or the Gravedigger in *Hamlet*. Susan Allen Ford offers an illuminating discussion of *Mansfield Park* in relation to *King Lear*, especially in relation to Nahum Tate's 1681 reworking of Shakespeare's play, which is the version that was performed throughout the eighteenth century and well into the nineteenth. Tate imagined the tragedy of King Lear with a new ending, a happy ending, in which Cordelia marries Edgar. As Ford points out, this revision may seem to undermine Shakespeare's purpose and plot, but it met with the full approval of Samuel Johnson, who said that the audience's acceptance of the happy ending granted it legitimacy ("'Intimate'" 179–80). In the case of *Mansfield Park*, on the other hand, many members of the reading audience disapprove of the abrupt happy ending. Ford shows how Austen shifts the focus of the story from father (Lear–Sir Thomas) to daughter (Cordelia-Fanny). Ford also elaborates on the linguistic parallels between *Mansfield Park* and *King Lear* ("Working Out"). See also Snyder. Calvo discusses *Mansfield Park* as a condition-of-England novel.

[4]As both Ford and H. R. Harris point out, Fanny's "never, never, never" may echo King Lear's famous lament, in which he says "never" five times (Ford, "Intimate" 192; H. Harris 317).

[5]The square brackets are those of the translator, George Whalley. Unlike many commentators who see catharsis or purification or purgation as something that happens in the emotions of the audience, I follow Whalley, who was following Gerald Else, in locating the purification in the action or story.

[6]My "'My Idea'" analyzes the discussion of chapels and clergymen in *Mansfield Park*.

[7]In his lecture on Austen, Whalley says that none of the tragedies with prosperous outcomes "has come to us among the few survivors from the Greek theatre" (133), but he must be misremembering the *Poetics* here, because *Iphigenia in Taurus* does survive. Austen may have learned Greek from her father (DeForest). If so, it is possible that she read both the *Poetics* and *Iphigenia*. Whether or not she read Aristotle or Euripides, however, she would have been familiar with the idea of the tragedy with a prosperous outcome from Shakespeare's plays, and from other sources such as Samuel Richardson's novel *Sir Charles Grandison* or Mozart's *Cosi Fan Tutte*, which also combine elements of tragedy and comedy.

[8]"[P]oiein—to make, do, fashion, perform" (Aristotle 44n1).

[9]Whalley believes that *Mansfield Park* may be best understood as a tragedy, but he does not specify what the morally serious action of the novel is, nor does he explore the importance of dialogue at the heart of the plot.

[10]For an analysis of Fanny's growth and development, including the testing of her virtue, see my *Jane Austen's Philosophy*, ch. 5.

[11]"For tragedy is a *mimesis* not of men [simply] but of actions—that is, of life." Aristotle says that characters "do not act in order to present their characters: they embrace their characters for the sake of the actions [they are to do]" (73).

Avenues, Parks, Wilderness, and Ha-Has: The Use and Abuse of Landscape in *Mansfield Park*

Inger Sigrun Bredkjaer Brodey

Landscape gardening provides an important entry into the world of *Mansfield Park*, a novel that can be challenging for students, especially when its heroine is contrasted with her livelier and better known counterpart in *Pride and Prejudice*. Familiarity with discourses surrounding landscape and gardening of the period helps modern readers better understand the symbolism embedded in Austen's careful descriptions of landed estates. *Mansfield Park* includes descriptions of, or allusions to, six separate estates—Mansfield Park, Mansfield parsonage, Sotherton, Compton, Thornton Lacey, and Everingham—and spends time on plans for relandscaping three of them. In particular, the extended treatment of Sotherton's improvements and Austen's explicit reference to Mr. Rushworth's idea of hiring the famous landscape gardener Humphry Repton (1752–1818) mark, at least superficially, the importance of landscape gardening to this novel. In fact, Austen's realism in the description of Sotherton in volume 1 is so detailed that it is possible to diagram many aspects of the estate. Her decision to name *Mansfield Park* after a place rather than an idea or an individual confirms the central role of nature and landscape in this novel.

In *Mansfield Park*, Austen uses her familiarity with the history and symbolism associated with the English garden (then in vogue all over northern and central Europe) to provide a key to many of the philosophical and ethical themes in the novel, such as the role of authority and civility, the relation between law and virtue, issues of tradition and change, and competing notions of moral education. She uses the English garden also to provide a key to the internal life of the heroine. Her work belongs to an eighteenth-century tradition in which central relationships in sentimental novels are defined by the heroine's connection to gardens.

Landscape has its advantages as a topic for teaching, in that it appeals to the contemporary student who enjoys visual cues. Accordingly, I am building this essay around visual tools, such as maps and films. I first introduce some of the historical context that students need to decipher Austen's symbolism; then I take a close view of the group excursion to Sotherton, a sequence that is fruitful for in-class study.

The name of Repton, the designer who helped establish landscape gardening as a polite art as well as a fashion, appears five times in *Mansfield Park*. Such specific historical referencing is unusual in Austen's mature works, so it is worth considering what Repton signifies in this novel. He was a master improver and, following in the tradition of Lancelot "Capability" Brown, an expert in relandscaping and rebuilding estates to maximize their beauty and grandeur. Repton greatly promoted the spread of English landscape gardening, not only by reshaping over four hundred estates in his thirty-year career but also by writing three major works on the subject published between 1796 and 1816. Austen could easily have read and certainly must have known Repton's very popular *Observations on the Theory and Practice of Landscape Gardening* (first published in 1803).

What distinguished Repton from other landscape gardeners was his ability as a salesman. He perfected a system of before-and-after watercolor images in order to sell his improvements to his clients. In his Red Books (so called because they were generally bound in red morocco leather), he would overlay a small flap of paper onto a watercolor painting of the estate. When lying flat, the picture would show the estate in its current form; the client, by lifting the flap, would see Repton's proposed changes.[1] Together, these before-and-after illustrations make an excellent tool in the classroom. Each Red Book included extensive text in which Repton described his improvements in the context of contemporary aesthetics. Although his opinions shifted over time and according to prevailing fashions, there were consistent qualities in his "improvements." Austen clearly found humor in the use of this term for all landscape changes, including alterations for the worse. One of Repton's goals was the removal or disguise of objectionable aspects of the prospect. The most common offenders were geometric arrangements that smacked of the former passion for the baroque in landscape design and straight lines that hinted at utilitarian or agricultural purposes, such as plotting or plowing. Avenues (two long parallel rows of trees that line a path or road) were also frequently broken up. For Repton, agriculture degraded the prospect from a manor house: "[W]e never see a park ploughed up, but we always attribute it to poverty," he writes in his Red Book for the Honing estate in Norfolk (qtd. in Williamson 122). In some cases, religious buildings, particularly churches in contemporary use, were deemed as unacceptable for a prospect as well—although ruined churches were considered picturesque. Mrs. Norris echoes this fashion in her descriptions of what she intended to do (and the Grants actually complete) at the Mansfield parsonage: namely, planting trees to block the churchyard from the view of the Parsonage.

> We did a vast deal in that way at the parsonage; we made it quite a different place from what it was when we first had it. You young ones do not remember much about it, perhaps. But if dear Sir Thomas were here, he could tell you what improvements we made; and a great deal more would have been done, but for poor Mr. Norris's sad state of health. . . . If it had not been for *that*, we should have carried on the garden wall, and made the plantation to shut out the churchyard, just as Dr. Grant has done.
>
> (63; vol. 1, ch. 6)

The irony here is increased by the fact that the clergymen find reminders of their calling unappealing to their aesthetic tastes.

Repton and others strove to open the prospect by removing trees and buildings in order to emphasize the grandeur of the estate and the social status of its owner. To enhance the drama of a view, Repton favored serpentine approaches to the great houses, which enlisted the element of surprise to dramatize one's first view of the estate. To create these approaches, he often needed to redirect public roads that had previously stopped in front of the manor houses or that had gone directly by them. These general (Reptonian) goals are implicit in Mr. Rushworth's use of the term *improvement* and his description of Repton's work at Compton:

> "I wish you could see Compton," said he, "it is the most complete thing! I never saw a place so altered in my life. I told Smith I did not know where I was. The approach *now* is one of the finest things in the country. You see the house in the most surprising manner. I declare when I got back to Sotherton yesterday, it looked like a prison—quite a dismal old prison."
>
> "Oh! for shame!" cried Mrs. Norris. "A prison, indeed! Sotherton Court is the noblest old place in the world."
>
> "It wants improvement, ma'am, beyond any thing. I never saw a place that wanted so much improvement in my life; and it is so forlorn, that I do not know what can be done with it."   (62)

The word "prison" evokes a need for the openness and liberation that Repton supplied to his clients.

Another frequent way in which landholders opened their prospects was by appropriating common land that had formerly served for tenant or subsistence farming. The utility and well-being of the common farmer were sacrificed for the sake of social status and fashion. It is this irreverent form of improvement that Austen evokes in Rushworth's dismissal of Sotherton's avenue:

> "[At Compton] [t]here have been two or three fine old trees cut down that grew too near the house, and it opens the prospect amazingly, which makes me think that Repton, or any body of that sort, would certainly have the avenue at Sotherton down; the avenue that leads from the west front to the top of the hill, you know," . . .
>
> Fanny, . . . who had been attentively listening, now looked at [Edmund], and said in a low voice,
>
> "Cut down an avenue! What a pity! Does it not make you think of Cowper? 'Ye fallen avenues, once more I mourn your fate unmerited.'"
>   (65–66)

One Red Book gives an example of an avenue sacrificed (or opened) for aesthetic purposes while Repton also publishes plans for improvement of his own, more modest estate (figs. 1 and 2). In order to enhance the view from his house,

Fig. 1. The view from Humphry Repton's own house before his proposed improvements (Repton, colored plate between pp. 232 and 233)

Fig. 2. Repton's house after improvements (Repton, colored plate between pp. 232 and 233)

Repton blocks out all signs of mercantile or agricultural activity—namely, the small plowed common field and the butcher shop. He tellingly improves his prospect by enclosing the small patch of common land and blocking out the impoverished, one-legged, one-eyed, one-armed ex-soldier who begs nearby (Duckworth, *Improvement* xxxii).

Although Rushworth (who is "rushing" to improve his "worth" both in fashion and in love) first initiates the topic and Mrs. Norris self-avowedly demonstrates great potential as an improver, the chief improver of the novel is Henry Crawford. Henry, "such a capital improver" (284; ch. 7), is always looking for new projects. We have direct evidence of his views of improvement, not only in his own alterations at Everingham and at his uncle's summer cottage but also in the plans he volunteers for Edmund's parsonage at Thornton Lacey:

> The farm-yard must be cleared away entirely, and planted up to shut out the blacksmith's shop. The house must be turned to front the east instead of the north—the entrance and principal rooms, I mean, must be on that side, where the view is really very pretty; I am sure it may be done. And *there* must be your approach—through what is at present the garden. You must make a new garden at what is now the back of the house; which will be giving it the best aspect in the world—sloping to the south-east. The ground seems precisely formed for it. . . . The meadows beyond what *will be* the garden, as well as what now *is*, sweeping round from the lane I stood in to the north-east, that is, to the principal road through the village, must be all laid together of course; very pretty meadows they are, finely sprinkled with timber. They belong to the living, I suppose. If not, you must purchase them. Then the stream—something must be done with the stream; but I could not quite determine what. (281–82; vol. 2, ch. 7)

The most striking features of Henry's plan are his concern for superficial impressions, such as "aspect" and "approach"; his cavalier disregard of expense, combined with complete disregard for current usages of the land ("the farmyard"); and the desire to block out all traces of village life (the blacksmith, the village, the road)—evidence of the very people Edmund will be trying to serve. Tom Williamson aptly calls this type of improvement the "landscape of exclusion" (100–09).

On the evidence of her other novels, Austen took "the duties and dignities of the resident land-holder" seriously and saw in them an ideal of stewardship (*Persuasion*, [Chapman] 138). She features landowners in other novels who exhibit this ideal and do not isolate themselves from the villages on and around their estates, particularly Mr. Knightley of *Emma*, and to a lesser extent Mr. Darcy of *Pride and Prejudice*. As Alistair Duckworth argues, "For Jane Austen, the estate as an ordered physical structure is a metonym for other inherited structures—society as a whole, a code of morality, a body of manners, a system of language" (*Improvement* ix; see also Quaintance).[2] When Fanny and the Bertrams approach Sotherton Court and notice all the run-down cottages, Maria remarks, "Those cottages are really a disgrace" (96; vol. 1, ch. 8). Whereas Maria merely sees them as an embarrassingly ugly blemish on her otherwise grand vista, Fanny witnesses an ethical failure on the part of Mr. Rushworth as landlord.[3] Similarly, when Henry tries to demonstrate his merit to Fanny, he does so by returning to Everingham and posing as a model landlord: he meets tenants and sees cottages on his own estate that he previously did not know had existed (469; vol. 3, ch. 10).

After giving students some historical background on Repton and landscape improvements and showing at least one pair of before-and-after illustrations, I have them take a close look at the group excursion to Sotherton (vol. 1, ch. 9). Students might find it helpful to draw a map, an approximation based on Austen's meticulous description. Figure 3 is a map that I created and find particularly helpful in class.[4] The narrator mentions that the terrace is the perfect spot for "fault-finding" (105; ch. 9), and this remark applies on a number of different levels. In fact, the whole discourse of landscape in these pages is packed with double entendre and metaphorical usages, particularly involving obliquely romantic remarks. For example, Mrs. Grant alludes to the presence of a new wife as the ultimate improvement for Sotherton, in response to Mr. Rushworth's complaints that the estate wants improvement: "'No wonder that Mr. Rushworth should think so at present,' said Mrs. Grant to Mrs. Norris, with a smile; 'but depend upon it, Sotherton will have *every* improvement in time which his heart can desire'" (62; vol. 1, ch. 6).

Similarly, the word *prospects* (often plural) is frequently used to describe one's chances of a good marriage: generally men improve the prospect of their estates, while women improve their prospects of marriage.[5] In both cases, *prospect* refers to our human ability to shape our surroundings and, by extension, our future. There is an analogy implied between the hubris of the matchmaker and the hubris of the improver. The improver, as Williamson writes, must have a "particular frame of mind: a breezy confidence, an ability to look at an existing piece of landscape and see its form not as God-given and inevitable but as provisional and changeable" (122). The double meanings of words like *improvement* and *prospect* help Austen reveal the self-serving pursuit of fashion and show that aesthetic concerns cannot be separated from practical and ethical considerations. "[Sotherton's terrace] was a good spot for fault-finding" indeed (105), and the faults revealed relate more to the young people visiting Sotherton than to the estate itself. Ultimately, the reshaping of landscapes in *Mansfield Park* is a direct indication of character and interpersonal relations.

The time spent on the tour of the manor house is eventually oppressive for all the young members of the group. Mary detests the banality of Mrs. Rushworth's detailed enumerations of family portraits; Maria and others tire of Mr. Rushworth's bumbling attempts to impress his fiancée with empty grandeur; and the more observant among the party sense an atmosphere of thwarted desires and unfulfilled expectations as well as the cumulative burdens of insincerity. By the end of the tour, the visitors at Sotherton Court crave escape from the ancient house.

Austen then stages the movements of her characters through a series of spaces, each separated from the next by a barrier. These, and the doors through them, are catalysts for the novel's moral and emotional dramas.

Door 1: "One Wish for Air and Liberty"

The narrator informs us:

> [T]he question of surveying the grounds, with the who and the how, was likely to be more fully agitated, and Mrs. Norris was beginning to arrange by what junction of carriages and horses most could be done, when the young people, meeting with an outward door, temptingly open on a flight of steps which led immediately to turf and shrubs, and all the sweets of pleasure-grounds, as by one impulse, one wish for air and liberty, all walked out. (104–05; vol. 1, ch. 9)

The phrasing of the long sentence itself allows the reader to experience the delayed gratification that this small escape provides. The reader too breathes in the fresh air with relief. The words "temptingly," "sweets," "pleasure," "impulse," and "liberty" in this passage, however, suggest that the freedom is somehow illicit. Although Mrs. Rushworth recommends that the young people move on to the wilderness, they prefer at first to "[disperse] about in happy independence" on the lawns and terrace. After a little while, the individuals "began to form into parties," seeming "naturally to unite," yet these unions are fraught with tension (105). Two are clear-cut love triangles: Mary-Edmund-Fanny and Maria-Henry-Rushworth. Julia reluctantly joins the older women, Mrs. Rushworth and Mrs. Norris, making another uncomfortable trio. These groupings foreshadow some of the desires that are expressed through responses to the landscape, such as another implicit love triangle—namely, Julia-Henry-Maria. The Sotherton sequence, like the theatrical chapters, lays desire and rivalry bare.

Door 2: Comfort in the Shade

The doors lead to a series of escapes, from the confinement of the house to the walled garden and bowling green of the lawn to the shady regularity of the wilderness to the more open expanses of the park (figs. 3 and 4). The doors mark a progression from enclosed formal and cultivated spaces to spaces that are gradually less cultivated and more open in appearance. Ironically, those

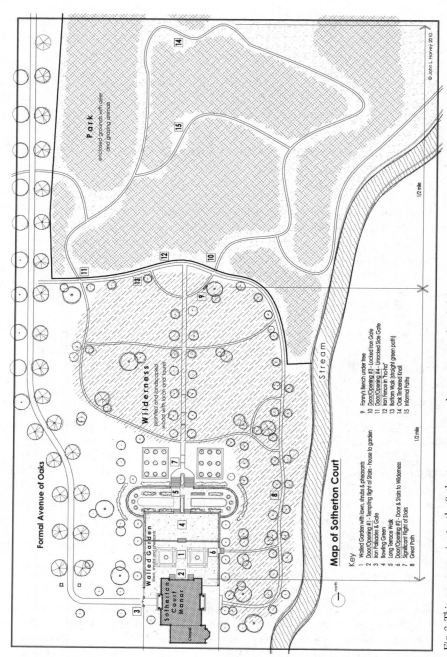

Fig. 3. This map approximates the Sotherton estate, according to Austen's detailed descriptions in the novel.

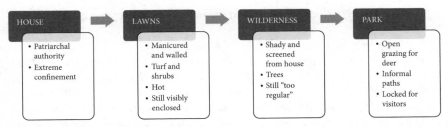

Fig. 4. Diagram of the young characters' movement through Sotherton Park, arrows representing thresholds the characters cross. The corresponding thresholds are numbered in fig. 3.

who pass through them are never as free as they could wish, and frustration persists: despite its name, the wilderness is "too regular," and the park, while promisingly open and "informal," must be entered through gates, most of which are locked.[6]

The transition from lawn to wilderness, just like the transition from manor house to lawn, is described as an escape and "refreshment" (107). The second door, in the middle of the lawns and presumably breaking the walled garden, enables this second escape. Miss Crawford initiates this departure, claiming that it is "insufferably hot" and posing the interesting rhetorical question, "Shall any of us object to being comfortable? Here is a nice little wood, if one can but get into it. What happiness if the door should not be locked." Mary assumes that the escape will not be granted: "[I]n these great places, the gardeners are the only people who can go where they like" (106), revealing the discrepancy she feels between what she wishes to do and what society expects of her class. The "wilderness," the narrator informs us, is a "planted wood of about two acres, and though chiefly of larch and laurel, and beech cut down, and though laid out with too much regularity, was darkness and shade, and natural beauty, compared with the bowling-green and the terrace. They all felt the refreshment of it, and for some time could only walk and admire" (106–07).

The provocative term *wilderness* designated a tract of land planted with trees and shrubs to provide meandering walks in the later eighteenth century, but it could also mean "wildness," land left uncultivated and therefore suggesting ungoverned and anarchic possibilities. The characters must literally leave the seat of patriarchal authority and ancient tradition that Mr. Rushworth himself calls "a prison," in order to taste the sweet liberty of the wilderness, where they are, or think they are, free from the burden of imposed authority as well as the demands of civility. The groups become individualized as desires increasingly shape the actions of the characters and their inhibition decreases. Yet ironically the wilderness is refreshing only in contrast to the openness and heat of the formal lawns. It provides a greater degree of privacy and anonymity, allowing Mary for example to renew the difficult conversation about Edmund's becoming a clergyman, and yet the trees are laid out "with too much regularity," symbolizing the continuing oppression of the manor house or society's regulations in general.

It is tempting to remember the desire for escape to the wilderness as gratifying only to the ever-restless Crawfords and the chronically dissatisfied Miss Bertrams—that is, the less honorable characters in *Mansfield Park*. But Austen carefully shows the reader that all the young people, even Edmund and Fanny, feel oppressed by the claustrophobic atmosphere of Sotherton Court. Inasmuch as all the characters are sensible of the restraints on them, it is the manner in which they respond to confinement and to authority symbols that sets them apart. As doorways 3 and 4 appear, the illicit desires of Henry, Maria, and Julia manifest themselves, as well as the seductive powers of both Henry and Mary Crawford.[7] Their actions in this fictional state of nature reveal deeper differences in character, which extend throughout the novel and foreshadow its ending.

Door 3: The Locked Gate

The central fixture (and central obstacle) in chapters 9 and 10 is a ha-ha. This ha-ha divides the wilderness from the park, and openings in the hedges and iron gates that line the upper edge of the ha-ha mark the next transition in (and imposition on) the characters' sense of liberty. As they approach the ha-ha, the trios break apart and couples emerge; disunity is caused by desires that conflict with conventions or expectations. Individuals—namely, Mr. Rushworth and Fanny—are hurt as they are excluded from the new formations. The ha-ha is first seen by the trio Fanny-Edmund-Mary, eliciting from Mary Crawford the memorably contradictory response: "'I must move,' said she, 'resting fatigues me.—I have looked across the ha-ha till I am weary. I must go and look through that iron gate at the same view, without being able to see it so well'" (112; vol. 1, ch. 9). Note that Mary recognizes the perversity of her desires: what she gains in relief from a feeling of oppression she will lose in actual view or prospect, as she descends (literally and figuratively) to the level of the iron gate. Her romantic prospects are, however, improved by the removal of Fanny from the scene.

In order to be able to visualize this scene, students will need to know what a ha-ha is (fig. 5). Christopher Hussey has credited the landscape gardener Vanbrugh with first popularizing the ha-ha in the 1730s (128). A ha-ha—or ha!ha!, as it was also called—is "[a] boundary to a garden, pleasure-ground, or park, of such a kind as not to interrupt the view from within, and not to be seen till closely approached; consisting of a trench, the inner side of which is perpendicular and faced with stone, the outer sloping and turfed; a sunk fence." Ha-has could keep livestock off carefully manicured lawns without marring the estate's picturesque scenic prospect with unsightly fences: since the ha-ha was a ditch, it would be hidden from sight at a distance. Repton explains that the different

Fig. 5. Diagram of a ha-ha (Repton and Repton 79). Many thanks to Chad Haefle and Tommy Nixon.

physical shapes of the ha-ha have to do with the kinds of creatures meant to be excluded in order to protect the pristine prospect and keep animals from nibbling on formal gardens. Whereas ditches might suffice for deterring cows, deer require higher fences. In some locations, Repton prefers hedges of thorns to disguise the presence of fences (59, 84–86).

The ha-ha in *Mansfield Park*, which separates the more manicured wilderness from the vast expanses of Sotherton's park, is visible to characters wandering in the wilderness at close range, not from the central, officially picturesque manor house and its lawns. Ha-has thus attempt to maintain order while also hiding the hand of the landscape gardener. They represent a masked, or hidden, imposition of authority. Whereas the straightforward fence suggests the visibility and unmistakability of law, the ha-ha may suggest society's *hidden* constraints, which would be the domain of conscience, or virtue, rather than of law. The ha-ha in *Mansfield Park* is an occasion for a moral dilemma that reveals much about the characters who respond to it. The ha-ha thus helps reveal the huge ethical domain not enclosed by law.

Repton is constantly concerned with the psychological effect of landscapes and barriers on his viewers, especially the viewers' presumed dislike of confinement: his central task in landscaping, it seems, is liberating and occupying their eyes and imagination. Mary Crawford is not alone in finding the view "through the iron gate" wearying and insufferable. Repton writes that where a fence or ha-ha "is higher than the eye, as it must be against deer, the landscape seen through its bars becomes intolerable" (86). Like Mary, he emphasizes the importance of freedom understood as movement and novelty.[8] Austen, however, thwarts most plans for improvement in *Mansfield Park*.

On discovering the locked gate, Maria sends Mr. Rushworth running off to retrieve the key from the house and allows Henry to seduce her into leaving the wilderness without waiting for Mr. Rushworth or his key: "[U]nluckily that iron gate, that ha-ha, give me a feeling of restraint and hardship," she cries. "Mr. Rushworth is so long fetching this key!" (115–16; vol. 1, ch. 10). Her seducer suggestively responds:

"And for the world you would not get out without the key and without Mr. Rushworth's authority and protection, or I think you might with little difficulty pass round the edge of the gate, here, with my assistance; I think it might be done, if you really wished to be more at large, and could allow yourself to think it not prohibited."

"Prohibited! Nonsense! I certainly can get out that way, and I will."

(116)

With Henry's help, Maria slips around the edges of the locked gate before Mr. Rushworth returns with the keys. Julia also leaves the wilderness through doorway 3 without waiting for the official sanction of Rushworth's key. Unlike Maria, she is not seduced and does not deliberate over her actions. Instead of deliberately "pass[ing] round" the gate, "Julia was vexed, and her temper was hasty," and she "immediately scrambled across the fence" (117–18). This is not a small feat, since Repton himself says, "[N]othing is so difficult to pass as a deep sunk fence" (81).[9]

It may seem silly to attribute such significance to actions so minor. Yet in Austen's novels in general, manners are morals writ small, and the reader, like a woman trying to gauge a suitor, needs to pay careful attention to details— especially in highly symbolic scenes such as the Sotherton excursion. It is no accident that the ha-ha scene is immediately preceded by Edmund's remarks on the interconnectedness of manners and morals: "[W]ith regard to [the clergy's] influencing public manners, Miss Crawford must not misunderstand me, or suppose I mean to call them the arbiters of good breeding, the regulators of refinement and courtesy, the masters of the ceremonies of life. The *manners* I speak of, might rather be called *conduct*, perhaps, the result of good principles" (109).[10]

The difference between Maria's and Julia's crossing of the ha-ha is analogous to the legal difference between first-degree and second-degree offenses or, in ethical terms, between vice and folly. Maria is deliberate where Julia is impulsive, behaviors that foreshadow their respective love affairs at the end of the novel: Maria consummates and persists in a long-desired adulterous relationship; Julia impulsively elopes to Scotland with Mr. Yates.

Door 4: The Unlocked Gate

Mary Crawford too bemoans the iron gate (door 3) but does not blatantly challenge its authority (she also leaves before Mr. Rushworth is sent to find the key, avoiding additional social problems). She finds a third way of relieving her sense of confinement or restraint. We learn, with Fanny, that Mary and Edmund walk alongside the ha-ha (symbolically flirting with danger) until "a side gate, not fastened, had *tempted* them" (120; my emphasis). The unlocked gates (doors 1, 2, and 4) represent temptation and escape yet also legitimate responses to oppression, whereas Henry's, Maria's, and Julia's responses to the locked gate (door 3) represent illicit or ill-judged responses. Maria is actually the only person who really wants to escape: Mary wants novelty and activity, as well as a tête-à-tête with Edmund; Julia wants not to be excluded from Henry's romantic attentions; and Fanny wants to see the park.

Insofar as the ha-ha and its gate symbolize the restraints dictated by society and Mr. Rushworth's key symbolizes its sanctioned propriety, the responses of the four females are interesting to compare: Maria and Julia Bertram both disregard even the appearance of propriety in their eagerness to satisfy their desires—and they overtly insult their host in the process; Maria's additional disrespect for Rushworth's authority is echoed in her subsequent affair; and Mary Crawford manages to satisfy her desires without directly breaking any of society's strict conventions, persisting until she finds not one but two unlocked gates to serve her purposes. Fanny alone neither violates nor feels threatened by the ha-ha.

Austen thus distinguishes between the authority that is imposed externally, with force, pomp, and circumstance, and the authority that is felt internally. To be strictly proper, in society's terms, is no guarantee of virtue. Virtue requires a conscience or sense of delicacy, which is lacking in all three females who cross the ha-ha. In the context of this "fault-finding" excursion, we learn of Julia, for example, that

> [t]he politeness which she had been brought up to practise as a duty, made it impossible for her to escape [society's demands—in this case, escape Mrs. Rushworth's dull company and slow pace]; while the want of that higher species of self-command, that just consideration of others, that knowledge of her own heart, that principle of right which had not formed any essential part of her education, made her miserable under it.
> (106; vol. 1, ch. 9)

In contrast, Fanny feels free not because she passes around or scrambles over all restraints to experience license, or comes to a conveniently open door that lets her rationalize her way out of a moral predicament, but because she finds actions that satisfy both what society demands and her own strict sense of propriety.

Without that "species of self-command," the Miss Bertrams are slaves of their passions and of circumstance. Fanny, though paradoxically stationary in the wilderness scene, actually has greater mobility. The Bertram sisters do not experience liberation from external restraints, because the lack of internalized restraint prevents them from achieving any moral freedom.[11] The suggestion is that the daughters of Sir Thomas and Lady Bertram never learned to tolerate any externally imposed restraint; because they never learned self-restraint, they also never learned to share in their own guardianship. Mary, too, cares only for outward politeness, although she is more successful in maintaining it than the Miss Bertrams. Sir Thomas, even after he returns home and witnesses the theatricals, still only cares about the surface—about politeness or the appearance of propriety: he restores his house to "its proper state" and "wipe[s] away every outward memento," dismisses the carpenter and the scene painter, hides all outward traces of the preparations, and burns "every unbound copy of 'Lover's Vows'" that meets "his eye" (223; vol. 2, ch. 2). Like a landscape gardener removing all traces of offending purposes from his prospects, he restores an "external smoothness," culminating in his call for music, which the narrator informs us, "helped to conceal the want of real harmony" (224).

The responses of the characters in the Sotherton scene reveal not only imperfect forms of rebellion but also the flawed moral education that shaped the characters, an education that did not provide some of them with self-knowledge, internal boundaries, or moral authority.[12] The desires and impulses set temporarily free or explored in the Sotherton scene will remain simmering under the decorums of gentility and determine the future course of these characters in *Mansfield Park*.

NOTES

[1] An interesting classroom activity would be to compare his Red Book drawings with the modern use of before-and-after advertisements in today's fashion magazines (including *Redbook*). One could consider what aspects of human nature this strategy appeals to. The comparison also brings out the similarity between landscaping and matchmaking (both improve prospects) that Austen brings forth. Several of Repton's works, including his illustrations, have been digitized and are available at Web sites such as www .archive.org.

[2] A new group of critics, such as Celia Easton and Mary Chan, challenge Duckworth's conclusions and suggest that several of Austen's sympathetic heroes, including Edmund Bertram, Henry Tilney, and George Knightley, benefited from enclosure.

[3] Everett writes elegantly on Austen and landlords.

[4] Figure 3 is based on Vladimir Nabokov's sketch from his lectures (31). It is also influenced by the estates often cited as a possible inspiration for Austen, particularly Stoneleigh Abbey. Jon Spence, following Nigel Nicolson, makes an eloquent argument that the chapel at Sotherton is based on the chapel at Stoneleigh. I would like to thank John Harvey for his assistance in drawing this map.

[5] Henry Crawford plays on this double meaning when he remarks to Maria at Sotherton Court, "Your prospects, however, are too fair to justify want of spirits. You have a very smiling scene before you" (115; vol. 1, ch. 10).

[6] It is helpful to give students abbreviated *OED* definitions in a class handout. A park is "[a]ny large enclosed piece of ground, usually comprising woodland and pasture, attached to or surrounding a manor, castle, country house, etc., and used for recreation, and often for keeping deer, cattle, or sheep." A wilderness is either "[a] wild or uncultivated region or tract of land, uninhabited, or inhabited only by wild animals; 'a tract of solitude and savageness'" (def. 1b) or "[a] piece of ground in a large garden or park,

planted with trees, and laid out in an ornamental or fantastic style, often in the form of a maze or labyrinth" (def. 1c). This second definition of *wilderness* dominates *Mansfield Park*.

[7] It is interesting that the ethical reading reflects primarily on the female characters, perhaps because they have considerably less mobility than their male counterparts and thus respond more tellingly to the rare opportunity to shape their own prospects with relative privacy. (I remind students of the rarity of sanctioned private conversations between men and women then.)

[8] Although I've used Repton as a source about the role of ha-has, Austen associates him primarily with the notion of improvement. She uses him for his symbolic valence, not for accuracy regarding specific designs. One could, in fact, easily imagine Repton's deciding to rid Sotherton of its ha-ha, as well as of its iron fences, gates, and palisades.

[9] John Wiltshire suggests additional allusions for the garden gate: "[I]t is appropriate that readers should feel that the garden's wilderness and pathways of dalliance remind them of Spenser, or *Paradise Lost*, or *A Midsummer Night's Dream* or *As You Like It*, and that the gate should suggest to some the wicket gate through which Christian passes after his confrontation with Mr. Worldly Wiseman in Bunyan's *Pilgrim's Progress*, or Marvell's 'iron gates of life.' Others may remember the scene in *Clarissa* in which the heroine is lured to betray herself by Lovelace, as Maria is by Henry, in front of a 'garden door'" (Introduction lvi.)

[10] If these warnings are not enough, Austen additionally layers an allusion to Genesis 3.1–6, another garden that serves as a focal point for a discourse on obedience and authority. In the Garden of Eden, we have an overt prohibition from the Creator, analogous to the anonymously locked gate at Sotherton. Henry's speech resembles the serpent's as Henry repeats and twists the meaning of Mary's prohibition.

[11] Susannah Fullerton astutely remarks that "Maria Bertram's progress through *MP* is graphically visualized by Jane Austen as a movement from one form of imprisonment to another, and her fate is vividly depicted through prison imagery. *MP* is, in fact, a novel about freedom—moral, sexual, and emotional—and most of its characters blunder from one form of confinement to the next in their search for greater liberty. The language of restraint and confinement is everywhere—the reference to slavery, Henry's role in the play which includes a spell in prison, Fanny's term of imprisonment in the little house in Portsmouth, etc. The subtle depiction of Sotherton Court as a prison reinforces all the important themes of the novel."

[12] It is interesting to follow the word "authority" as it progresses through the novel. Authority begins as the almost exclusive attribute of Sir Thomas, but by the end of the novel, as the moral center of Mansfield Park shifts and as Fanny matures, it is attributed to her. When Susan arrives, we learn that Fanny has adopted a new "office of authority" (459; vol. 3, ch. 9). An excellent exercise is to have students do an electronic word search of "authority" and analyze how its meaning changes. This change is the central point of Brodey, "Papas." See also Brodey, *Ruined* 13, 27, 41–42, 108.

Samuel Johnson and
the Morality of *Mansfield Park*

Deborah J. Knuth Klenck

To keep students from dismissing Fanny Price as a prig, as they often do if they read *Mansfield Park* directly after *Pride and Prejudice*, I have found it helpful for them to read the novel along with the writings of Samuel Johnson, a teacher of Jane Austen—and of Fanny Price, because Fanny is certainly the novel's central moral conscience. In the earliest biography of Austen, her brother Henry tells us that "her favourite moral writers were Johnson in prose, and Cowper in verse" (H. Austen 7).[1] Reading Johnson with *Mansfield Park* can change the tone of the conversation about the novel and show students aspects of this novel they might otherwise overlook. Many topics from Johnson's essays anticipate the concerns of *Mansfield Park*, from garden design to Shakespeare, from travel writing to novel reading, from tyrannical parents to self-indulgent children: issues that Austen uses, among other purposes, to distinguish right from wrong, Fanny from Mary. I have used Johnson's *The Rambler* (1750–52), *The Dictionary of the English Language* (1755), and *Rasselas* (1759) as companion texts with *Mansfield Park* to help students think about both Austen's content and form. There are also distinct advantages to pairing Johnson with *Mansfield Park* in survey-of-the-novel courses.

In teaching fiction, I try to avoid discussions of fictional characters we like or dislike, as if they were real people. Nevertheless, when as formidable a critic as Lionel Trilling pronounces, "Nobody, I believe, has ever found it possible to like the heroine of *Mansfield Park*," something must be done ("*Mansfield Park*" [*Moral Obligation*] 296). In this essay I give examples of Johnsonian reasons to like Fanny while judging Mary Crawford, along the way confirming Mrs. Norris as the character we all love to hate. My purpose is to help students appreciate that Austen's novel goes beyond the courtship plot, that there is a cogent set of moral imperatives structuring the philosophy and practice of her work. Austen herself did not scruple to refer to liking characters: an example is Emma, "whom no one but myself will much like" (Austen-Leigh), and the author's affection for Fanny is evident in her proprietary reference to "My Fanny" at the end of the novel (533; vol. 3, ch. 17). Perhaps it is no coincidence that Austen also refers to the author of *The Rambler* as "my dear Dr. Johnson" in a letter to her sister (Le Faye 121; letter 50).

Austen sketches Fanny's character, in part, through Fanny's opinions—most, though not all, "formed" by Edmund (76; vol. 1, ch. 7)—on many topics. One such topic, a crucial one that recurs in the novel, is the landscape. While the class considers the ironic plan to "improve" an estate by cutting down its avenue of trees (65–66; ch. 6) or Maria Bertram's symbolic decision to squeeze past the locked iron gate with Henry Crawford (116; ch. 10), the conversation can turn to a later passage, from volume 2, chapter 4, in which the bored Mary has taken up Fanny as a walking companion, now that Maria's marriage has removed both Bertram sisters from the neighborhood. As the girls talk in the Grants' shrubbery, their words are a measure of the many significant contrasts between them:

> "This is pretty—very pretty," said Fanny, looking around her as they were sitting together one day: "Every time I come into this shrubbery I am more struck with its growth and beauty. Three years ago, this was nothing but a rough hedgerow along the upper side of the field, . . . and now it is converted into a walk, . . . and perhaps in another three years we may be forgetting—almost forgetting what it was before. How wonderful, how very wonderful the operations of time, and the changes of the human mind!" And following the latter train of thought, she soon afterwards added: "If any one faculty of our nature may be called *more* wonderful than the rest, I do think it is memory. There seems something more speakingly incomprehensible in the powers, the failures, the inequalities of memory, than in any other of our intelligences. The memory is sometimes so retentive, so obedient—at others, so bewildered and so weak—and at others again, so tyrannic, so beyond controul!—We are to be sure a miracle every way—but our powers of recollecting and of forgetting, do seem peculiarly past finding out." (243)

Typically, Mary is "untouched and inattentive" to Fanny's meditation, and Fanny politely converts it to a compliment to Mary's half sister ("I must admire the taste Mrs. Grant has shewn in all this. There is such quiet simplicity in the plan of the walk!"), as she goes on to apologize for her enthusiasm: "You will think me rhapsodizing; but when I am out of doors . . . I am very apt to get into this sort of wondering strain" (244). When Mary finally responds to what Fanny modestly calls her "rambling fancy," Mary fails to engage with either the "wonder" of the evergreens or the praise of her sister's garden design:

> "To say the truth," replied Miss Crawford, "I am something like the famous Doge at the court of Lewis XIV, and may declare that I see no wonder in this shrubbery equal to seeing myself in it. If any body had told me a year ago that this place would be my home, that I should be spending month after month here, as I have done, I certainly should not have believed them!—I have now been here nearly five months!" (244)

It is fun to observe that Mary Crawford uses some form of the first-person pronoun nine times—never self-deprecatingly—in the course of this short speech.[2]

But Johnson helps us examine other words in the passage. Fanny's "train of thought" about memory and forgetting may be informed by Boswell's record of

Johnson's "nice distinction" between "to remember and to recollect" (Boswell 1162–63). John Wiltshire points out that "Fanny's reflections are reminiscent of Johnson's essays on Memory in the *Rambler* and the *Idler*" ("Explanatory Notes" 696).[3] *Rambler* number 41 says that

> Memory is the purveyor of reason, the power which places those images before the mind upon which the judgment is to be exercised, and which treasures up the determinations that are once passed, as the rules of future action. . . . It is, indeed, the faculty of remembrance, which may be said to place us in the class of moral agents,

a definition that seems to form the basis for Fanny's association between memory and the "miracle" of creation (*Rambler* 3: 223).[4]

Even though it is Fanny who apologizes for wondering, Mary Crawford's "wonder[ing]" at "seeing [her]self" in the shrubbery may remind us of *Rambler* 137's opinion of the act of wondering:

> It may be remarked . . . that ignorance is often the effect of wonder. It is common for those who have never accustomed themselves to the labour of enquiry, nor invigorated their confidence by conquests over difficulty, to sleep in the gloomy quiescence of astonishment, without any effort to animate enquiry or dispel obscurity. . . . [T]hey therefore content themselves with the gaze of folly   (*Major Works* 222)

Mary's thoughts hardly ever follow anything so rigorous as a "train," and her self-regarding comparison of herself with the Doge shows that five months in the country have taught her nothing about country life.[5] She paid no attention to the lesson of an earlier exchange with Edmund, when she insisted how "astonished" she was to find no horse and cart available to collect her harp from Northampton (68; vol. 1, ch.6). Edmund patiently attempted to correct her ignorance: "You could not be expected to have thought on the subject before, but when you *do* think of it, you must see the importance of getting in the grass." Edmund's italics show his emphasis that there are some things Mary "must" learn, but even as in this conversation she promises, "I shall understand all your ways in time," she contradicts herself by repeating the "true London maxim, that every thing is to be got with money" (69). Fanny remarks on the "wonderful" human memory but does more than wonder. Her mind has been trained in what Johnson calls the "labour of enquiry": her library in the East Room (which includes Johnson's ironically named *Idler* essays) demonstrates the discipline of her leisure hours. Mary's failure to attend to Fanny's observations about nature, or even to Edmund's simple agricultural facts, denotes not only intellectual but also moral lassitude.[6]

The relationship between Fanny and Mary in volume 2, as Fanny well perceives, is brought about only by the absence of more appropriate companions for Mary and promoted by both Edmund and Henry to further their courtship plans. (Henry's courtship of Fanny might be as much a product of his boredom as Mary's friendship for Fanny is a refuge for her in the "quietest five months I have ever passed" [244; vol. 2, ch. 4].) The "sort of intimacy" between the two girls is not really friendship but rather "an intimacy resulting principally from Miss Crawford's desire of something new" (242). The contrast between the girls' awkward nonconversations and actual friendship is clearer when we read *Rambler* 64, which makes the crucial distinction that for friendship to be "at once fond and lasting, there must not only be equal virtue on each part, but virtue of the same kind" (*Rambler* 3: 341).

In Johnson's view—and in Austen's—true friendship is good preparation for and analogous with a good marriage. Johnson's allegorical correspondent Hymenaeus sends the *Rambler* three letters chronicling his search for a wife (nos. 113, 115, and 167). He has his brushes with an assortment of inappropriate women before settling down with Tranquilla, with whom he finds complete agreement about the definition of the married state: "We considered marriage as the most solemn league of perpetual friendship, a state from which artifice and concealment are to be banished for ever, and in which every act of dissimulation is a breach of faith" (*Major Works* 245 [*Rambler* 167]).[7] Hymenaeus's comparison of marriage with friendship can open a discussion of the jealous competition between Maria and Julia for the attentions of Henry Crawford and the general theme of what Johnson calls "dissimulation" (245)—a word that does not appear in Austen—throughout the novel. Hymenaeus's concern about marital "artifice and concealment" becomes Mary Crawford's frank, or more cynical, assertion that almost all marriages involve being "taken in" (53; vol. 1, ch. 5).

In *Mansfield Park*, the motif of role-playing is pervasive, most obviously in the rehearsals of *Lovers' Vows* but also in the many other personae adopted for effect, particularly by the Crawfords. Henry's changes of persona are the most numerous and varied, from purported suitor to Julia (52) to landscape architect (72; ch. 6, and 283; vol. 2., ch. 7) to devil-may-care lady-killer seeking to make "a small hole in Fanny Price's heart" (267; ch. 6) to aspiring naval officer (275) to naval mentor (346; ch. 13) to literary critic (390; vol. 3, ch. 3) to would-be preacher (395) to selfless suitor and finally to reckless seducer. But even Maria Bertram's veering between the role of the absentminded flirt who "does not recollect" the avenue of oak trees at Sotherton to the role of the estate's future mistress, completely familiar with its topography, partakes of this sort of posturing (65; vol. 1, ch. 6; and 97; ch. 8).[8]

Austen's characters, even with their realistic personalities, often reflect the values of Johnsonian archetypal characters. Mary's glib dismissal of Henry's elopement with Maria as an "*etourderie*" (506; vol. 3, ch. 15) proves that her character comprehends precious little virtue, none of it "of the same kind" as Fanny's. Edmund has always overlooked or explained away Mary's flaws; they painfully burst upon him only in his final conversation with Mary about what she refers to lightly as "the folly" of Henry and Maria (525; ch. 16), what Edmund considers a "dreadful crime" and a "sin" (529). *Rambler* essays, like Edmund's speeches, are not afraid of such moral language, which Mary dismisses as "[a] pretty good lecture upon my word. Was it part of your last sermon?" (530). One of the *Rambler's* anonymous correspondents relates a dream vision of an allegorical figure of Religion, "the offspring of Truth and Love, and the parent of Benevolence, Hope and Joy," who has a sermon of her own to deliver:

> "The true enjoyments of a reasonable being," answered [Religion] mildly, "do not consist in unbounded indulgence, or luxurious ease, in the tumult of passions, the languor of indolence, or the flutter of light amusements. Yielding to immoral pleasures corrupts the mind. . . . Whoever would be really happy must make the diligent and regular exercise of his superior powers his chief attention."   (*Rambler* 3: 239–40 [*Rambler* 44])

Mary's attitude of bravado, both in her final exchange with Edmund and in many earlier exchanges, shows her faults to be, as he finally discerns, "faults of principle . . . of blunted delicacy and a corrupted, vitiated mind" (528; vol. 3, ch. 16). We might think back to her first offense against Fanny, monopolizing Fanny's horse, because Mary's "enjoyment of riding was such, that she did not know how to leave off. . . . [T]o the pure genuine pleasure of the exercise, something was probably added in Edmund's attendance . . . and something more in the conviction of very much surpassing her sex in general by her early progress" (78; vol. 1, ch. 7). Mary's defense of her inconveniencing Fanny is no defense whatever:

> "My dear Miss Price," said Miss Crawford, as soon as she was at all within hearing, "I am come to make my own apologies for keeping you waiting—but I have nothing in the world to say for myself—I knew it was very late, and that I was behaving extremely ill; and, therefore, if you please, you must forgive me. Selfishness must always be forgiven you know, because there is no hope of a cure."   (80)

Mary has made the witty choice to name her vice as a means of explaining it away.

Another character with distinct Johnsonian antecedents is the novel's almost archetypal villain, Mrs. Norris. Johnson depicts several women who personify forms of what he called domestic tyranny, in particular Tetrica in *Rambler* 74 and Lady Bustle in *Rambler* 51. Sir Thomas only very belatedly comes to understand how his daughters have been spoiled by their aunt's "excessive indulgence and flattery" (535; vol. 3, ch. 17); earlier he assumed that Mrs. Norris errs only because "her kindness did sometimes overpower her judgment" (223; vol. 2, ch. 2). Students, hearing more of Mrs. Norris's dialogue than Sir Thomas does and having the narrative voice to guide them, will damn Mrs. Norris from the first, not least for her constant belittling of Fanny for "who and what she is"

(172; vol. 1, ch. 15). Johnson's Tetrica—her name is the Latin adjective for "gloomy"—reminds us of Mrs. Norris's most obvious failings. Johnson identifies "benevolence [as] the chief duty of social beings," a duty "fatally disable[d]" by "ill-humour . . . a species of depravity in the highest degree disgusting and offensive" (*Rambler* 44: 23 [*Rambler* 74]), words echoed in Sir Thomas's reprimands to Fanny (367; vol. 3, ch. 1). Johnson shrewdly says that peevishness is "employed . . . by tyranny in harrassing subjection," a neat summary of Mrs. Norris's satisfaction in her mistreatment of Fanny (*Rambler* 4: 25).

Tetrica's dictatorial advice also reminds us of Mrs. Norris's exaggerated household parsimony: "If many servants are kept in a house, [Tetrica] never fails to tell how Lord Lavish was ruined by a numerous retinue" (26 [*Rambler* 74]). Long after she has left off housekeeping at the Parsonage, Mrs. Norris keeps track of the Grants' extravagance there, including their cook's unduly high wages (35–36; vol. 1, ch. 3). One of the most unpleasant manifestations of Mrs. Norris's grasping attitude is her mistreatment of servants. From her airy suggestion that the Bertrams' governess need earn no extra fee when Fanny becomes one of her charges (10; ch. 1) to her triumph in refusing the carpenter's son a free lunch during the building of the theater (166–67; ch. 15), Mrs. Norris finds no opportunity for saving, at someone else's expense, too petty. But Austen's peevish character is much more complicated than any of Johnson's allegorical figures: she is comic but also frightening—Fanny and William are "horror-struck at the idea" of her accompanying them on the journey to Portsmouth (430; vol. 3, ch. 6). Her self-delusion is so profound that she even considers herself to be useful and benevolent. After arranging for the Bertrams to take on Fanny, Mrs. Norris "might so little know herself, as to walk home to the Parsonage . . . in the happy belief of being the most liberal-minded sister and aunt in the world," but her "love of money was equal to her love of directing" (9; vol. 1, ch. 1).

Johnson's Lady Bustle is another prototype for Mrs. Norris: she is a country matron who never shows real hospitality to a guest, always beset as she is with "anxious earnestness" about some domestic trifle. One unhappy guest of Lady Bustle, Cornelia, writes to the *Rambler*, "I was surprised . . . to find, instead of the leisure and tranquillity, which a rural life always promises, . . . a confused wildness of care, and a tumultuous hurry of diligence" (*Rambler* 3: 273–79, 274 [*Rambler* 51]). Mrs. Norris's constant interruption of Sir Thomas's first hour at his own fireside after his long absence in Antigua with suggested exertions (for the servants) is a comic riff on this characteristic, echoing both Johnson's use of "bustle" and "tranquillity": she is "trying to be in a bustle without having any thing to bustle about, and labouring to be important where nothing was wanted but tranquility and silence" during Sir Thomas's exciting account of his encounter with pirates (211; vol. 2, ch. 1). In a later scene, when William, at his uncle's invitation, recounts his experience of "every variety of danger, which sea and war together could offer," his aunt repeats this behavior. "Mrs. Norris could fidget about the room, and disturb every body in quest of two needlefulls of thread or a second hand shirt button in the midst of her nephew's account of a shipwreck" (275; ch. 6). Lady Bustle, too, has "no curiosity after the events of a war, or the fate of heroes in distress." Tellingly, Cornelia points out that "[w]ith regard to vice and virtue [Lady Bustle] seems a kind of neutral being. She has [i.e., recognizes] no crime but luxury" (*Rambler* 3: 278).

For Austen, Mrs. Norris's thrift is a failing rather than a virtue, as several nuanced *Rambler* essays help make clear. Though Johnson, who was no stranger to poverty, celebrates frugality in two *Rambler* essays (nos. 53 and 57), in others he calls into question misguided excesses of parsimony.[9] A misadventure brings Hymnaeus into contact with "the calm, the prudent, the economical Sophronia," who "discoursed with great solemnity on the care and vigilance which the superintendence of a family demands; [and] observed how many [families] were ruined by confidence in servants" (*Major Works* 207–11, 210 [*Rambler* 113]). Hymenaeus satisfies himself that "whatever I might suffer from Sophronia, I should escape poverty," and he almost goes through with the marriage. He learns his intended's true nature when she summarily "turned her [maid] out at night for breaking six teeth in a tortoise-shell comb," leaving her "destitute among strangers . . . in danger of perishing in the streets, or of being compelled by hunger to prostitution" (210). In *Rambler* 138, household economies so engross the widow Mrs. Busy that she neglects her children (*Rambler* 4: 364–69). From cadging roses from the Bertrams' garden (84–85; vol. 1, ch. 7) to "spunging" plants, eggs, and a cream cheese from the Rushworths' housekeeper (123; ch. 10) to making off from Mansfield Park with yards of green baize curtains (228; vol. 2, ch. 2), Mrs. Norris is invariably self-serving in her directing.

The most explicit connection between *Mansfield Park* and Johnson's work is *Rasselas*. After only the first week of her stay at home at Portsmouth, Fanny ruefully adapts one of *Rasselas*'s most epigrammatic sentences: "Fanny was tempted to apply [to the two houses] Dr. Johnson's celebrated judgment as to matrimony and celibacy, and say, that though Mansfield Park might have some pains, Portsmouth could have no pleasures" (454; vol. 3, ch. 8; *Major Works* 377 [*Rasselas*]). Of all the quotations in Austen's work, including the trite tags memorized by the young Catherine Morland in *Northanger Abbey* and the even triter tags quoted pompously by Mrs. Elton in *Emma*, this reference to Johnson's "celebrated judgment" is the most conspicuous quotation we hear from the authorial voice.[10]

A brief text, *Rasselas* can be fitted into most syllabi and offers a surprising number of connections with Austen's work. For one thing, there is equal treatment of the sexes: the philosopher Imlac teaches both Rasselas and his sister, Nekayah, and extends his instruction, without patronizing, even to Nekayah's attendant, Pekuah. There is a parallel between this instruction and Edmund's serious conversations about books, astronomy, and moral values with Fanny, unlike his glancing interchanges with his brother, his sisters, or even with Mary Crawford.

In pursuit of their "choice of life," Rasselas and Nekayah divide their researches into lives other than their own stultifying sojourn in the Happy Valley: Rasselas studies life at court, Nekayah studies domesticity. Each evening they report to each other. Nekayah herself has become "too long accustomed to the conversation of Imlac and her brother to be much pleased with childish levity and prattle" among young women: her observations about courtship and married life make up one of the most sustained considerations of the "choice of life" in the work (374; chs. 25–29). Among her discoveries is the triviality of most young women's lives. The Bertram sisters illustrate this triviality from their very first appearance, "making artificial flowers or wasting gold paper" (16; vol. 1, ch. 2).

Having grown up exiled from her parents (not unlike Fanny), Nekayah ideal-izes the relations between parents and children. "An unpractised observer," she notes, "expects the love of parents and children to be constant and equal," but she finds that it is not. She describes the evil of sibling rivalry for parental af-fections, anticipating how Fanny is crushed by the realization of how little she means to her parents, in contrast with her brothers, especially the favorite, Wil-liam (S. Johnson, *Major Works* 376 [*Rasselas*]; 450–51; vol. 3, ch. 8).[11] Nekayah also mentions discord between husbands and wives and difficulties caused by management of—and even blackmail by—servants, a subtopic in the novel that takes in both Mrs. Price's slatternly maid of all (or no) work and the elder Mrs. Rushworth's maidservant, whose threats to reveal Maria's elopement pre-cipitate the novel's dénouement (521 and 526; 3: ch. 16).

Reading Johnson with Austen, whether in an Austen seminar or in a survey of the British novel, helps place Austen in literary history, as an heir to the eighteenth century. This contextualization is an important corrective to nine-teenth- and twentieth-century tendencies to relegate her work to a special cat-egory.[12] Johnson also clarifies Austen's place in literature that follows her. For example, in a course that surveys the British novel, even if only the nineteenth century is considered, students who get to Thackeray's *Vanity Fair* might recog-nize the importance of Becky Sharp's contempt for "Johnson's '*Dixonary*'" (41; ch. 1). Reading Gaskell's *Cranford*, whose characters revere rather than reject Johnson, students can appreciate the distinction between Mrs. Norris's mean-minded parsimony and the poignantly charming economies of Miss Matty, who carefully uses a single candle during solitary evenings, making sure to burn each of the pair so that, when company calls, the candles can be lit together (41–45). Mrs. Busy and Mrs. Norris are forerunners of Mrs. Jellyby in Dick-ens's *Bleak House* (though the state of housekeeping at the Jellybys' [34; ch. 4] owes much to the Prices' life at Portsmouth). What George Eliot describes in *Felix Holt* as Mrs. Transome's habit of "doctoring" servants and tenants, enjoy-ing "every little sign of power her lot had left her," may also owe something to Mrs. Norris and her Johnsonian counterparts (28; cf. Austen, *Mansfield Park* [Wiltshire] 221; vol. 2, ch. 2).

Assignments could include brief class presentations by students who have pur-sued a dictionary exercise, studying key words from *Mansfield Park* as defined by Johnson, with special attention to Johnson's choice of illustrative quotations.

Many words will work in this context: a few examples are *attend*, *duty* (a word that Trilling alleges "grates on our moral ear" ["*Mansfield Park*" (*Moral Obligation*) 299]),[13] *friendship*, *gratitude*, *habit*, *oblige*, *price*, *principle* (a word that Wiltshire points out is important from the first paragraph of the novel nearly to the last),[14] and *temper*.

Writing assignments might include a discussion of courtship in *Mansfield Park* in the light of one or more of the *Rambler* essays on marriage (nos. 18, 35, 39, 45, 113, 115, and 167). For example, the anonymous correspondent of *Rambler* 35, an eligible man in possession of a considerable estate, shows real compassion for the young women he meets:

> I saw not without indignation, the eagerness with which the daughters, wherever I came, were set out to show; nor could I consider them in a state much different from prostitution. . . . As I knew these overtures not to proceed from any preference of me before another equally rich, I could not but look with pity on young persons condemned to be set to auction, and made cheap by injudicious commendations. . . .
>
> (*Rambler* 3: 192–93 [*Rambler* 35])

The sadder but wiser author of this letter is, despite his insight, now married to Mitissa, who, he finds, "had taken a husband only to be at her own command, and to have a chariot at her own call" (194), a pattern for Maria Bertram's decision to marry Mr. Rushworth to gain "the enjoyment of a larger income than her father's, as well as . . . [a] house in town" (44; vol. 1, ch. 4). *Rambler* 35 obviously opens possibilities for discussion of Sir Thomas's unseemly eagerness to marry off Maria (and later Fanny) to a rich suitor, but it also invites us to consider the advertising value of the display of Mary Crawford with her harp: "A young woman, pretty, lively, with a harp as elegant as herself; and both placed near a window, cut down to the ground, and opening on a little lawn . . . was enough to catch any man's heart" (76; ch. 7). The dry wit of this passage suggests that the window displaying Miss Crawford's accomplishments might as well be a shopwindow.

The contrast between the city and the country is an equally rich topic. For example, the London socialite Euphelia complains in a letter to the *Rambler* about her predicament during a long visit to an aunt in the country: "I walk because I am disgusted with sitting still, and sit down because I am weary with walking" (*Rambler* 3: 230 [*Rambler* 42]). An engaging creative assignment would be to invite students to write an imitation of such an unintentionally self-condemnatory letter to the *Rambler*, in the voice of one of Austen's characters. This project engages students with Austen's Johnsonian intersection between morality and style. Euphelia's letter is easily adapted for Mary Crawford (with the additional advantage that students will learn the all-important change that the word *disgust* has undergone over time). Another entertaining character is the air-headed London socialite Bellaria, who complains that the restless round of her life leaves no time for reading (*Major Works* 257–60 [*Rambler* 191]).[15]

As Euphelia's and Bellaria's letters underline their authors' blindness to their own faults, another candidate for a letter-to-the-*Rambler* assignment is Mrs. Norris. Martin Price observes that Mrs. Norris's devotion to "principle" is nothing more than "the *reductio ad absurdum* of low-minded greed and high-toned viciousness" (84). A letter of self-congratulation from Mrs. Norris to the *Rambler*, outlining her economies and philanthropies, would be an exercise in devastating irony.

Another exercise could be in close reading, where students analyze Austen's prose in relation to Johnson's style. Pursuing such a project, they might find that Austen is not as "difficult to catch in the act of greatness" as Virginia Woolf claimed ("Jane Austen at Sixty" [Watt] 23).[16] An excellent choice for such a study would be the last *Idler*, a text from Fanny's library, on "last things" (*Major Works* 304–06 [*Idler* 103 (104)]). Such truisms as "Value is more frequently raised by scarcity than by use. That which lay neglected when it was common, rises in estimation as its quantity becomes less" (305) can be taken as glosses on many aspects of the novel, including its conclusion.[17]

Fanny is particularly susceptible to the word *last*. (She has Scott's *Lay of the Last Minstrel* by heart and quotes it in vol. 1, ch. 9, and vol. 2, ch. 10.) She is affected when it is her "last time" to have breakfast with William at Mansfield Park, his "last morning" (325 and 326; vol. 2, ch. 10; repeated on 327; ch. 11), or the "last time of seeing" Mary Crawford, whom she does not even like: "[H]er feelings could seldom withstand the melancholy influence of the word 'last.' She cried as if she had loved Miss Crawford more than she possibly could" (414; vol. 3, ch. 5). Johnson tells his (last) readers, "Those who never could agree together shed tears when mutual discontent has determined them to final separation; of a place which has been frequently visited, though without pleasure, the last look is taken with heaviness of heart" (305). Fanny duly weeps over inanimate objects she sees for the "last time." Though looking forward to her visit to Portsmouth, she has "tears for every room" at Mansfield Park the night before her journey (431; ch. 6).[18]

Studying Fanny's sentimentality over last things should make it clear that Austen's heroine is not a moral paragon. Fanny is subject to occasional gentle teasing, as here. Another such moment shows her indignant because Edmund has forgotten her while he takes Mary riding: "[I]f [Fanny] were forgotten the poor mare should be remembered" (79; vol. 1, ch. 7). Fanny is not perfect: she deceives herself here, or pretends, that her feelings are for the horse. At the end of the novel, "[n]ot even Fanny had tears for Aunt Norris—not even when she was gone for ever" (539; vol. 3, ch. 17), so Fanny is only human.

Dr. Johnson's works open a rich array of possibilities for informed readings of *Mansfield Park*, and combining Johnson and Austen can afford pleasure to instructor and student alike. Even if Fanny does not become a favorite character, students can better appreciate how Austen recalls Johnson's writings on moral character as she creates her complex fictive characters.

NOTES

I have studied *Mansfield Park* with Paul Pickrel at Smith College, Martin Price at Yale University, and many undergraduates during over thirty years at Colgate University: all these readers have taught me about this complicated novel.

[1] A general list of Austen's reading, based on literary allusions in her works, including her letters, was compiled by R. W. Chapman and includes Boswell's *Journal of a Tour to the Hebrides* and *Life of Johnson*; Johnson's *Idler, Dictionary, Rasselas*, and *Journey to the Western Islands of Scotland*; and Hester Thrale Piozzi's *Letters to and from the late Samuel Johnson LL.D.* ("Index 1" 317–28).

[2] Wiltshire identifies Mary's reference to this anecdote of Voltaire, pointing out that Austen would know it through Johnson's letter to Hester Thrale, as she then was, in 1773, a letter published in *Mrs. Hester Lynch Piozzi's Letters to and from the Late Samuel Johnson* (1788). The first volume of this collection would be the source from which Austen quotes in one of her letters. Johnson writes, "You remember the Doge of Genoa who being asked what struck him most at the French Court, answered 'Myself'" (Wiltshire, "Explanatory Notes" 696n10). It might be interesting to contemplate whether Mary's own source is Johnson or whether Austen imagines her referring directly to Voltaire's *Siècle de Louis XIV* (1751)—or to an excerpt from some collection, in French or in translation, of witty extracts, which would indeed prove the Doge and his remark to be "famous."

[3] Wiltshire also cites a passage from *Rasselas* that Fanny may be echoing here with her reference to the memory as "sometimes tyrannic." Imlac warns his young tutees not to mock the delusions of an astronomer: "There is no man whose imagination does not sometimes predominate over his reason. . . . No man will be found in whose mind airy notions do not sometimes tyrannize" ("Explanatory Notes" 696n10; S. Johnson, *Major Works* 405 [*Rasselas*, ch. 44]).

[4] Wherever possible, I cite *Major Works* as the most comprehensive yet inexpensive collection of Johnson available for undergraduate courses. *Rasselas* and the "Preface to Shakespeare" and many other texts in this one-volume edition are useful in relation to *Mansfield Park*. But not all of the Johnson essays I discuss are collected in this volume; other *Rambler* essays are cited, as this one is, from *The Yale Edition of the Works of Samuel Johnson* (*Rambler*).

[5] In *Rambler* 8, Johnson emphasizes that true piety requires a "voluntary employment of our mind in the contemplation of its excellence, its importance, and its necessity." "To facilitate this change of our affections, it is necessary that we weaken the temptations of the world, by retiring at certain seasons from it" to indulge in "solitary meditation" (*Rambler* 3: 40). Mary has retired, reluctantly, to the country but has failed to practice any such meditation.

[6] In this connection, Fanny's reflections on nature show fellow feeling with the urban Johnson's surprising reflections on spring, in *Rambler* 5 (*Rambler* 3: 25–30).

[7] The list of women Hymenaeus has encountered before meeting Tranquilla, including "Imperia" and "Charybdis," affords many useful comparisons with the marital discords of *Mansfield Park* (*Rambler* 4: 252 [*Rambler* 115]). Further *Rambler* essays on marriage provide such characters as the scolding Furia, the flighty Zephyretta (no. 18), and the "vain, glittering, and thoughtless" heiress Melanthia (*Major Works* 200 [*Rambler* 39]).

[8] Even the early discussion among the young people of whether the absent Fanny is out or not out (56–57; vol. 1, ch. 5) raises the issue of playing a role: like so many indica-

tions overlooked by Edmund, the Crawfords' explanation of the distinction betrays their slippery moral values, while Edmund distinguishes between girls who behave with "real modesty" and those who "are always acting upon motives of vanity" (58). When we look at the novel this way, we can appreciate more fully Fanny's repeated protestation, "I cannot act," "I really cannot act" (171; ch. 15).

[9] In later life, Johnson practiced considerable personal charity, taking to live with him various penurious friends.

[10] Jeffrey Meyers points to another close (though unacknowledged) echo of Johnson, comparing Hymenaeus's statement in *Rambler* 115, "I was known to possess a fortune, and to want a wife" (*Rambler* 4: 248), with the opening sentence of *Pride and Prejudice* (39–49, 40).

[11] Wiltshire observes that Nekayah's observations about "family dynamics" have many parallels in content and style with Austen's analysis of the Price household ("Explanatory Notes" 724).

[12] Vladimir Nabokov refers to the author as "Miss Austen" (10); Virginia Woolf calls her "singularly blessed" (McNeillie 9); Lionel Trilling finds it "extraordinary" that Emma "has a moral life as a man has a moral life" ("*Emma*" 38); and F. R. Leavis considers her an introduction to the "great tradition" though not exactly belonging to that tradition (1–27). Critical praise for Austen has often marked her as unique, at least for her sex. To show that Austen has roots in eighteenth-century style and substance ("There has been one infallible Pope in the World," she wrote to Cassandra on 26 October 1813, alluding to *An Essay on Man* [Le Faye 245 (letter 940)]) hardly detracts from her greatness in the tradition of the novel.

[13] Trilling's dismissal of *duty* is especially doubtful when we recall how the word is used in Austen's novel to describe a young woman's response to a proposal. Maria twice considers it her "duty" to marry Mr. Rushworth (44; vol. 1, ch. 4). Lady Bertram's "only rule of conduct, the only piece of advice" to Fanny during her entire stay at Mansfield Park is that "it is every young woman's duty to accept such a very unexceptionable offer as [Henry Crawford's]" (384; vol. 3, ch. 2).

[14] Introduction lii (from 4; vol. 1, ch. 1; to 536; vol. 3, ch. 17]. Robert Scholes refers to "principle" as a "most important word in the vocabulary of both" Samuel Johnson and Jane Austen" (382).

[15] The city/country problem is the topic of *Rambler* 46 and 124 and *Idler* 80.

[16] According to Hermione Lee, Woolf's praise of a scene in *Mansfield Park* contains "no attempt to explain the technical devices which create the emotion; quite the reverse, it is left as a mystery" (101): "[I]t is midday in Northamptonshire; a dull young man is talking to rather a weakly young woman on the stairs as they go up to dress for dinner, . . . from triviality, from commonplace, their words become suddenly full of meaning, and the moment . . . fills itself; it shines; it glows" ("Jane Austen" [*Common Reader*] 201–02).

[17] Wiltshire notes the affinity between *Mansfield Park*'s volume 3, chapter 5, and the last *Idler* ("Explanatory Notes" 717).

[18] Mary Crawford too is inclined to mark off her relationship with Edmund as a series of lasts, including "the last time that [Mary] will ever dance with [him]" (311; vol. 2, ch. 9) and the "last, last interview of friendship" (525; vol. 3, ch. 16), in which he sees her true character for the first time (528).

Reading Aloud in *Mansfield Park*

Laura Dabundo

> The subject of reading aloud was farther discussed. . . . [T]hey . . . talked over the too common neglect of the qualification, the total inattention to it. . . .   (392; vol. 3, ch. 3)

By the time that Jane Austen wrote *Mansfield Park*, she had mastered many strategies of narration beyond description, dialogue, and action to develop and reveal character and advance plot. But this novel is unique in her canon for another device: the continual use of reading aloud both as a feature of the text and as a subject discussed in it. This device is borrowed from her family practice and the widespread public interest at the time in "private theatricals" (Gay, "Pastimes" 341–42). Families like the Austens and the Bertrams engaged in producing full-scale plays with varying degrees of accomplishment in stagecraft and presentation. A corollary to theatricals and related to their success was practicing for the performance and reading aloud, and these activities take place several times in *Mansfield Park*, in connection with the staging of *Lovers' Vows* and in other contexts too. For instance, when Tom Bertram convalesces near the end of the novel, his brother reads to him. Reading aloud is evening entertainment in *Mansfield Park*; Lady Bertram notes that, "she [Fanny] often reads to me out of those books" (389; vol. 3, ch. 3). Henry Crawford reads aloud from Shakespeare's *Henry VIII* to Lady Bertram, Edmund, and Fanny as part of his courtship of Fanny, after which Edmund and Henry discuss the "too common neglect" of reading aloud. In *Mansfield Park*, characters in the novel actually discuss reading aloud, especially with respect to church services. Instructors teaching this novel can highlight reading aloud to deepen students' connection to the book and to the characters.

A focus on reading aloud is especially appropriate in teaching *Mansfield Park* because the literature classroom is a place where dramatic reading may bring characters and the narrator's voice to life for modern students. When both instructor and students read aloud dialogue and narration thoughtfully, the novel's drama, poignancy, and humor often become more apparent than when the book is read silently and in solitude. Thus reading aloud *in* the novel can be illuminated by the reading aloud *of* the novel, and students become better able to articulate its effects as they engage in it themselves. "Reading aloud is especially effective with Austen's novels, partly because she wrote dialogue so dramatically and partly because she so deeply knew the hidden layers of each of her characters. When the narrator's voice is also read aloud, it adds stage directions, insight into tones of voice, and sometimes irony to the vivid dialogue" (Folsom, "Privilege" 7). With Austen, reading aloud can be both a subject and a means of instruction.

Some sections of *Mansfield Park* that might profitably be read aloud in class are passages from the Sotherton expedition in chapters 9 and 10 of the first volume, the interior tour of the house and chapel and also the perambulations around the wood and wilderness outside the house. In these scenes, the conversations of the characters reveal a complex interplay of disguised and revealed motivation and emotion. The many voices in these scenes offer a range of opportunities for students to try out by means of voice the expression of the moods and tones of the characters.

Reading aloud was the television or Internet of Austen's era, the domestic engine of the passing of time. In *A History of Reading*, Alberto Manguel singles out the Austen family as exemplary of reading aloud: "At Steventon rectory in Hampshire, the Austen family read to one another at all times and commented on the appropriateness of each selection" (122). He adduces several instances from the Austen family records and concludes that reading aloud "gives the versatile text a respectable identity, a sense of unity in time and an existence in space that it seldom has in the capricious hands of a solitary reader" (123). Austen herself was reported to read aloud very well by those in her circle who were privileged to hear her (Leithart 43–44). Students might be asked, once they have begun reading aloud in *Mansfield Park*, if the performance does indeed transform the experience, as Manguel suggests.

In addition to having evidence that the Austen family enjoyed reading aloud, we know that Austen's older brothers staged plays at home, first in the dining room of the Steventon rectory and later in the barn they converted to a playhouse in the 1780s, when Austen was young and impressionable (Leithart 43). Evidently their father, the Reverend George Austen, approved of this activity, or it would not have continued.

Like the Austen family, the Bertrams and Crawfords decide to present a play at *Mansfield Park*. They select Elizabeth Inchbald's *Lovers' Vows*, a translation of the German playwright August von Kotzebue's *Das Kind der Liebe*. The Inchbald translation was wildly popular in the late eighteenth century and still performed in the early nineteenth century, and it is likely that the first readers of the novel knew its plot and characters. The young people in the novel adopt parts congenial to their personal interests, in a play that is concerned with "families, wronged women, class division, and young lives dictated by family circumstances," as noted by a biographer of Inchbald (Jenkins 418), themes all relevant to the Bertrams and the Crawfords. Isobel Armstrong points out that the frank presentation of issues of sex and illegitimate birth in *Lovers' Vows* might well have rendered the play risky for the Bertrams to perform while Sir Thomas is away (66–74). In order to help students grasp the complexity of the chapters that contain the preparation for the play, the teacher can make clear that the Austen family enjoyed theatricals and that Austen herself took pleasure in the legitimate theater. Why do Fanny and Edmund disapprove of the idea of performing a play? Why do they disapprove of this play in particular? What is the danger for Maria Bertram when she engages in scenes of passionate feeling with someone other than her intended husband?

Students will be able to see that reading aloud lines intended for characters in a play may cause emotions and desires just beneath the surface of the actors' tangled lives to bubble upward and out. Edmund and Fanny see the danger of *Lovers' Vows* to their family, for it is an emotionally fraught drama. A question that will provoke class discussion is, Should this play be performed by these young people? Because several editions of the novel include the playscript, students can sort out which characters in the novel take which parts in the play (see the essay by Susan Allen Ford in this volume). The class might read aloud the two crucial scenes (1.1 and 3. 2) to grasp the dangers for the actors in playing these parts.

All the characters are caught up in the rehearsals in *Mansfield Park*, and Fanny first becomes important to the other characters when the task of prompter falls to her. She is especially needed by Mr. Rushworth, whose lack of intelligence seems to explain his ineptitude in mastering his short part in *Lovers' Vows*. His inability explains why Maria "could not, did not like him" (234; vol. 2, ch. 3); he brags about his number of speeches and then cannot learn them.

Lovers' Vows takes over Mansfield Park. Downstairs, Maria and Henry assiduously practice, earning for themselves the arch epithet from Mary "those indefatigable rehearsers" (198; vol. 1, ch. 18). They utilize the words of love scripted for the imaginary son and mother, Frederick and Agatha, as license to speak what they should not say to each other. The first scene in act 1 allows Henry and Maria to enact an affectionate reunion, expressing a mutual tenderness that Maria actually feels. Maria is certainly more sincere in using the words of another to express her true feelings than Henry. The two are acting, of course, not just reading aloud, which is an important distinction. The dialogues between Agatha and her son provide plenty of opportunities for close bodily contact, which others in the household sometimes espy. Henry and Maria are saying and doing what is forbidden under the terms of her engagement, but being in the play provides the license.

Meanwhile, upstairs, Fanny is sought as a reading partner by both Edmund and Mary in what is her private, inviolable East Room retreat, and now she must listen to them read their emotional parts to each other. The character Mary plays and the words she reads allow her to express feelings for Edmund directly. These words are especially painful for Fanny because Edmund as Anhalt is being seduced by Amelia, his pupil. Since this relationship reproduces Fanny's own to Edmund, the dialogue makes Fanny forget herself, lose herself as the prompter and find herself in the love triangle. Reading aloud has made real what the characters feel but were constrained from expressing. The crisis point for this part of the plot, at which the first volume and the *Lovers' Vows* rehearsal end before the curtain ever rises, is the return of Sir Thomas. His return is preceded by the cast's suddenly importuning Fanny to read Mrs. Grant's lines in Mrs. Grant's absence from the final rehearsal. Henry says, "You have only to *read* the part" (201). Students will understand that in this novel's world, there is no mere reading of a part, for to read is to commit to a part, to take part. Fanny is about to be trapped into being part of the play, but the return of Sir Thomas spares her.

An important episode of reading aloud in *Mansfield Park* focuses on Shakespeare. After Henry Crawford has proposed to Fanny, he and Edmund come into a room where Lady Bertram tells the men that Fanny has just been reading aloud to her. Trying to discern what Shakespeare play Fanny was reading, Henry figures out that she chose *Henry VIII*. Students may not be familiar with this late play. Why might it have been Fanny's choice? The parallels between cast-off Katherine and humiliated Fanny, both facing patriarchal oppression, suggest that Fanny was reading aloud Katherine's lines bewailing Katherine's situation (Folsom, "Part" 70–71):

> Alas, I am a woman, friendless, hopeless.
> . . . Ye turn me into nothing. Woe upon ye,
> And all such false professors! Would you have me
> (If you have any justice, any pity,
> If ye be anything but churchmen's habits)
> Put my sick cause into his hands that hates me?
> . . . What can happen
> To me above this wretchedness?   (3.1.79–123)

These are resonant lines for someone who ". . . like Fanny, finds herself friendless, transplanted from her home to a hostile territory where no one can protect her" (Folsom, "Part" 73): Spanish-born Katherine is in England, Portsmouth-born Fanny in Mansfield Park. "For readers who think of Fanny as too passive, in her choice of *Henry VIII* to read aloud is evidence of her secret resistance to Bertram family pressure" (74). Students might read aloud these words of Katherine in the light of Fanny's circumstances, especially after her confrontation with her uncle in the East Room, and consider if Fanny is indeed using these lines to assert herself and express her terrible loneliness. Henry reads what the narrator terms "the best scene or the best speeches" of *Henry VIII*. His dramatic reading reaches "a variety of excellence beyond what [Fanny] had ever met with" (389; vol. 3, ch. 3).

Henry achieves this excellence not just by choosing which speeches to read but also by performing with "dignity or pride, or tenderness or remorse, or whatever were to be expressed . . . with equal beauty.—It was truly dramatic" (390; vol. 3, ch. 3). Susan Harlan argues that he has the ability to distinguish among the characters by differences of inflection, tone, and accent, in accord with Romantic interpretations of Shakespeare: "In extracting the characters from the play and conveying, or performing, the differences between them, Crawford performs a task similar to that of many contemporary critics . . ." who studied Shakespearean characters as the acme of his art (44). Hazlitt (246–49) and Coleridge, for instance, among other critics of the age, said that one can hear in the mind's ear the genius of Shakespeare in the characters and their voices.

It is no wonder that Maria Bertram melts under Henry's charms. Henry may enact emotions that he does not feel, but his performance is powerful. Fanny does not capitulate to that power as her cousin does, but Edmund, watching her watching Henry as he reads so well, "was amused and gratified by seeing how she gradually slackened in the needle-work, . . . how it fell from her hand . . . and at last, how the eyes which had appeared so studiously to avoid him through- out the day, were turned and fixed on Crawford." The spell his reading casts, a "charm," as Austen writes (390), is testimony to his power to give life to the written word. As Harlan says, "Henry Crawford appropriates Shakespeare's lan- guage as a vehicle by which he performs himself" (43), and he uses that ability to seduce young women. Does his skill as an actor demonstrate that he needs to be acting a role in order to reveal a personality?

Henry and Edmund actually have a conversation about reading aloud, and they comment on their experience as listeners. They discuss "the want of man- agement of the voice, of proper modulation and emphasis, of foresight and judg- ment, all proceeding from the first cause, want of early attention and habit . . ." (392), and Fanny's keen attention to this exchange tells us how important it is. The conversation also indicates Austen's knowledge of the skills of reading aloud for an audience or a congregation.

Henry and Edmund's discussion of reading aloud is connected to the delivery of the liturgy in church. Reading scripture and liturgy, along with preaching, constituted the church service with which these characters were familiar and is relevant to the novel because of Edmund's impending ordination. Edmund expresses surprise at "how little the art of reading aloud has been studied," even "in my profession," for listening to it is a part of the weekly experience of churchgoing. As for preaching, Mary Crawford has said, earlier in the novel in the chapel at Sotherton, that a clergyman should have "the sense to prefer Blair's sermons to his own" (108; vol. 1, ch. 9), in other words, to appropriate another's language and thought in a manner very like acting. This comment foregrounds the role of clergyman as a performer, which appeals to Henry's sense of the minister's making a show, having an appreciative audience.

The two young men continue to talk about Edmund's obligations as a cler- gyman of the church to read well out loud. "'Our liturgy,' observed Crawford, 'has beauties, which not even a careless, slovenly style of reading can destroy; but it has also redundancies and repetitions, which require good reading not to be felt'" (393; vol. 3, ch. 3). A reader may discern, in Henry's observations, the thoughts of the author, who, as the daughter and sister of clergymen, has given thought to the delivery of a service. The clergy must be able to read aloud well in order to be effective in their charge.

The responsibilities of the clergy are the subject of a conversation earlier in the novel, when Henry asks if he might rent Thornton Lacey and improve it while Edmund as clergyman still lives at Mansfield Park. That question leads Sir Thomas to say that "Edmund might, in the common phrase, do the duty of Thornton, that is, he might read prayers and preach, without giving up Mansfield Park; he might ride over, every Sunday, to a house nominally inhabited, and go through the divine service" (288; vol. 2, ch. 7) by reading it, by standing before the congregation and intoning the words. However, neither Sir Thomas nor Edmund approves of this way of fulfilling a clergyman's duty. They believe that a clergyman must be rooted in his parish to truly do his duty. They agree that it is essential to do more than read aloud. Meaningful clerical reading aloud parts ways from the thespian accomplishment, in which actors take on roles and efface themselves: a clergyman must mean what he says. Students might consider what distinction the novel is drawing here between studied performance and genuine engagement and self-expression.

This discussion of reading aloud in the church recalls another about reading and listening in the novel. In Mrs. Rushworth's guided tour of the family chapel at Sotherton, Fanny praises the observance of family prayers, now abandoned at Sotherton, which formerly allowed a household to share in hearing words read aloud. What Edmund and his father see in the clergyman's dwelling in his parish is his role in the community. He must speak the words of the church services to a group in which he is an abiding, participating member. Reading aloud sacred language, the service of the church from the aptly named *Book of Common Prayer*—*common* indicating the shared, routine gathering of a community—is a vital aspect of a connection that binds people together. Austen surely saw this significance, because she wrote prayers for family services based on the English prayer book (Chapman, *Minor Works* 453–57).

Students might reflect on whether reading aloud can still form communities in this way, bringing readers and listeners together, forming a community, not necessarily a religious one but certainly tied by commonly valued interests and aims. A "learning community" is a valid term for what can happen in a college course, and literature instructors have an opportunity to create a classroom that becomes a community. Examining instances of reading aloud in *Mansfield Park* and talking about what they mean may turn the literature classroom into a community of learners, bound by this novel and their rich experiences of it and now aware of this transaction. The words of others read aloud may help create a community, and students who form a community in their class may become a part of a larger community that knows and appreciates the greatness of this novel.

TEACHING *MANSFIELD PARK* IN THE BROADER POSTCOLONIAL CONTEXT

Mansfield Park and the Pedagogy of Geography

Lynn Voskuil

When students first find out that *Mansfield Park* lies at the center of a decades-long critical controversy—one, moreover, that has been urgently politicized—they are often quite perplexed. What is it about this story of the modest, unassuming Fanny Price, they wonder, that could possibly have generated this kind of response? If we want to teach (as I do) the debates provoked by Edward Said's controversial reading of this novel, their perplexity is pedagogically useful. A classroom filled with genuinely puzzled and curious students is a gift, of course, one that most of us know is not frequently given. In the case of *Mansfield Park*, student bewilderment usually sparks its own generative sense of urgency without much professorial prompting: new readers, as well as repeat readers newly attuned to the novel's critical status, are rightly intrigued by the sense that their reading of a two-hundred-year-old book has current relevance.

Their perplexity, however, also signals the considerable pedagogical challenges of using Said and related theorists to help students understand this relevance. For example, the Saidian approach seems counterintuitive: "Where do we see imperialism in the novel?," students often want to know. How might we use that question in pedagogically effective ways? In this essay, I suggest a few strategies for using Said that may themselves seem counterintuitive. Though I make no promises to mute my own position on this particular critical controversy, my goal here is neither to endorse nor to refute a generally postcolonial or Saidian approach to *Mansfield Park*. Instead, I want to offer some reflections about how we might use that approach to help our students understand the theoretical contexts of this novel without supplanting a focus on the primary text.

A quick look at Said's important piece and at a few of the essays Said's piece inspired will underscore the pedagogical challenges raised. Initially published in 1989 in a volume inspired by the work of Raymond Williams, Said's "Jane Austen and Empire" builds on Williams's interpretations of landscape and space in *The Country and the City*, arguing that what Williams notes as the "'dramatic extension of landscape and social relations'" in late-Victorian imperial culture ([*Raymond Williams*] 152) should be extended in geography and time—going back to the late eighteenth century, in fact, just before Austen began publishing her novels. Said devotes most of his relatively short piece to analyzing the spatial relations in the novel: Fanny's movement to Mansfield Park, Sir Thomas's journeys to Antigua and back to England, the claustrophobic domesticity of Portsmouth, the ideological and moral resemblances between Sir Thomas's control of the English estate and the colonial plantation, and so on. In the final few pages, Said discusses what he calls the "casual references to Antigua" and other colonies in the novel—Lady Bertram's request, for example, that the voyaging William Price bring back two shawls for her from the East Indies—references that stand for "something significant 'out there'" (161). Although such references are a powerful feature of Said's argument, he does not analyze them much.

As everyone now knows, Said's essay generated its own industry in Austen studies. Interestingly, however, many of the critics who build on his work focus much more closely on those Antiguan references than on the larger claims Said advances about imperialist conceptions of geography and space, a focus that leads them to search for more such references in the novel and to construct a contextual edifice to explain them. As John Wiltshire notes ("Decolonising" 313), a favored passage has thus become the scene where Fanny mentions how she questioned Sir Thomas about the Antiguan slave trade but was met with a "dead silence," as she puts it, after his reply (231; vol. 2, ch. 2). Brian Southam's "The Silence of the Bertrams" is typical in this regard. Because such essays focus on references that are glancing at best, critics must supply a context for what remains unsaid, and that context is not only historically distant but also deeply complex in evidentiary terms. The result is exemplified by Joseph Lew's essay, a learned piece that ranges widely over the parliamentary context of *Mansfield Park*, the politics of slavery after the French Revolution, and political theory contemporary with Austen. When done well, such work is impressive. For example, although Elaine Freedgood does not analyze *Mansfield Park* per se, she focuses on similarly glancing references to "things" in several canonical nineteenth-century novels—calico curtains in *Mary Barton*, mahogany furniture in *Jane Eyre*, Magwitch's tobacco plug in *Great Expectations*—and advances an innovative theory of metonymic reading that goes a long way beyond contextual reading to suggest how ideas of empire may have resonated in the nineteenth-century popular imagination.

But however persuasive such scholarship might be, it nonetheless favors the omissions and elisions in the texts we teach, the moments when characters don't speak and the scenes where seemingly insignificant objects or settings are considered only fleetingly. Such readings, of course, originated neither with Said's Austen essay nor with those of his followers; they are part of a complex history of literary theory that is beyond the scope of this essay. What interests me here is not that history per se but how the logic of such theoretical frameworks affects our teaching of *Mansfield Park* by raising particular kinds of pedagogical challenges. Teaching moments of textual elision, or grounding pedagogy in narrative silence, requires an approach that differs significantly even from what we usually do with "close reading," a practice that attends to details on the page. In contrast, asking our students to interpret Maria and Julia's silence that Fanny says followed Sir Thomas's reply to her question—matter that lies between the lines, so to speak, and not on the page—requires a degree of speculation that quickly becomes counterproductive without at least a minimal knowledge of the social, historical, and ideological context that produced the question. How should we approach such challenges without supplanting a focus on the primary text? Even if we no longer think of novels like *Mansfield Park* as our New Critical forebears did, most of us—myself included—want and need to stay focused on the literary texts we love to teach rather than revert to history lectures.

I explored these issues recently when I taught a graduate course on nineteenth- and early-twentieth-century fiction, a course whose heuristic was the novel and social space. *Mansfield Park* was situated at the beginning of the course to establish the key ideas and concepts for the semester. We followed it with Gaskell's *Mary Barton*, Dickens's *Bleak House*, Gissing's *The Odd Women*, Wells's *The War of the Worlds*, Conrad's *Nostromo*, Forster's *Passage to India*, and Woolf's *Mrs. Dalloway*, an array of texts that enabled us to range over landed estates, urban Manchester and London, colonial cities and landscapes, and even the global territories implied by Wells. With its emphasis on the spaces of the estate, the seaside port town, the central metropolis, and the unrepresented colony, *Mansfield Park* turned out to be an excellent place to begin. But rather than focus on its casual references to Antigua in our discussions, we took Said's notion of social space as our point of departure, which let us sidestep some of the potential logical and pedagogical difficulties presented by a focus on textual omission.

On the face of it, Said's notion of social space would not seem to lessen more difficulties than it raises: an elusive and knotty abstraction, it is resistant to the concrete demands of the classroom, even an advanced classroom. For a graduate seminar, I could—and did—assign critical texts to help us think it through. In addition to the novels, we read Said's 1993 *Culture and Imperialism*, which includes the Austen essay in a more developed form; Williams's *The Country and the City*; and Franco Moretti's *The Atlas of the European Novel, 1800–1900*. Our best discussions, however, were prompted not by the secondary material but by our uses of it to analyze the novels. In the section of *Culture and Imperialism* entitled "Narrative and Social Space," just prior to the Austen material, Said develops his idea of social space at some length, defining it initially and simply as "space to be used for social purposes" but stressing much more strongly the geography that grounds it. "Underlying social space," he writes (in a sentence I used as the epigraph for our course), "are territories, lands, geographical domains, the actual geographical underpinnings of the imperial, and also the cultural contest" (78). In practical terms, this definition meant that our discussions tended to notice the uses of space in *Mansfield Park* and other novels rather than, say, the narrative structures or modes of characterization. We analyzed closely the garden scene at Sotherton, Fanny's return to Portsmouth and her response to that space, and the expanses of the Bertram estate. We compared the geographic locations of London, Portsmouth, Antigua, and Mansfield Park, noticing what kinds of activities and interactions they prompted among characters. Many students used maps in their presentations (Moretti's book was particularly helpful in this regard) to highlight how characters inhabited their social spaces. One student used maps of London in the 1890s to show how Gissing's character Monica Madden navigated the urban landscape on trains and on foot—a presentation that showed, with concrete specificity, how class and gender issues were integrally related to social and geographic space in late-Victorian London. The shift from a narrative and temporal focus to a spatial one sharpened our analysis considerably, in part because it provoked us to notice and struggle with features we might formerly have dismissed or overlooked as background or setting.

A good graduate class, of course (as this one was), will need only a bit of prompting to use a heuristic framework productively and contribute actively to the shaping of a seminar. Similar strategies also work in undergraduate classrooms, however, with appropriate modifications for less advanced students; and there are now excellent, widely available sources for developing such strategies. The British Library, for example, has *Online Gallery*, a Web site with an amazing array of maps and related visual materials available for use in the classroom (www.bl.uk/onlinegallery/); the resolution of the maps is excellent, and they can be viewed and studied carefully with a user-friendly zoom function. Particularly helpful for the analysis of *Mansfield Park* (and of Austen in general) is the library's *Crace Collection of Maps of London*, which contains hundreds of estate maps and plans, many of them beautifully crafted, that may be analyzed to help students grasp the geographic sense that shaped the use and representation of the British landed estate.

The late-eighteenth-century *Plan of an Estate Situate at Millbank Westminster Belonging to the Marquis of Salisbury*, for example, designates the variable uses of land on the estate with inks and markings of different colors; it also includes the actual names and premises of the estate's thirty tenants, all easily readable. Other useful materials are available on the Web sites of Britain's National Archives and various regional archive offices. *The Sutherland Collection* is an online archive maintained by the Staffordshire and Stoke-on-Trent Archive Services and contains thousands of documents—maps, letters, diaries, estate records—that relate to the management and use of estate land and architecture in Staffordshire for over ten centuries (www.sutherlandcollection .org.uk/). The owners of this family archive made it available not only to professionals but also to the general public, in order to stimulate interest in the use of historical and archival documents. For teachers interested in Austen's allusions to Humphry Repton and the picturesque landscape controversy, some of Repton's Red Books are also now available online (*Humphry Repton's Red Books* [www.themorgan.org/collections/works/repton/]). Finally, the British government's huge collection of nineteenth-century ordnance survey maps offers yet another resource (www.bl.uk/onlinegallery/onlineex/ordsurvdraw/).

How might these materials be used in an undergraduate classroom? At the University of Houston, we have a variety of options: courses taught wholly in person; courses taught wholly online; and what we call a hybrid course, which involves both live and virtual instruction. I have used maps very profitably in a Monday-Wednesday-Friday hybrid course, for which I teach two classes in person and the third online. With this structure, I analyze one document in class with my students—the Westminster estate plan mentioned above, for example—and then link a few additional documents to our *Blackboard* site for students to analyze on their own for the third session. (I don't teach the online classes in real time but give students a time frame, usually from Wednesday afternoon to Monday morning, in which to analyze the materials and then post comments, respond to prompts, or work together in small, online groups. I log in periodically to check on their progress or add my own comments if necessary.) This structure allows us to establish a framework for our analysis and discussion but remain focused on the novel during live classes.

The use of maps and related documents in the undergraduate classroom clearly gives students a concrete sense for the setting and background of historically distant novels like *Mansfield Park*; it also offers them the opportunity to work with archival materials, something many students have never experienced. My aim in using such documents is to stimulate their sense of context or discovery and provide a visual schematic of what Said calls the "geographical sense" that shapes *Mansfield Park*. This additional representation, in an alternative visual medium, helps us see how cultural attitudes toward geography and land prompt certain ways of using it and representing it aesthetically. "The geographical sense . . . makes possible the construction of various kinds of knowledge," Said writes in *Culture and Imperialism*, "all of them in one way or another dependent upon the perceived character and destiny of a particular geography" (78). While I don't usually assign long sections of Said to undergraduate students, I do want them to think about how this "geographical sense" works.

A brief discussion of three maps shows how this lesson might be taught with *Mansfield Park*. Beginning with the Westminster estate map, I use a variety of questions to stimulate in-class discussion and help students understand what they're viewing. Why does the marquis of Salisbury have all these tenants, for instance? Why doesn't he just live on the land himself? What might we surmise is the difference between Benjamin Hodges—a tenant who leases a number of spaces: a "House and Garden," "Distillery Sheds and Yard," other "Gardens," a "Meadow," and so on—and R. Jenkins, whose lease is only for a cottage and garden? What can we infer about the work of these two men and their uses of the land they rent from the marquis? What can we deduce overall about the uses of land, coded by color on this map? Moving back to the novel, we discuss a few passages that the maps illuminate, the passage that narrates Sir Thomas's return from Antigua, for example, when he "had to reinstate himself in all the wonted concerns of his Mansfield life, to see his steward and his bailiff—to examine and compute—and, in the intervals of business, to walk into his stables and his gardens, and nearest plantations" (223; vol. 2, ch. 2). After viewing the estate map, how do we judge his management of his estate? Another useful passage occurs later in the novel, when Henry Crawford, eager to impress Fanny, "had begun making acquaintance with cottages whose very existence, though on his own estate, had been hitherto unknown to him" (469; vol. 3, ch. 10). How could these cottages (and their inhabitants) exist on his estate without his knowledge? How does his management of his estate compare with that of Sir Thomas? What is the connection of their estate management—an activity not generally conducive to sustaining reader interest—with the marriage plot of this novel?

After some class discussion of this estate map and its relation to the novel, I provide links to other maps relevant to *Mansfield Park*, and students are required to view them at home or in the library, on their own, before contributing to online discussion or preparing for another live class. Two examples are *Portsmouth* (1797) from the British Library's collection *Ordnance Survey Drawings*, and *A Chart of the Antilles, or, Charibbe, or, Caribs Islands, with the Virgin Islands* (1784), from the library's *Caribbean Views*. *Portsmouth* is an early ordnance survey map, authorized by the government at a time when the French threat to English security was palpable (the ordnance surveys and mapping of Britain continued, however, throughout the nineteenth century). Portsmouth's location on the English Channel at the very "mouth of the port" meant that the city was militarily as well as commercially significant. My discussion prompts for this map point students to the dual importance of Fanny's home town, and concrete questions direct them to the map's features. Where is Portsmouth situated in relation to London? (To answer this question, they must find a basic map of England on their own.) In relation to France? What are dockyards, and why are they so prominently marked? What can we infer about the kinds of work that people did in Portsmouth? How does this map differ from the estate plan we viewed in class? Why are there no tenants' plots delineated? I can't always predict what students will say in response to these prompts, and this unpredictability almost always takes the discussion in productive directions.

Chart of the Antilles is an especially useful map for discussing how "the geographical sense" constructs knowledge. In addition to providing a more conventional cartographic view, as if drawn from above, this map includes individual profile sketches of all the Caribbean islands (including Antigua) as they appeared to sailors approaching by sea. Why might the mapmaker have included such views? Why isn't there a similar view of the Isle of Wight in the map of Portsmouth? The headnote reads, "[The islands] are named Windward Islands by the Spaniards, as well as by the French, the Dutch, and the Danes; while the English, who consider the position of those Islands respectively to Barbadoes, give them the name of Leeward Islands, or Leeward Charibbe Islands." Why are all these nations mentioned? Why does it matter that they call the Caribbean Islands by different names? We link these maps to our subsequent discussions of Fanny's return to Portsmouth—perhaps the walk around the dockyards Fanny takes with Henry Crawford toward the end of the novel—or to one or two of the Antiguan references in the novel. With our maps in mind, the Antiguan references make more sense but don't require a lengthy, explanatory lecture.

There are a number of pedagogical advantages to using such materials. The students are intrigued by the alternative representational mode of the maps and estate plans. Challenged to make sense of unfamiliar materials, they turn back to the novel with renewed curiosity and new analytic tools. Especially important to me is that the maps challenge our conventional uses of Said and related theorists to teach novels like *Mansfield Park*. I can teach what I consider to be one of Said's most valuable contributions—an acquaintance with the "geographical sense"—without devoting an exorbitant amount of class time to explaining postcolonial theory or to providing the kind of contextual historical knowledge that is necessary to understand the novel's glancing references to Antigua. Students learn to cultivate this "geographical sense" by working with archival materials themselves instead of trying to memorize what I tell them— a form of engagement, as much research has shown, that deepens and strengthens the learning process.

The maps also enable us to sidestep the now ubiquitous and often reductive practice of "othering," a mode of reading derived from Said's analysis of how the West has represented non-Western "others" (and now frequently referenced in the verb form "to other" and in the gerund form "othering"). In his *Orientalism*, the concept of the other is complex and grounded in his exceptional knowledge of French, German, and British orientalism across several centuries. Unfortunately, othering also lends itself to facile literary applications, and in my experience the concept is difficult to complicate or dislodge once students have absorbed its reductive uses. By redirecting their energies to the analysis of geographic materials, I help them develop tools that enable them to fashion their own readings of *Mansfield Park* instead of simply memorizing mine or regurgitating those of other critics.

Obviously, my emphasis on these kinds of materials and approaches bespeaks my own convictions about what's at stake when we teach novels like *Mansfield Park* to students in the twenty-first century. At a time when international policy makers are still dealing with the effects of the nineteenth- and twentieth-century "geographical sense" of both Western and non-Western cultures, I want to alert my students to these issues in the literature we read and give them analytic tools to view those issues carefully and critically. At the University of Houston,

I don't need to work hard to show them why this analysis matters. Our student body draws largely from the Houston-Galveston metropole, reflecting the area's richly diverse ethnic mix and representing its large and vibrant Hispanic, Vietnamese, and South Asian communities. As first- or second-generation immigrants from these global regions, many of my students are intimately and experientially acquainted with what Derek Gregory, a geographer, has called "the colonial present." It would be wrong to ignore this fact in the classroom. At the same time, I do not want to teach students exactly what they should think about a work of literature—and especially not what political conclusions they should draw from it. The authority structures of the classroom are too fraught with complexities and inequalities to justify the inculcation of what could appear as dogma to many of our students, whatever the stripe of our own political beliefs. Happily, teaching *Mansfield Park* as a novel about space, place, and geography allows me to address the diverse pedagogical goals and convictions I have outlined here: to speak to the theoretical contexts of the novel, to keep the focus on the text itself, and to give my students some useful tools for understanding our current global and geographic crises.

"That Was Now the Home":
Nationalism and Imperialism in *Mansfield Park*

Lisa Kasmer

Students who haven't yet read Austen's novels sometimes view them as innocuous romantic tales. However, the new historical attention that literary critics have brought to her work in the last few decades has made her political and social relevance difficult for a teacher to ignore. Claudia L. Johnson (*Jane Austen*) and Marilyn Butler (*Jane Austen*) both read Austen's novels in the political context of the late eighteenth century, and *Mansfield Park* has also received attention in postcolonial studies, though scholars are divided in their conclusions.[1] Brian Southam and Joseph Lew both view the novel as a politically savvy text with abolitionist leanings, while Edward Said places it in context of the British Empire's interests at home and abroad. These critics do not suggest that Austen speaks directly about national politics but instead that she highlights these concerns through her portrayal of the Mansfield Park family and estate. Gary Kelly's assertion that anti-Jacobinic novels "reduce large political and public issues to their everyday, domestic, commonplace consequences in individual domestic experience" defines this metonymic relation between the nation and the estate in *Mansfield Park* (289).

Introducing students to this way of reading the novel, I argue that Austen's commitment to a nationalist narrative and yet awareness of the unacknowledged foundations of that confident narrative make *Mansfield Park* ambiguous: Fanny Price comes to value the abundance and moral order of the landed estate even as her status as a poor relation and as a native of Portsmouth clearly reveal the estate's undergirding in a restrictive social order and embattled colonialist interests.

In his work on nationalism, Said argues that ideals surrounding national identity must necessarily involve amnesia regarding a nation's history, since "[n]ational identity always involves narratives. . . . But these narratives are never undisputed or merely a matter of the neutral recital of facts" ("Invention" 177). National identity necessarily involves "the invention of tradition," which is "a method for using collective memory selectively by manipulating certain bits of the national past, suppressing others, elevating still others in an entirely functional way. Thus memory is not necessarily authentic, but rather useful" (179).

During the Regency period, Britain's national pride, spurred by successes in the Napoleonic War like the 1805 victory in Trafalgar, may have made Austen, like others, sense the need for a clear national narrative. Those gathered at Mansfield listen admiringly to William Price's naval exploits, Sir Thomas acknowledging William's "good principles, professional knowledge, energy, courage, and cheerfulness" and Henry Crawford his "glory of heroism, of usefulness" (275; vol. 2, ch. 6). The novel honors the moral fortitude and order of command associated with the national navy's strength but also suggests that paternal authority, strict social hierarchy, and religious cohesion are its corollaries in the Mansfield estate. The novel's political confidence about the navy does not mask the reality of the estate's and the nation's troubling social inequities and ties to colonialism.[2] *Mansfield Park* suppresses and manipulates national history and politics to create a "useful" national narrative but one that is inauthentic because it occludes a painful past.

Said's commentary ("Invention") can be supplemented by referring students to Benedict Anderson's earlier *Imagined Communities: Reflections on the Origins and Spread of Nationalism*, first published in 1983 (see esp. ch. 1). Anderson helpfully defines the nation as "an imagined political community—and imagined as both inherently limited and sovereign." Through this envisioned community, he suggests a shared worldview as defining the nation: "It is *imagined* because the members of even the smallest nation will never know most of their fellow-members, meet them, or even hear of them, yet in the minds of each lives the image of their communion" (6). The constructed nature of the national narrative in *Mansfield Park* suggests that the entity of the nation exists in the conscious and unconscious beliefs and hopes of a people rather than in definite political or social criteria. Austen relays this idea by having Fanny come to feel such a kinship and interest in the Bertram family and estate.

In the opening chapters of *Mansfield Park*, Fanny has no clear national consciousness. After the ten-year-old is consigned to Mansfield under the benevolent design of assisting Lady Bertram's sister, Fanny's supposedly inferior intellect and memory are the subject of self-satisfied discussion among the Bertrams. When Maria and Julia report that Fanny knows nothing of "the chronological order of the kings of England, with the dates of their accession, and most of the principal events of their reigns!," Mrs. Norris replies, "Very true, indeed, my dears, but you are blessed with wonderful memories, and your poor cousin has probably none at all. There is a vast deal of difference in memories, as well as in everything else, and therefore you must make allowance for your cousin, and pity her deficiency" (21; vol. 1, ch. 2). The statement that Fanny has "probably none [no memory] at all," senseless as it is, marks her as the ideal cipher for promoting a national narrative.

Along with Fanny's ignorance of monarchical history, the Bertram girls mock her limited view of the British Empire and the globe, reporting that "my cousin cannot put the map of Europe together—or my cousin cannot tell the principal rivers in Russia—or she never heard of Asia Minor." When asked how she would go to Ireland, Fanny says, "she should cross to the Isle of Wight," just off the coast from her home in Portsmouth. The girls ridicule her for designating it as "*the Island*, as if there were no other island in the world" (20). Like other social critics of her time, such as Maria Edgeworth and Mary Wollstonecraft, Austen criticizes the rote learning that passed for education in the upbringing of young ladies, but there is another significance latent in these comments. Fanny at this stage has local knowledge but no learning. It can be helpful to mention that the Isle of Wight, like Portsmouth itself, was important in British history—it was, for example, the island to which Charles I, the Stuart monarch, fled in 1647. The Bertram sisters, with their information (but no intellectual curiosity) are ignorant of the significance of Fanny's "*Island*," but their reported conversation signals a potential national consciousness in this exchange, a consciousness that develops in the novel's account of Fanny's education.

The narrator of *Mansfield Park* writes that Edmund has "formed" Fanny's mind through his suggestions for her education (76; vol. 1, ch. 7). A baronet's second son who will become a member of the clergy, he represents both the ruling class and its moral recuperation from association with dissipation. Under his tutorship, Fanny acquires Christian ethics and genteel taste. She sanctions both Anglican tenets and the moral authority of the landed gentry, especially over the lower orders, when she decries Sotherton's abandoning the custom of gathering the whole household for prayer in the chapel on its grounds. This ritual, if it is enforced by the patriarch of the estate, she implies, binds the community through shared belief. While visiting Sotherton, only Fanny shows an interest in the ancestry of the estate, which proclaims Britain's glory; she listens with "unaffected earnestness to all that Mrs. Rushworth could relate of the family in former times, its rise and grandeur, regal visits and loyal efforts" (99; ch. 9). Her response to Rushworth's extensive plans for improvements to Sotherton suggests, however, that she fears that the traditions embodied in the landed estate are gradually being destroyed. She worries that Rushworth's proposed changes will destroy the "grandeur," and the regality and loyalty embodied in the estate's ancestry, all images evocative of allegiance to the British nation. Indeed, Henry Crawford's characterization of himself as a "devourer" for his avid support of improvements denotes a violent desecration through these changes to the estate (72; ch. 6).

When the conversation shifts to the role of the clergy in contemporary English society, Edmund asserts that "as the clergy are, or are not what they ought to be, so are the rest of the nation" (109; ch. 9), thus reiterating one of the principal aims of the Evangelical movement in the Anglican church, which was to strengthen "the nation" through moral improvement. Fanny's enthusiastic concurrence in Edmund's opinions on such matters shows how fully she has absorbed both his ethical values and his sense of obligation—the obligation of the ruling class. Yet Fanny herself is, and remains, on the periphery of this class.

Fanny's disapproval of Elizabeth Inchbald's *Lovers' Vows*, a play dealing with the pursuit of secret love affairs, shows again how fully Fanny has adopted Edmund's ideology. Without explicitly saying so, she defers to Sir Thomas's absent authority. The playscript itself undermines the immutability of class hierarchy and patriarchal control. It includes Amelia's confessing her love for her tutor, Anhalt, even though her father has chosen Count Cassel as her future husband and thus underscores the social—and, in a larger sense, national—threat of the Jacobinic ideals. But the play's disturbing potential goes beyond this: in flirting with Henry Crawford during the rehearsals, Maria openly violates the standards of decorum expected of the dutiful daughter of a baronet and begins a process that ultimately damages not only her personal life but the standing of the Mansfield estate itself.

Fanny is a gifted and intellectually curious young woman. Under Edmund's guidance, her education progresses. She becomes more and more aware of, and interested in, the world around her in its social and political aspects. Her awareness also comprises a progressive identification with the ruling-class family that signals an adoption of, or acquiescence in, the mythology of the national narrative. It is the ambiguous quality of her position that makes this aspect of the novel so puzzling but also so fascinating.

One key instance for illuminating this paradox has been analyzed by postcolonial critics. In response to the conversations with her uncle concerning his dealings in Antigua, Fanny mentions to Edmund that she loves "to hear [her] uncle talk of the West Indies" (230; vol. 2, ch. 3), and, in a much disputed passage, she reminds Edmund of her asking her uncle about the slave trade and adds that she did not continue to question him because of the "dead silence" that followed her question and his reply (231). While Said reads this silence as revealing Fanny and Austen's complicity in Britain's involvement with the slave trade, Southam asserts that Austen shows Fanny to be a "friend of the abolition" ("Silence" [*Mansfield Park*] 498). More recently, George E. Boulukos took postcolonialist readings of the novel to task for regarding that "dead silence" as either a complete indictment or acceptance of Britain's attitudes on slavery. Distinguishing between the politics of slavery and colonialism, he views Austen as supporting an ameliorist view of slavery. In particular, he interprets the silence concerning the slave trade as a criticism of the Bertram children's lack of interest in their father's (and, I would add, the nation's) business: he argues that the "moral failing . . . is the indifference of Fanny's cousins to their father and to his slaves" (362).[3] One salient point then is the domestic one: Fanny is interested in history, social politics, and the estate; her cousins, the beneficiaries, are not. Tom, Maria, and Julia, who inherit the wealth and social prestige of the ruling family, are interested in nothing but their pleasures. Fanny's questioning of Sir Thomas about the slave trade reveals a concern for both her guardian's business in Antigua and her nation's holdings there, a concern that is morally correct in the context of the Bertram home and, in a larger sense, of Fanny's status as a British citizen.

Austen acknowledges the devastation colonialism has wreaked on England; she acknowledges less the devastation it has wreaked on the colonies. The portrayal of Sir Thomas on his return from Antigua as "burnt, fagged" and with a "worn look of fatigue" suggests forcefully the cost that his involvement in the torrid zone of the colonies has on the English (208–09; vol. 2, ch. 1). His absence from his family to attend to their estates is the immediate cause of its moral decay. Further, his commitment to a crucial source of the family's wealth alienates him from that very family, with the result that a telling pervasive "sameness and gloom" follows his return (229; ch. 3).

A second key passage for understanding the national and moral issues the novel raises occurs during Fanny's enforced visit to her birth family in Portsmouth. Schooled by Edmund, and used to the luxuries of Mansfield, Fanny condemns her surroundings, especially after the departure of William to join his ship and fight for his country: "[T]he home he had left her in was — Fanny could not conceal it from herself — in almost every respect, the very reverse of what she could have wished. It was the abode of noise, disorder, and impropriety. Nobody was in their right place, nothing was done as it ought to be. She could not respect her parents, as she had hoped" (450; vol. 3, ch. 8). "[N]othing was done as it ought to be" is the phrase of an enlightened observer who sees the household from a position of moral authority.

More significant still is the passage in which Fanny in her thoughts compares Mansfield Park with her home in Portsmouth:

> At Mansfield, no sounds of contention, no raised voice, no abrupt bursts, no tread of violence was ever heard; all proceeded in a regular course of cheerful orderliness; every body had their due importance; every body's feelings were consulted. If tenderness could be ever supposed wanting, good sense and good breeding supplied its place; and as to the little irritations, sometimes introduced by aunt Norris, they were short, they were trifling, they were as a drop of water to the ocean, compared with the ceaseless tumult of her present abode. (453–54)

This passage is a telling evocation of a delicate young woman whose nerves are frayed. The exaggeration of the clichéd phrase "they were as a drop of water to the ocean" is Austen's signal that Fanny's assessment here is not the narrator's.

Nevertheless, students will clearly see that although Fanny admits the neglect at Mansfield in the phrase "[i]f tenderness could be ever supposed wanting," she is in effect mythologizing the estate she has left.[4] "[N]o abrupt bursts, no tread of violence was ever heard"? Wasn't a painful scene in Mansfield preceded by "a heavy step" at which Fanny "trembled" and begins to "tremble again" as she recalls "[t]he terror" of Sir Thomas's previous visits to the East Room (360; vol. 3, ch. 1)? "[T]he little irritations, sometimes introduced by [A]unt Norris"? She ignores those, too, because at this moment need, or longing, overrides memory. Austen shows Fanny's willingness to obliterate the truth when Fanny endorses the "good sense and good breeding" so strongly associated with the British upper and ruling classes. In her journey toward a true place in the Bertram household and a truer view of her homeland, she must repress the trauma inherent in the estate of Mansfield Park: the plight of her family and of the poor in general, necessitated by England's social hierarchy as well as by the colonialism underlying the nation's imperialist commercial enterprises.

Fanny's mythologizing of Mansfield is akin to, or perhaps a version of, the national British narrative. It glosses over and in fact misrepresents or belies the truths of cruelty, oppression, and exploitation on which Mansfield is founded, in order to construct an image of stability, calm, and order. Fanny is thus here the consciousness through which the naked facts of imagined national history are allowed to speak. Austen therefore provides, in the novel, an analogy of the very process of imperialist consolidation that many critics have thought *Mansfield Park* itself performs.

Mansfield's grandeur is delicately balanced with social criticism of its institutional foundations. Fanny's education into a critical awareness of the world is simultaneously an account of her acculturation into the ideology of the ruling class; it also uncovers the role that repression and imagined community play in the construction of a national narrative. This complex process of suppression and the equivocations it demands are revealed in the opening of the final chapter of the novel. Austen makes clear the distress residing just under the surface of Britain's national narrative in the denouement of *Mansfield Park*, in which Fanny returns to Mansfield Park as wife and daughter: "Let other pens dwell on guilt and misery. I quit such odious subjects as soon as I can, impatient to restore every body, not greatly in fault themselves, to tolerable comfort, and to have done with all the rest" (533). The narrator refuses to dwell on possible guilt and misery, just as the narrative of the nation in *Mansfield Park* does not dwell on national guilt and misery, in order to proclaim Britain's greatness. The abruptness of this refusal to dwell is a signal that the complexities that the novel has uncovered are now to be abandoned.

Through this critical approach to *Mansfield Park*, students begin to see beyond the romantic entanglements in the novel and witness the dense cultural and political insinuations in Austen's work. Class discussion of Said's and Anderson's theories on the emergence of nationalism enables students, before they approach *Mansfield Park*, to explore Austen's engagement with slavery, colonialism, and imperialism. As they become more familiar with the political and social milieu of the long eighteenth century, they also engage more fully in reading *Mansfield Park*, since they begin to see the contemporary relevance of the issues of nationalism and of home in Austen's novel.

NOTES

In this essay, quotations of *Mansfield Park* are from the Norton Critical Edition (ed. Johnson).

[1] The Norton Critical Edition of the novel, based on Austen's revised 1816 manuscript, which has a strong introduction by Johnson, an Austen scholar, works well for taking this theoretical approach in the classroom, because this edition contains condensed versions of critical responses by Southam (493–98), Lew (498–510), and Said (490–93).

[2] In *Jane Austen and the Navy*, Southam details Austen's depiction of the Royal Navy in her novels.

[3] Boulukos argues that Sir Thomas is compelled by economics to attend to the plantation in Antigua but that "economic motives, in the discourse of the time, would by no means impinge on the sense that his mission was also a moral one" (373).

[4] Susan Fraiman points out that Austen intends the irony in Fanny's statement that "Mansfield is now the home," because "[t]he Mansfield we have seen has been nothing but contention, jealousy, and insensitivity to others" (810).

"You Do Not Know *Me*":
Reformation and Rights in *Mansfield Park*

Paula Loscocco

When we get to *Mansfield Park* at the end of my eighteenth-century survey, there are three things I want students to do. First, I want them to analyze the textual patterns that govern the novel's portrayal of human conscience and consciousness. Second, I want them to appreciate how those patterns relate to contemporary debates about obligation, authority, liberty, rights, and redemption. Finally, I want them to consider the possibility that Austen's preimperial novel is a postcolonial text that explores issues of power through a heroine whose distinguishing features are her obscured voice and contingent story line.

This project is made difficult by the vexed relation between Austen studies and postcolonial studies. Postcolonial theory effectively began in 1978 with Edward Said's *Orientalism* and achieved influential articulation in his 1993 *Culture and Imperialism*. In "Jane Austen and Empire," Said is unable to resist what he himself recognizes as a "rhetoric of blame" when he asserts that Austen and *Mansfield Park* participate in the "complete subordination" of the oppressed "colony" to the colonizing European "metropolis" ([*Culture*] 96, 90). Far from asserting any kinship between preimperial culture and postcolonial consciousness, he assumes their essential conflict.

The relation between postcolonial studies and Austen studies has improved since 1993, however, as fresh scholarship has enriched both fields. Postcolonial studies now brings a mix of concerns to its exploration of people, culture, and power across time and space. Understanding modernity as the period marked by people moving in global ways, Andrew Smith outlines the field: the "project of postcolonial literary studies begins with the sense that 'other' places and stories are suddenly visible and vocal in the heart of the metropolis, courtesy of mass migration and new forms of communication" that allow for "writing back" (244–45). In this context, he adds, the "emblematic figure of the migrant" is "an appropriate self-image" for postcolonial identity (259), and cultural insight in a mobile and polyvocal world derives from the "*in-between* space[s]" of hybridity, liminality, and translation (248). Smith also notes that postcolonial studies is now grounded in "the recognition that those 'other' places have been there from the very beginning of modern Western literary tradition" (245). Sunil Agnani similarly seeks "to broaden the purview" of postcolonial studies "retrospectively to the European Enlightenment, since this is the period in which many of the questions of sovereignty, rights, and so on were formed" (Yaeger 645).

Recent studies of *Mansfield Park*, in turn, have brought the social, political, and economic debates of the early nineteenth century to bear on the novel. While some of this work aims merely to prove Austen's imperialist or abolitionist credentials, several historically grounded and sensitive readers have explored how her engagement with cultural debate brings her characters and their dilemmas into more precise focus. My own students are quick to apply their knowledge of colonial history (from other courses) and eighteenth-century debates about power and culture (from our readings of Aphra Behn, Samuel Johnson, William Cowper, Phillis Wheatley, and Olaudah Equiano) to *Mansfield Park*. My challenge as a teacher is to make sure that we begin and end with Austen's novel: I want us first to analyze the novel as a meaningfully structured text; next, to set its represented struggles in the context of its time; and only then to consider how the novel functions as a postcolonial work.

My strategy for keeping students grounded in textual analysis is to reveal in *Mansfield Park* traces of a major hermeneutic tradition that Austen inherited and used—namely, patterns of reading and interpretation that derive from the English Reformation. Although there is a great difference between the Protestant Reformation of the sixteenth century and the world of early-nineteenth-century Anglicanism, Reformation traditions of discerning individual duty, locating sources of legitimate authority, and seeking redemption persist in *Mansfield Park*, especially in its heroine's struggles to determine her responsibility to others and herself. Once students see these Reformation patterns of reading and interpretation in the novel, they recognize them in the novel's engagement with the debates of its time.

I use excerpts from other texts as background for *Mansfield Park*. First, I provide the class with two models of Reformation reading: one simple, populist, and accommodating; the other complex, rigorous, and austere. I link the simpler model of Reformation reading to Samuel Richardson's *Pamela*, which we read in excerpts as a comic foil to Austen's darker novel. I link the more demanding model of Reformation reading to *Mansfield Park*, using it to highlight Fanny Price's urgent pursuit of moral thought and feeling—a pursuit made more difficult by its taking place not in the theological sixteenth or seventeenth century but in the secular nineteenth.

I introduce students to Reformation hermeneutics by offering them emblematic texts by William Tyndale (c.1494–1536), on the one hand, and Desiderius Erasmus (c.1467–1536) and John Milton (1608–74), on the other. All three writers assume the primacy of sacred text, as well as the priority of the individual soul, whose salvation depends on what and how a person reads. But where Tyndale imagines a single, normative, and capacious Scripture through which readers enter into universal communion, Erasmus and Milton understand the Bible as a difficult and fragmented text that demands the entire skill and labor of a single learned reader seeking his own salvation.

Once we have these two models of Reformation reading in place, I point to their spectral presence in eighteenth-century and early-nineteenth-century fiction, tracing the outlines of Tyndalean textual principles in Richardson's *Pamela* and Miltonic principles in *Mansfield Park*. I argue that Austen implicitly rejects Tyndale as inadequate to the demands of the preimperial world but that her use of Miltonic habits of interpretation makes clear that whatever sources of authority exist in 1814, they are more obscure and less promising of salvation than even Milton imagined. A great deal of the novel's power and poignancy comes from our seeing that Fanny's determined efforts to find her way suggest the heroic persistence of Reformation habits in a post-Reformation world.

We begin with Tyndale's 1531 "A Pathway into the Holy Scripture," a translation of Martin Luther's prologue to the New Testament. Tyndale's articulation of the Protestant principle of *sola scriptura*—the supreme authority of a universally accessible Scripture—still packs a revolutionary punch by setting the individual reader over all figures of worldly authority: "[I]t hath pleased God to send unto our Englishmen . . . the Scripture in their mother tongue, considering that there be in every place false teachers and blind leaders, that ye should be deceived of no man" (489). *Sola scriptura* may put religious agency in the hands of the reader, but what that reader discovers in his encounter with the Bible is his innate depravity: "In all my deeds I must have the law before me, to condemn mine unperfectness. For all that I do (be I never so perfect) is yet damnable sin, when it is compared to the law" (493). But if the "law" of the Hebrew Bible condemns the reader, the "promises" of the Christian Bible offer him salvation: "I must also have the promises before mine eyes, that I despair not; in which promises I see the mercy, favour, and good will of God upon me in the blood of his Son Christ, which hath made satisfaction for mine unperfectness" (493).

Discovering his depravity by reading the Old Testament, a Christian keeps reading to find his salvation in the New Testament. Tyndale amplifies the satisfaction provided by Protestant textual salvation by imagining a community of readers gathered within the Word itself. If everyone can read (through primers and catechisms) and Scripture is available to all (through print translations), then everyone can access God's "promises" and enter into textual communion: "These things . . . to know, is to have all the Scripture unlocked and opened before thee, so that if thou wilt go in and read, thou canst not but understand. . . . And now because the lay and unlearned people are taught these first principles . . . [,] they read the Scripture and understand and delight therein" (509–10). By the time we finish with Tyndale, we know the basic elements of English Reformation hermeneutics, elements we recognize (in altered form) when we get to *Pamela* and *Mansfield Park*. These are the agency of the individual soul (or conscience or consciousness), the authority of Scripture (or other texts), the pursuit of salvation (or duty or integrity) through reading (or reflection or remembrance), and the presence (or absence) of a community of readers and a space within which that community might gather.

Tyndale's "Pathway" contrasts with Erasmus's and Milton's more demanding model of Reformation humanism. In Reformation humanism, learning, analysis, and interpretation replace simple literacy, and the Christian reader is on his own with God's Word, requiring neither community nor space. Because Erasmus demands scriptural expertise, for example, he focuses not on lay or unlearned readers but on the theologian: in a 1515 letter, he insists on "learning[,] without which a true judgement . . . is impossible," and he argues that knowledge is "so important for understanding the holy scriptures that it seems to me gross impertinence for anyone to assume the name of theologian if he is ignorant of" it (170–71, 160–61). Erasmus's particular emphasis is on scriptural languages—"[I]f in the present state of the world you persuade yourself that you can have a true understanding of theology without a knowledge of languages, especially of the one in which most of the holy scriptures have come down to us, you are entirely wrong"—but his general focus is on "human learning" and "the books of men" (161).

A hundred and thirty years later, in book 2, chapter 19, of the 1644 second edition of *The Doctrine and Discipline of Divorce*, Milton collapses the distinction between Erasmus's theologian and Tyndale's everyman. He also locates Scripture's difficulty not in its source languages but in the only partial legibility of its own discourse. Making proper sense of a cryptic and fragmented sacred text, Milton argues in 1644, is the hard work of individual salvation:

> [T]here is scarse any one saying in the Gospel, but must be read with limitations and distinctions, to be rightly understood; for Christ gives no full comments or continu'd discourses, but . . . speaks oft in Monosyllables, like a maister, scattering the heavenly grain of his doctrin like pearle heer and there, which requires a skilfull and laborious gatherer; who must compare the wordes he finds, with other precepts, with the end of every ordinance, and with the general *analogy* of Evangelick doctrine.   (338)

There is little here of Tyndale's easy sense that to read the English Bible is to understand one's salvation. Milton's scriptural scholar faces a challenging text that he must read "with limitations and distinctions" to reach an "Evangelick" interpretation. He must also be a "skilfull and laborious gatherer" in his Master's textual fields, which are open to him not as Tyndale's Scripture is open to a "delight[ed]" community of saints but as a harvested field is open to the scattered gleaners who must seek their difficult livings on it.

Milton's stern and solitary version of Reformation hermeneutics is a far cry from the universal community of Tyndale's mother-tongue Bible. It is an equally far cry from *Mansfield Park*, despite that novel's portrayal of Fanny Price as a textual gatherer who struggles to piece together authority and agency from the limited fragments of reading, thought, and feeling at her disposal. Nevertheless, the Miltonic model illuminates our discussion of *Mansfield Park*: Austen portrays Fanny's pursuit of moral agency through reading and reflection as an implicitly humanist endeavor, even as Austen uses the humanist model to measure just how far Fanny's world has come from its Reformation roots.

Reformation hermeneutics haunt the 1740 *Pamela* and the 1814 *Mansfield Park*. I begin with *Pamela* both to demonstrate the presence of Reformation principles of reading and interpretation in eighteenth-century fiction and to set up a comparison with *Mansfield Park*. I make short work of *Pamela*, focusing on elements of text and reading familiar from Tyndale. Richardson's heroine emerges here as a second Tyndale, offering her story as a plainspoken, widely disseminated, and scriptural text, the reading of which saves the rake, the institution of marriage, and the local Anglican Church.

Like Tyndale, Pamela insists on her soul's integrity and its inalienable freedom from human authority: "[H]ow came I to be his Property? What Right has he in me?" she asks Mrs. Jewkes, referring to Mr. B. (Richardson 126). "[L]et my Assent be that of a free Person, mean as I am," she writes to Mr. B., "and not of a sordid Slave" (139). "O Sir," she writes to Mr. Williams, "my Soul is of equal Importance with the Soul of a Princess, though my Quality is inferior to that of the meanest Slave" (158).

As Tyndale perceives all souls to be captivated by sin, finding release only in the Gospel, so Pamela, a captive cut off from society, family, and her own liberty, turns to the psalter. "I remembering the 137 Psalm to be a little touching," she writes, "[I] turn'd to it, and took the Liberty to alter it to my Case more" (140). Michael Austin notes that Pamela's psalm and story are treated as Scripture by the other characters (7). Like Tyndale's gospel, her letters are recovered with difficulty, read with ease, and transformative of those who understand them. As soon as Mr. B. has read even part of Pamela's story, he resolves to marry, plights himself to her, and promises his "everlasting Truth and Fidelity" (Richardson 275). Once he has read her psalm, he has his soul purged by Mr. Williams, an event Pamela celebrates as the effect of her "Papers" (309).

Like Tyndale, finally, Richardson envisions a community of scriptural readers, though unlike Tyndale he houses them not in the Bible but in the Anglican Church. Pamela's story saves not just Mr. B. but the several institutions with which he is affiliated—his family, neighborhood, local church, and manorial chapel. When she hears that the chapel "has not been us'd for two Generations, for any thing but a Lumber-room," she replies, "I hope it will never be lumber'd again, but kept to the Use, for which, as I *presume*, it has been consecrated" (276–77). No sooner said than done: the characters repair to the restored chapel to debate texts for Sunday's sermon; they worship at the local church, Pamela's father psalming and Mr. Williams preaching; they conduct a parallel service at home, using her psalm and its source; and Mr. B. and Pamela return to the chapel to wed. Pamela's epistolary scripture serves as a conduit to the literal spaces of Anglican marriage and worship. This is comfort indeed both to her community of saved readers and to the Anglican Church, which is thereby rerooted in Tyndalean principles of textual salvation and community.

"[C]reepmouse" Fanny is no Pamela (171; vol. 1, ch.15), but students come to regard her as a braver and more heroic figure than her dauntless predecessor. Fanny conforms to Milton's image of a "skilfull and laborious gatherer" of textual "grain," but she operates in a post-Reformation world that lacks his guarantees of sacred text and salvation. Compelled as she is by the humanist mandate to piece together what discursive fragments she can find—if not from Scripture then from books, feeling, and memory—she persists, though she does so without expectation of redemption or communion.

Like Pamela, Fanny is committed to the Reformation principle of spiritual autonomy—the individual's right to and responsibility for her own conscience. "[Y]ou will make [Henry Crawford] every thing," Edmund tells Fanny. "'I would not engage in such a charge,' cried Fanny in a shrinking accent—'in such an office of high responsibility!'" (406; vol. 3, ch. 4). Henry later repeats Edmund's sentiment: "When you give me your opinion, I always know what is right. Your judgment is my rule of right." "Oh, no!—do not say so," Fanny cries, "We have all a better guide in ourselves, if we would attend to it, than any other person can be" (478; ch. 11).

Despite the urging of "a better guide in ourselves," however, Fanny's world is not one in which a person might read (as in Tyndale) or interpret (as in Milton) or adapt (as with Pamela) a Scripture capable of saving souls. Though texts abound in *Mansfield Park*, they are secular, not sacred, even in churches. Though her reading matters to her, it provides more comfort than clarity, and it neither promises nor delivers redemption. And though she values shared reading, mainly with Edmund but even with Henry, such reading creates no community and hallows no space. There is no "Evangelick doctrine" to secure texts in *Mansfield Park* and therefore no guarantee—of anything. In this context, the spectral presence of Reformation notions of scripture, textual salvation, and a community of readers—signaled in part by Fanny's insistence on the "better guide" of free conscience—identifies Fanny as a belated Reformation humanist struggling for interpretive authority in a dismayingly secular world.

The scene at Sotherton chapel in volume 1 dramatizes Fanny's difficulty, not least because of the scene's contrast with chapel scenes in *Pamela*. In Richardson, the heroine's story redeems its readers, leading them to restore chapel, church, and home as sacred spaces within which the Anglican neighborhood recommits itself to scriptural Protestantism. In Austen, the characters enter a chapel that is—and remains—dead space. "I am disappointed," Fanny tells Edmund. "This is not my idea of a chapel. There is nothing awful here, nothing melancholy, nothing grand. Here are no aisles, no arches, no inscriptions, no banners. No banners, cousin, to be 'blown by the night wind of Heaven.' No signs that a 'Scottish monarch sleeps below'" (100; ch. 9). The starkness of her position as a literary (not scriptural) reader seeking satisfaction (not salvation) is striking. Standing on supposedly consecrated ground that highlights the episode's spiritual stakes, Fanny uses Scott's "Lay of the Last Minstrel" as authorized text; she engages with the "Lay" in humanist fashion, culling from it what she needs, comparing it with what she sees before her, and putting it in the context of "awful . . . Heaven"; and her collaboration with Edmund allows her to perceive the "nothing . . . nothing . . . nothing" before her. Unlike Pamela's scriptural story, however, Fanny's literary labor transforms, reforms, and redeems no one and nothing. The company passes out of the still and silent chapel, and by the end of the chapter even Fanny's community of two has disbanded.

Once students have seen Fanny at Sotherton, they perceive her as a belated Reformation humanist throughout *Mansfield Park*. She loves "her books—of which she had been a collector, from the first hour of her commanding a shilling" (178; vol. 1, ch. 16), and she acquires a secular canon of Macartney, Crabbe, Johnson, Shakespeare, Cowper, and Wordsworth. Her moral insights spring from textual sources, as we see when she cites Cowper's "Ye fallen avenues" at dinner (66; ch. 6), the "poetry" of natural sublimity at the glee (132; ch. 11), and the value of "a rambling fancy" in Mrs. Grant's shrubbery (244; vol. 2, ch. 4). And she enjoys a master-scholar relationship with Edmund, from his tutorials early on (25; vol. 1, ch. 2) to his late survey of her reading at the end of volume 1 (183; ch. 16). In every instance, however, her quest for clarification and satisfaction runs up against the insufficiency of her materials. We get an ironic glimpse of this insufficiency when Edmund, choosing Mary Crawford and *Lovers' Vows*, leaves Fanny to Macartney's text: but "there was no reading, no China, no composure for Fanny" (183). We smile at her melodramatic misery here, but the gentle comedy allows for serious insight: her flashes of literary illumination leave her unredeemed, her books fail to ease her aching heart, and her reading never affects the novel's action.

If Fanny's world constitutes a fallen realm of post-Reformation reading and reflection, her perseverance in trying "to find her way to her duty" is all the more noteworthy (180). It suggests both her fidelity to an inner guide and her determination (in Milton's words) to "compare the words [she] findes, with other precepts, and with the end of every ordinance, and with the generall *analogie* of Evangelick doctrine." William Deresiewicz is surely right when he characterizes Fanny's use of memory to turn misery into comfort as both Wordsworthian and Romantic ("*Mansfield Park*" 58–59), but the Romanticism he draws attention to has distinctly Reformist roots. Cold, lonely, and disenfranchised, especially in her East Room sanctuary, Fanny searches her virtual library of memory, thought, and feeling, using her "better guide" to arrive at whatever principles inform her conduct elsewhere in the novel—including her decisions not to act, to forgo the supervision of another's soul, to assert the autonomy of a person's inner self, and to guard the privacy of desire.

We see how Fanny links Reformation notions of the soul's authority to Romantic ideas about self-authorizing consciousness by analyzing two East Room scenes: the scene during the theatricals in volume 1, in which she seeks duty and comfort through memory and reflection, and the scene before the ball in volume 2, in which she "remain[s] to tranquillise herself" after Edmund's confession of feeling for Mary (306; ch. 9). Struggling with "stab[bing]" misery and jealous reservations, Fanny pushes herself to "principle[d]" resolution:

> It was her intention, as she felt it to be her duty, to try to overcome all that was excessive, all that bordered on selfishness in her affection for

Edmund. . . . She would endeavour to be rational, and to deserve the right of judging [Mary and caring for Edmund] by a sound intellect and an honest heart.

She had all the heroism of principle, and was determined to do her duty. (307)

We cannot help but admire her determination to avoid "selfishness," reserve her right to her own affections and judgments, and comfort herself as best she can here. Austen checks our admiration, however, when she teases her heroine for poring over Edmund's half-written and discarded note: "[S]he seized the scrap of paper . . . as a treasure beyond all her hopes," admiring not only its willfully misapprehended content but its occasion, style, handwriting, even alphabetical characters (307). But it is a resonant tease. In her parody of a soul searching for redemptive meaning in an authorized but challenging text, Austen lightly links this episode backward in time, to the earlier East Room scene in which Fanny finds her way to duty and comfort through emotion recollected in tranquillity; to the Sotherton chapel scene, in which she discovers Anglican absence through Reformation reflection; perhaps to Richardson's chapel scenes, with their mix of Tyndalean and Anglican interpretive principles; and perhaps even to Milton's image of Reformation reading alone in the fields of God's Word.

We are not required to hear this echoing sequence. But when we do hear it, we realize that the sacred space that interests Austen most in *Mansfield Park* is not an actual chapel or church, or even the secular chapel that is Fanny's East Room, but Fanny herself. Volume 3 opens with Sir Thomas's occupation of the East Room and includes Fanny's removal from Mansfield to Portsmouth; throughout both, Fanny asserts the inviolability of her inner life within the several spaces of her mind, heart, and body. Where she once struggled to find duty and comfort, she now protects the autonomy and privacy of her consciousness, in defiance of patriarchal power, social obligation, even love. Her self-possession gives students pause. When they see Fanny as her own chapel, embodying and protecting the freedom and privacy of her self-authorizing consciousness, they recall Tyndale's assertion of the scriptural reader's freedom from worldly power as well as his image of Scripture as shelter for saved readers. They also discern the Reformation underpinnings of nineteenth-century debates about human rights.

When Sir Thomas visits Fanny, his attempts to "guide" her run up against the humanist presence that has been gathering force in her and in the novel. His decent offer of a "comfortable" fire and his assertion of avuncular prerogative or "duty" seem painfully literal, for example, given her earlier efforts to secure duty and comfort for herself in this same room (367, 360; vol. 3, ch. 1). Worse is the gap that opens between what he intends and what we hear when he levels his most serious charge against her: "You have now shewn me, that you can and will decide for yourself, without any consideration or deference for those who have surely some right to guide you—without even asking their advice" (367).

Sir Thomas is more right than he realizes here: the "right" of self-direction is precisely what Fanny claims for herself, though she claims it as principle, not crime. Indeed, the challenge of external authority makes the revolutionary nature of her self-possession manifest. When Sir Thomas responds to her refusal with the outrage of an indulgent but authoritarian uncle, guardian, father, or master, she silently defies him by plotting to protect the privilege of her heart and mind. She is "miserable for ever" for angering him (370), but she "would rather die than own the truth" and "she hope[s] by a little reflection to fortify herself beyond betraying it" (365).

Fanny's defiant guarding of her consciousness "by a little reflection" recurs later in volume 3. After Mary has left her in the East Room, Fanny rejoices that "she had escaped . . . without detection. Her secret was still her own; and while that was the case, she thought she could resign herself to almost every thing" (421; ch. 5). As with Sir Thomas, she hides the double "secret" of her feelings and self-fortifications, but we get a glimpse of both later on. Alone in Portsmouth, "almost vexed into displeasure and anger, against Edmund" for a self-absorbed letter about Mary, Fanny ends her reading with sudden insight: "Edmund, you do not know *me*" (492). In this one line of "secret declaration" (491), Fanny takes ownership of Edmund's ignorance of her heart; she redefines the "truth" or "secret" she hid from Sir Thomas and Mary to include her very self ("*me*"); and she asserts her self-knowledge and voice, on the one hand, and her right to keep both to herself, on the other.

Given *Mansfield Park*'s commitment to sifting through textual fragments in pursuit of hard-won self-authorization, students are startled by the novel's final chapter: "Let other pens dwell on guilt and misery. I quit such odious subjects as soon as I can, impatient to restore every body, not greatly in fault themselves, to tolerable comfort, and to have done with all the rest" (533). Students recognize that in providing her characters with essentially universal "restor[ation]," Austen acts as the savior of her novel, a deus ex machina who reminds her readers of no one so much as Tyndale's God. Students are even more startled when Austen hands them her pen: "I purposely abstain from dates on this occasion, that every one may be at liberty to fix their own, aware that the cure of unconquerable passions, and the transfer of unchanging attachments, must vary much as to time in different people" (544). Her offer to readers to cowrite the novel's ending is limited to determining exactly how and when Fanny is incorporated into marriage, family, and estate at Mansfield Park. But by inviting them to feel "at liberty" to sift through text, memory, and feeling for their own "different" chronologies and conclusions, Austen opens the door to readings that build not on her Tyndalean ending but on her larger narrative's Miltonic commitment to individual agency and authority through humanist textual labor. And such readings build not on the final chapter of *Mansfield Park* but on the final chapter in which Fanny is her own person—in Portsmouth.

In Portsmouth, before Henry's visit, the Bertram catastrophes, and her return to Mansfield Park, Fanny experiences genuine autonomy. Working upstairs with

Susan, she remembers the East Room and its books: "[A]fter a few days, the re-membrance of the said books grew so potent and stimulative, that Fanny found it impossible not to try for books again" through a circulating library (461; vol. 3, ch. 9). This is a pivotal scene of humanist reflection in which "remembrance" realizes itself and consciousness becomes "potent and stimulative" enough to push Fanny to find, read, and teach essential texts. We are as "amazed" as she is at her "being anything in *propria persona*, amazed at her own doings in every way; to be a renter, a chuser of books! And to be having any one's improvement in view in her choice!" (461). For a brief moment, the world is all before Fanny: she is her own woman, a chooser of books and occupations, and the founder of a female seminary.

Fanny does not head out into the world, but imagine if she had. Imagine if she had left not only Mansfield but Portsmouth, that maritime gateway to the great and terrible Atlantic. Imagine Fanny as she might have been, had Henry and Edmund never come: a disenfranchised adoptee of a well-meaning but authoritarian family, a young woman who has already found her way to duty, comfort, and self-possession through reading and reflection, an independent being poised to leave home altogether, "stimulat[ed]" by the "potency" of her own heart and mind to seek the liberties of work, community, perhaps even independent residence.

In 2004, Smith imagined the postcolonial figure as a global migrant. But students know that Wheatley was a global migrant in 1761 when she was brought from Africa to Boston as a slave, and again in 1773 when she left the home of her mistress and adoptive mother and set sail for England, seeking health, publication, and the first anniversary of the Mansfield antislavery case. I do not argue for Fanny as a latter-day Wheatley but I do acknowledge intriguing parallels—not only in personal situation (to a degree) but in a shared commitment to achieving self, voice, and redemption through reading and reflection. Only a flight of imagination allows us to assert a continuum between Fanny's Portsmouth achievement—the transformation of self-possession into autonomous action—and an actual woman's pursuit of personal, professional, and political freedom. But it may be a flight worth taking to appreciate emancipation as the legal realization of the original Reformation concept of redemption.

NOTES ON CONTRIBUTORS

Regulus Allen is associate professor of English at California Polytechnic State University, San Luis Obispo. She is the author of essays on William Hayley's contributions to the Romantic sonnet revival and eighteenth-century depictions of African female beauty.

Inger Sigrun Bredkjaer Brodey is Bank of America distinguished term associate professor in the Department of English and Comparative Literature at the University of North Carolina, Chapel Hill. Her *Ruined by Design: Shaping Novels and Gardens in the Culture of Sensibility* (2008) places Austen in the context of British and Continental political philosophy, landscape gardening, and the history of the novel.

Pamela Bromberg is professor of English at Simmons College. She has published essays on Margaret Atwood, Margaret Drabble, William Blake, Lillian Hellman, and Jane Austen. Her research and teaching interests include the development of the English novel, eighteenth-century British literature, postcolonial literature, African literature, and critical theory.

Julia Prewitt Brown is professor of English at Boston University. Her books include *The Bourgeois Interior: How the Middle Class Imagines Itself in Literature and Film* (2008), *Cosmopolitan Criticism: Oscar Wilde's Philosophy of Art* (1997), and *Jane Austen's Novels: Social Change and Literary Form* (1979). Her current project is a book on the bildungsroman and its afterlife in film.

Laura Carroll is lecturer in educational development at La Trobe University in Melbourne, Australia. She is the author of book chapters and essays on Austen films, Austen book illustration, teaching *Persuasion*, literature and dance, Shakespeare's women, and book collecting. Her current project is a book on Jane Austen and learning.

Monica F. Cohen is adjunct assistant professor of English and comparative literature at Columbia University. She is the author of *Professional Domesticity in the Victorian Novel: Women, Work and Home* (1998) and essays on Austen's *Persuasion*, Brontë's *Villette*, and Eliot's *Daniel Deronda* and *Felix Holt*.

Laura Dabundo is professor of English at Kennesaw State University. She is the author of *The Marriage of Faith: Christianity in Jane Austen and William Wordsworth* (2012) and the editor of *The Encyclopedia of Romanticism: Culture in Britain, 1780s–1830s* (2009), and *Jane Austen and Mary Shelley and Their Sisters: Romantic Women's Fiction in Context* (2000).

Dorice Williams Elliott is associate professor of English at the University of Kansas. She is the author of *The Angel out of the House: Women's Philanthropy and Gender in Nineteenth-Century England* in 2002 and essays on Elizabeth Gaskell, Hannah More, Sarah Scott, Sarah Trimmer, Charles Reade, Jane Austen, servants and industrial workers, and Australian female convicts.

Sarah Emsley is a writer in Halifax, Nova Scotia. She is the author of *Jane Austen's Philosophy of the Virtues* (2005) and the editor of *Jane Austen and the North Atlantic*

(2006) and Edith Wharton's *The Custom of the Country* (2008). Her essays on Jane Austen have appeared in *Persuasions* and *Persuasions On-line*. She is currently working on a novel.

Marcia McClintock Folsom is professor of Literature and chair of the Department of Humanities and Writing at Wheelock College. She is the editor of two MLA Approaches to Teaching volumes, on Austen's *Pride and Prejudice* and *Emma*, and she contributed an essay to *Approaches to Teaching Woolf's* To the Lighthouse.

Susan Allen Ford is professor of English and Writing Center coordinator at Delta State University. She is the author of essays on Jane Austen and her contemporaries, Shakespeare, the gothic, and detective fiction. Her current project is a book entitled "Jane Austen's Great Readers."

Penny Gay is professor emerita of English at the University of Sydney. She is the author of *Jane Austen and the Theatre* (2002), *The Cambridge Introduction to Shakespeare's Comedies* (2008), and *As She Likes It: Shakespeare's Unruly Women* (1994). Her essay "*Emma* and *Persuasion*" appears in the second edition of *The Cambridge Companion to Jane Austen*.

Peter W. Graham, professor of English at Virginia Tech, studies British literature and culture, especially Austen, Byron, Darwin, and the Romantics. His books include *Jane Austen & Charles Darwin: Naturalists and Novelists, Articulating the Elephant Man, Don Juan and Regency England*, and *Byron's Bulldog*.

Lisa Kasmer is associate professor of English at Clark University. She is the author of *Novel Histories: Women Writing History, 1760–1830* (2012) and essays on Mary Shelley and eighteenth-century women critics. Her research and teaching interests are eighteenth-century and Romantic British literature and women's writing. Her current project is a study of trauma in emergent British nationalism.

Deborah J. Knuth Klenck is professor of English at Colgate University. She is the author of essays on Jane Austen and Alexander Pope. At Colgate, she directs the honors program in English and the London study group. Her current project is on rituals of courtship in Austen.

Karyn Lehner is a PhD candidate in the English program at La Trobe University, Melbourne. Her research focuses on horse riding, the female image, and the erotic in English and Australian nineteenth-century novels. She is studying the role that horses and other companion animals play in Austen's work.

Paula Loscocco is associate professor of English at Lehman College, City University of New York. She edited *Katherine Philips (1631/32–1664): Printed Works 1651–1729* (2007). She is the author of essays on Philips, Milton, early modern psalms, theory and early women writers, teaching *Clarissa*, and Sterne. Her current project is a book entitled "Phillis Wheatley's Miltonic Poetics."

Anne Mallory is assistant professor of English at East Carolina University. She is the author of an essay on boredom and counterrevolution in Edmund Burke's *Reflections on the Revolution in France*. Her research interests include British Romanticism, nineteenth-century literature, and psychoanalytic theory.

Kay Souter is director of learning environments, research, and evaluation at Deakin University. She is coeditor of *An Endless Winter's Night: An Anthology of Mother-Daughter Relationships in Indian Literature* and *Physical and Virtual Learning Spaces in Higher Education*. She is coauthor of *Beckett and Bion: The (Im)Patient Voice in Psychotherapy and Literature*.

Lynn Voskuil is associate professor of English at the University of Houston. She is the author of *Acting Naturally: Victorian Theatricality and Authenticity* (2004) and essays on nineteenth-century British literature and culture, women's studies, and empire studies. Her current project is a book entitled "Horticulture and Imperialism: The Garden Spaces of the British Empire, 1789–1914."

John Wiltshire is adjunct professor in English at La Trobe University in Melbourne, Australia. He is the author of *Samuel Johnson in the Medical World: The Doctor and the Patient, Jane Austen and the Body: "The Picture of Health," Recreating Jane Austen*, and *The Making of Dr. Johnson*. He is the editor of the Cambridge University Press edition of Austen's *Mansfield Park*. *The Hidden Jane Austen* is his most recent book (2014).

SURVEY PARTICIPANTS

Pauline W. Beard, *Pacific University*
Toby R. Benis, *Saint Louis University*
Nicholas Birns, *The New School, Eugene Lang College*
Soledad Cabellero, *Allegheny College*
Melissa Edmundson, *University of South Carolina*
Thomas Fair, *Adams State College*
Marc Falkenberg, *Lincoln Park High School (Illinois)*
Elizabeth Fay, *University of Massachusetts, Boston*
Suzanne Ferriss, *Nova Southeastern University*
Paul Fry, *Yale University*
Kathy Gentile, *University of Missouri, St. Louis*
Lynda Hall, *Chapman University*
Jocelyn Harris, *University of Otago (New Zealand)*
Emily Hipchen, *University of West Georgia*
Claudia L. Johnson, *Princeton University*
Manjushree Kumar, *Jai Narain Vyas University (Jodhpur, India)*
Jackie Labbe, *University of Warwick*
Beth Lau, *California State University, Long Beach*
Nathaniel Leach, *Cape Breton University*
Kathleen Lundeen, *Western Washington University*
Barbara Mann, *University of Toledo*
Burton Melnick, *University of Lausanne*
Victoria Myers, *Pepperdine University*
Emily Rohrbach, *Hamilton College*
Francesca Saggini, *Istituto di Studi Anglo-Germanici (Italy)*
Richard C. Sha, *American University*
Scott Simpkins, *University of North Texas*
Mary Simonis, *Merion Mercy Academy (Pennsylvania)*
Rana Tekcan, *Istanbul Bilgi University (Turkey)*
Katie Trumpener, *Yale University*
Clara Tuite, *University of Melbourne (Australia)*
Amy Watkin, *Concordia College*
Cheryl Wilson, *Indiana University of Pennsylvania*
Juliette Wells, *Manhattanville College*

WORKS CITED

Abrams, M. H. *A Glossary of Literary Terms*. 7th ed. Fort Worth: Harcourt, 1999. Print.

Alexander, William. *The Costume of China*. London, 1805. Print.

———. *Picturesque Representations of the Dress and Manners of the Chinese*. London, 1814. Print.

Anderson, Aeneas. *A Narrative of the British Embassy to China*. London, 1795. Print.

Anderson, Benedict. *Imagined Communities: Reflections on the Origin and Spread of Nationalism*. New York: Verso, 1983. Print.

Aristotle. *Poetics*. Trans. George Whalley. Ed. John Baxter and Patrick Atherton. Montreal: McGill–Queen's UP, 1997. Print.

Armstrong, Isobel. *Jane Austen:* Mansfield Park. New York: Penguin, 1988. Print.

Armstrong, Nancy. *Desire and Domestic Fiction: A Political History of the Novel*. Oxford: Oxford UP, 1987. Print.

Auerbach, Nina, "Jane Austen's Dangerous Charm: Feeling As One Ought about Fanny Price." J. Austen, *Mansfield Park* [ed. Johnson] 445–57.

Austen, Henry. Preface. "Biographical Notice of the Author." 1818. J. Austen, *Northanger Abbey* 3–8.

Austen, Jane. *Emma*. 1816. Ed. Richard Cronin and Dorothy McMillan. Cambridge: Cambridge UP, 2005. Print.

———. *Emma*. Ed. Stephen Parrish. New York: Norton, 2000. Print. Norton Critical Ed.

———. *Jane Austen's Letters*. 1952. Ed. R. W. Chapman. London: Oxford UP, 1969. Print.

———. *Later Manuscripts*. New York: Cambridge UP, 2008. Print.

———. *Mansfield Park*. Ed. R. W. Chapman. 3rd ed. Oxford: Clarendon, 1987. Print. Vol. 3 of *The Novels of Jane Austen*.

———. *Mansfield Park*. Ed. J. M. Dent. Illus. C. E. Brock. London, 1908. Print.

———. *Mansfield Park*. Ed. Claudia L. Johnson. New York: Norton, 1998. Print.

———. *Mansfield Park*. Ed. Jane Stabler. Oxford: Oxford UP, 2003. Print. Oxford World's Classics.

———. *Mansfield Park*. Ed. June Sturrock. Ontario: Broadview, 2001. Print.

———. *Mansfield Park*. Ed. Kathryn Sutherland. Harmondsworth: Penguin, 1996. Print.

———. *Mansfield Park*. Ed. John Wiltshire. Cambridge: Cambridge UP, 2005. Print.

———. *Mansfield Park*. Illus. Hugh Thomson. London: Macmillan, 1894. Print.

———. *Mansfield Park*. London, 1814. *Google Books*. Web. 12 Apr. 2010.

———. *Mansfield Park*. 2nd ed. London, 1816. *Google Books*. Web. 12 Apr. 2010.

———. *Mansfield Park*. 1814. *Project Gutenberg*. Web. 26 Feb. 2014.

------. *Northanger Abbey*. Ed. Barbara M. Benedict and Deirdre Le Faye. Cambridge: Cambridge UP, 2006. Print.

------. *The Novels of Jane Austen*. Ed. R. W. Chapman. 5 vols. Oxford: Clarendon, 1965–66. Print.

------. "Opinions of *Mansfield Park*." Chapman, *Minor Works* 431–35.

------. *Persuasion*. Ed. R. W. Chapman. 3rd ed. Oxford: Oxford UP, 1987. Print. Vol. 5 of *The Novels of Jane Austen*.

------. *Persuasion*. 1818. Ed. Janet Todd and Antje Blank. Cambridge: Cambridge UP, 2006. Print.

------. *Pride and Prejudice*. Ed. Donald J. Gray. New York: Norton, 1966. Print.

------. *Pride and Prejudice*. Ed. Pat Rogers. Cambridge: Cambridge UP, 2006. Print.

------. *Selected Letters*. Ed. Vivien Jones. Oxford: Oxford UP, 2004. Print.

Austen-Leigh, James Edward. *A Memoir of Jane Austen*. 1871. *Project Gutenberg*. Web. 26 Feb. 2014.

Austin, Michael. "Lincolnshire Babylon: Competing Typologies in Pamela's 137th Psalm." *Eighteenth-Century Fiction* 12.4 (2000): 1–14. Web. 1 Apr. 2009.

Babb, Howard S. *Jane Austen's Novels: The Fabric of Dialogue*. Columbus: Ohio State UP, 1962. Print.

Bander, Elaine. "The Other Play in *Mansfield Park*: Shakespeare's *Henry VIII*." *Persuasions* 17 (1995): 111–20. Print.

Barrow, John. *Some Account of the Public Life, and a Selection from the Unpublished Writings, of the Earl of Macartney*. 2 vols. London, 1807. Print.

------. *Travels in China*. London, 1804. Print.

Bartlett, John. *Bartlett's Familiar Quotations*. New York: Little, 1982. Print.

The Beauties of Shakespeare. 5th ed. London, 1790. Print.

Bennett, Robin L., et al. "Genetic Counseling and Screening of Consanguineous Couples and Their Offspring: Recommendations of the National Society of Genetic Counselors." *Journal of Genetic Counseling* 11.2 (2002): 19–119. *SpringerLink*. Web. 18 Feb. 2014.

Blau, Peter M. *Exchange and Power in Social Life*. 1964. New York: Wiley, 1986. Print.

Boswell, James. *Life of Johnson*. Oxford: Oxford UP, 1998. Print.

Boulukos, George E. "The Politics of Silence: *Mansfield Park* and the Amelioration of Slavery." *Novel: A Forum on Fiction* 39.3 (2006): 361–83. *JSTOR*. Web. 17 Aug. 2013.

Bradley, A. C. "Jane Austen: A Lecture." 1929. Littlewood 2: 119–217.

Brodey, Inger Sigrun. "Papas and Ha-has: Rebellion, Authority, and Landscaping in *Mansfield Park*." *Persuasions* 17 (1995): 90–96. Print.

------. *Ruined by Design: Novels and Landscape in the Culture of Sensibility*. New York: Routledge, 2008. Print.

Brown, Julia Prewitt. *The Bourgeois Interior: How the Middle Class Imagines Itself in Literature and Film*. Charlottesville: U of Virginia P, 2008. Print.

Burlin, Katrin Ristkok. "Games." Grey 179–83.

Burrows, John F. "Style." Copeland and McMaster [1997] 170–88.

Butler, Marilyn. *Jane Austen and the War of Ideas*. Oxford: Oxford UP, 1975. Print.

———. "*Mansfield Park*: Ideology and Execution." Simons 19–33.

Byatt, A. S., and Ignês Sodré. *Imagining Characters: Six Conversations about Women Writers: Jane Austen, Charlotte Brontë, George Eliot, Willa Cather, Iris Murdoch, Toni Morrison*. London: Vintage, 1997. Print.

Byrne, Paula. *Jane Austen and the Theatre*. New York: Hambledon, 2001. Print.

Calvo, Clara. "Rewriting Lear's Untender Daughter: Fanny Price as a Regency Cordelia in Jane Austen's *Mansfield Park*." *Shakespeare Survey* 58 (2005): 83–93. Print.

Capsopoulos, Meegan. "*Mansfield Park* and *Lovers' Vows*: Tutor's Report." Memo to Penny Gay. 4 May 2010. TS.

Carr, Raymond. *English Fox Hunting*. London: Weidenfeld, 1976. Print.

Carroll, Laura, and John Wiltshire. "Jane Austen, Illustrated." Johnson and Tuite 62–77.

Chan, Mary M. "Mansfield Park as Greenhouse: 'The Effect of Education' in *Mansfield Park*." *Persuasions On-line* 27.1 (2006): n. pag. Web. 25 Feb. 2014.

Chandler, Steve, and Terrence W. Hill. *Two Guys Read Jane Austen*. Bandon: Reed, 2008. Print.

Chapman, R. W. "Chronology of *Mansfield Park*." J. Austen, *Mansfield Park* [ed. Chapman] 554–57.

———. "Index of Characters, Etc." J. Austen, *Northanger Abbey* 313–16.

———, ed. *Minor Works*. Oxford: Oxford UP, 1987. Print. Vol. 6 of *The Novels of Jane Austen*.

A Chart of the Antilles, or, Charibbe, or, Caribs Islands, with the Virgin Islands. *Caribbean Views*. British Lib., n.d. Web. 4 Aug. 2010.

Clarkson, Thomas. *The History of the Rise, Progress, and Accomplishment of the Abolition of the African Slave-Trade by the British Parliament*. London: Longman, 1808. *Google Books*. Web. 18 Aug. 2013.

Clifford, Katrina. "Lovers' Vows." Message to Penny Gay. 16 Sept. 2008. E-mail.

Coleridge, Samuel Taylor. "Shakespeare." *The Portable Coleridge*. Ed. I. A. Richards. New York: Penguin, 1978. 410–37. Print.

Colman, George, the Younger. *The Heir at Law*. London, 1808. Print.

Copeland, Edward. "Money." Copeland and McMaster [1997] 131–48.

Copeland, Edward, and Juliet McMaster, eds. *The Cambridge Companion to Jane Austen*. Cambridge: Cambridge UP, 1997. Print.

———, eds. *The Cambridge Companion to Jane Austen*. 2nd ed. Cambridge: Cambridge UP, 2011. Print.

Cowper, William. *Poems: Volume 2, Containing* The Task, An Epistle to Joseph Hill, Esq., Tirocinium; or, A Review of Schools, *and* The History of John Gilpin. London, 1785. Print.

———. "The Task." *Cowper's Task*. Ed. Francis Storr. London: Rivingtons, 1874. 62–63. Print.

Cumberland, Richard. *The Wheel of Fortune: A Comedy*. 2nd ed. London, 1795. Print.

Darwin, Erasmus. *A Plan for the Conduct of Female Education in Boarding Schools*. London: Joseph Johnson, 1797. Print.

Davidson, Jenny. "A Modest Question about *Mansfield Park*." *Eighteenth-Century Fiction* 16.2 (2004): 245–64. Print.

Davies, Paul S., and Harmon R. Holcomb, eds. *Conceptual Challenges in Evolutionary Psychology: Innovative Research Strategies*. Dordrecht: Kluwer Academic, 2001. Print.

Davis, Natalie Zemon. *The Gift in Sixteenth-Century France*. Madison: U of Wisconsin P, 2000. Print.

DeForest, Mary. "Jane Austen: Closet Classicist." *Persuasions* 22 (2000): 98–104. Print.

Deresiewicz, William. *Jane Austen and the Romantic Poets*. New York: Columbia UP, 2004. Print.

———. "*Mansfield Park*: Substitution." Deresiewicz, *Jane Austen* 56–85.

Derrida, Jacques. *Given Time: 1: Counterfeit Money*. Trans. Peggy Kamuf. Chicago: U of Chicago P, 1992. Print.

Dickens, Charles. *Bleak House*. 1853. Ed. Osbert Sitwell. London: Oxford UP, 1994. Print. New Oxford Illustrated Dickens.

Dingley, R. J. "Henry Crawford between Tragedy and Comedy in Jane Austen's *Mansfield Park*." *Studies in Iconography* 14 (1995): 306–08. Print.

Dodd, William. *The Beauties of Shakespear*. 3rd ed. Vol. 3. London, 1780. Print.

Donovan, Robert Alan. "The Mind of Jane Austen." Weinsheimer 109–27.

Downie, A. J. "The Chronology of *Mansfield Park*." *Modern Philology*, forthcoming.

———. "Rehabilitating Sir Thomas Bertram." *Studies in English Literature* 50.4 (2010): 739–58. Print.

Duckworth, Alistair. *The Improvement of the Estate*. 1971. Baltimore: Johns Hopkins UP, 1994. Print.

———. "'Spillikins, Paper Ships, Riddles, Conundrums, and Cards': Games in Jane Austen's Life and Fiction." Halperin 279–97.

Easton, Celia. "Jane Austen and the Enclosure Movement: The Sense and Sensibility of Land Reform." *Persuasions* 24 (2002): 71–89. Print.

Edwards, Thomas R. "The Difficult Beauty of *Mansfield Park*." *Nineteenth-Century Fiction* 20 (1965): 51–67. Print.

Eliot, George. *Felix Holt, the Radical*. 1866. Ed. Fred C. Thompson. Oxford: Oxford UP, 1980. Print.

Eliot, Simon, and Jonathan Rose, eds. *A Companion to the History of the Book*. Malden: Wiley, 2007. Print.

Eliot, T. S. "Burnt Norton." *The Complete Poems and Plays, 1909–1950*. New York: Harcourt, 1980. 117–22. Print.

Elliott, Dorice Williams. "The Gift of an Education: Sarah Trimmer's *Oeconomy of Charity* and the Sunday School Movement." Zionkowski and Klekar 107–22.

Emsley, Sarah. *Jane Austen's Philosophy of the Virtues*. New York: Palgrave, 2005. Print.

————. "'My Idea of a Chapel' in Jane Austen's World." *Persuasions* 24 (2002): 133–42. Print.

————. "The Tragic Action of *Mansfield Park*." *Persuasions On-line* 28.1 (2007): n. pag. Web. 8 Oct. 2013.

Enfield, William. *The Speaker*. New ed., corrected. London, n.d. Print.

Erasmus of Rotterdam. Praise of Folly *and* Letter to Maarten Van Dorp. Trans. Betty Radice. New York: Penguin, 1993. Print.

Everett, Nigel. "The View of Donwell Abbey." *The Tory View of Landscape*. New Haven: Yale UP, 1994. 183–203. Print.

Farrer, Reginald. "Jane Austen, *ob*. July 18, 1817." 1917. Littlewood 2: 177–98.

Festa, Lynn. "Losing One's Place in *Mansfield Park*." *Eighteenth-Century Novel* 6–7 (2009): 429–63. Print.

Fleishman, Avrom. *A Reading of* Mansfield Park: *An Essay in Critical Synthesis*. Minneapolis: U of Minnesota P, 1967. Print.

Folsom, Marcia McClintock, ed. *Approaches to Teaching Austen's* Emma. New York: MLA, 2005. Print.

————. "Part of an Englishwoman's Constitution: The Presence of Shakespeare in *Mansfield Park*." *Persuasions* 28 (2006): 65–80. Print.

————. "Power in *Mansfield Park*: Austen's Study of Domination and Resistance." *Persuasions* 34 (2012): 83–98. Print.

————. "The Privilege of My Own Profession: The Living Legacy of Austen in the Classroom." *Persuasions On-line* 29.1 (2008): n. pag. Web. 1 June 2010.

Ford, Susan Allen. "Fanny's 'Great Book': Macartney's Embassy to China and *Mansfield Park*." *Persuasions On-line* 28.2 (2008): n. pag. Web. 18 Aug. 2013.

————. "'Intimate by Instinct': *Mansfield Park* and the Comedy of *King Lear*." *Persuasions* 24 (2002): 177–97. Print.

————. "'It Is about *Lovers' Vows*': Kotzebue, Inchbald, and the Players of *Mansfield Park*." *Persuasions On-line* 27.1 (2006): n. pag. Web. 18 Aug. 2013.

————. "Working Out a Happy Conclusion: *Mansfield Park* and the Revision of *King Lear*." *Sensibilities* 27 (2003): 95–110. Print.

"Forestall." *Oxford English Dictionary Online*. Oxford UP, 2013. Web. 30 Sept. 2013.

Forster, E. M. *Howards End*. Toronto: Bantam, 1985. Print.

Fraiman, Susan. "Jane Austen and Edward Said: Gender, Culture, and Imperialism." *Critical Inquiry* 21.4 (1995): 805–21. *JSTOR*. Web. 2 May 2006.

Freedgood, Elaine. *The Ideas in Things: Fugitive Meaning in the Victorian Novel*. Chicago: U of Chicago P, 2006. Print.

Fuller, Miriam Rheingold. "Crawfords on the Couch: A Psychoanalytical Exploration of the Effects of the 'Bad School' on Henry and Mary Crawford." *Persuasions* 28 (2006): 13–30. Print.

Fullerton, Susannah. "Mansfield Park." *Country Houses in Jane Austen's Novels—* Mansfield Park. Jane Austen Soc. of Australia, 16 Aug. 2000. Web. 25 Feb. 2014.

Gaskell, Elizabeth. *Cranford*. Ed. Elizabeth Porges Watson. London: Oxford UP, 2011. Print. Oxford World's Classics.

Gay, Penny. *Jane Austen and the Theatre*. Cambridge: Cambridge UP, 2002. Print.

———. "Pastimes." Todd, *Jane Austen in Context* 337–45.

Genette, Gérard. *Paratexts: Thresholds of Interpretation*. Trans. Jane Lewin. Cambridge: Cambridge UP, 1997. Print.

Gilbert, Sandra M., and Susan Gubar. *The Madwoman in the Attic: The Woman Writer and the Nineteenth-Century Literary Imagination*. 2nd ed. New Haven: Yale UP, 2000. Print.

Gilson, David. "Later Publishing History, with Illustrations." Todd, *Jane Austen in Context* 121–59.

Gissing, George. *The Odd Women*. Ed. Arlene Young. Peterborough: Broadview, 1998. Print.

Graham, Peter W. "'An Entangled Bank': Sibling Development in a Family Ecosystem." Graham, *Jane Austen* 47–86.

———. "Falling for the Crawfords: Character, Contingency, and Narrative." *ELH* 77.4 (2010): 867–91. Print.

———. *Jane Austen and Charles Darwin: Naturalists and Novelists*. Aldershot: Ashgate, 2008. Print.

Greetham, David. "What Is Textual Scholarship?" Eliot and Rose 21–32.

Gregory, Derek. *The Colonial Present: Afghanistan, Palestine, Iraq*. Oxford: Blackwell, 2004. Print.

Grey, J. David, ed. *The Jane Austen Companion*. New York: Macmillan, 1986. Print.

"Ha-ha." *Oxford English Dictionary Online*. Oxford UP, 2013. Web. 10 Oct. 2013.

Halperin, John, ed. *Jane Austen Bicentenary Essays*. Cambridge: Cambridge UP, 1975. Print.

Harding, D. W. "Regulated Hatred: An Aspect of the Work of Jane Austen." *Scrutiny* 8 (1940): 346–62. Print.

Harlan, Susan. "'Talking' and Reading Shakespeare in Jane Austen's *Mansfield Park*." *Wordsworth Circle* 39.1–2 (2008): 43–46. Print.

Harris, H. R. "Jane Austen's Venture into Tragedy." *Contemporary Review* June 1998: 314–18. Print.

Harris, Jocelyn. "*Pride and Prejudice* and *Mansfield Park*." Copeland and McMaster [2011] 39–54.

Hazlitt, William. "Conversations of James Northcote, Esq., R. A." *The Complete Works of William Hazlitt*. Ed. P. P. Howe. Vol. 11. New York: AMS, 1967. 185–320. Print.

Holmes, Samuel. *The Journal of Mr. Samuel Holmes, Serjeant-Major of the Eleventh Light Dragoons*. London, 1798. Print.

Home, John. *Douglas: A Tragedy*. 1757. London, 1791. Print. Vol. 3 of *Bell's British Theatre*.

Honan, Park. *Jane Austen: Her Life*. New York: Fawcett, 1987. Print.

Hoyle, Edmond. "The Game of Speculation." *Hoyle's Games Improved*. Ed. Charles Jones. London, 1800. iv. *Eighteenth Century Collections Online*. Web. 15 Aug. 2010.

Hussey, Christopher. *The Picturesque*. London: Cass, 1967. Print.

Inchbald, Elizabeth. *Lovers' Vows*. 5th ed. London, 1798. J. Austen, *Mansfield Park* [ed. Wiltshire] 555–629.

Jenkins, Annibel. *I'll Tell You What: The Life of Elizabeth Inchbald*. Lexington: U of Kentucky P, 2003. Print.

Johnson, Claudia L. "Introduction: Austen and the Text of *Mansfield Park*." J. Austen, *Mansfield Park* [ed. Johnson] xi–xxi.

———. *Jane Austen: Women, Politics, and the Novel*. Chicago: U of Chicago P, 1988. Print.

———. "Jane Austen's Relics and the Treasures of the East Room." *Persuasions* 28 (2006): 217–30. Print.

———. "*Mansfield Park*: Confusions of Guilt and Revolutions of Mind." C. Johnson, *Jane Austen* 94–120.

Johnson, Claudia L., and Clara Tuite, eds. *A Companion to Jane Austen*. Malden: Wiley, 2009. Print.

Johnson, Samuel. *The History of Rasselas, Prince of Abissinia*. Ed. J. P. Hardy. Oxford: Oxford UP, 1968. Print.

———. *Major Works*. 1984. Ed. Donald Greene. Oxford: Oxford UP, 2000. Print.

———. *The Rambler*. Ed. W. J. Bate and Albrecht B. Strauss. New Haven: Yale UP, 1969. Print. Vols. 3–5 of *The Yale Edition of the Works of Samuel Johnson*.

Kavanagh, Julia. "Miss Austen's Six Novels." 1862. Littlewood 1: 356–74.

Kelly, Gary. *Women, Writing, and Revolution, 1790–1827*. Oxford: Clarendon, 1993. Print.

Keymer, Thomas, and Jon Mee, eds. *The Cambridge Companion to English Literature*. Cambridge: Cambridge UP, 2004. Print.

Kierkegaard, Søren. *Either/Or: A Fragment of Life*. Trans. Alastair Hannay. New York: Penguin, 1992. Print.

Kirkham, Margaret. *Jane Austen, Feminism, and Fiction*. New York: Methuen, 1986. Print.

Knox, Vicesimus. *Extracts, Elegant, Instructive, and Entertaining, in Poetry*. 1783. London, 1791. Print.

Landry, Donna. "Learning to Ride at Mansfield Park." Park and Rajan 56–73.

Lane, Maggie. "Star-gazing with Fanny Price." *Persuasions* 28 (2006): 150–65. Print.

La Rochefoucauld, François de. *Collected Maxims and Other Reflections*. Trans. E. H. Blackmore, A. M. Blackmore, and Francine Griguère. Oxford: Oxford UP, 2007. Print.

———. *Maximes et réflexions diverses*. Paris: Garnier, 1977. Print.

Leavis, F. R. *The Great Tradition*. London: Chatto, 1948. Print.

Leavis, Q. D. Introduction. *Mansfield Park*. By Jane Austen. London: McDonald, 1957. vii–xviii. Print. Illustrated Classics.

Lee, Hermione. "Virginia Woolf's Essays." *The Cambridge Companion to Virginia Woolf*. Ed. Sue Roe and Susan Sellers. Cambridge: Cambridge UP, 2000. 91–108. Print.

Le Faye, Deirdre, ed. *Jane Austen's Letters*. New ed. Oxford: Oxford UP, 1997. Print.

Leithart, Peter. *Jane Austen: Christian Encounters*. Nashville: Nelson, 2009. Print.

Lew, Joseph. "'That Abominable Traffic': *Mansfield Park* and the Dynamics of Slavery." *History, Gender, and Eighteenth-Century Literature*. Ed. Beth Fowkes Tobin. Athens: U of Georgia P, 1994. 271–300. Print.

Lewes, G. H. "The Great Appraisal." 1859. Southam, *Jane Austen: The Critical Heritage* 148–66.

Linkiewicz, Deirdre. "*Lovers' Vows* Workshops." Memo to Penny Gay. Oct. 2008. TS.

Littlewood, Ian. *Jane Austen: Critical Assessments*. 4 vols. East Sussex: Helm Information, 1998. Print.

Manguel, Alberto. *A History of Reading*. New York: Penguin, 1996. Print.

Mansfield Park. Dir. David Giles. BBC World Films, 1983. Film.

Mansfield Park. Dir. Iain B. MacDonald. Prod. Company Pictures and WGBH Boston Video, 2008. Film.

Mansfield Park. Dir. Patricia Rozema. Perf. Frances O'Connor and Jonny Lee Miller. Miramax, 1999. Film.

Mauss, Marcel. *The Gift: The Form and Reason for Exchange in Archaic Societies*. Trans. W. D. Halls. New York: Norton, 1990. Print. Trans. of *Essai sur le don*. 1950.

McIntyre, Alasdair. *After Virtue*. Notre Dame: U of Notre Dame P, 2007. Print.

McKeown, Ailish. "*Lovers' Vows*." Memo to Penny Gay. July 2010. TS.

McMaster, Juliet. "Class." Copeland and McMaster [1997] 115–30.

McNeillie, Andrew, ed. *The Essays of Virginia Woolf*. Vol. 2. New York: Harcourt, 1987. Print.

Meyers, Jeffrey. "Samuel Demands the Muse: Johnson's Stamp on Imaginative Literature." *Antioch Review* 66 (2007): 39–49. Print.

Michaelson, Patricia Howell. *Speaking Volumes: Women, Reading, and Speech in the Age of Austen*. Stanford: Stanford UP, 2002. Print.

Miller, D. A. *Jane Austen; or, The Secret of Style*. Princeton: Princeton UP, 2003. Print.

Miller, Nancy K. "Emphasis Added: Plots and Plausibilities in Women's Fiction." *PMLA* 96.1 (1981): 36–48. Print.

Milton, John. *Complete Prose Works of John Milton*. Vol. 2. Ed. Ernest Sirluck. New Haven: Yale UP, 1959. Print.

Monaghan, David. "In Defense of Patricia Rozema's *Mansfield Park*." *Persuasions* 28 (2006): 59–64. Print.

Moore, Edward. *The Gamester: A Tragedy*. London, 1753. Print.

More, Hannah. *Coelebs in Search of a Wife*. 12th ed. London: Cadell and Davies, 1809. Print.

———. *Thoughts on the Importance of the Manners of the Great to General Society*. London: Cadell and Davies, 1809. Print.

Moretti, Franco. *Atlas of the European Novel, 1800–1900*. London: Verso, 1998. Print.

Morgan, Susan. *Sisters in Time: Imagining Gender in Nineteenth-Century British Fiction*. Oxford: Oxford UP, 1989. Print.

Musser, Joseph F., Jr. "William Cowper's Rhetoric: The Picturesque and the Personal." *SEL* 19 (1979): 515–31. Print.

Nabokov, Vladimir. "Jane Austen: *Mansfield Park*." *Lectures on Literature*. Ed. Fredson Bowers. San Diego: Harcourt, 1980. 9–60. Print.

Nicolson, Nigel. *The World of Jane Austen*. London: Weidenfeld, 1991. Print.

Osteen, Mark, ed. *The Question of the Gift: Essays across Disciplines*. New York: Routledge, 2002. Print.

"Park." Def. 1b. *Oxford English Dictionary Online*. Oxford UP, 2013. Web. 25 Feb. 2014.

Park, You-me, and Rajeswari Sunder Rajan, eds. *The Postcolonial Jane Austen*. New York: Routledge, 2000. Print.

Pedley, Colin. "'Terrific and Unprincipled Compositions': The Reception of *Lovers' Vows* and *Mansfield Park*." *Philological Quarterly* 74 (1995): 297–316. Print.

Perry, Ruth. *Novel Relations: The Transformation of Kinship in English Literature and Culture, 1748–1818*. Cambridge: Cambridge UP, 2004. Print.

Plan of an Estate Situate at Millbank Westminster Belonging to the Marquis of Salisbury. *British Library Online Gallery*. British Lib. Board, n.d. Web. 10 July 2010.

Plates to Staunton's Account of the Embassy to China. London, 1796. Print.

Plumptre, Anne, trans. *The Natural Son*. By August von Kotzebue. London, 1798. Print.

Poovey, Mary. *The Proper Lady and the Woman Writer: Ideology and Style in the Work of Mary Wollstonecraft, Mary Shelley, and Jane Austen*. Chicago: U of Chicago P, 1984. Print.

Portsmouth. Ordnance Survey Drawings. British Lib. Board, n.d. Web. 3 Aug. 2010.

Price, Martin. *Forms of Life: Character and Moral Imagination in the Novel*. New Haven: Yale UP, 1983. Print.

Pride and Prejudice. Dir. Robert Z. Leonard. MGM, 1940. Film.

Quaintance, Richard. "Humphry Repton, 'Any Mr. Repton,' and the 'Improvement' Metonym in *Mansfield Park*." *Studies in Eighteenth-Century Culture* 27 (1998): 365–84. Print.

Repton, Humphry. *Observations on the Theory and Practice of Landscape Gardening*. London: T. Bensley for J. Taylor, 1803. Print.

Repton, Humphry, and J. Adey Repton. *Fragments on the Theory and Practice of Landscape Gardening*. London: T. Bensley and Son for J. Taylor, 1816. Print.

Richardson, Samuel. *Pamela*. Ed. Thomas Keymer and Alice Wakely. New York: Oxford UP, 2001. Print.

Said, Edward. *Culture and Imperialism*. New York: Vintage, 1994. Print.

———. "Invention, Memory and Place." *Critical Inquiry* 26. 2 (2000): 175–92. Print.

———. "Jane Austen and Empire." Said, *Culture* 80–97.

———. "Jane Austen and Empire." *Raymond Williams: Critical Perspectives*. Ed. Terry Eagleton. Boston: Northeastern UP, 1989. 150–64.

———. *Orientalism*. New York: Vintage, 1978. Print.

Sales, Roger. *Jane Austen and Representations of Regency England*. London: Routledge, 1994. Print.

———. "*Mansfield Park*: The Regency Crisis and the Theatre." Sales, *Jane Austen* 87–131.

Scholes, Robert. "Dr. Johnson and Jane Austen." *Philological Quarterly* 54.1 (1975): 380–90. Print.

Schrift, Alan D., ed. *The Logic of the Gift: Toward an Ethic of Generosity*. New York: Routledge, 1997. Print.

Scott, Walter. Rev. of *Emma*, by Jane Austen. *Quarterly Review* 14.27 (1815): 188–201. Print.

———. *The Lay of the Last Minstrel*. 2nd ed. London, 1805. Print.

Selwyn, David. "Games and Play in Jane Austen's Literary Structures." *Persuasions* 23 (2001): 15–28. Print.

———. "Toys and Games." *Jane Austen and Leisure*. London: Hambledon, 1999. 261–75. Print.

Shakespeare, William. *King Henry VIII; or, All Is True*. Ed. Jay L. Halio. Oxford: Oxford UP, 1999. Print.

———. *Measure for Measure*. Ed. Jonathan Crewe. New York: Penguin, 2000. Print.

———. *A Midsummer Night's Dream*. *The Complete Works*. 2nd ed. Ed. Stanley Wells and Gary Taylor. Oxford: Oxford UP, 2005. 401–24. Print.

———. *Othello*. Ed. E. A. J. Honigmann. 3rd ed. Walton-on-Thames: Nelson, 1997. Print. Arden Shakespeare.

Shea, Alison. "'I Am a Wild Beast': Patricia Rozema's Forward Fanny." *Persuasions* 28 (2006): 52–58. Print.

Sheridan, Richard Brinsley. *Six Plays*. New York: Farrar, 1957. Print.

Simons, Judy, ed. Mansfield Park *and* Persuasion. New York: St. Martin's, 1997. Print.

Smith, Andrew. "Migrancy, Hybridity, and Postcolonial Literary Studies." *The Cambridge Companion to Postcolonial Studies*. Ed. Neil Lazarus. Cambridge: Cambridge UP, 2004. 241–61. Print.

Snyder, Susan. *The Comic Matrix of Shakespeare's Tragedies:* Romeo and Juliet, Hamlet, Othello, *and* King Lear. Princeton: Princeton UP, 1979. Print.

Souter, Kay Torney. "Jane Austen and the Reconsigned Child: The True Identity of Fanny Price." *Persuasions* 23 (2001): 205–14. Print.

Southam, Brian. *Jane Austen and the Navy*. New York: Hambledon, 2000. Print.

———, ed. *Jane Austen: The Critical Heritage*. New York: Barnes, 1968. Print.

———. "The Silence of the Bertrams." *Times Literary Supplement* 17 Feb. 1995: 13–14. Print.

———. "The Silence of the Bertrams." J. Austen, *Mansfield Park* [ed. Johnson] 493–98.

"Speculation." *Oxford English Dictionary Online*. Oxford UP, 2013. Web. 9 May 2014.

Spence, Jon. *The Leighs: The Revelations of Stoneleigh*. Jane Austen Soc. of Australia, 13 Jan. 2004. Web. 25 Feb. 2014.

Staunton, George. *An Authentic Account of an Embassy from the King of Great Britain to the Emperor of China*. London: G. Nicol, 1797. Print. 3 vols.

Sterne, Laurence. *A Sentimental Journey through France and Italy*. Introd. Virginia Woolf. London: Oxford UP, 1960. Print.

Stovel, Bruce. "Once More with Feeling: The Structure of *Mansfield Park*." *Persuasions On-line* 27.1 (2006): n. pag. Web. 20 Aug. 2013.

Sturrock, June. "Money, Morals, and *Mansfield Park*: The West Indies Revisited." *Persuasions* 28 (2006): 176–84. Print.

Sulloway, Frank. "Birth Order, Sibling Competition, and Human Behavior." Davies and Holcombe 39–83.

———. *Born to Rebel: Birth Order, Family Dynamics, and Creative Lives*. New York: Pantheon, 1996. Print.

Sutherland, Kathryn. Introduction. J. Austen, *Mansfield Park* [ed. Sutherland] xi–xl.

———. "Jane Austen and the Invention of the Serious Modern Novel." Keymer and Mee 244–62.

———. *Jane Austen's Textual Lives: From Aeschylus to Bollywood*. Oxford: Oxford UP, 2005. Print.

Tanner, Tony. Introduction. *Mansfield Park*. By Jane Austen. Ed. Tanner. New York: Penguin, 1966. 7–36. Print.

———. *Jane Austen*. 1986. Basingstoke: Macmillan, 2007. Print.

———. "Original Penguin Classics Introduction by Tony Tanner." *Sense and Sensibility*. By Jane Austen. Ed. Ros Ballaster. London: Penguin, 2003. 356–83. Print.

———. "The Quiet Thing: *Mansfield Park*." Tanner, *Jane Austen* 142–75.

Thackeray, William Makepeace. Vanity Fair: *Authoritative Text, Backgrounds, Criticisms*. Ed. Peter Shillingsburg. New York: Norton, 1994. Print.

Todd, Janet, ed. *The Cambridge Introduction to Jane Austen*. New York: Cambridge UP, 2006. Print.

———, ed. *Jane Austen in Context*. New York: Cambridge UP, 2005. Print.

———. "Mansfield Park." Todd, *Cambridge Introduction* 75–93.

Tolstoy, Leo. *Anna Karenina*. Trans. Richard Pevear and Larissa Volokhonsky. New York: Penguin, 2000. Print.

Tomalin, Claire. *Jane Austen: A Life*. New York: Knopf, 1997. Print.

"Tragicomedy." *The New Princeton Encyclopedia of Poetry and Poetics*. Ed. Alex Preminger and T. V. F. Brogan. Princeton: Princeton UP, 1993. Print.

Trilling, Lionel. "*Emma* and the Legend of Jane Austen." *Beyond Culture*. New York: Viking, 1965. 31–55. Print.

———. "In *Mansfield Park*." Littlewood 4: 41–56.

———. "*Mansfield Park*." Austen, *Mansfield Park* [ed. Johnson] 423–34.

Tyndale, William. "A Pathway into the Holy Scripture." *The Works of the English Reformers: William Tyndale and John Frith*. Ed. Thomas Russell. Vol. 2. London: Ebenezer Palmer, 1831. 489–510. *Google Books*. Web. 20 Aug. 2013.

Waldron, Mary. "The Frailties of Fanny: *Mansfield Park* and the Evangelical Movement." *Eighteenth-Century Fiction* 6.3 (1994): 259–81. DigitalCommons@ McMaster, n.d. Web. 11 Feb. 2014.

———. *Jane Austen and the Fiction of Her Time*. Cambridge: Cambridge UP, 1999. Print.

Watt, Ian, ed. *Jane Austen: A Collection of Critical Essays*. Englewood Cliffs: Prentice, 1963. Print.

Weinsheimer, Joel, ed. *Jane Austen Today*. Athens: U of Georgia P, 1975. Print.

Wells, Juliette. "A Harpist Arrives at Mansfield Park: Music and the Moral Ambiguity of Mary Crawford." *Persuasions* (2006): 101–14. Print.

Whalley, George. "Jane Austen: Poet." *Jane Austen's Achievement*. Ed. Juliet McMaster. London: Macmillan, 1976. 106–33. Print.

Whately, Richard. Rev. of *Northanger Abbey* and *Persuasion*, by Jane Austen. Littlewood 1: 318–34.

Wheatley, Phillis. *Complete Writings*. Ed. Vincent Carretta. New York: Penguin, 2001. Print.

Wilde, Oscar. "The Picture of Dorian Gray." *Collins Complete Works of Oscar Wilde*. Glasgow: Harper, 1999. 17–159. Print. Centenary ed.

"Wilderness." Defs. 1b, 1c. *Oxford English Dictionary Online*. Oxford UP, 2013. Web. 25 Feb. 2014.

Williams, Raymond. *The Country and the City*. New York: Oxford UP, 1973. Print.

Williamson, Tom. *Polite Landscapes: Gardens and Society in Eighteenth-Century England*. Baltimore: Johns Hopkins UP, 1995. Print.

Wilson, Edmund. "A Long Talk about Jane Austen." *Classics and Commercials: A Literary Chronicle of the Forties*. New York: Farrar, 1950. 196–203. Print.

Wiltshire, John. "Commentary on the Text." J. Austen, *Mansfield Park* [ed. Wiltshire] 633–38.

———. "Decolonising *Mansfield Park*." *Essays in Criticism* 53 (2003): 303–22. Print.

———. "'Eloquent Blood': The Coming Out of Fanny Price." Wiltshire, *Jane Austen* 62–109.

———. "Explanatory Notes." J. Austen, *Mansfield Park* [ed. Wiltshire] 639–738.

———. *The Hidden Jane Austen*. Cambridge: Cambridge UP, 2014. Print.

———. Introduction. J. Austen, *Mansfield Park* [ed. Wiltshire] xxv–lxxxvi.

———. *Jane Austen and the Body: "The Picture of Health."* Cambridge: Cambridge UP, 1992. Print.

———. "*Mansfield Park, Emma, Persuasion*." Copeland and McMaster [1997] 58–83.

———. *Recreating Jane Austen*. Cambridge: Cambridge UP, 2001. Print.

Woolf, Virginia. "Jane Austen." Littlewood 1: 439–42.

———. "Jane Austen." *The Common Reader*. 1st ser. New York: Harcourt, 1925. 191–206. Print.

———. "Jane Austen at Sixty." Watt 15–24.

Wordsworth, William. "Lines Composed Five Miles above Tintern Abbey." Wordsworth, *William Wordsworth* 49–56.

————. "Simon Lee, the Old Huntsman." Wordsworth, *William Wordsworth* 16–18.

————. *William Wordsworth*. Ed. Stephen Gill. Oxford: Oxford UP, 2010. Print. Twenty-First-Century Oxford Authors.

Yaeger, Patricia. "Editor's Column: The End of Postcolonial Theory? A Roundtable with Sunil Agnani, Fernando Coronil, Gaurav Desai, Mamadou Diouf, Simon Gikandi, Susie Tharu, and Jennifer Wenzel." *PMLA* 122.3 (2007): 633–51. Print.

Yeazell, Ruth B. "The Boundaries of *Mansfield Park*." *Representations* 7 (1984): 133–52. Print.

Zajonc, R. B., and Frank Sulloway. "The Confluence Model: Birth Order as a Within-Family or Between-Family Dynamic?" *Personality and Social Psychology Bulletin* 33 (2007): 1187–94. Print.

Zionkowski, Linda, and Cynthia Klekar, eds. *The Culture of the Gift in Eighteenth-Century England*. New York: Palgrave, 2009. Print.

INDEX

Approaches to Teaching World Literature

To purchase MLA publications, visit www.mla.org/bookstore.

Achebe's Things Fall Apart. Ed. Bernth Lindfors. 1991.

Arthurian Tradition. Ed. Maureen Fries and Jeanie Watson. 1992.

Atwood's The Handmaid's Tale *and Other Works*. Ed. Sharon R. Wilson,
    Thomas B. Friedman, and Shannon Hengen. 1996.

Austen's Emma. Ed. Marcia McClintock Folsom. 2004.

Austen's Mansfield Park. Ed. Marcia McClintock Folsom and John Wiltshire.
    2014.

Austen's Pride and Prejudice. Ed. Marcia McClintock Folsom. 1993.

Balzac's Old Goriot. Ed. Michal Peled Ginsburg. 2000.

Baudelaire's Flowers of Evil. Ed. Laurence M. Porter. 2000.

Beckett's Waiting for Godot. Ed. June Schlueter and Enoch Brater. 1991.

Behn's Oroonoko. Ed. Cynthia Richards and Mary Ann O'Donnell. 2014.

Beowulf. Ed. Jess B. Bessinger, Jr., and Robert F. Yeager. 1984.

Blake's Songs of Innocence and of Experience. Ed. Robert F. Gleckner and
    Mark L. Greenberg. 1989.

Boccaccio's Decameron. Ed. James H. McGregor. 2000.

British Women Poets of the Romantic Period. Ed. Stephen C. Behrendt and
    Harriet Kramer Linkin. 1997.

Charlotte Brontë's Jane Eyre. Ed. Diane Long Hoeveler and Beth Lau. 1993.

Emily Brontë's Wuthering Heights. Ed. Sue Lonoff and Terri A. Hasseler. 2006.

Byron's Poetry. Ed. Frederick W. Shilstone. 1991.

Works of Italo Calvino. Ed. Franco Ricci. 2013.

Camus's The Plague. Ed. Steven G. Kellman. 1985.

Cather's My Ántonia. Ed. Susan J. Rosowski. 1989.

Cervantes' Don Quixote. Ed. Richard Bjornson. 1984.

Chaucer's Canterbury Tales. First edition Ed. Joseph Gibaldi. 1980.

Chaucer's Canterbury Tales. Second edition. Ed. Peter W. Travis and
    Frank Grady. 2014.

Chaucer's Troilus and Criseyde *and the Shorter Poems*. Ed. Tison Pugh and
    Angela Jane Weisl. 2006.

Chopin's The Awakening. Ed. Bernard Koloski. 1988.

Coetzee's Disgrace *and Other Works*. Ed. Laura Wright, Jane Poyner, and Elleke
    Boehmer. 2014.

Coleridge's Poetry and Prose. Ed. Richard E. Matlak. 1991.

Collodi's Pinocchio *and Its Adaptations*. Ed. Michael Sherberg. 2006.

Conrad's "Heart of Darkness" and "The Secret Sharer." Ed. Hunt Hawkins and
    Brian W. Shaffer. 2002.

Dante's Divine Comedy. Ed. Carole Slade. 1982.

Defoe's Robinson Crusoe. Ed. Maximillian E. Novak and Carl Fisher. 2005.

DeLillo's White Noise. Ed. Tim Engles and John N. Duvall. 2006.

Dickens's Bleak House. Ed. John O. Jordan and Gordon Bigelow. 2009.

Dickens's David Copperfield. Ed. Richard J. Dunn. 1984.

Dickinson's Poetry. Ed. Robin Riley Fast and Christine Mack Gordon. 1989.

Narrative of the Life of Frederick Douglass. Ed. James C. Hall. 1999.

Works of John Dryden. Ed. Jayne Lewis and Lisa Zunshine. 2013.

Duras's Ourika. Ed. Mary Ellen Birkett and Christopher Rivers. 2009.

Early Modern Spanish Drama. Ed. Laura R. Bass and Margaret R. Greer. 2006.

Eliot's Middlemarch. Ed. Kathleen Blake. 1990.

Eliot's Poetry and Plays. Ed. Jewel Spears Brooker. 1988.

Shorter Elizabethan Poetry. Ed. Patrick Cheney and Anne Lake Prescott. 2000.

Ellison's Invisible Man. Ed. Susan Resneck Parr and Pancho Savery. 1989.

English Renaissance Drama. Ed. Karen Bamford and Alexander Leggatt. 2002.

Works of Louise Erdrich. Ed. Gregg Sarris, Connie A. Jacobs, and
    James R. Giles. 2004.

Dramas of Euripides. Ed. Robin Mitchell-Boyask. 2002.

Faulkner's As I Lay Dying. Ed. Patrick O'Donnell and Lynda Zwinger. 2011.

Faulkner's The Sound and the Fury. Ed. Stephen Hahn and Arthur F. Kinney. 1996.

Fitzgerald's The Great Gatsby. Ed. Jackson R. Bryer and Nancy P. VanArsdale. 2009.

Flaubert's Madame Bovary. Ed. Laurence M. Porter and Eugene F. Gray. 1995.

García Márquez's One Hundred Years of Solitude. Ed. María Elena de Valdés and
    Mario J. Valdés. 1990.

Gilman's "The Yellow Wall-Paper" and Herland. Ed. Denise D. Knight and
    Cynthia J. Davis. 2003.

Goethe's Faust. Ed. Douglas J. McMillan. 1987.

Gothic Fiction: The British and American Traditions. Ed. Diane Long Hoeveler
    and Tamar Heller. 2003.

Poetry of John Gower. Ed. R. F. Yeager and Brian W. Gastle. 2011.

Grass's The Tin Drum. Ed. Monika Shafi. 2008.

H.D.'s Poetry and Prose. Ed. Annette Debo and Lara Vetter. 2011.

Hebrew Bible as Literature in Translation. Ed. Barry N. Olshen and
    Yael S. Feldman. 1989.

Homer's Iliad *and* Odyssey. Ed. Kostas Myrsiades. 1987.

Hurston's Their Eyes Were Watching God *and Other Works*. Ed. John Lowe. 2009.

Ibsen's A Doll House. Ed. Yvonne Shafer. 1985.

Henry James's Daisy Miller *and* The Turn of the Screw. Ed. Kimberly C. Reed and
    Peter G. Beidler. 2005.

Works of Samuel Johnson. Ed. David R. Anderson and Gwin J. Kolb. 1993.

Joyce's Ulysses. Ed. Kathleen McCormick and Erwin R. Steinberg. 1993.

Works of Sor Juana Inés de la Cruz. Ed. Emilie L. Bergmann and Stacey Schlau. 2007.

Kafka's Short Fiction. Ed. Richard T. Gray. 1995.

Keats's Poetry. Ed. Walter H. Evert and Jack W. Rhodes. 1991.

Kingston's The Woman Warrior. Ed. Shirley Geok-lin Lim. 1991.

Lafayette's The Princess of Clèves. Ed. Faith E. Beasley and
   Katharine Ann Jensen. 1998.

Writings of Bartolomé de Las Casas. Ed. Santa Arias and Eyda M. Merediz. 2008.

Works of D. H. Lawrence. Ed. M. Elizabeth Sargent and Garry Watson. 2001.

Lazarillo de Tormes *and the Picaresque Tradition*. Ed. Anne J. Cruz. 2009.

Lessing's The Golden Notebook. Ed. Carey Kaplan and Ellen Cronan Rose. 1989.

Works of Naguib Mahfouz. Ed. Waïl S. Hassan and Susan Muaddi Darraj. 2011.

Mann's Death in Venice *and Other Short Fiction*. Ed. Jeffrey B. Berlin. 1992.

Marguerite de Navarre's Heptameron. Ed. Colette H. Winn. 2007.

Works of Carmen Martín Gaite. Ed. Joan L. Brown. 2013.

Medieval English Drama. Ed. Richard K. Emmerson. 1990.

Melville's Moby-Dick. Ed. Martin Bickman. 1985.

Metaphysical Poets. Ed. Sidney Gottlieb. 1990.

Miller's Death of a Salesman. Ed. Matthew C. Roudané. 1995.

Milton's Paradise Lost. First edition. Ed. Galbraith M. Crump. 1986.

Milton's Paradise Lost. Second edition. Ed. Peter C. Herman. 2012.

Milton's Shorter Poetry and Prose. Ed. Peter C. Herman. 2007.

Molière's Tartuffe *and Other Plays*. Ed. James F. Gaines and
   Michael S. Koppisch. 1995.

Momaday's The Way to Rainy Mountain. Ed. Kenneth M. Roemer. 1988.

Montaigne's Essays. Ed. Patrick Henry. 1994.

Novels of Toni Morrison. Ed. Nellie Y. McKay and Kathryn Earle. 1997.

Murasaki Shikibu's The Tale of Genji. Ed. Edward Kamens. 1993.

Nabokov's Lolita. Ed. Zoran Kuzmanovich and Galya Diment. 2008.

Works of Ngũgĩ wa Thiong'o. Ed. Oliver Lovesey. 2012.

Works of Tim O'Brien. Ed. Alex Vernon and Catherine Calloway. 2010.

Works of Ovid and the Ovidian Tradition. Ed. Barbara Weiden Boyd and
   Cora Fox. 2010.

Petrarch's Canzoniere *and the Petrarchan Tradition*. Ed. Christopher Kleinhenz
   and Andrea Dini. 2014.

Poe's Prose and Poetry. Ed. Jeffrey Andrew Weinstock and Tony Magistrale. 2008.

Pope's Poetry. Ed. Wallace Jackson and R. Paul Yoder. 1993.

Proust's Fiction and Criticism. Ed. Elyane Dezon-Jones and
   Inge Crosman Wimmers. 2003.

Puig's Kiss of the Spider Woman. Ed. Daniel Balderston and Francine Masiello. 2007.

Pynchon's The Crying of Lot 49 *and Other Works*. Ed. Thomas H. Schaub. 2008.

Works of François Rabelais. Ed. Todd W. Reeser and Floyd Gray. 2011.

Novels of Samuel Richardson. Ed. Lisa Zunshine and Jocelyn Harris. 2006.

Rousseau's Confessions *and* Reveries of the Solitary Walker. Ed. John C. O'Neal and Ourida Mostefai. 2003.

Scott's Waverley Novels. Ed. Evan Gottlieb and Ian Duncan. 2009.

Shakespeare's Hamlet. Ed. Bernice W. Kliman. 2001.

Shakespeare's King Lear. Ed. Robert H. Ray. 1986.

Shakespeare's Othello. Ed. Peter Erickson and Maurice Hunt. 2005.

Shakespeare's Romeo and Juliet. Ed. Maurice Hunt. 2000.

Shakespeare's The Taming of the Shrew. Ed. Margaret Dupuis and Grace Tiffany. 2013.

Shakespeare's The Tempest *and Other Late Romances.* Ed. Maurice Hunt. 1992.

Shelley's Frankenstein. Ed. Stephen C. Behrendt. 1990.

Shelley's Poetry. Ed. Spencer Hall. 1990.

Sir Gawain and the Green Knight. Ed. Miriam Youngerman Miller and Jane Chance. 1986.

Song of Roland. Ed. William W. Kibler and Leslie Zarker Morgan. 2006.

Spenser's Faerie Queene. Ed. David Lee Miller and Alexander Dunlop. 1994.

Stendhal's The Red and the Black. Ed. Dean de la Motte and Stirling Haig. 1999.

Sterne's Tristram Shandy. Ed. Melvyn New. 1989.

Works of Robert Louis Stevenson. Ed. Caroline McCracken-Flesher. 2013.

The Story of the Stone (Dream of the Red Chamber). Ed. Andrew Schonebaum and Tina Lu. 2012.

Stowe's Uncle Tom's Cabin. Ed. Elizabeth Ammons and Susan Belasco. 2000.

Swift's Gulliver's Travels. Ed. Edward J. Rielly. 1988.

Teresa of Ávila and the Spanish Mystics. Ed. Alison Weber. 2009.

Thoreau's Walden *and Other Works.* Ed. Richard J. Schneider. 1996.

Tolstoy's Anna Karenina. Ed. Liza Knapp and Amy Mandelker. 2003.

Vergil's Aeneid. Ed. William S. Anderson and Lorina N. Quartarone. 2002.

Voltaire's Candide. Ed. Renée Waldinger. 1987.

Whitman's Leaves of Grass. Ed. Donald D. Kummings. 1990.

Wiesel's Night. Ed. Alan Rosen. 2007.

Works of Oscar Wilde. Ed. Philip E. Smith II. 2008.

Woolf's Mrs. Dalloway. Ed. Eileen Barrett and Ruth O. Saxton. 2009.

Woolf's To the Lighthouse. Ed. Beth Rigel Daugherty and Mary Beth Pringle. 2001.

Wordsworth's Poetry. Ed. Spencer Hall, with Jonathan Ramsey. 1986.

Wright's Native Son. Ed. James A. Miller. 1997.